THE LEES OF VIRGINIA

Thomas Lee, 1690–1750

PRESIDENT OF THE COUNCIL, COMMANDER IN CHIEF AND
ACTING GOVERNOR OF VIRGINIA

THE LEES OF VIRGINIA

Biography of a Family

By

BURTON J. HENDRICK

With Illustrations

"The family of Lee . . . has more men of merit
in it than any other family." —*John Adams to
Samuel Cooper, February 28, 1779*

BOSTON
LITTLE, BROWN, AND COMPANY
1935

THE ATLANTIC MONTHLY PRESS BOOKS
ARE PUBLISHED BY
LITTLE, BROWN, AND COMPANY
IN ASSOCIATION WITH
THE ATLANTIC MONTHLY COMPANY

PRINTED IN THE UNITED STATES OF AMERICA

PREFACE

In 1825, Richard Henry Lee, of Leesburg, Virginia, published his two-volume *Memoir of the Life of Richard Henry Lee,* his grandfather, and in 1829 followed this with a two-volume *Life of Arthur Lee, L.L.D.* As biographies these books are not to be seriously regarded, but they contain a large amount of information and correspondence useful to the student of the Lee family. In 1891 Mr. Worthington Chauncey Ford published three volumes of the letters of William Lee — a selection from the voluminous correspondence of that Revolutionary leader; and, in 1911 and 1914, Professor James Curtis Ballagh issued, in two volumes, *The Letters of Richard Henry Lee.* These and the family genealogical work, *Lee of Virginia* (1895), by Dr. Edmund Jennings Lee, are the printed sources concerning this Virginia clan. There are, in addition, several manuscript collections. The most valuable are the Lee papers in the libraries of Harvard University, the University of Virginia, the Virginia Historical Society of Richmond, the American Philosophical Society of Philadelphia, and the Pennsylvania Historical Society. Of particular importance are the documents of the Shippen family, — affiliated with the Lees through the marriage, in 1762, of Alice Lee, of Stratford, to Dr. William Shippen, Jr. — now in the Library of Congress. The author extends his thanks to these institutions for placing at his service their indispensable Lee archives. He also is under obligations to the Marquess of Lansdowne, for sending copies of the valuable Arthur Lee letters in the library of Bowood, to Mrs. William Boothe, of Alexandria, Virginia, for giving access to the letter books of her ancestor, William Lee, and to Miss Sarah Lee, of Washington, for kindly permitting an examination of the papers of Thomas Sim Lee, revolutionary governor of Maryland.

Mr. Cazenove Gardner Lee, Jr., of Washington, D. C., present antiquary of the Lee family, and intimate student of its annals in all its generations, has been especially kind in making available his records and personal knowledge.   The unremitting hospitality of the Library of Congress, and the aid of the chief of its Division of Manuscripts, Dr. J. Franklin Jameson, have facilitated researches at every point.   The New York Public Library, rich in materials concerning American history, has treated the writer with that courtesy and painstaking interest one invariably receives from its able staff.   Professor Samuel Flagg Bemis, of Yale University, was good enough to permit the reading of the manuscript (since published) of his invaluable *Diplomacy of the American Revolution.*   Dr. Edmund C. Burnett, of the Carnegie Institution of Washington, whose *Letters of Members of the Continental Congress* has added immeasurably to the understanding of that era, furnished many hints and much tonic criticism.   Professor Thomas P. Abernethy, of the University of Virginia, and Mrs. Abernethy suggested several sources of material.   To Mr. Edward Weeks, of the Atlantic Monthly Press, the author is indebted for valuable literary criticism.   For reading certain chapters and making worth-while suggestions, thanks are extended to Mr. Fairfax Harrison, of Washington, and Dr. Earl G. Swem, librarian of William and Mary College, Williamsburg, Virginia, whose recently published *Index* has made the study of Virginia history a far simpler process than it has previously been.

B. J. H.

WASHINGTON, D. C.
May 21, 1935

INTRODUCTION

THE following pages attempt the study of a social and political development which seems, at first, alien to America, but which exercised an incalculable effect upon the rise of the United States. Virginia history, especially in the eighteenth century, presents an organization in which family was the predominant unit. Influential families arose in other sections of the Atlantic seaboard, — the patrician Quakers of Pennsylvania and the patroons of New York immediately come to mind, — but it is doubtful whether elsewhere an aristocratic oligarchy, consisting of a dozen or fifteen "houses," obtained supreme power in the state. The phenomenon is especially remarkable because Virginia started existence as a democratic society, with practically universal suffrage and equal distribution of land. After the Restoration of the Stuarts, however, an engrossing process began which, decade by decade, placed the Old Dominion's richest possessions, and with them political and social power, in the control of a few aggressive clans. The "feudal" character of this group can be easily exaggerated; that it was a reproduction in America of the higher social existence of England is a fable which modern historical study has dispelled; yet the fact remains that Virginia, more preëminently than her sister commonwealths, is the state of the family, the one American community in which an effort was made, and for a time succeeded, to create something resembling hereditary lines of nobles — in fact if not in name — who basked in a popularly conceded right to rule its fortunes.

The history of one of these tribes should have at least an antiquarian interest. The Lees are especially worthy of attention because, for two centuries, they stood well at the top of Virginia life, because they present a succession of engaging characters, and because they have exercised great influence on the American state. They illustrate, perhaps better than their brother clans, the Virginia system in its most beneficent phase. In them all the important epochs in Virginia life are exemplified. They were Stuart adherents in the early time, servants of the crown for the first three quarters of the eighteenth century, revolutionists and founders of a new nation in 1776. From the landing of the first Lee in 1640 to the rise of the Confederacy in 1861, there were few crises that did not find Lees in the foremost ranks. The element of caste — of family predominance — is persistent in every generation. The last Lee who operated in the grand style — the military leader of the Confederacy — was as much an eighteenth-century Virginian gentleman as the Lees who signed the Declaration and did so much to pilot the colonies through Revolutionary troubles. Henry Adams, in his acid sketch of his Harvard classmate, "Rooney" Lee, detects this same persistence of type. This Lee also had "the Virginia habit of command, and took leadership as his natural habit." He was as little suited to the atmosphere of Harvard and Boston as a "Sioux Indian to a treadmill." "Rooney" Lee, son of the then Colonel Robert E. Lee, was, said Adams, "a gentleman of the old school," living in other times, and always conscious, if not of present problems, of the vast importance to American growth of "that leadership" exercised by his ancestors.

Significantly this Virginia leadership cannot be described without frequent allusion to the Adams *gens* itself — a family cohort with which the Lees, in mental endowment, in political standpoint, even in a certain dourness and crankiness of behavior, had much in common. "Rooney" Lee and Henry Adams were closer, at least in family tradition, than the Bostonian seemed to understand. In the early seventeenth century America was roughly divided into south Virginia and north Virginia — the latter region including the territory afterward known as New England. The identity of purpose which these geographical expressions symbolized came to full realization in 1776. It was personified in the coöperation of the families of Lee and Adams. Without their sympathetic union there would have been no Declaration of Independence, at least at that time, which was the indispensable time. It is probably not too much to say that there would have been no Revolution and consequently no United States of America without the association established between Virginia and New England. When meditating some drastic step in the Continental

Congress, Jefferson was wont to say, in his reminiscent old age, "We always counted Virginia and the four New England states on our side, and then looked around to see where we could find two more to make a majority." Thus was the United States made a nation. In taking a leading part in bringing together these two "countries," as both Virginia and Massachusetts called themselves in 1776, — countries so different in most concerns of life, — the Lees reached their epic stage, and exercised an influence on the growth of the American empire that endures.

The type of society and public life they represented has gone, and gone forever. Probably there was not much in its essential manifestations that the present generation would care to resurrect. What could be more distant from the present manner of American life than public men who underwent careful self-education for their tasks — who, highly cultured in a general sense, spent years in the scholastic investigation of such a matter as government? Men of leisure, born with a sense of responsibility as citizens, looking to labor in legislative chambers as their birthright, accorded by popular will that high position which had become with them a family inheritance — the fact that such an order once existed witnesses the transformation that has taken place in American affairs. They had personal attributes also which have vanished as completely as has the Latin-quoting statesman from the British House of Commons. They were gifted with fine love of social amenity, of intercourse of man with man; they lived in an age of conversation and correspondence; the mass of letters exchanged by the Lees with friends, not only in Virginia, but in all America, and at times with intellectual leaders in Europe, discussing particularly political topics and problems of government, is one of the most splendid legacies of that leisured time. Only a rash soul would picture this old Virginia, with its great plantations, its slaves, its upper class, full of snobbishness and of social oppression, its less fortunate lower stratum of whites, as superior to the present era. But the mere fact that such an order once held sway in this country and wrought great things for their descendants is interesting. It forms a humane and charming episode in the nation's annals — a kind of quiet interlude in the rushing progress of American life. That is a sufficient reason for telling its story.

CONTENTS

Part IV

THE LEES OF LEESYLVANIA

ILLUSTRATIONS

PART I

VIRGINIA'S GOLDEN AGE

I

THE "EMIGRANT"

I

THE founder of the family of Lee came to Virginia in the latter part of 1640, and presently acquired a plantation of fifteen hundred acres on the north side of the York. His name was Richard; he evidently was a man of standing in England; his condition on emigration, if not affluent, was fairly substantial, and his political and economic progress began almost immediately on the day of his arrival. Concerning his ancestral origin nothing is definitely known. This statement probably comes as a surprise, for much has been heard, in connection with the Virginia Lees, of the Lees of Coton, of Ditchley, or of one or another of the dozen or so families of Lee, or Lea, or Leigh, or Lega, whose beginnings run back to the Plantagenets. Yet the patriarch of the Virginia Lees has not been identified with any of these lines. The simple fact is that we do not know who Richard Lee was; that is, we do not know the names of his father or mother, or the place and date of his birth. Even the last name of his wife has not been handed down. In 1933 the Heralds' College in London attested Richard Lee as the son of Richard, younger son of Coton Hall, and Elizabeth Bendy, his wife, but, in the opinion of those best qualified to judge, on unsatisfactory evidence. The first two generations in Virginia never claimed descent from this distinguished house. One of the closest friends of the "Emigrant" was John Gibbon, member of the Heralds' College in his day, who, in his still valued work on heraldry, describes Colonel Richard as of "the Lees of Shropshire," and reproduces his coat of arms, which is the generic "fesse chequy and eight billets" of the Shropshire Lees, but not that of the family of Coton. This is the escutcheon displayed by the first two generations in Virginia, on tombstones, drinking cups, and communion plate; however, as there were several families of Lee in the county of Salop, all entitled to these quarterings, the seeker of exact knowledge is still left in the dark. William Lee, in 1771, described his ancestor as "of a good family in Shropshire," and that was probably all that was accurately known then, and certainly all that is known to-day, concerning the origin of one of America's most distinguished stocks.

That general rewriting of colonial history under way for the last quarter of a century has dealt rather destructively with Virginia legend. In particular the popular impression has been dispelled that the Old Dominion was peopled largely by English aristocrats. Not country gentlemen, or "Cavaliers," but chiefly the mercantile and commercial classes apparently laid its foundations. The Byrds, London goldsmiths; the Fitzhughs, maltsters; the Carys, merchants; the Ludwells, mercers; the Allertons, tailors; the Blands, members of the skinners' guild — such are a few of Virginia's leading families whose immediate ancestors in England happen to be known. Of many others, still more distinguished in American history, not even this much has been established. A few years ago one of Virginia's ripest historical scholars, William G. Stanard, published a monograph on "several hundred emigrants to Virginia whose parentage is known or former residence indicated by authentic records": in this compendium many of Virginia's most conspicuous names, such as Carter, Beverley, Jefferson, Harrison, Madison, Marshall, Mason, — and Lee, — are not enrolled. That is, no "authentic records" can be cited that fix the "parentage" of the English progenitors of these families. Many, however, could undoubtedly trace their ancestry to patrician lines. England, at the time of the Virginia settlement, was full of men, sprung of lofty lineage and entitled to noble escutcheons, who were themselves shopkeepers, merchants, and even artisans. They were the consequences of that familiar phenomenon in British life, the younger son. When titles and family estates all went to the oldest male heir, the brothers, unless they were advantageously married, or provided for in the church, the army or navy, or public employment, were left to shift for themselves, and in most cases they and their descendants were quickly eliminated from the gentry. Whatever their station, however, these disregarded cadets clung fiercely to their pride of birth, bore the family arms to which they had a legal claim, and commonly, in devotion to church and king, upheld the opinions of the class from which they were descended. Many acquired wealth, but lacked that social distinction for which, as connections of important English families, they yearned. To them the vast, beckoning expanse of the New World opened like a Promised Land. Here they could acquire estates that, in size and fertility, put the ancestral acres to shame; here they could resume their birthright as country gentlemen; and here too, with an apparently inexhaustible demand for tobacco, they could gain wealth and power.

That Richard Lee was a member of this substantial order may be confidently assumed. Undoubtedly he was *armiger,* entitled to the bearings of the Lees of Shropshire; according to family tradition he was a London merchant, possibly in the tobacco trade. Quite likely he was more closely allied to his ancestral line than most of his Virginia contemporaries were to theirs; if not a younger son of the Lees of Coton, or Langley, or Acton Burnell, or another of the Shropshire Lees, not improbably he was the son of a younger son. He was a man of substance and ambition, with aspirations to a social and public career that would be difficult to achieve in England. Like millions of Europeans since, Lee came to America to improve his condition, but there were probably other motives than the purely practical. That tendency, always marked in Richard's descendants, to combine the idealistic and the utilitarian was evident also in him. He lived in a time of expansive national fervor. Elizabeth was no more, but the spaciousness of her spirit was still abroad. England was outgrowing her historic confines and reaching into new worlds. The outburst of a great literature, the rise of new conceptions of freedom, Britain's military triumphs on land and sea, had given all Englishmen a new birthright. This new England was symbolized by America, which then meant Virginia, a name that signified a new faith in Britain and her star. In the minds of Englishmen of the seventeenth century, "Virginia" exercised a wonder and magic that we to-day can hardly comprehend. To Americans of the present time, Virginia is an ancient state of the Union, chiefly famous for the leaders contributed in the early days of the Republic; but to Elizabethan and Jacobean Englishmen, Virginia was a vast geographical expanse, extending from Florida to Canada and vaguely westward to the Pacific Ocean, a continent divinely set apart to the power and glory of England. When Spenser dedicates the *Faerie Queene* "to the most high, mightie and magnificent empresse Elizabeth . . . by the Grace of God Queene of England, Fraunce, and Ireland and of Virginia," we can fairly feel the triumphant crescendo of that culminating title, just as we feel it when, glancing on old maps, we find the Atlantic Ocean entitled "The Virginian Sea." England, with Virginia, was no longer a little island cooped up in the North; now English institutions, English speech, and the English race were to spread in all quarters of the earth. Someone has called Jamestown the "cradle of the Republic," but it is the cradle also of Canada, Australia, New Zealand, and South Africa, — of all the lands which English civilization has reached, — for with the founding of Jamestown begins that extension of England into two hemispheres which is the greatest fact in modern history.

The colonization of America was a necessity of England's progress; without it, the island would sink into the comparative insignificance from which it had so recently and so brilliantly emerged. That an energetic and farseeing man like Richard Lee would experience this universal impulse may be taken for granted. His great-grandson William instanced, as his outstanding trait, "an enterprising spirit," and all through Richard's career this quality was manifest, but never more so than on the day when, with his bride, he embarked on one of those tiny ships that then formed the fragile link between England and her struggling Western Empire. He was to play his rôle in one of the greatest of historic dramas — the outflow of the English race into all sections of the globe.

2

Not improbably the transatlantic voyage served Richard and Ann, his wife, also as a wedding journey. The fact that all their children were born after their arrival in Virginia would indicate

Richard Lee II, 1647–1714

Richard Lee, The Founder, d. 1664

that, at the time of sailing, they were young and recently married. As to their appearance and bearing there is more reliable evidence than that concerning their origin, for their portraits, which hung for nearly a century in Stratford Hall on the Potomac, are still in existence. Ann Lee was clearly a woman of dignity and breeding, erect, stately, serene, framed by nature to be the mother of a race of pioneers. The same self-confidence and satisfaction shine forth in every lineament of Richard. The large features, — characteristic of the Lees for three generations, — the great nose, frank and open eyes, unlined face, double chin, expanding chest, and well-fed body, proclaim a man at ease with himself and his neighbors. William Lee describes his great-grandfather as of "sound head, good stature and comely visage," and doubtless solid virtues, rather than scintillating talents, marked his days; the feeling is that of a man painstaking, far-seeing, quiet, acquisitive, thoughtful, deliberate. The place selected for his first establishment reënforces this impression. The Virginia of 1640 consisted of a few straggling plantations along the James; the territory to the north, the valleys of the York, the Rappahannock, and the Potomac, had so far enticed few adventurers. Richard, however, boldly "seated" himself on the farther side of the York, region of the still unreconciled Powhatans, who, in 1622, had fallen upon the settlers, almost annihilating them, and who, in 1640, were known to be awaiting another favorable opportunity to strike. The first Lee sojourn was on Tindal's Point, directly opposite that promontory which, two centuries afterward, became famous as Yorktown; but this was apparently a temporary outpost, for, in 1642, Richard's first patent appears on the Virginia records — 1000 acres on Poropotank Creek, an estuary of the York, about twenty miles from its mouth. Here again the man's "enterprising spirit" is displayed. In this wild region there were no other settlers: how jealously the natives regarded the land north of the York was shown two years afterward, when, in a peace treaty following another massacre, the whole section was placed aside eternally for the red man, encroachment of whites in this hunting ground being made a felony.

Despite this prohibition, Richard added year by year to his holdings in what is now Gloucester County, until the estate reached an aggregate of nearly 1500 acres. In extent, as well as in primeval charm, and even in exposed location, it accorded well with the owner's froward spirit. That Richard loved the spot is evident from the persistent manner in which he kept increasing his fields, and from the name "Paradise" which he gave it. No more beautiful place could be found in Virginia. Here the lordly York still retained a width of three miles; its wooded banks, an unbroken fringe of oak, pine, poplar, and cypress, were gay with many-colored wild flowers, while great natural vineyards, with huge clusters of grapes, and fruit trees — crab-apple, cherry, plum, persimmon — had been growing from immemorial time. Brilliantly plumaged birds, most of them new to Englishmen, filled the air with cries and song, the creeks and rivulets were thick with trout, and the ground was so covered with strawberries, far larger and sweeter than anything known in Europe, that, as an early Virginia chronicler wrote, one could scarcely walk in the forest without staining the feet with the "blood of this fruit." There were dogwoods such as no Englishman had ever seen, violets and roses blossoming in English profusion, while the sun shone with a brilliance that must have startled a voyager from London. Not the least attraction was the richness of the soil — a fruitful loam that had been accumulating for uncounted ages seemingly with the particular mission of heaping riches in the lap of the tobacco planter.

One likes to linger over this early Virginia, with its sunshine, its fruits, its flowers, its white man's civilization — a Virginia still unvexed by the problems that made much of its history so tragic. In Richard's time the Cavaliers are supposed to have given character to Virginia life; that first primeval Lee estate, however, disclosed few evidences of a "baronial" existence. Those fine country houses were to appear in another century, but none had been built in Richard's time. Indeed, in the entire seventeenth century there was probably not one Virginia "mansion" that rose above the commonplace. Richard Lee's house, if it resembled the prevailing habitation of his class, was a barnlike unpainted structure of wood, one and a half stories high, with gabled roof, and enormous outside brick chimneys at both ends, almost as wide as the house itself. Crude as it seemed in outward appearance, the place still had a rough-and-ready charm. In addition to the abundant native flowers, favorite plants had been imported from England — phlox, marjoram, thyme; and Richard, like his fellow Virginians, took vast pride in his peach and pear orchards, which, in budding season, made the place an animated glory. As in the later Virginia, kitchens and servants' quarters were in separate buildings and cabins, the whole collection surrounded by a stockade, not so much for protection from Indians as from swine, sheep, and cattle, which had free run of the country.

The interior was more cheery tnan the external aspect. The rooms were few and cramped, but the furnishings were not especially different from those of a family in prosperous station at home. Lee and the English country squire both did their shopping in the same place — the several marts of London. All their household appurtenances — beds, carpets, window hangings, tables, chairs, even tapestries, china, kitchen utensils — were the same. The planter sent his tobacco overseas direct to the Virginia Exchange in London; and in appropriate time the vessel appeared again at his wharf, bringing back all the personal and household supplies needed by a gentleman of breeding. The Virginia plantations were thus a kind of suburb to Great Britain, and Richard was far closer to London, and far more neighborly to "home," than to New England. The general aspect, however, was one of loneliness. The greater part of the estate, even though it had been "seated" several years, had changed little from earliest days, and endless forests that had so charmed the eyes of John Smith and his associates, as they entered the James in 1607, still reigned amid the silence.

But it was not until one had carefully observed the industrious workers that the contrast presented to the subsequent Virginia would have been so startling. The men and women bending over tobacco plants, the girls busy with milk pail and churn, the household servants hurrying about their tasks — all these were strangely unlike those immemorially associated with Virginia and the South. For all had skins as white as that of the master himself. Probably not a solitary negro ever appeared on Richard's farm. So far as the manual workers were concerned, Paradise looked like a piece of agricultural England, bodily transported to American soil. In truth that was precisely what it was. Virginia began its career, and for nearly a century maintained it, as a "white man's" country. Of negro slavery, and the complications it was to introduce in the South, and the part it was to play in the history of his descendants, Richard Lee knew little. About 40,000 persons were living in Virginia at the time of his death, and probably not more than 500 were black folk, the vast majority being members of that famous group of empire builders known as "indented servants." This signified, among other things, that the Old Dominion started life not as a slave-owning aristocracy but as a democratic society. Great estates were not parceled out by the king to favored retainers, as is too commonly supposed; rather the original planting followed lines not dissimilar to the American homestead laws of the nineteenth century. Thus Richard Lee did not cross the Atlantic with a parchment from Charles I, awarding him, in feudal tenure, a vast domain in the wilderness; he came with the patrimony that was assigned to every "emigrant," a mere fifty acres each for himself, wife, and such servants as he might bring. Every settler, whether peasant, artisan, or country gentleman, was entitled to these fifty acres, and no more. Even to obtain such a limited estate he must "seat" and cultivate his farm; should he fail to build a home and plant his crops, the land reverted, after a reasonable period, to the common store. This privilege, available to lord or churl, was known as "head-right," and the most practical way by which an ambitious planter could increase his holdings was to acquire the head-rights of pioneers less fortunate than himself.

In the social state of England at the time this was not particularly difficult. The English countryside was full of agricultural workers unable to earn a living, and English cities, especially London, were swarming with a wretched proletariat, without hope in present or future. Essentially these men and women represented excellent English stock, precisely the material out of which sturdy nations can be formed; emigration not only was the solution of their personal problems, but provided a new country with the kind of settlers it required. Many succeeded in making the voyage unaided, obtained on arrival the fifty acres offered as an incentive to settlement, and laid the basis of a small, landowning Virginia yeomanry. A far greater number, lacking the price of transportation, sold themselves, for a specific period, to Virginians prepared to assume the cost of the voyage. Not only did the importing capitalist acquire their labor "for their time," but something that was even more coveted — the head-right, the fifty acres in absolute ownership, that was inherent in each voyager. The deed by which Richard Lee secured his thousand acres on Poropotank Creek tells in its seventeenth-century phraseology a story that is comprehensive in its implications of democratic enterprise. This document recites that the land is due Richard "for his own personal adventure, his wife Ann, and John Francis, and by assignment from Thomas Hill, Florentine Paine and William Freeman, of their right of land due for the transportation of seventeen persons." The last three names were undoubtedly those of ship captains, who had brought over the "seventeen persons" as a private speculation, expecting to sell them and their "rights" on landing — a fairly safe gamble, for workers of this type were in great demand. The "persons" in question, humbly anonymous, soon found themselves hard at labor on Lee's plantation, and their blood, as well as that of thousands of others purchased by Richard and his contemporaries, flows in the veins of Virginians of all classes to-day. For, after seven years of bondage, spent happily or otherwise, according to the nature of the proprietor in whose hands they fell, the "indented servants" became free, upstanding men and women and were usually allotted, on emancipation, presents of clothes and little patches of land on which a new life could be begun. Most rose to positions of decent self-respect, and not a few to posts of honor and dignity.

From the perspective of a happier day the lot of the indented servant seems a hard one; for the period of his service he was really a white slave, and as such was bought and sold, given as wedding present to children, bequeathed in wills along with horses, cows, and other livestock of the estate, just as was his successor, the African bondman. Yet it is hardly necessary to point out the excellent historic purpose he served. For nearly the first hundred years this system of peopling Virginia prevailed. Had the black man not driven the white servant from the plantation,

how different would have been the story of Virginia and the
South! Those white English field workers and those English
milkmaids are thus a part of the sunshine and natural brilliancy
with which Virginia history, and that of the Lee family, begins.
The change from white to black, which became definitely established fifty years after the first Richard's death, was one of the
greatest calamities in modern history. Certainly the Lees themselves so regarded it, for, from 1750 to 1861, they were outspoken enemies of "the institution." Their antislavery feelings
are an important phase of the family story — convictions that
were perhaps an inheritance from "Emigrant" Richard, the proud
master of several plantations, all cultivated by an industrious and
happy company of Anglo-Saxons.

3

The reason for believing that Richard Lee was no starveling
waif of the British aristocracy, but a man of substance, is that
soon after arrival he invested so largely in head-rights and acquired such good-sized estates. In modern money, the price of
an indented servant could hardly have been less than $200; the
seventeen that Richard almost immediately purchased, therefore,
must have represented an outlay of about $3500 — and he fol-
lowed this up with other more extensive acquisitions. The reason for thinking that his family connection in England was important is that he quickly obtained political recognition and, in
brief time, became the right-hand man of Sir William Berkeley,
royal governor, and thus, at least on the official side, second man
in the colony. No settler would be acceptable to Berkeley who
was not of influence in England, and not strongly attached to the
royal cause. Berkeley was an aristocrat of deepest hue, a Stuart
adherent almost grotesque in his adoration; with him caste was
everything; he would not have joined a young man's fortunes to
his own, and rapidly advanced him to the highest positions in the
state, if that young man had not been politically sound on the
question then so violently agitating England — the struggle between king and Parliament — and well recommended on ancestral
lines. It is safe to conclude, therefore, that Richard was a fol-

lower of Charles — if not a ferocious one like Berkeley, yet of unquestioned loyalty.

This governor with whom he was to become coadjutor in ruling the colony has left an odious memory in Virginia, yet, during Lee's time, only the more ingratiating sides of his character were apparent; he was still Virginia's "darling," as the old historian, Beverley, calls him, and Richard died before the man's shocking qualities came to public notice. To modern eyes Berkeley, in his choleric moods, seems a kind of Peter Stuyvesant; like Peter, too, he was not lacking in bravery, nor in ability to make his denunciations effective. But he had other qualities that the doughty Dutchman did not possess. In Richard's day Berkeley showed traces of exquisite English breeding; he was still the gentleman who, sprung from one of the most distinguished English families, had been trained at Oxford, had spent his early years chiefly at the court of Charles I, had entertained the world of fashion with his wit and learning and the pleasure-loving public with his plays. "Thence to the theatre," writes Mr. Pepys, January 28, 1660, "where I saw again 'The Lost Lady,' which do now please me better than before." This was the most successful of Berkeley's writings — a tragi-comedy which Dodsley included in his edition of English plays. In 1642–1660 Berkeley was still the Berkeley of gold braid and lace cuffs, of sword and velvet coat, of courtly bows and smiles, and the governor who maintained an affectionate feeling towards the backwoods populace and even tolerated the exercise of limited popular rights.

Occasionally, indeed, the vigorous sides of his character came to the front, but not in ways that alienated public regard. Certainly Berkeley's savage methods of suppressing Indian insurrection did not lessen his popularity. Even his proposal to massacre all Indian braves and sell their squaws and children into slavery to pay the cost of extermination did not shock a community that had just passed through the Indian attacks of 1644. Neither did Berkeley's violent attachment to episcopacy and Archbishop Laud, and his pleasant habit of putting in the pillory and subjecting to public whippings those who spoke disrespectfully of His Grace, disturb Virginians of that time, practically all of whom were

Anglicans. His Excellency's hatred of Quakers, "that pestilential sect," would not have been misplaced in the New England of the time; and his edict banishing all Puritans from Virginia shows that the Old Dominion, like the region farther north, was not entirely free from religious persecution.

In this early period, however, Berkeley's public agitations, in the eyes of the populace, were not the important things. The man himself was liked and honored as a worthy representative of his king. His "graces of a soft and winning exterior" were aptly domiciled in his estate at Green Spring, on the James, four or five miles from Jamestown, one of the few brick buildings in the colony, where he dwelt contentedly with his 1500 apple trees, peach orchard, windmill, gardens, stables for eighty horses, and even his state coach — though just where this impressive equipage was used, in the roadless Virginia of Berkeley's day, is a mystery. An ornate chatelaine, even more arrogantly Tory than her lord, was Lady Berkeley, born a Culpeper, and in his affection for her the old governor's amiable side is disclosed. To his "dear and virtuous wife, the Lady ffrances Berkeley," — the words are from Berkeley's will, — was bequeathed Green Spring. "If God had blessed me with a far greater estate I would have given it all to my most dearly beloved wife." When Berkeley wrote those words he was unconsciously adding to the possessions of the Lees. Not long after her husband's tender departure, Lady Frances married Philip Ludwell, an ancestor of the Stratford Lees, and in this way Green Spring and other Berkeley riches ultimately passed into the hands of Richard Lee's descendants.

No man could make substantial progress in Virginia officialdom from 1642 to 1650 without the favor of this man. "During the civil war between Charles I and the Parliament," writes the family biographer, "Richard Lee and Sir William Berkeley, being royalists, kept the colony to its allegiance." That seems to have been the part set aside for the first Lee in American history. Clerk of the Quarter Court in 1641, a few months after arrival; attorney-general in 1643 — the first incumbent of that office, so far as official records reveal; sheriff of York County in 1646; burgess of York County in 1647; secretary of state in 1649 — such was the continuous succession of dignities by which Lee ultimately reached the highest of all, membership in the Council. There is something in the regular order by which the first Lee and his successors ascended the offices of state that reminds one of the steady progress by which the Roman youth, member of a favored gens, started with his ædileship and steadily advanced to the Roman Senate. And the prime qualities demanded in both cases were the same: character and ability, indeed, played their part, but indispensable requirements were also wealth and social station. Certainly this was the case in the greatest honor at the disposal of Virginia's body politic, in Richard's time and afterward. To be a Virginia councilor was, comparatively speaking, a higher honor than the Roman Senate, for the members were few — sometimes half a dozen, sometimes ten, finally twelve.

One needs to be deeply imbued in the Virginian atmosphere to understand the exalted significance of this distinction. Councils there were in other colonies, but none possessed quite the prestige that attended this body in the Old Dominion. It was unblushingly aristocratic in character; one might almost say of the Council, as Lord Melbourne remarked of the Order of the Garter, "Thank God, there's no damned merit about it." It was an honor to which a member must be born; and, in Virginia, "conciliar" families occupied a little niche of their own, like the elder statesmen in Japan. The councilor was nominally appointed by the king, and thus reposed in the glamour of being a "royal" officer, as contrasted with those vulgarly chosen by the electoral mob; in practice the king acted on the advice of his governor, — that is, Berkeley, — whose letters, suggesting candidates, again reflect the social requirements invariably insisted upon. That the individual suggested was a man of "family and fortune"; that he had an estate sufficiently large to bear the duties of the office — these qualities were always advanced, even before his personal virtues and talents. The fact that appointment usually — though not invariably — lasted for life; the great influence wielded in government; the heavy financial emoluments that attended the office; the immunities the members enjoyed — these circumstances gave this unusual body a prestige, both political and social, that no American legislative organization has since enjoyed. This eminence was perhaps not so pronounced in Richard's time as afterward, for the colony was small and struggling, and castes are never so rigorously drawn in an undeveloped society as in one definitely settled; but even then it was the prime dignity in the state. Emigrant Richard Lee became a member of this group in 1651, and every succeeding generation of his family, until the Council's extinction by the new republican order that rose in 1776, occupied a seat around its green baize table in the Virginia capitol. As the office itself at this time carried no salary, or only a nominal one, the fattest employments were usually assigned councilors — they became collectors of port duties, naval officers, and the like. The richest of these conciliar plums fell to Richard Lee, for he attained the highest executive office in the colony, next to Berkeley — that of secretary of state. His occupations were many, since a variety of tasks, which in a more complicated government are entrusted to several heads, were, in that primitive organization, comprised in one man. It requires no great exercise of the imagination to picture Richard in his modest Jamestown office, performing his functions as keeper of records, affixer of the Virginia seal to official documents, bestower of marriage licenses upon expectant couples, controller of passports, judge of applicants for land titles and claims to head-rights, grantor of licenses to trade or hunt wild hogs, recorder of wills, collector of fines — the office had a Pooh-Bah aspect, even in that microscopic state. For each official act a definite fee was allowed, paid, as was everything else, in tobacco. The aggregate amounted to a tidy sum; and all this time Richard was reaping a handsome revenue from his plantations. Pioneering was evidently not a thankless job, and, of that close corporation which was Virginia in his day, the secretary of state was a valiant beneficiary.

Yet, after all, how much is known of this Richard Lee? Of his character, his tastes, his recreations, his notions of life, his treatment of his friends, his inmost thoughts on the great happenings, intellectual and political, of his time? Most that we gather must be inferred from such information as is derived from records. This kind of material is not inconsiderable or to be disregarded; yet of living testimony of men who knew him face to face, and can furnish that kind of data that enables one to frame a flesh-and-blood human being — such glimpses are scanty. In

all the chronicles of the period Richard Lee makes an occasional
appearance, but early Virginia writing is sketchy and not given to
personal memoirs or to delineation of character.   And Virginia
itself was the scene of few startling events in Richard's time.   Its
chronicle is the story of a great, historic proceeding — one of the
greatest in human annals: the arrival of settlers; the parceling out
of land; the establishment of homes in a wilderness; the cultivation of a single crop; and, more important, the cultivation of
human qualities that served their end in time to come — independence, a hard preparedness for the struggle of life, love of
friends and neighbors, allegiance to domestic affections, pride in
family and region, ineluctable devotion to causes and beliefs.   One
terrible Indian massacre — that of 1644, when the red men made
a last ferocious attempt to exterminate the whites; difficulties
with Maryland over its appropriation of Virginia soil; restrictions
adopted against religious dissenters — these were the provincial
concerns that make up the formal history of the time.   The events
that really stirred Berkeley and Lee were taking place in England,
and these events were big indeed.

Only one witness emerges to enlighten us on Richard's part in
these transactions, but his evidence is illuminating.   John Gibbon
(1629–1718) — already referred to — is still important enough
to occupy more than a page in the *Dictionary of National Biography*.   Gibbon was a great-granduncle of the historian of Rome,
who devotes to him several engaging paragraphs in his autobiography.   He was a soldier and traveler, an astrologer and poet
— though, according to his kinsman, Edward Gibbon, not an impeccable one; his Toryism was quite unspeakable, surpassing that
of Berkeley himself.   Among his many books, only one survives,
his *Introductio ad Latinam Blasoniam,* still highly valued by
writers on heraldry — a potpourri of Latin and English, of
biography and heraldic science, with occasional casting of royal
horoscopes.   The book contains a passage of interest concerning
Richard Lee.   "A great part of anno 1659 I lived in Virginia,
being most hospitably entertained by the Honorable Collonel
Richard Lee, some time secretary of State there; and who after
the King's martyrdom hired a Dutch vessel, freighted her himself, went to Brussels, surrendered up Sir William Barcklaie's

old commission (for the government of that Province) and received a new one from his present Majesty (a loyal action and
deserving my Commendation)." There is no reason to doubt
the truth of this statement. Gibbon obtained it, of course, from
Richard Lee's own lips, while he was his guest — quite a protracted one, of a year's stay — in Virginia; the report was probably common at the time. The action was precisely the one that
Sir William Berkeley would have taken, and Richard Lee, his
secretary of state, who was making constant transatlantic trips,
was the messenger he would have chosen. The period referred to
is that of Charles's sojourn at Breda from February to June, 1650,
just before his fatal invasion of England, ending in the rout of
Worcester. Charles I, by his "martyrdom," having ceased to be
king, Berkeley's commission as governor of Virginia no longer
had force, and its surrender was in accordance with the usual procedure. Charles II's new commission, to the same office, was of
little practical value in view of his military state. It was, indeed,
a little comedy that Richard Lee and the Stuart prince played in
the "court" of the royal exile, useful chiefly as a manifestation of
Virginian loyalty. Perhaps Charles would have done better had
he accepted the invitation that Richard is said to have extended on
this occasion — to cross the ocean, make his home in that Virginia which was still loyal, and bide his time. However, the rash
young man's decision to try the issue with Cromwell saved the
colony from what would probably have been an inconvenient and
not altogether edifying guest.

Yet Virginia, from the outbreak of the civil war, remained
faithful to the Stuart kings. If Richard Lee's public task had
been to maintain this loyalty, his administration proved a success.
Not that the times in Virginia were especially troublous. After
all, England was a long distance away; her excitements concerned
the colony only remotely; Virginia's business was raising tobacco
and building a state, and parliamentary wrangles and religious
arguments did not divert the Dominion from this task. Even
Richard, we feel, sincere as were his royal sentiments, never approached the feverish agitation of Berkeley. The state of most
Virginians was the same. In the counties south of the James, a
few Roundhead sympathizers occasionally lifted up their voices

for Cromwell; most of these, Puritans, unpopular on general principles, were presently sent packing to that disloyal country, New England, as outspoken for Parliament as Virginia was for king. It took a royal beheading to arouse Virginia's deeper emotions. Then the tones of Berkeley and his legislature were heard throughout the land. Cromwell may have subdued England and made way with its king, but he had not conquered Virginia. A special meeting of the General Assembly declared that Charles I was "undoubtedly sainted" and denounced his executioners as guilty of "traiterous proceedings." All in Virginia upholding the crime were to be regarded as "accessories after the fact" and punished in accordance with the laws of England. Berkeley's defiance went further; his obedient Assembly acclaimed Charles II king, and resolved that anyone who should "insinuate any doubt or scruple" as to his rights to the throne should be guilty of "high treason."

Such a challenge was not likely to be ignored, and presently a British fleet appeared before Jamestown, demanding its surrender in the name of the Commonwealth. This *dénouement* brought out both sides of Berkeley's character. His preparations for resistance, the construction of fortifications, and the impressment of Dutch vessels into service display the man in his Peter Stuyvesant vein; the remarkable terms of surrender obtained evinced again his innate shrewdness and common sense. Great Britain and Virginia parleyed almost like equal independent powers, and the surrender was made on terms that enhanced Virginia's honor. In return for acknowledging the Cromwellian régime, Virginia became practically a self-governing republic; in the next ten years it was far freer than it had ever been under the Stuarts. Proscriptions usual on such occasions were foregone, the use of the English prayer book for a year was secured, — provided there were no prayers for the king, — and everybody was guaranteed the continued possession of his land. These Virginia negotiators disclosed their comprehension of the part the land-grant system — the fifty acres for every "person transported" — played in their prosperity, for a special clause in the treaty provided that this privilege should remain.

The new régime naturally ended Berkeley's career as governor

and Lee's as secretary of state.   Richard's name vanished from
the list of councilors, and the several offices that yielded such
agreeable emoluments now passed into the hands of faithful
Roundheads.   He met this new crisis in his life with dignity —
far more dignity than Berkeley displayed, for the ousted governor
made no secret of his rage and chagrin.   Shaking the dust of
Jamestown, with its new Puritan House of Burgesses and Council, Berkeley retired to his country estate at Green Spring, with its
gardens and plum trees, and converted it into a kind of sanctuary
for royalists, who now began to arrive in hundreds.   Only technically were Berkeley and his guests acquiescent in the new order;
stories came from this retreat telling of high revelry, of toasts to
King Charles and curses to Cromwell.   Richard Lee was not so
brazen or vituperative in his seclusion.   His retirement was
quieter, less antagonistic to the forces in power — and also not
without profit.   Perhaps, like his celebrated descendant two hundred years afterward, Richard's disposition was to accept an established situation; having lost the righteous fight, he acquiesced,
without rancor, in the new government, and resolved to play in
it, if not an enthusiastic, at least a conciliatory part.   Indeed, one
of the legal documents of the time refers to Richard Lee as a man
who had been "useful and faithful to the Commonwealth" —
though the nature of his service is not explained.   Unlike
Berkeley, who remained close to Jamestown, with an ear open for
disloyal gossip, Richard withdrew to a section of Virginia that
was a four days' journey from the capital.   In the southern part
of what was afterward called the "Northern Neck," roughly the
area between the Rappahannock and the Potomac, was one of
those estuaries of the Chesapeake which Virginians call "creek";
it was a broad and deep body of tidewater, which, after flowing
inland for a short space, divided in two — its separate branches
in turn splitting into different streams.   From this sinuous
tendency it was known as "Dividing Creek."   So adapted was the
sea frontage for a harbor that, until recent years, Baltimore
steamboats used it as a landing place, and in the seventeenth century no better vantage point could be imagined for that shipping
business which the planter carried on.   The adjoining land, extremely fertile, was wild; in fact, treaty with the Indians made

settlement by white men on its soil a felony. Ten years before, Richard had ignored a similar prohibition, applying to the country north of the York, and now again he urbanely disregarded a foolish law and began encroaching on the Indian preserves. Once more he chose an unpeopled land, and pitched his tent in a wilderness. In Northumberland County, — not yet, however, set aside as a county, — Lee, in the course of the next ten years, established two plantations, at the same time constantly adding to his possessions on the York. Making some kind of accommodation with the Indians, here Lee built a rough planked house and spent the rest of his days.

The new "seat" was not lacking in natural beauty, for the magnificent expanse of the Chesapeake was always before the proprietor's eyes; there being no official duties to perform, Lee could concentrate on what, from this time forth, became the serious business of life, the heaping up of land that would make his descendants secure. All these new possessions he acquired, as he had those on the York, by the purchase of head-rights. *"Ne incautus futuri"* — such was the heraldic motto of the Lees, further emphasized, on the family crest, by the image of a squirrel nibbling a nut. No more fitting injunction could be imagined, and no man was ever less careless of the future than Lee. Land! land! land! — that was the goal of Richard's last ten years. He was not the founder of one family, but of several; for the subsequent lines of Lee nearly all established their seats on soil which the great ancestor put together at this time. Lee Hall, Ditchley, Cobb's Hall, Mount Pleasant — these and other estates were carved out of Richard's seventeenth-century sequestrations. Up the Potomac, from the mouth to the site of Washington, it would be hard to find any choice piece of river front that escaped Richard's eye. One of his greatest tracts included the plantation afterward known as Mount Vernon. Richard's hand even reached over the river and added a Maryland grant to his domain, destined to become the Blenheim of the Maryland Lees. The cultivation of Paradise and of his two estates in Northumberland actively went on, but the extensive acres assembled in this new Virginia region, the Potomac, were reserved for a later day. It was the Cavaliers who gave this section prominence. There, in the years from 1650 to 1660, came scores of families that were destined to play a great part in another revolution — this time taking sides against an English king. Lee undeniably felt an affiliation with this company; the land was rich, and possessed those advantages indispensable to successful tobacco growing, plenty of landings on the river. Though Lee at bottom disapproved the Commonwealth, there really was no ground for personal grievance. Cromwell's hand rested lightly on Virginia; its Roundhead governors showed no hostility to royalists in bestowing lands; at any rate there was no discrimination against Lee, and the great planter accepted titles as contentedly from "the keepers of the Liberties of England" as he had formerly from "Sir William Berkeley, with the advice and consent of the Councell of State."

The fact is that Lee was becoming a rich man — probably the richest Virginian of his day. Wealth then was land, and Richard died the greatest landholder of his generation. Afterward, when the country was opened to the west, larger proprietors appeared, — Fairfax, Byrd, Carter, Fitzhugh, — but no Virginian, in 1664, the year of Richard's death, equaled his 13,000 acres of rare tobacco soil. John Gibbon, Richard's heraldic friend, estimated his "faire estate in Virginia" at £2000 a year. In that era this was a princely income — probably unmatched by any planter of the time. But Richard was more than a capitalist in land. In several of the ships plying between Virginia and England he was a partner. That he was a large tobacco trader in London, with his own warehouse and countinghouse, is apparent. Indeed, in the Commonwealth period, Richard was a man of two countries, England and Virginia, crossing and recrossing the Atlantic almost as frequently as a modern American captain of industry; not improbably he spent more time in London than on the Chesapeake. And now he gratified the ambition that inspired all "younger sons" of his day — he became a country gentleman in England, the owner of a fine and reasonably large estate about three miles from the metropolis. For ages an old Roman road had crossed the county of Essex — a favorite approach to London, through the varying centuries, of Roman legions, Canterbury pilgrims, mediæval wayfarers, and subsequent modern traffic of all kinds. The Anglo-Saxon word for road is *strat* (or *stræt*) — hence the English *street;* this *strat,* at a point about four miles from London, crossed a river — appropriately called the River Lea — by an ancient ford; and on old maps the famous thoroughfare is called the "Strat by the ford." How one of the most famous of Virginia's colonial houses gets its name needs no further explanation.

At the junction with the River Lea stood the town of Stratford-atte-Bowe — the village where Chaucer's Prioress learned her un-Parisian French; three miles to the east a sleepy village, called Stratford-Langthorne, — or Langton, — had mused for centuries. To-day the whole section, comprising the boroughs of East and West Ham, is a woeful melange of factories, docks, railroad stations, and slums, for rapacious London has engrossed it all, just as rapacious New York has swept over the old villages of Bloomingdale and Harlem; in Richard Lee's time, however, the country had much of its ancient ecclesiastical flavor. The land, sweeping southward to the Thames, was all meadow, divided by pretty mill streams, artificially deflected between two arms of the River Lea, dotted by mills, orchards, and an occasional peasant's cottage. "Then the Lea, presently uniting its streams, runs with a gentle current into the Thames, whence the place is called Lea mouth." The ruins of the old Cistercian Abbey of Langthorne were visible in Richard's day. A writer of his own time describes the view towards West Ham from the bridge at Stratford, whence he saw "the remains of a monastery pleasantly watered about with several streams, and the meadows near the mills planted around with willows."

Whether Richard purchased this estate himself or obtained it as inheritance is not known, but the likelihood is that it represented profit from his Virginia plantations. What more desirable home for a rich Virginia tobacco planter whose climb to fortune had not dulled his love of English country life? This was the estate that made Lee, according to his will, "lately of Stratford-Langton, in the County of Essex, Esquire." One should not miss the significance of that "Esquire"; it was almost a title, as well-defined as Baron or Marquess; it meant that the possessor was the proprietor of land, with tenants of his own, and Richard's use of the appellation was a kind of clarion call, proclaiming the achievement of his goal. And the life Richard led in Stratford-Langton was certainly that of the substantial class. Each morning his coach appeared, and drove the master to his London countingroom; every evening it came rumbling back over the Strat-by-the-Ford, depositing a silver-buckled, knee-breeched gentleman at his door. That Richard was still "in trade" did not detract from his glory, for the London merchant in that time was held in high social esteem. How much time Richard spent here cannot be said. His visits, however, were frequent, and not improbably several of his children were born in this English house. The section is full of reminders of the subsequent Stratford on the Potomac. Skirting the country on the north is Epping Forest — a name given to the section that similarly encroaches on the Virginia estate. Possibly that strange architecture of the Westmoreland Stratford derives from the same region. The most conspicuous mansion at Stratford-Langton was Ham House, built probably in the time of Queen Elizabeth and occupied by a succession of distinguished Englishmen — among them that Dr. Fothergill who, in the eighteenth century, became a close friend of Arthur Lee. It had the same form of the letter "H," the same two pointed roofs, and a conspicuous feature was a row of splendid Virginia cedars, said to have been the first transplanted to England. This house is no longer standing, but surviving prints disclose a remarkable similarity, in general outlines, to the Virginia Stratford.[1] Thomas Lee, Richard's grandson and builder of Stratford, visited London in 1716. Naturally he went to West Ham to survey the old Lee seat in Essex, and must have many times inspected Ham House, its most conspicuous architectural ornament. What more likely than that it should have given him the exterior conception of his meditated Virginia home, just as the English village of his ancestor gave him the name of his Virginia estate?

When Richard settled in Essex, he evidently intended to make this country home his permanent abiding place. His Virginia career had been ended by Cromwell; his tastes were for a culti-

---

[1] See page 234 of *History of the Parishes of East and West Ham,* by Katherine Fry, London, 1888.

vated life; his children's future, backed as it was by wealth, seemed to offer a fairer prospect in the old country than on the shores of the Chesapeake. John Gibbon relates that Lee was prepared to put his Virginia property in the hands of a steward, that he himself had been selected, and that Richard had even set aside one of his daughters as Gibbon's wife! Yet Richard's frequent returns to Virginia show that the Old Dominion was exerting a powerful contrary spell. It seems almost as though something like a struggle were taking place — that the conflicting pulls of East and West were always at work. Should he make his definite home at Stratford-Langton, one worthy of his ancestors, or should he fix the family seat for all time in the country where he had fared so well? When in Virginia, the charm of English life and English tradition proved irresistible; as soon as Richard found himself on the English estate, the sunlit waters of the Chesapeake and the glamour of a new nation rising in the forest began tugging in the other direction. His family — six sons and two daughters — were growing up; two of the boys had been placed in Oxford; where could these and the others best be established in life? In 1659, the decision had evidently been made — for England; in this year Lee, with Gibbon, crossed to Virginia, to settle his affairs and make arrangements for permanent departure. But suddenly an event in England changed all their plans. That was the Restoration, in May 1660, of Charles II. This opened a new prospect for Berkeley and Lee in Virginia, where the old régime was set up again, Berkeley in his place as governor and Lee again in the Council.

Richard, however, did not return as secretary of state, and the likelihood is that he had no wish to reassume the arduous duties of this office. For he was getting old and had had a difficult, if interesting, life. Existence at far-away Dividing Creek offered a more pleasant prospect than the troublous era which now began in Jamestown. And so Richard spent his last days in this distant fastness, still active in his favorite occupation of adding to his lands. At the time of his death, head-rights had been acquired of ninety-four "persons," entitling him to another 4700 acres — a claim which his oldest son promptly and successfully asserted. And again, in this ultimate period, the yearning for England returned. In the latter part of 1662, Richard, with his whole family of wife and eight children, — several of them very young, — crossed the ocean and took up residence at Stratford-Langton. If this translation was made with an idea of definite settlement, the mood quickly changed again — and this time for good. Hesitation was now at an end — the Lees were not to be Englishmen, but Virginians. That country, in Richard's twenty-five years' sojourn, had become more than a tobacco farm; it was already showing the beginnings of empire.

Let Richard's will tell the story. "In the name of God, amen. I, Colonel Richard Lee . . . being bound upon a voyage to Virginia aforesaid, and not knowing how it may please God to dispose of me in so long a voyage . . . do make, ordain and declare this my last will and testament." Now he burned all his bridges. The English estate was ordered to be sold and its furnishings distributed among his children. The following instruction was added in case the foreboding in this preliminary sentence should be fulfilled: "Also my earnest desire is that my good friends will, with all convenient speed cause my wife and children (all except Francis if he be pleased) to be transported to Virginia and to provide all necessary for the voyage." Another son, Richard, at Oxford, had won distinction as a scholar — so much that influential churchmen had asked the father to permit him to remain in England to be ordained. Lee was assured that the young man would be preferred and ultimately reach high position. But Lee was emphatic. The die had been cast. Virginia was to be the future family seat, and Richard, Junior, with the rest, sailed home.

The elder Lee's apprehension was not realized. He safely made the voyage and resumed the old life at Dividing Creek. But never again did he visit England or see the ruins of the Abbey of Langthorne. He died at Cobb's Hall, Dividing Creek, in the early part of 1664. Three centuries have obliterated all traces of Richard's tomb — but somewhere, in the old graveyard at Cobb's Hall, on the Chesapeake, the founder of the Lees is buried. A sycamore, six feet thick, is commonly pointed out to-day as marking the site of his resting place.

II

THE REVOLUTION OF 1676

I

To the student of American democracy, the first two generations of the Lees have particular interest. So tenacious is the legend of Virginia "Cavaliers" that the seventeenth-century province remains, in the popular mind, a magnificent expanse of huge estates, a land of transplanted English noblemen, maintaining a splendor fairly mediæval. Yet the word "cavalier" has properly a meaning political, not social; it signifies an active supporter of the king, a fighter in the royal armies, and can hardly be descriptive of an emigrant, like Richard Lee, who came to America in 1640, two years before the outbreak of English civil war. Following the execution of Charles I, a fair-sized company of undoubted Cavaliers sought refuge in the friendly colony, but, compared with the inflowing of humble folk that followed throughout the seventeenth century, their number must have been unimportant. Certainly not all the 150,000 [1] settlers who reached Virginia from 1600 to 1704 could have represented this heroic breed. In fact, probably very few came from prosperous or Cavalier state; the immigrants, as a mass, were agricultural workers, or proletarian city dwellers, who sought the New World like millions of their brethren since, as a means of improving their social and economic status. And these more numerous pioneers formed the basis of Virginia's population. In the preceding chapter a glimpse has been suggested of Richard Lee's first plantation on the River York and of the Anglo-Saxon bondmen who cultivated it. The statistics of subsequent emigration suggest the sequel. The white retainer is

---

[1] The figure is an estimate of Professor Thomas J. Wertenbaker of Princeton, to whose studies of the Virginia population in the colonial period all writers on the subject, including the present one, are greatly indebted.

no longer exclusively a tobacco serf; he has graduated from that order and become a proprietor himself. He has toiled for the period, usually four years, necessary to pay the cost of passage, has acquired a modest tract of his own, constructed a little frame house, married, and raised a large family of freemen. His holding averages perhaps a hundred acres; so far as comfort and happiness are concerned, Virginia, in its great prosperity previous to the Restoration, presents one of the most fortunate spots on the earth's surface. Its basis is this yeoman class, industrious, intelligent, independent; voting, as proudly as the Cavalier, for members of the House of Burgesses, occasionally sitting in that body themselves. Thus the Tidewater, from the Potomac to the James, dotted with thousands of rough planked homesteads, has become the seat of an agricultural small landholding democracy such as Jefferson is afterward to picture as the most blessed state of mankind.

But the family of Lee more closely — though not too closely — approximated the type of Virginian that has passed into legend. In size it was typical of its age; Richard's will makes provision for six sons and two daughters. In many respects the document pictures the type of family organization prevalent then and afterward. The most promising of the sons, John and Richard, in accordance with a practice that lasted until the Revolution, were set aside for schooling in English universities; at Oxford the oldest, and principal heir, John, received a medical degree, and the second son, Richard, also obtained his education. From earliest settlement great planting families invariably chose one scion for life in London, as tobacco merchant. It was his business, first of all, to receive the crops from the ancestral estate, sell them in the London market, and send back in turn the supplies of clothing, furniture, farm utensils, and other manufactured articles needed on the Potomac; usually he owned or chartered one or more ships which were dispatched to Virginia in the spring, there loaded with hogsheads of tobacco and reëmbarked for London. Richard's will, instructing his trustees to sell his English possessions and transport his family to Virginia, makes one reservation — "except Francis, if he be so pleased." This Francis had evidently displayed business qualities; he was therefore the one set aside for a mercantile career. Such Virginians — and this was the case with Francis — were usually lost to the Old Dominion. They commonly married English wives, not infrequently reached good status in England, and left descendants who were absorbed in the English population.

Besides John, Richard, and Francis, the second generation comprised three other sons, one of whom, Hancock, became the founder of a notable line.   The Hancock Lees, indeed, have an especially significant history, for they were a joint product of New England and Virginia, in a way symbolizing that future union of the two sections, under the leadership of Virginia and Massachusetts statesmen, which exercised so decisive an influence in the Revolution.   Richard Lee, of Dividing Creek, and Elder Brewster, of the *Mayflower* pilgrimage and of the Plymouth colony — who could ask for more representative American ancestry?   Such were the progenitors of the Hancock Lees.   One of the richest voyagers on the *Mayflower* was Isaac Allerton, also one of the most cantankerous, for, after marrying Brewster's daughter Fear, and quarreling with fellow Puritans over certain business phases of their enterprise, he suddenly took his departure, lived for some time at Marblehead, where trouble again broke out, then moved to New Amsterdam and finally to New Haven, where he died in 1658.   His son, also named Isaac, similarly liked to wander, his excursions ultimately ending in Westmoreland County, Virginia, where he became the close friend of John Lee and Henry Corbin and co-builder with them of an un-Puritanical banqueting hall at the junction of their estates.   His daughter's marriage with the original Hancock Lee produced an adventurous group of Americans known as the Ditchley line, from the name of their "mansion" on the Chesapeake.   A grandson — this one also named Hancock — was one of the first pathfinders in Kentucky, fellow explorer and close friend of Daniel Boone, founder of Leestown on the Ohio, and surveyor for the Ohio Company.   A daughter of Ditchley, marrying into the Taylor family, gave the United States its twelfth President, the hero of the Mexican War, old "rough and ready" Zachary.

2

Richard's oldest son and principal heir, John Lee, embodied many of the qualities that have passed into history as Virginian.

He is a charming though fleeting figure in the family story, for he died, unmarried, at twenty-eight. Educated at Oxford as a physician, he apparently did not studiously follow his craft — at least not to the extent of ignoring the main purpose of life, which was having a good time. Shooting, fishing, militia training and its attendant jollifications, took up more of John Lee's time than his learned trade. He was the first of the Lees to establish the family seat on the Potomac, the region with which it was to be identified for the next two hundred years, for he was probably the builder of Mount Pleasant, the house near Machotick Creek, on the estate of 2600 acres awarded him by his father's will. An even more famous architectural achievement was the "Banquetting Hall" referred to above. Its purposes, solemnly enshrined in official documents, gave the flavor of the man, as well as of his partners. John Lee, Allerton, and Corbin signed a contract to entertain, in turn, their "men, masters and friends yearly" — "for the better preservation of that friendship which ought to be between neighbors." Other memorials of John Lee indicate tastes harmonizing with this association. An inventory of his estates lists his saddles, guns, fishing equipment, pistols, "gray suits with silver buttons," "gloves with silver tops," and other appurtenances of dashing, open-air Virginia. Public duties had not been avoided, for John had served as high sheriff and burgess from Westmoreland, and had been commissioner to safeguard the county against the "Susquehannock" Indians, already, in 1672, planning those attacks which had such momentous consequences. But most of the few glimpses obtained of John Lee identify his name with hospitality and friendship. Appropriately enough, the one surviving memento is a silver drinking cup, presented by John to Queen's College, Oxford, and still preserved in its dining hall. It attests John's loyalty to the house of Stuart, for such gifts were piously made, in the period of his residence, to replace the silver which loyal Oxford had melted to reënforce the treasury of the king. It has proved a godsend to present-day genealogists, for it is decorated with the arms of the Lees of Shropshire, thus being another link in the evidence tracing Lee descent to that stock.

There was nothing of the roisterer in John's brother Richard, who fell heir to his wide-extending acres. Richard was as home-

keeping and sedate as the elder had been free-ranging and obstreperous.   Everything known of the second Richard portrays a man
thoughtful, serious, quiet, devoted to the domestic virtues, deeply
loyal in his political convictions, prepared, at times, to sacrifice
personal fortune for things in which he believed.   Richard's surviving portrait indicates a man of melancholic, even saturnine
disposition.   The grim face, eyes searching and cold, and deeply
indented lines show traces of care, perhaps of suffering; it seems
unlikely that this man enjoyed a happy-go-lucky career — rather
that life presented problems, difficulties, even moments of despair.
All the Lee characteristics stand out boldly — the oval face, big
nose, and double chin; here also appear the family dignity and
pride; that the second Richard was a stickler for principles and
tradition, perhaps contemptuous of the "rabble," not given to
hasty, unconsidered speech — all this is evident.   The lively
humor apparent in John it seems unlikely that Richard shared;
existence in his view was clearly something that must be justified
to God and man.   Richard's Latin epitaph, in Burnt House Fields,
Westmoreland, strengthens this impression.   It describes him as
born of *antiqua familia,* and here, cut deep in marble, again appears the statement that the Virginia Lees spring from the county
of Salop.   It recalls the zeal with which Richard had fulfilled his
public duties, and pays tribute, as a culminating virtue, to the
piety with which he had always served God.   As a more worldly
note, the inscription tells how Richard excelled in Greek and Latin
and in all other forms of humane letters.   And so the man stands
forth — pious, learned, conservative, bookish, devoted to the
public good.

Possibly the second Richard's serious face is merely a reflection
of days consumed in study.   For over two generations there was
an illuminating collection of papers in the Lee family — a series of
notes in Greek, Latin, and Hebrew, kept in Richard's handwriting.
He evidently preferred "the languages," even for personal memo-
randa.   Naturally, great business shrewdness could not be looked
for in a character of this type, and the fact is that Richard did not
manifest his father's talent for accumulation; the large inheritance remained intact under his direction, but did not grow.   A
grandson, William, comments on these lost opportunities ruefully,

almost reproachfully. "He neither improved nor diminished his paternal estate, though in that time he might with ease have acquired what would produce at this day a most princely revenue." William looks askance at his improvident ancestor, much as the contemporary New Yorker looks back on his great-grandfather, who failed to purchase, for a few hundred dollars, uptown farms now bisected by Fifth Avenue. And the Potomac River was Virginia's Fifth Avenue — its great artery of traffic as well as a favorite seat of wealth and fashion.

Who could conscientiously blame this scholar for failing as an operator in real estate? The "inventory" of Richard's library has survived, in itself a sufficient commentary on the man. Merely to glance over the titles gives the headache. A planter finding surcease in patristic writings and mediæval theology — the type was not so rare as may be thought, but no early Virginia collector of books goes quite so deep as Richard. Who to-day, even of the learned, breaks his teeth over Florus Franciscus, Paulus Orosius, Aretus, Corderius, and many others of like kidney? Such trivial reading as appears is usually in the classics; all the traditional writers are there, from Homer to Horace — Lucian, Vergil, Ovid, and "Tulley." Montaigne, too, was apparently a favorite — a fact that makes one deal gently with Richard's literary tastes. The man was likewise a devotee of French and Italian. Ariosto and Voiture and Balzac (he of the *Letters*) are found incongruously touching elbows with a vast assortment of pietistic reading — *Learn to Die, The Mischief of Sin, Hear the Church! Divine Breathings, A Glimpse of Eternity,* and plenty more in the same vein. Richard, as already noted, so impressed his instructors at Oxford that they wished him to remain in England and enter the Church. One almost thinks, in surveying this library, that a mistake was made in failing to fit him into the Establishment. Richard's selection of political volumes similarly brings out the man's convictions. Who but the blindest followers of divine right would fill his shelves with such folios as these: *Government and obedience as they are directed by Scripture, The Accomplished Courtier, Power Communicated by God to the Prince.* A robust antipopery note resounds in such a challenge as *Europe a Slave unless England break her chains.* In the whole list there is not a trace of Shakespeare, Spenser, Milton, Dryden, and other almost contemporary lights of English literature; no Restoration drama sullies the shelves; significantly the only poets of Richard's own time are Cleveland, the Cavalier laureate, and Butler, whose *Hudibras* is one long diatribe against the Puritans.   In the catalogue only a single caption suggests the more urbane side of Virginia existence, for Richard's library did contain a volume on *The Art of Distillation.*

Lee's studies did not keep him from the official station which, from this time forward, became almost hereditary in the family. That grandson William, quoted above, shows querulousness also on this point: "He was of the council in Virginia and also other offices of honor and profit, though they yielded little to him." Not only was the second Richard burgess, councilor, naval officer, and receiver of duties on the Potomac River, but likewise colonel of the Westmoreland militia.   For Richard promptly moved into Mount Pleasant on his brother's death.   The house stood on a lowland near the Potomac; it was built, probably, of wood, and exclusively surrounded by a brick wall.   Here Richard lived out his dignified days, a man of weight, respected not only for his station, but for his character.   All references to him in contemporary writings are favorable.   He frequently appears in the letters of William Fitzhugh, whose son married Richard's daughter Ann.   "You are not Yorkshire enough," writes this occasionally sententious planter, "to set the course of your advice by the compass of your interest."   A discerning compliment, eloquently expressed!   Richard manifested another prudence which appeared in his descendants.   He chose his wife with judgment. A single marble slab to-day covers the graves of Richard and Lettice Lee, — for such was her charming name (more formally Lætitia), — a name that was afterward one of the favorites among the daughters of the clan.   Not improbably written by Richard himself, for her death took place in 1706, eight years before his own, the Latin inscription sets forth the virtues especially desired in Virginia gentlewomen of the time.   Thus Lettice was "a dutiful wife," "a most loving mother of her children," "charitable to the poor," and "kind to all the world."   According to the same legend Lettice was the daughter of Henry Corbin,

generosus, — gentleman well born, — and probably in that circumstance she rendered her contribution to the family breed. Her portrait, that of an amiable, placid woman, justifies the lapidary compliments, yet the significant point must not be forgotten: through Lettice the strength of the Corbin family was transmitted to the Lees. And it was a genuine addition. Her father, Henry Corbin, had been a boon companion of John, one of his associates in building the "Banquetting Hall"; he was an indubitable Cavalier, coming to Virginia in 1654, taking up an estate that adjoined the first Richard's patents on the Machotick, a seat which, under the name of Peckatone, ultimately became the most magnificent in Westmoreland. The family went back to the Middle Ages in England, — it is one of the few Virginia trees that can be definitely established, — and was to play an important part in Virginia history. In addition to securing a charming and loving helpmeet, the second Richard thus reënforced the Lee blood with the enterprise and character of one of the most forceful of Potomac houses.

3

In politics Richard was an active and irreconcilable die-hard. His loyalty to the reigning house went further than his father's. That devotion to theology and learning which precluded the increase of his estates added fervor to his love of prince and absolutism. The times put these qualities to the severest test, for that phenomenon known to succeeding generations as a "depression" was almost the uninterrupted course of Richard's day. The prosperous economic era of the first Richard's time, when every man lived in a land of plenty, seemed to have passed forever. Man and nature combined to heap misery on the devoted colony. Hurricanes of violence hitherto unknown, hailstorms and epidemics, added their destruction to high taxes, debts, widespread poverty, and attacks by the Dutch on commerce, for, just as the vigorous Hollanders, then at war with England, entered the Thames and wrought havoc almost as far as London, so they came into the James and riddled and plundered Virginia tobacco ships. Indian outbreaks from the North kept the planters in constant anxiety. The whole thing culminated in the first American revolution, which broke out in 1676, just one hundred years before America was made a free republic.

According to the old historian Beverley, among the causes of Bacon's Rebellion were "the heavy restraints and burdens laid upon this [tobacco] trade by act of Parliament in England." The Navigation Law of 1661, to which the writer refers, did more than produce conditions that led to this immediate outburst, for it embodied the policy, the point of view, that made inevitable the separation of Great Britain and her American colonies. The underlying conception was precisely the same as that which prompted the Stamp Act of 1765 and all the other legislation that received its answer at Bunker Hill and Yorktown. An enlightened colonial policy was a lesson that England learned slowly; the modern view — essentially a product of the nineteenth century — did not gain the upper hand early enough to keep the American provinces within the British Empire. Englishmen were led to establish companies for the settlement of America largely for compensatory reasons. England, as an economic power, was incomplete; for products indispensable to its existence, notably shipping materials, — masts, timber, tar, rosin, and the like, — the island kingdom was dependent on foreign countries, especially on the Baltic, which might be closed on a moment's notice, with resultant national ruin. To obtain such essentials, in lands under English control, was the motive for planting colonies; the motive, that is, was exclusively an English one — the purpose in mind was the good of England, not the development of new nations beyond the seas. That these outlying regions might develop an independent consciousness, national purposes, and a manner of life entirely distinct from the intentions of the mother country — this is an idea that, for the nearly two hundred years that Virginia remained under the British crown, was not widely comprehended in England. But this conception gained quick predominance in Virginia itself, and the two points of view were brought into violent contention when the Navigation Laws suddenly brought the Virginia economic system to ruin.

Up to 1660 the Dominion had what was practically a world market for its single crop, tobacco. All Europe, from Russia and the Baltic countries to Italy and Spain, yearly competed for the output of the Tidewater planters. This competition naturally led to high prices, which in turn led to the rapid expansion that marked the first Richard's day — an expansion that dotted the landscape with thousands of small farms, interspersed occasionally by a large plantation. But the Navigation Laws provided that tobacco could henceforth be sent to only one country — England; that Americans could import goods only from the mother land; and that all commerce should be carried only in English ships. Obviously, in passing such legislation, — legislation entirely consonant with the political thought and mercantile economy of the day, — Parliament was not thinking of colonial welfare, but only of what was regarded as the advantage of the British Isles.

A generation that has lived through the era 1915–1930 hardly needs instruction as to the consequences of such a change. Indeed the status of Virginia, from 1660 to 1680, strongly represents the agricultural era through which the United States is now passing. Just as American farmers, under pressure of world war, enormously extended their acres and increased their crops, only to suffer bankruptcy when the demand suddenly ceased, so the Virginia tobacco planter, in the epoch of the first two Richard Lees, adjusted his one industry to the demands of a world market — which suddenly vanished when the Navigation Laws restricted their output to a single country, England. The cause of the distress that followed was precisely the same as that which has reduced the present-day American farmer to misery — the loss of foreign trade. Just as wheat fell from a dollar a bushel in 1929 to thirty-five cents in 1932, so Virginia tobacco, selling for fourpence a pound in 1650, dropped to half a penny in 1667. The resultant calamity was comparatively far greater in Virginia in 1660 than in the United States in 1932, for tobacco was the only crop — the only source of income that made the country self-supporting. In two or three decades the large planters found a way of overcoming this disadvantage, but the intervening period was one of continuous misery, especially for the small proprietors.

And tobacco rotting on the farms and the dilapidation that overtook the farms themselves were not the only form of suffering. All kinds of political oppression accompanied economic distress.

Just as Charles and his party, after the Restoration, began destroying English liberties, so their heavy fist fell upon Virginia. No
part of his realm had shown such loyalty as Virginia, and no
part did the king treat with such callous ingratitude. The suffrage was restricted so that only a small part of the citizenry could
vote. The authority of the House of Burgesses was all but extinguished. A House elected in 1661 proved so subservient to
Berkeley that it was kept in power for fifteen years, and during
this time the wishes of the populace were unrecognized in Jamestown. It was a period of one-man rule, — that of Berkeley, —
and a rule that represented, in every detail, the voice of autocracy
at home. This political "boss," whose exclusion from office during the Commonwealth had only whetted his natural taste for
despotism, now, under the Restoration, promptly put his heel
on the democratic idea that had prevailed in that peaceful interval.
Thus the popular outburst of 1676 was both agrarian and political
— an uprising of the unemployed against the large planting class,
and of a citizenry determined not to lose privileges exercised in
the preceding half century. The Revolution of 1676, in its purposes, thus almost duplicates the more successful revolt of 1776,
in which both political and economic independence was also the
stake. In the latter uprising the Lees were leaders on the popular
side; it is interesting, therefore, to examine the family attitude
in the rebellion that served as prologue.

The changes in thinking wrought by a hundred years were startling. To the second Richard young Nathaniel Bacon was no enlightened herald of new things, and to Bacon the scholarly recluse
embodied all the evils he was seeking to destroy. Could Richard
be revivified and learn that this detested swashbuckler had become a modern hero, the first performer in a drama that had its
blossoming in the American republic, he would be mystified and
shocked. Probably that republic itself would not receive his
blessing, for the man who spent days absorbing such volumes as
Power Communicated by God to the Prince would not understand
such heresy as political authority residing in the people. For
that, as explained by present-day historians, is the principle for
which Bacon fought. On the personal side Bacon has always
been a compelling figure. He flames, like a backwoods D'Ar-

tagnan, amid the desolation of the time — forceful, gallant, risk-
ing and losing everything in what he regarded as a sacred cause.
School-book illustrations have imprinted on the memory Bacon's
defiance of Berkeley, as, hand on sword hilt, he confronted him
before the Jamestown courthouse and forced the cowering governor to his will; and his secret, midnight burial in the York, or
some other unknown spot, has enshrined his martyrdom with a
mystery stimulating to romance.   Seldom has a revolutionary
leader so united in one person oratory that stirred the most sluggish and military prowess that brought unvarying success; Bacon
was both the Patrick Henry and the George Washington of the
rebellion of 1676.   Beverley, who hated Bacon as cordially as did
Lee, but for whom the man clearly had a positive attraction, hits
him off well.   "This gentleman had been brought up at one of
the Inns of Court and had a moderate fortune.   He was young,
bold, active, of an inviting aspect and powerful elocution, in a
word, he was in every way qualified to lead a giddy and unthinking multitude.   Before he had been three years in the country,
he was, for his extraordinary qualifications, made one of the Council, and in great honor and esteem among the people."   As to
Bacon's power over men, one fact suffices: he started his movement
in June 1676, with a few ragged vagabonds for followers, and in
less than a month all Virginia, except the Berkeley "clique," was
solidly behind him.   In one swift action Berkeley's troops were
scattered and that gentleman driven in flight to his ships, leaving
Bacon master of Jamestown; had Bacon not died of a sudden and
mysterious fever, there is little doubt that he would have made
considerable trouble for the royal troops which Charles was preparing to send, and that the mother country would have been
compelled, a century before that situation actually arose, to face
the problem of suppressing a rebellious province three thousand
watery miles away.   The leader who pushed things to this extreme was twenty-nine years old, a cadet of one of the great families of England, that of Lord Chancellor Francis Bacon and
himself a product of Cambridge University — perhaps the first
American colonist who had thought deeply on the strange problems
presented by this experiment of planting new English nations on
foreign soil.

For Bacon was not only the Patrick Henry and George Washington of 1676; he was the Thomas Jefferson as well. Ostensibly he was assembling forces to fight the Indians, who were massacring and torturing in several parts of Virginia — to perform a duty that Berkeley had neglected; but his final aims were profound. Berkeley's repeated refusal to permit popular levies was not surprising; he knew that Bacon, after suppressing the red men, would turn his ragged soldiers against his own inviolate person, for the redress of long-standing grievances — and this is what happened. Bacon's real offending, in conservative quarters, was his assertion of the people's right to control their destinies. "The rabble give out that they should have their own lawes," writes an indignant commentator of the time. That was just the point. Berkeley had so completely abolished all forms of popular rule and concentrated all political power in himself that those whom he called "rag-taile and bob-taile" were looking back longingly to the republic that Virginia had been during the Oliverian era. Berkeley himself had been a beneficiary of this system, for the House, in 1659, on the eve of the Restoration, had chosen him chief executive — an act afterward sustained by a commission from his "sacred majesty." In Bacon's proclamation an odious word, recently popularized in England, was used to describe the little circle which, with Berkeley at the head, held Virginia in its grip. That was "cabal." One of its most determined members was Richard Lee. Practically all Richard's compatriots of Westmoreland took Berkeley's side, and the Lees were foremost in assailing the rebel. In all the excitements of the time and in the fifty years that followed, not a word is forthcoming from this family that betrays any swerving from the royal cause. The loyalty the first Richard brought from England to Virginia still, in the mind of the Lees, constituted the beginning and end of colonial politics.

In the midst of all this misery and injustice, another word, of quite different implication from "cabal," suddenly flamed into the consciousness of this overburdened province — to burst into a brilliant prominence and then to die out, and remain quiescent for nearly a century. This uncouth term — "the People" — appeared in all Bacon's proclamations and speeches. His manifesto, reciting needed reforms, is signed "Nathaniel Bacon, General by the consent of the People"; prophetically, as though seeing ahead one hundred years, this document is entitled "The Declaration of the People," and is filled with ideas, and even words and sentences, that bring to mind Jefferson's arraignment of George III. It catalogues, item by item, the wrongs the people had suffered at Berkeley's hands, just as Jefferson lists the grievances of the colonies against the British king. "Unjust taxes," "consent of the people," "we, the commons of Virginia," "we declare and doe desire a prime union," "he hath levyed forces without an assurance or the consent of the people" — does it all not have a familiar sound?

But Bacon's quarry was the "cabal" — the little inner ring who were ruling Virginia, and ruling it, according to this fervent pamphleteer, in their own interest, engrossing its lands and revenues. "Let us trace these men in authority and favor to whose hands the Dispensation of the country's wealth has been committed . . . and see what sponges have sucked up the public Treasury." And who were these culprits? Bacon frames a kind of "thou art the man" indictment, specifically naming those responsible for Virginia's sad state. After elevating Berkeley to the place of head conspirator, he adds: "And we further declare these the ensuing persons to have been his wicked and pernitious consillers aiders and assisters against the Commonalty in these our civil commotions." Here follow the names of 19 prominent Virginians, conspicuous among whom is Richard Lee. Bacon's roll of dishonor, indeed, almost forms a Social Register of the Virginia of that date. And he does more than name the offenders — he demands that they be surrendered for trial and punishment. "We do further demand that the said Sir William Berkeley, with all the persons in this list, be forthwith delivered up, or surrender themselves, within four days after the notice hereof, or otherwise we declare as followeth; That in whatsoever house, place, or ship any of the said persons shall reside, be hide [hidden] or protected, Wee doe declare, that the owners, masters, or inhabitants of said places, to be confederates and traitors to the people and the estates of them, as alsoe of the aforesaid persons, to be confiscated." Nor was this mere proletarian bombast. Bacon meant every word he said, and in at least one case his threat of pursuit and capture was successfully carried out. Berkeley saved his skin by fleeing to Accomac; his confederates found refuge in a variety of places; but Richard Lee was seized and held prisoner for seven weeks. The details set forth in public records show that he was ungently dealt with. Had Bacon not suddenly died, and the rebellion in consequence been quashed, there is no doubt that, for a period at least, all the fine estates put together by the first Lee would have been devoted to the common good. After order had been restored appeals were made by loyal sufferers to the government for redress. In these appeals the name of Richard Lee conspicuously appears. "Major Richard Lee, a loyal discreet person worthy of the place to which he was recently advanced of being one of his majesty's Council in Virginia and as to his losses we are credibly informed they were very great and that he was imprisoned by Bacon above seven weeks together, at least one hundred miles from his own home, whereby he received great prejudice to his health by hard usage and very greatly to his whole estate by his absence." To what extent Richard was reimbursed there is no record, but as restitution to loyal subjects who had suffered in their behalf was not a favorite practice of the Stuarts, it is not likely that this petition brought much relief.

Bacon's death ended the insurrection; his forces, having lost their leader, were scattered and rapidly overwhelmed; in American annals he figures as a splendid failure and as a harbinger of 1776. Perhaps it was just as well; certainly the infant American colonies, in 1676, were too immature to set up for themselves, even had Bacon lived and won — which is not likely, for a colony of 50,000 people could not indefinitely have withstood the British Empire. Berkeley's savage reprisals — the hangings and confiscations — recall the behavior of James II after the Monmouth Rebellion and have left an indelible stain on his memory. Good-natured King Charles II was shocked and outraged; "he has hanged more men in that naked country," he remarked, "than I have for the murder of my father." When Berkeley came to London, in 1677, to explain his bloody assize, Charles treated him with contempt, and the old man died, in misery, soon afterward.

4

In the first assertion of popular rule on American soil the tribe of Lee thus can claim no share.   And presently Richard appears again in the scanty literature of the day, this time in an episode that reveals the man's loyalty, sincerity, and that spirit of accommodation which has seemed innate in the Lees from the first.   "I find also," writes William Fitzhugh to George Luke, a kinsman, October 27, 1690, "you are in a hopeful way of managing that concern of the Collector's place, especially now that Col. Lee, in whose hands it is, by refusing to take the appointed oath to King William, etc. it is said he has made himself incapable of bearing any office or place."   Fitzhugh refers to an event that was a sensation of the day.   After the death of Charles II, Richard remained still faithful to the Stuarts.   Even though James II was a papist — no ogre was more monstrous to the Virginian of that time — and had finally abandoned his kingdom and fled, to become a resident of Versailles and pensioner of Louis XIV, still he was, in Richard's eyes, the Lord's anointed and therefore rightful king. And so the second Lee did not accept the "glorious Revolution" of 1688, would not acknowledge William and Mary as lawful sovereigns, and refused to take the oath of allegiance.   As a result, he lost his position in the Council and the lucrative office which Fitzhugh — human nature changes so little! — was now urging his friend to enter the scramble for.   In this Richard was out of tune with Virginia, even with his own planter class.   Most Potomac aristocrats had thoroughly tired of the wretched dynasty and joyfully welcomed William and Mary to the throne.   Richard stuck to his principles, at least for a time — but now that sober, practical sense for which the family is famous came to the front.   William and Mary proved to be just and liberal rulers; under them England rapidly advanced to glory and power, while Virginia also entered on a new career of happiness.   Everybody about him, Richard perceived, was contented and prosperous. Why should he, almost alone of Virginia's great characters, hold out for a vanished and despised régime?   Like his father after the rise of Oliver, like his descendant at Appomattox, Richard therefore accepted the reign of things as they were.   He took the oath of allegiance and his grateful country restored him to the Council.

Richard makes one farewell appearance on the historic stage, again as a foe to democracy and upholder of the ancient régime. His final days witnessed a transformation in Virginia society, from a popular to an aristocratic basis, and in this he was an active influence on the conservative side.   This means that the favorite Virginia system of land grant, based on head-right, disappeared, its place taken by the feudal tenure that had guided European destinies for centuries.   The essence of the Virginia democracy, of course, was this method of distributing the soil.   Certain historians, such as Alexander Brown, have insisted that Virginia's early planting represented a deliberate, conscious determination to set up in America a democratic society, directly opposed to everything for which Stuart England stood.   Frederick Jackson Turner upholds a slightly different thesis.   The Virginia seventeenth-century democracy was not a transplantation from England, but a direct outgrowth of conditions in Virginia itself, the most important being the fee ownership of land by its cultivators, great and small.   Only when this land system was supplanted by one almost essentially the same as that of England did the celebrated Virginia aristocracy develop — an aristocracy that grew as immediately out of the aspects of Virginia life as did that of England out of the Norman Conquest.   According to both the Brown and the Turner interpretation, the democratic era that rose in 1776 was merely a reversion to the original Virginia type, the reëstablishment of that anti-Stuart society which existed in the seventeenth century.

The fifty acres for each settler — slightly reminiscent of the "forty acres and a mule" that became the watchcry of certain pioneers in the nineteenth century — formed the basis of Virginia's "planting" for the first hundred years.   Even that arch-Tory Berkeley made no attempt to change it, for, as already pointed out, the head-right scheme was something he and his followers insisted on inserting in the "treaty" by which Virginia rendered allegiance to Cromwell.   The man who destroyed this democratic order was Charles II — probably not deliberately, for Charles never considered closely the outcome of his acts, but effectively.   It was merely one phase of that destruction of Virginia's liberties that followed the Restoration. To Charles Virginia was a personal property, to be used in ways that would best promote his interests and pleasures. That here was the beginning of a great American nation was a conception that never crossed his mind. America was simply so much real estate, which he could grant to friends in the same generous fashion in which he gave dukedoms to the spurious heirs of Lady Castlemaine and Nell Gwynne. In 1673 Virginia awoke to the fact that this genial monarch had made a free gift of the colony to two royal favorites, Lord Arlington and Lord Culpeper. The howl that rose from one end of the colony to the other deafened the royal ears, and Charles, debonair as always, rescinded the grant.

At about the same time, however, the king revived another gift which had been made, in 1649, to seven of his faithful followers, but which had naturally fallen into abeyance with the subsequent rise of the Commonwealth. This was the territory known as the Northern Neck, the fruitful land lying between the Potomac and the Rappahannock, extending indefinitely westward — an area of about 5,000,000 acres. One of the original grantees was Lord Culpeper, father of the Culpeper to whom, with Arlington, an unsuccessful attempt had been made to transfer the whole colony. Culpeper had evidently set his heart on becoming a lord of Virginia; for a few years he served as royal governor — not with great success or popularity; in 1681 he bought out all his associates and set up his claim as sole proprietor of the Northern Neck. The claim was allowed by Charles, but caused much resentment in Virginia. Many of the colony's greatest families — including the Lees — had acquired, by head-right, large estates on the Potomac, of which they were absolute owners; they showed no eagerness to receive these territories from Culpeper on what was essentially a feudal tenure. Culpeper died in 1688, leaving his rights to his daughter Catherine, widow of Lord Fairfax, herself ultimately bequeathing the property to her son, Lord Thomas Fairfax. For more than twenty years the Culpeper-Fairfax family and the Potomac "barons" were deadlocked. Lord Baltimore's proprietary of Maryland had not proved too successful an experiment in government, and the Potomac planters were not tamely disposed to see their independent domain transformed into

anything resembling it.   They repeatedly appealed to the king to
annul the grant; they attempted to buy off the Fairfax family;
and, when all these and other representations failed, maintained an
attitude of sullen opposition.   By 1700 not a solitary planter had
attorned to the new proprietor — that is, had shifted his feudal
allegiance to the Fairfax family.

To the Fairfaxes the prospect was thus a gloomy one; so long
as the most influential men in the Northern Neck remained aloof,
their power of leasing lands and collecting quitrents was little
more than a pretension.   But suddenly the whole situation
changed.   Almost as if by magic, the planters and the Fairfaxes
came to terms and began that friendly association which lasted
until the Revolution.   The historian Beverley explains this sudden
brightening of the Fairfax skies.   "At last," he says, "Colonel
Richard Lee, one of the Council, an inhabitant of the Northern
Neck, privately made composition with the Proprietors themselves for his own land.   This broke the ice, and others were induced to follow so great an example, so that by degrees they were
generally brought to pay their Quit Rents into the hands of the
Proprietors' agents."   That this act was the greatest force in
establishing the Fairfaxes definitely in their extensive domain is
apparent, and that the Lee family did not suffer for their kind
intervention the sequel disclosed.

What Richard's attorning meant was that he acknowledged
the Fairfax family as liege lord, and was prepared to pay those
annual quitrents formerly paid to the king.   The practical outcome was to destroy the head-right system in this part of Virginia.   Henceforth settlers were to obtain land in the Northern
Neck from the Fairfax family, on lease, not freehold.   Almost
simultaneously the head-right system — comparable to modern
American homestead laws — came to an end, settlers in other
regions being obliged to purchase farms from the land office in
Williamsburg.   Thus Richard's last appearance is again that of
a compromiser and an upholder of privilege.   His accommodation
was another blow at Virginia democracy, and a powerful influence
in perpetuating that rule of class which was the predominating
force in Virginia for the first half of the eighteenth century.   The
first Richard had acquired his Potomac lands by head-right, but

his successors, in the eighteenth century, added to their domain only by consent of the Fairfax family.   In other words, there now ensued, in the Northern Neck, a system of feudal tenure, with direct allegiance to a feudal lord.   Richard's satisfaction, and probably the only one at which he aimed, was the establishment of quiet where there had previously been unrest, and the beginning of new and more prosperous times.   Probably once more this transaction evinced that tendency to accept determined facts which has characterized the family to modern times.   A final appeal in behalf of the Potomac planters had been made to William and Mary, but this had been more coldly repelled than their prayers to Charles and James.   The sad fact was that the Culpeper-Fairfax family stood high in the favor of William III, for it had been one of the leaders in transferring the British crown to the Dutch stadtholder.   In these circumstances even a less complaisant and practical man than the second Richard would have seen the futility of continued resistance.   The Fairfaxes, he observed, were established in the Northern Neck for all time, and Virginia might just as well reconcile itself to this new situation.   And that a great bulwark of democracy had vanished with the disappearance of the old land system probably did not greatly disturb this arch-feudalist and upholder of the divinity of kings and the rights of the upper class.

Richard lived to witness the office of the Fairfax proprietary set up on his own estate of Mount Pleasant with his own son in charge.   Thus, in a small colonial way, he had played the part of a General Monk, firmly settling a Virginia dynasty on its throne; and, in accordance with accepted usage, had gathered in his reward.   For fifteen years after his attorning, Richard Lee survived in scholarly seclusion, with his dead languages and tobacco fields, at peace with the men and politics of his time, watching the rise of a new Virginia, obtaining, in his last days, glimpses of that era in colonial history which was afterward to be known as the "golden age."

III

THE "PRESIDENT OF VIRGINIA"

I

WITH the rise of the Stratford Lees the family interest began to extend beyond the borders of old Virginia and to develop leadership on Continental lines. Under the first two Richards — from about 1640 to 1714 — Virginia was all Tidewater; the complicated patterns made by the Chesapeake, the four rivers and their endless bays, estuaries, creeks, and "runs," and the intervening plantations, large and small, comprised that American "frontier" so precious to the modern historian. Virginia, even as far west as the present Mount Vernon, was uncultivated woodland; two years after the second Richard's death, 1714, Governor Spotswood and his "Knights of the Golden Horseshoe" crossed the Blue Ridge Mountains and gazed upon the Shenandoah, but the settlement of this region was regarded as a matter for coming centuries. The second generation occasionally heard the almost mythical words "Ohio" and "Mississippi" — but that vast territory, though, according to the Virginia charter, part of the Old Dominion, engaged the imagination of only the most adventurous. The fact is that the first two Richards were not Americans, hardly even Virginians; they were merely transplanted Englishmen; their ambitions and political ideas were all derived from the mother land; to them Virginia was really an English county, accidentally separated from England by a great stretch of water, as much a part of the ancient soil as the Shropshire from which they came. A voyage to England in those days meant "going home," and the conceptions of the British squirarchy in all important concerns of life — church, politics, social relationships — were immutable law on the Potomac and the James.

But with the third generation came a new outlook; a new spirit

of confidence and new loyalties seemed to find expression in the
grim and substantial pile of Stratford. Not grace of architecture
but solidity, assurance, and permanence were its prevailing notes.
The million and more of bricks that went to make the structure
were baked on the premises, of good Potomac clay, and similarly
the building symbolized a new America — crude, unformed, yet
individual, aspiring, and self-reliant. And the firmness and independence marked in every line of Stratford presently became the
salient qualities of its residents. The building signalized and
witnessed the transition of Virginia from a subservient colony
into a masterful commonwealth, and it became the fate of its
proprietor to act a leading rôle in that development. When John
Adams wrote, in 1779, that the Lees of Virginia had produced
more men "of merit" than any other American family, it was the
sons of Stratford that he had in mind. When Thomas Lee, its
builder, proudly styled himself, in his official reports to the British
Lords of Trade, the "President of Virginia," he was asserting,
perhaps unwittingly, that new position of leadership which was
to play its part in forming a new nation.

Stratford was built sometime between 1725 and 1730; the
plans of the original Richard were now rapidly bearing fruit.
Practically all the hopes entertained for his descendants had been
fulfilled. No instinct was quite so strong in Richard's mind, and
that of his contemporaries, as "family"; his reason for abandoning civilization and settling in the wilderness had been to acquire
extensive lands, to strengthen his fortunes, to found his own
distinctive line. It was an ambition that was quickly achieved.
The story of the Lees in this respect is quite different from that of
the New England tribe of Adams, a family with which it was
subsequently to be associated most sympathetically in public affairs. For three generations the descendants of the original
Adams were to plod along as simple farmers, in no way distinguished from thousands of their compeers. The Lees, on the other
hand, immediately on arrival, took rank with the first half-dozen
families of Virginia. Great estates, the highest offices in the colony, leadership in social life, and widespread personal repute — all
these things they possessed when the Adams yeomen were deriving
a sweaty living from difficult soil. From the beginning the annals

of Virginia fairly bristle with the name, and in the eighteenth century not a vestry in Westmoreland, not a Council or a House of Burgesses, came together in which the Lees were not represented.   They reveled not only in Virginia's dignities, but in its fleshpots.

This preëminence was appropriately domiciled in the many Lee estates rising along the Potomac.   The patriarch Richard had secured these acres when they were all forest, inhabited by a few straggling savages, and now, in the third generation, his farsightedness was reaping its reward.   Nor had the earliest acquisitions departed from the line.   The Lees, once possessed of a portion of the earth's surface, clung to it with a tenacity that was fairly aristocratic.   Like those great city landlords, the Astors, they could not let it go.   The old estate on the York, Paradise, where the "Emigrant" first seated himself, remained in the family for a century and a half, and in the third generation was being cultivated by Francis Lee, son of the second Richard.   A succession of Henrys — culminating finally in General Henry, "Light Horse Harry" of the Revolution, and General Robert E. Lee — had started their careers at Lee Hall, on the Machotik, and a few miles east of Stratford lived George Lee, one of the most interesting of the lot — a young man, born in England of an English mother, and educated in English schools, who never saw Virginia until his twentieth year, but who, answering the westward call, came to the land of his fathers about 1734 and made it his permanent home.   George is chiefly famous for having married, in 1752, the recently widowed Mrs. Lawrence Washington, and for collecting, from her half brother-in-law, George, £82 a year as rental of Mount Vernon.   In this commanding estate Mrs. Lawrence had a life interest, absolute ownership, under her husband's will, reverting to George Washington after her death.   There was an element of revengeful human nature in George Lee's exaction, for the Lee and Washington families had quarreled many years, and engaged in apparently endless lawsuits over the ownership of Mount Vernon.   The Lees had a patent from Sir William Berkeley, given to Richard, while the Washingtons held a grant from Lord Culpeper.   Victory finally perching on the Washingtons, the Lees were left in not too friendly a mind.   George Lee

enjoyed his landlordship for about ten years, when Mrs. Lawrence's death released the property to the other George.

In Maryland, on the Patuxent, lived Philip, progenitor of the
Catholic Lees — a branch destined to play a patriotic rôle in the
Revolution. The Lees in Maryland achieved prominence not
unlike their brethren of Virginia. They became members of
the Council, of the Continental Congress, and, in Thomas Sim
Lee, produced a governor and Revolutionary patriot, especially
zealous in providing men and supplies for the Southern army.
Despite attempts to prevent the "Romanization" of the Maryland
Lees, — Philip left property to his wife on condition "that she
remain a Protestant," — Thomas Sim, in 1771, married Mary
Digges, daughter of one of Maryland's most prominent Catholic
families, and, a little before his death, became a convert to his
wife's faith. His services as a citizen were especially valuable in
the Maryland convention of 1788, called to ratify the new constitution; he was an ardent Federalist and strong supporter of Washington's administration.

The plantations on Dividing Creek, to which the "Emigrant"
had withdrawn after the rise of Cromwell, were still, for a hundred years, cultivated by his heirs — Ditchley by the descendants
of Hancock Lee, and Cobb's Hall by the descendants of Charles
Lee. A third Richard, son of the second Richard, was living in
England with an English wife, as tobacco merchant, on Virginia
Walk. This transference to England by Richard was unusual,
for he was the oldest son, inheritor of the principal family estates;
in accordance with custom he should have remained in Virginia
and ascended the several steps of political preferment, finally
reaching his hereditary niche in the Council. Instead, he married
an English wife, Martha Silk, — an "heiress," says the family
record, — and lived his days in "Goodman's Fields, parish of
Whitechapel, Middlesex." Possibly his three children, George
— that George who married the widow of Lawrence Washington
— and Lettice and Martha, resented this desertion; at any rate
all three, arriving at maturity, left England, settled in Virginia,
and made alliances with "baronial" families. And it so happens
that, in the third generation, not the first son, but the fourth, became the family head. This fourth son proved to be the ablest of

his tribe, up to that time, and the founder of that Stratford branch which was destined to play so conspicuous a part in American history. Certainly his eldest brother, Richard, treated Thomas generously. In payment "of a peppercorn only on the feast day of the birth of our Lord" Thomas rented from the London tobacco merchant the plantation of Mount Pleasant, on the Potomac, — a house and estate of 2500 acres, — which at this time was the appointed seat of the family head. Though this homestead was destroyed by fire a few years afterward, the land still holds one precious memorial, for the family graveyard is still intact. "Burnt House Fields" it was called in honor of the conflagration; and for a hundred years after all traces of the family had disappeared, sons and daughters were taken back here for a final resting place.

2

For the most part all the other Lees have been obscured by the brilliance of the Stratford line. Yet its founder started life under far less favorable circumstances than most of his generation. Born in 1690, son of the scholarly and recalcitrant Richard, the boyhood of Thomas Lee was passed in difficult times. His father's attitude towards younger sons was the prevailing one of his age and social caste; they might be appropriate objects of paternal affection, but, so far as family prestige was concerned, descendants of secondary consideration. And Thomas, being a fourth son, received less attention than was commonly lavished on cadets. Even his schooling was neglected. The learning in which the father shone so brilliantly was regarded as unsuitable for this obscure stripling. Preparatory training at Eton, four years' residence at Oxford, followed by studies at Inns of Court — this was the common fate of Virginia hopefuls, but not of Thomas Lee. That he had an exceedingly vigorous mind and an eagerness for knowledge evidently escaped observation. His mental equipment was therefore limited to the rudiments, — reading, spelling, ciphering, — probably imparted by one of those learned indented servants, Oxford graduates down on their luck, who occasionally sold themselves, "for their time," to the lords of Westmoreland. Thomas Lee, wrote his son, was a boy of "strong natural parts," but his education was only such as could be picked up on a tobacco farm.

When it came to sharing in the Lee estates, this same disregard of younger sons kept him outside the breastworks. A slim hundred and fifty acres in Northumberland, a thousand or so in Maryland — such were the crumbs that fell to Thomas from his father's bountiful table. However, this family oversight proved a blessing. It put the young man on his mettle, and stimulated the spirit of independence that marked his afterlife. Thrown upon his own resources, Thomas proceeded to overcome these two great handicaps — lack of fortune and deficiencies of education. That he should conquer the first and acquire riches by his own exertion is not surprising — many have done that, before Thomas and since; but that, on the intellectual side, he should similarly have been a self-made man almost puts him in a class apart.

He was particularly ashamed of his want of classical learning. That was a serious defect, for Latin and Greek, in the Virginia of that day, were not only evidences of culture but hallmarks of the gentleman. One noticed their absence as one noticed the absence of good manners. Philip Fithian tells in his diary of young Bob Carter, sadly lacking in "the languages," but much in love with Betty Tayloe of Mount Airy. "The young lady's mother told him last Sunday that until he understands Latin he will never be able to win a young lady of family and fortune for his wife." Whether this unhappy fate was the incentive in Thomas Lee's case is not recorded, yet it is the fact that, after reaching manhood, Thomas purchased Greek and Latin textbooks, ground away in solitude, spurning tutorial assistance, until, as his son William records, he became "a tolerable adept." In this performance we have the man. Pride, ambition, aggressiveness, determination — these qualities, manifested in an unassisted conquest of ancient learning, were the ones that made Thomas Lee the foremost Virginian of his day; foremost, that is, in his influence on American history. On Thomas the spirit of primeval Richard had descended, vastly enhanced — the spirit of acquisition, of restlessness, of increasing family prestige, of engrossing political power and serving the state. Similarly the favorite family anecdote concerning Thomas reveals a talent for looking into the future. Some day these American colonies — so ran his prophecy — would become an independent nation and find their capital in the area to which he was devoting so much attention, the borders of the Potomac between the Great and Little Falls. This vaticination may be a myth, yet the fact remains that Thomas Lee's imagination turned from the Tidewater region that, in his father's day, seemed to be the natural limit of Virginia and reached into the land of the Hyperboreans, which was then the mysterious Western country.

For nearly a hundred years the portrait of Thomas hung in Stratford Hall, looking benignantly, proudly, perhaps a little haughtily, on his descendants — men who, although distinguished enough themselves, felt a little awe in its presence. A namesake grandson, Thomas Lee Shippen, has recorded his emotions under the penetrating gaze. One can excuse the florid style, for the underlying feeling is sincere. "Stratford, whose delightful shades formed the comfort and retirement of my wise and philosophical grandfather, with what mixture of awe and pious gratification did I explore and admire your beauties! What a delightful occupation did it afford me, sitting on one of the sofas of the great Hall, to trace the family resemblance in the portraits of all my dear mother's forefathers, her father and mother, her grandfather and grandmother, and so on upward for four generations. There is something truly noble in my grandfather's picture. He is dressed in a large wig, flowing over his shoulders (probably his official wig as President of the Council) and in a loose gown of crimson satin, richly ornamented. But it is his physiognomy that strikes you with emotion. A blend of goodness and greatness; a sweet yet penetrating eye, a finely marked set of features and a heavenly countenance, such as I have almost never seen. Do not think me extravagant; my feelings were certainly so when I dwelt with rapture on the portraits of Stratford and felt so strong an inclination to kneel to that of my grandfather — it was with difficulty that my uncles,[1] who accompanied me, could persuade me to leave the hall and look at the gardens, vineyards, orangeries, and lawns which surround the house."

[1] These uncles were Richard Henry Lee and Arthur Lee.

Probably Thomas Lee would have smiled at this veneration, for there are evidences that he had a sense of humor and that the dreary routine and adherence to conscience, conspicuous in the father, were tempered, in the son, by a deeper knowledge of his fellow men. For his face, in addition to the exalted qualities set forth by the grandson, is a human one, displaying the generous features of the Lees — the large head, assertive jaw, sympathetic but all-observant eyes; and, at the same time, it evinces dignity and charm. And that Thomas had his gentle side a few scraps of surviving writing disclose. Frequently the most revealing of colonial documents are not letters, speeches, and contemporary recollections, but wills. That of Thomas, "all written in my own hand," as it records, is especially so. In it the man portrays his qualities of mind and temperament — his deep religious feeling, his sense of paternal responsibility, devotion to friends, dislike of cheap ostentation, directness of purpose, even his decision of character and imperiousness. Above all the domestic affections appear as the strongest in his nature. Evidently the two beings who chiefly occupied his heart were his wife and mother. The grief of Thomas was fresh when the following lines were penned, for his wife Hannah died January 25, 1750, and the will was composed February 22 — just one month afterward. "I desire that I may be buried between my Late Dearest Wife and my honoured Mother, and that the bricks on the side next my wife may be moved, and my Coffin placed as near hers as possible, without moving it or disturbing the remains of my mother." The testamentary admonitions were strictly observed, and to-day, in Burnt House Fields, lie the three graves, situated immutably as the Lord of Stratford had ordained.

The wife so affectingly commemorated was an important accession to the House of Lee. Perhaps the fact that the fourth generation saw the family's full maturity may be in considerable measure owing to her. In tracing the origin of distinguished lines too exclusive emphasis is commonly laid on the masculine side. Despite modern scientific knowledge there is still too great a tendency to overlook the well-established biological truth that one derives as much from the mother as the father, perhaps even more. The Stratford Lees, in their marriages, strengthened the

HANNAH HARRISON LUDWELL, 1701–1750

WIFE OF PRESIDENT THOMAS LEE

stock by observing this rule.   Of the wife of the first Lee unfortunately nothing is known — not even her name and birthplace; the wife of his son, Lætitia Corbin, as already noted, was a
member of one of the most progressive clans in Virginia.   And
when Thomas joined his fortunes with a family long conspicuous
for the aggressiveness — even pugnacity — of its sons and daughters, he was instinctively acting in conformity with the highest
eugenic law.   In colonial Virginian history the name of Ludwell constantly appears, even more frequently than that of Lee.
At times it resounded from one end of the colony to the other.
Had the family not become extinct before the Revolution, it
would undoubtedly have played an important rôle in that proceeding.   "An old stander in the country, Col. Philip Ludwell,"
is the way that Beverley refers to Hannah Lee's grandfather, and
there is a robustness in the phrase that directed the man's every act.
Tradition ascribes to the Ludwells a Germanic origin; they may
have been descendants of Protestant refugees who fled to England in the sixteenth century; and possibly the fierceness, tactlessness, and "rash and fiery temper" that kept the colony constantly
embroiled can be thus explained.   The Ludwell behavior, however, suggests also the sturdiness of English stock, especially the
constant struggle maintained by Philip against the Virginia governors, who, after Bacon's Rebellion, adopted a studied programme
for the destruction of colonial liberties.   Ludwell's hostility to
these encroachments, his love of combat, his gift for vituperative
epigram, and his contempt for empty and pretentious officials
give vivacity to this period in Virginia history.   They also frequently brought him into conflict with the royal power.   His
characterization of the king's emissary, Colonel Jeffreys, as "a
pitiful little fellow in a periwig" — made, the official record discloses, after imbibing "half a flagon of Syder" — resulted in
Philip's expulsion from the Council and the loss of his place as
collector of York River.   But the man was not dismayed.   As
leader of the Green Spring faction he championed the popular
cause against succeeding governors.   Restored to the Council,
he was again expelled, but with the Virginia masses Ludwell's
popularity was great, and that Virginia retained some of her
privileges, despite the attacks of Charles and his minions, is usu-

ally credited to Ludwell and his associates. Finally, perhaps exhausted by these embroilments, Ludwell retired to London, where he died at an advanced age, leaving his Virginian interests and political battles in the hands of his son, Philip II, a man, in arrogance and fighting spirit, not unlike the old campaigner. This second Philip was the father of Hannah Ludwell and grandfather of the Revolutionary Lees. His wife, Hannah's mother, was a James River Harrison, and thus, through her, the blood of the family that was to produce two Presidents of the United States and many men eminent in other fields passed into the Stratford line.

To what extent Hannah Ludwell inherited the ancestral qualities is not definitely known. Yet the frequent manifestation, in her descendants, of Ludwell force and especially Ludwell arrogance and cantankerousness, as well as their disposition to champion popular rights, even against the throne, shows that at least she played a rôle in transmitting uncompromising qualities. Legend ascribes to Hannah a certain harshness of behavior, chiefly apparent in devotion to her eldest son in preference to the rest, and one of her descendants, the biographer of Richard Henry Lee, accuses her of callous partiality. It is clear that, first of all, Hannah was the aristocrat, completely absorbed in the glory of the Ludwell name, an idolizing daughter of her father, probably more loyal to family than to persons. To Americans she must always be a notable figure, for no American woman has achieved her record as the mother of famous sons. At least her physical traits appeared in her children. Up to her time the Lee physiognomy had been large, big-featured, but now their lineaments take on a more delicate character. Hannah's surviving portrait — companion piece to the one of her husband that so moved the admiration of Thomas Shippen — strongly contrasts, in this respect, with the rather uninteresting faces of the two Mrs. Richards. Though far from a beautiful woman, Hannah Ludwell's small, sharply cut features, the slightly petulant tilt of head, dainty ears, thin lips shadowing the faintest suggestion of a smile, and sprightly, intelligent eyes, suggest that something new has come into the House of Lee. That there was a little acid in Hannah's nature may well be believed; neither would one be sur-

prised to find a touch of wit and human understanding.   Certainly
there was plenty of acid — almost malignity — in her sons, and
possibly the traits in Arthur and William Lee that, in the Revolution, so disturbed the serenity of Benjamin Franklin can be traced
to Hannah, first mistress of Stratford, and to her quarrelsome
and public-spirited forbears.   A man who, like Philip Ludwell,
twice had the distinction of being expelled from the Virginia
Council might naturally transmit positive and disagreeable qualities to his great-grandsons.

3

Thomas Lee and Hannah Ludwell were married in 1722, and
took up residence at Mount Pleasant, his father's house, leased, as
noted above, from his senior brother, Richard.   Already Thomas
had taken his first stride to success.   The land hunger so powerful in his grandfather now broke into life anew.   More fortunate
brothers might inherit the choicest Lee possessions; still Virginia
was an imperial domain, and, especially in the northern region and
in the beautiful wilderness to the west, held opportunities as great
as those that had confronted the earliest colonist.   "Go north,
young man!" might have been the advice proffered by some colonial Virginia Greeley — north, and then west!   All that was
needed was energy; ready money was not so necessary.   Lee's
business training — and, first of all, he was a man of business —
had already sharpened his judgment.   In thinking of his career,
one somehow calls to mind George Washington.   Lee was forty-
two when Washington was born and was therefore hardly a contemporary, nor, in his period of supremacy, would he have been
complimented by too close an identification with the young gentleman of Wakefield.   The Washingtons were a family of repute and
weight, but not, in the matter of social eminence, quite in the
same class with the Lees.   The little cottage on Pope's Creek in
which Washington was born shrank into insignificance when
compared to Stratford; neither had the Washingtons attained political station of similar consequence.   Washingtons had sat in
the House of Burgesses, but none had attained the acme of political distinction, membership in the Council.   Nor had relations

between the two families been the most cordial; their difference over the possession of Mount Vernon has already been set forth. Despite superficial divergences, Thomas Lee and George Washington had much in common. Both were, above all, outdoor men, devoted far more to country life than to the political experiences that came their way; other concerns, especially those of the new country, evidently had more attraction than legislative duties. Like Washington, Lee loved to watch his crops develop and to make the tour of his plantations, and a constant reaching out into new fields was a prevailing impulse in the life of both. Like Washington, this Lee was a Virginian of the most undeviating allegiance, yet he was also an impassioned American, and was held imaginatively spellbound by the future of the continent. The eyes of both saw beyond the Blue Ridge hills, beyond the Alleghanies, reveled in the valleys of the Ohio and the Mississippi, and both alike became large landholders in the country originally sacred to La Salle and Marquette. The first view we gain of Washington is that of a young man, tramping over old Prince William County with surveyor's tools, mapping the Fairfax proprietary; yet a generation before, Thomas Lee had explored this same country, probably the first white man to traverse much of the forest which his successor finally reduced to something resembling scientific outline.

For Thomas Lee, like Washington, started life under the patronage of the Fairfax family. The initiation brought him into conflict with a far more powerful tribe, at that time headed by "King" Carter of Corotoman. No colonial figure more magisterially portrays the legendary Virginia aristocrat, and certainly none was so powerful, imperious, and ferociously energetic; and that Thomas Lee, in his twenty-first year, unhesitatingly ran athwart the Carter course tells much for his spirit. The feud that had its beginnings then ceased only with Carter's death, twenty years afterward. In 1713, by a combination of circumstances, young Thomas Lee became resident agent of the Fairfax family in the Northern Neck; absolute manager, that is, of the 5,000,000 acres that then comprised the Culpeper-Fairfax proprietary. It was a post of great influence and potentiality, so important that, for the preceding ten years, it had been the personal

province of King Carter.   During that period this Virginia monarch had been collecting rents and making land grants in the
Northern Neck, and, incidentally, laying the basis of that empire
of 300,000 acres that was to make him the greatest of Virginia
landlords.[1]   In 1710 died Margaret, Lady Culpeper, widow of
the original grantee, leaving the Virginia proprietary to her daughter Catherine, widow of Lord Fairfax.   This young lady never
saw Virginia, her interest in that region being purely monetary.
As soon as leases were made, and the lands settled, quitrents became payable to the absentee owner — a source of income that, if
properly conserved, might mean a considerable annual sum.
About 1712 Lady Catherine showed dissatisfaction with the pit-
tances transmitted overseas, a dissatisfaction inflamed by letters
from Virginia suggesting that, if she changed her resident agent,
more could easily be squeezed from the property.   Lady Fairfax
appealed for advice to Thomas Corbin, Virginia tobacco merchant
in London.   This Corbin was Thomas Lee's uncle, and his partner was Richard Lee, Thomas's brother.   Young as he was,
Lee's capacity for business had impressed his relatives in London,
who at once proposed him to Lady Fairfax as King Carter's successor.

The Fairfax family were under obligations to the Lees; as
already noted, it was the second Richard who, by attorning to the
proprietor for his estates, had done much to fix the Culpepers
solidly on their land.   Nominally the newly appointed agent was
Edmund Jenings, uncle of Thomas Lee, but the young man, his
associate, had absolute control.   A land office was opened at
Mount Pleasant, and Thomas began making grants on a lavish
scale.   At that time Germans were pouring into northern Virginia, zealous for landholdings; industrious and sober-living,
they made desirable settlers; the historic part they played in opening up northern Virginia and the Shenandoah was facilitated by
the business office maintained by Thomas Lee.

The change of agent from Carter to Thomas Lee had important
consequences, not only for Lee personally, but for the future
American nation.   Carter was a mighty Virginian in his day,

[1] Except, of course, the Fairfaxes, who, as proprietaries, belonged in a class
apart.

— probably the most powerful as a Virginian, — but his influence did not materially extend beyond his native soil, and he therefore cuts no particular figure in the nation's annals. But Lee's administration of the Fairfax proprietary had Continental importance, for it caused him to focus interest on the Western country and presently led him to penetrate a territory far more extensive than the Fairfax domain. That his private fortunes were benefited is true. Thomas never approached the Carter record, but he did fairly well, not far from 30,000 acres passing to his descendants. All Fairfax agents commonly made land grants to themselves; that was one of the prerogatives of the office, part of its compensation, not frowned upon by the proprietors. Nevertheless, it must be recorded to Thomas's credit that none of his Fairfax properties were acquired while he was agent. After four years his Uncle Jenings came home and ostensibly took charge, — though Thomas was still the active man, — and then the Lee annexations began. The long horseback peregrinations which Thomas made, in his painstaking way, over the entire Fairfax possessions, besides qualifying him for the job, gave side lights on the most desirable locations. Eight Fairfax land grants are accredited in the Virginia records to Thomas Lee. Several cover places famous in state and nation. His imagination constantly hovered over the region that now includes the District of Columbia. This was then wild country; perhaps, as a boy, Thomas had penetrated so far with rod and gun; and now, as a young man, he gathered in 16,000 acres, located between the Great and Little Falls. Commerce rather than agriculture directed this particular adventure; for the valley of the Potomac, as the future highway to the West, appealed to Lee just as it afterward appealed to Washington.

This western impulse presently carried Thomas into even more outlying countries. In Fauquier he obtained 4200 acres, land on which his descendants founded the city of Warrenton. In Loudoun several thousand more were put together, the town of Leesburg being the present monument to these transactions. And so Thomas went, ignoring, for the most part, the lower Potomac, always seeking new fields, north and west. The one spot in Westmoreland towards which his longing eyes were cast was "The

Cliffs" — "Hollis Cliffs," as the highlands of the Potomac are denominated on Jefferson's map.   "I want to buy the Cliffs," he
wrote his brother Henry from London, in 1716, when paying a
visit to British relations, and in 1717 this wish was realized.   One
day a representative of the Pope family ceremoniously presented to
Thomas Lee a handful of earth and a twig — ancient symbolic
confirmation of the transference of the 1400 acres on which Stratford was constructed.[1]   The exact date of building is not known,
but there is no doubt that it was finished and occupied by 1730.

For Lee's westward ambitions spread far beyond the borders
of Virginia.   Spotswood's explorations fired Thomas, as they
had fired other westward-looking Virginians.   The time was not
far back when the Blue Ridge Mountains were looked upon as the
final barrier; just west of that obstruction, it was commonly believed, lay the great South Sea — that is, the water now known
as the Pacific Ocean.   But this was suddenly revealed as the
Shenandoah, a valley of unparalleled beauty and fertility.   Virginia claimed not only this land, but everything west of the Alleghanies.   The Old Dominion's vaulting ambition was eloquently
echoed by Thomas Lee, who, in one of his letters to the Lords of
Trade, written as acting governor, thus described the boundaries
of Virginia: "the Atlantic on the east, North Carolina on the
south, the Potomac on the north, and, on the west, the Great
South Sea, including California."   The addendum was not superfluous, for in 1749 California was believed to be an island!
By this time, it is clear, the tremendous extent of Virginia's inheritance — an inheritance owing rather to ignorance of geography than design — had dawned upon an aspiring people.   Its
exploration and settlement became the ruling impulse of Thomas's
life.

His story now becomes involved in European politics, for Virginia's title to this mighty territory, so eloquently defined by
Thomas Lee himself, encountered the pretensions of two European powers — Spain and France.   The more immediate stumblingblock was France, for the visions of Lee and his associates

[1] For many facts concerning the Virginian land system acknowledgment is
made to two invaluable works, *Virginia Land Grants* and *Landmarks of Old
Prince William,* by Fairfax Harrison.

were, for the present, limited to the valley of the Ohio, the North American soil to which France was then effecting most determined claim. As sovereignty then went, the French argument rested on acceptable grounds. Had not La Salle and Joliet, in the latter part of the seventeenth century, sailed in birch-bark canoes down the Mississippi River to its mouth, site of the present New Orleans? Had not Marquette and other Jesuit fathers performed miracles of exploration that strengthened French possession? That settled the matter, for, in the international law of the seventeenth century, these feats gave Louis XIV all the lands drained by the Mississippi, the Ohio, and their tributaries — about two thirds of the present United States. And France was displaying characteristic French tenacity in holding the territory her noble and saintly navigators had won. When Thomas Lee looked westward to this Ohio and Mississippi country and formed the grandiose plan of appropriating a slice, he found himself confronted by an even more formidable obstacle than King Carter. The greatest military and political power in Continental Europe stood there, ready to frustrate his plans. If Great Britain were nourishing ambitions in the Western wilderness, she showed no signs; not a foot of the territory was in her possession, not an English settlement, not an English fort, not a solitary English soldier, had been established there. But the French were giving substance to their claims all over the country. From Quebec to New Orleans they were entrenched in a crescent of frontier towns, while the English settlements formed a straggling fringe along the Atlantic seaboard. That the encompassing Gaul proposed to hold his Anglo-Saxon brother to this water front was plain; almost like a vise, the Frenchmen were closing in on the West and North. They had established several *entrepôts* for trading with the Indians, whom, in wily Gallic fashion, they were making hostile to land-grabbing English. While the English had remained quiescent, the ancestral enemy had taken steps that seemed inevitably to make the Mississippi and Ohio valleys — the section now famous in the American economy and in American politics as the Middle West — an everlasting empire of the most Christian king.

4

Meanwhile Lee had run the full course of Virginia honors.   In 1732 he was advanced to the Council — stepping into a vacancy caused by King Carter's death.   Sixteen years later he became "President of Virginia" and "Commander-in-Chief" — that is, president of the Council and soon afterward acting governor. Almost his first report to the Lords of Trade and Plantations pictured him as a political philosopher of authentic English breed. "The French are intruders into this America," he wrote, blandly ignoring conspicuous facts to the contrary.   That was the keynote of his administration.   It signalized the settled purpose of his life.   No English missionary or peltry trader had sailed down the Ohio and Mississippi, planting metal plates at river mouths, thus ensuring title to a territory considerably larger than Europe. It fell to Thomas Lee to take the lead in a proceeding that remedied this defect.   One point the Frenchman had overlooked. When Marquette and La Salle made their excursions, claimants to this domain already existed; not only claimants, but human beings whose ancestors had been in possession for untold centuries.   One might reasonably argue that Indians who had hunted and fished and planted wigwams in the Northwest country all these ages, and maintained there a sort of sovereignty, might be regarded as rightful proprietors.   Supposing these tribes, or the chiefs who acted as their spokesmen, should assign their ancestral inheritance to their good English friends — would not that transaction outweigh the accomplishments of French explorers? At least that seemed logical to the spirit of British — and Lee — enterprise.   Circumstances were working in their favor.   The somewhat unstable affections of the Iroquois, or Six Nations, were now inclining to Virginia.   All this land that had been so haughtily appropriated by the French these famous Indians claimed for their own.   That their pretension was a little unsubstantial is true.   Their grandfathers had defeated and enslaved the Shawnees, who once ruled supreme north of the Ohio, and thus the Iroquois were lawful sovereigns on grounds universally recognized — the right of conquest.   Virginia diplomacy, there-

fore, now concentrated on the accommodating red man, and
Thomas Lee was appointed diplomat in chief.

One May morning, in 1744, a sloop cast off from the landing
at Stratford, wafted on its way by the huzzas of men, the boom-
ing of cannon, and the sighs and smiles of women. In place of
honor sat Thomas Lee, senior of two commissioners — the other
was William Beverley — appointed by Virginia to go to Lancaster, Pennsylvania, and there enter into a treaty with the Six
Nations. This excursion proved to be the most important diplomatic negotiation, up to that time, for the little yacht sailing from
Stratford that May morning represented Britain's first serious
answer to French encroachments. The outcome was the Treaty
of Lancaster — a treaty by which the Six Nations transferred
to Virginia all their ancestral territory in the country west of
the Great Mountains. On this scrap of paper and certain sentences in the Treaty of Utrecht was based Great Britain's claim
to the Northwest, the land which, after the Seven Years' War,
was shifted from French to English sovereignty, and which, in
the Treaty of Paris, was handed over to the new United States.
Out of this generous domain the states of Kentucky, Ohio, Indiana, Illinois, Wisconsin, Michigan, and part of Minnesota have
subsequently been carved.

The proceedings that led to so glorious a result possibly lacked
a little in the dignity of history. The story can be read in detail,
for it formed the subject of one of the most celebrated pamphlets
of the time: "A treaty, held at the town of Lancaster, Pennsylvania, with the Indians of the Six nations, in June, 1744. Philadelphia: printed and sold by Benjamin Franklin at the New
Printing Office near the Market, 1744." Interest in the negotiations proved so keen that enterprising Ben issued his account
almost as soon the sessions adjourned, and probably no publication of his press ever afforded that realistic philosopher keener
enjoyment. The solemn red men, clothed in gorgeous regalia,
smoking their pipes and drinking their rum, pledging undying
devotion, in all their natural eloquence, to the "Great King across
the seas"; the belts of wampum and "Jo-hahs" that ended each
oration; the gifts of camlet coats and gold-braided hats; banquets,
punch bowls, ceremonial dances — here is a specimen of the way

in which a whole continent ultimately passed from its native proprietors to white men.   At times Canassatego and brother sachems seemed to have glimmerings of this fate.   "You English have come settling on our lands like a flock of birds," he remarked; presently, however, there were more belts of wampum, more "Jo-hahs," more rum, more encomiums on the English, more denunciations of the French, and a final swearing of friendship between Iroquois and Virginians that should endure forever. Thomas Lee made several speeches, appearing as mouthpiece for Assarogoa, Indian name for the governor of Virginia.   Disregarding oratory, Thomas, in his first address, came instantaneously to the point.   Laying down the customary string of wampum, this forthright gentleman said: "We have a chest of new goods and the key is in our pockets.   You are our brethren; the Great King is our common father, and we will live with you as children ought to do in peace and love.   We will brighten the chain and strengthen the Union between us, so that we shall never be divided, but remain friends and brethren as long as the sun gives us light."

"We are glad to hear that you have brought with you a big chest of new goods," the Indian spokesman replied, "and that you have the key in your pockets.   We do not doubt that we shall have a good understanding on all points and come to an agreement with you."   Thomas had set forth the kernel of the situation.   For £200 in cash, and £200 in knives, hatchets, kettles, jew's-harp, and other valuable considerations of like quality, the Six Nations, fiercest and most courageous of aborigines, put marks on a parchment, transferring to Virginia that land which became so celebrated in American history as the Northwest Territory.   When Thomas and his associates sailed back to Stratford, their reception should have been more fervid than their departure; Great Britain finally had a valid claim — valid for the statesmanship of that epoch — to territory which subsequently developed into one of the world's greatest agricultural and industrial empires.   What a small matter the Dutch purchase of Manhattan Island for twenty-four dollars appears when contrasted with this stupendous transaction, in which enormous stretches of prairie, great lakes, mountains of iron and copper, untold millions of farm lands, and thousands of miles of navigable rivers were the stake! At the present time 25,000,000 Americans inhabit this region.

A great triumph for Thomas and his companions, yet much history was to be made and many battles fought, before Montcalm and Wolfe, on the Plains of Abraham, were to decide whether the claim founded on La Salle's canoe trip, or the one based upon the Treaty of Lancaster, was to shape the future of the North American Continent. In the steps that precipitated the final crisis Lee again played a provocative part. "The French are intruders into this America" — this conviction remained an abiding one, and, fortified by Indian concessions, he undertook to make the threat effective. Nothing so strengthened paper sovereignty as actual settlement, but up to 1748 few Englishmen had set foot in the trans-Alleghany land. That was the weak point in the British position and steps were now taken to remedy the defect. In 1748 was organized the first Ohio Company, with Thomas Lee as president. The whole enterprise, indeed, was very much a family affair. Other members were Thomas's sons, Philip Ludwell Lee and Thomas Ludwell Lee; his nephew, Richard Lee; his future son-in-law, Gawin Corbin; the future father-in-law of his son, John Tayloe; and such associated "Barons of the Potomac" as Lawrence and Augustine Washington, Robert Carter, — not the "King," but his son, — and George Fairfax, cousin of the proprietor. Thus practically all the Virginians concerned were part and parcel of that oligarchy of landholders which then ruled the colony. The Ohio Company — still more so its successors — has suffered at the hands of modern historians, who picture it as a classic illustration of that "land-grabbing" habit which is supposed to have been the chief occupation of the fathers of the Republic. Even the fact that George Washington afterward entered the charmed circle has not redeemed its reputation. That Thomas Lee, as well as his associates, suffered from the prevailing passion for land ownership; that, in fine, he hoped to make money out of the fertile lands to the west — all that is true; it is true also that he had public motives. He was a man of historic imagination, and just as Cecil Rhodes, a century and a half later, placed his hand on a map of Africa and expressed his determination to make that "all red," so Thomas Lee, meditating on the Ohio and the Mississippi valleys, decided that the Almighty had designed this section of the planet not for French but for English occupancy. In his letters to the Privy Council in London this ambition is constantly coming to the front. French encroachment, and the necessity for circumventing it, are always in his mind. His very first petition to the Lords of Trade, asking for 200,000 acres — afterward increased to 500,000 — south and north of the Ohio, gave, as the great purpose in view, "settling the countrys upon the Ohio and extending British trade beyond the mountains of the western confines of Virginia." Sir William Gooch, when royal governor, showed little interest in furthering this appeal; the reason, he wrote to London, was his fear that the grant "might make trouble with the French"; but this anxiety did not disturb Thomas Lee.

In 1749 the Master of Stratford, as senior councilor, became president of the Council and, in the absence of the king's representative, acting governor of Virginia. Just as, when a young man, he had traveled over the Fairfax domain, so now, in the vigor of his sixtieth year, he made a tour of the colony, sailing down its rivers in sloops, penetrating its forests on horseback, gathering material for a report to the Lords of Trade on Virginia, its extent, its peoples, its reserves, its future. It is a document that calls to mind — in a modest way — Jefferson's *Notes on Virginia,* published fifty years afterward. The experience fired Lee's heart anew for the Ohio Company, and again his purpose, as he describes it, is "to extend the British Empire." "It will, I apprehend," he writes, "be good policy to encourage the Dispositions of the People, to extend and cultivate the lands on the other side the Great Mountains; as well as foreign protestants to import themselves; which will make this the strongest frontier that is in any of the king's dominions in America, since the lands are rich on the Alligany and the Ohio, where, I am told, more people can conceivably settle than at this time inhabit Pennsylvania, the Jerseys and New York." The government should explore all this region, he insisted, and make a "compleat map of Virginia." "The country is very fertile and more so the farther we extend west and the lands richer after we have passed the Ridge of Mountains." And always Thomas kept a suspicious eye on the French. "The French claim to the Mississippi is not just" — thus imperiously that subject is dismissed. With "presents" they were constantly inciting the Indians to attack the English and were already weaning the Six Nations from the Treaty of Lancaster. Why should not Virginia retaliate in kind? Lee's favorite proposal was to fill up the new lands with German immigrants — the "protestants" mentioned in the passage quoted. At that time Virginia levied "parish dues" on all citizens, irrespective of creed, for the support of the Anglican Church. As an inducement to settlement, Lee urged that these be remitted to such German Lutherans as took up tracts. When it came to the natives Lee was just as practical as at Lancaster. "If we make presents to the Indians, as the French do, and so combate them with their own weapons, the Indians, being really inclined to the British interest, will not forsake it, while they are used as well as they are by the enemy: they are faithful allies and nothing but dire necessity can give the French power to debauch them."

The fact is that Thomas Lee is a forgotten American statesman — one of the most farseeing minds developed in the colonial era. If his methods of handling Indian problems did not rise above the morality of his time, — and of succeeding time, — he had, as few men in the eighteenth century had, a picture of the West as the future home of English-speaking peoples. His influence in making the country north of the Ohio part of the United States is something the present generation should not overlook. He died in 1750, when the Ohio Company had just started its explorations. What might have been accomplished had Lee lived can only be estimated. Even before his death, however, the first great westward steps had been taken. Lee's final act was to send Christopher Gist — the same frontiersman who afterward piloted Washington through the Alleghany wilderness — to travel over the country, establish a trading post, and carefully note and report the locations most suitable to settlement. Though the first Ohio Company subsided in the welter of the French and Indian War, certain definite things in the van of empire had been accomplished. Gist's travels had made the country well known and paved the way for settlement after the Revolution. The Ohio Company had laid out the road across the mountains which subsequently formed the route of pioneer migration. As one motors to-day along the great concreted highway he is traversing the route taken by Lee's agents in their first approach to the lands of the Ohio Company. The present city of Cumberland is a post established by the same enterprise. But the Ohio Company's greatest influence was on international politics. It brought to a climax the rivalry in America that had been smouldering for so many years between England and France. The French reply to the negotiation at Lancaster was the expedition of Céloron, who sailed up the Ohio, approaching closer and closer to Virginia, building forts in most exasperating fashion, and raising the French flag at decisive points. The French establishment at Fort Duquesne, the present site of Pittsburgh, proved the final straw. Only one way of determining the rival pretensions now remained. Washington's trips to the Alleghany, Braddock's defeat, and finally the world war of the eighteenth century, involving America, Europe, and Asia — all these followed in the train of Lancaster and the Ohio Company. The verdict of history at least has sustained Thomas Lee's declaration that "the French are intruders into this America." Even his insistence that Virginia — that is, English America — properly extended to the Pacific, "including California," is now seen to have been no empty boast.

5

The influence of a widening horizon of this kind necessarily became spiritual as well as social and economic. If the "aspects of nature" do much in forming national character, the expansion of Virginia to the Ohio and the Mississippi must have exercised magic on the Virginian mind. The realization that the colony was no mere fringe on the Atlantic, but extended, in an apparently unlimited reach of mountains, rivers, plains, and lakes, indefinitely to the west, inevitably instilled a sense of pride and leadership. That Thomas Lee did much to arouse this new consciousness has already been made plain; the degree to which the Western country entered the life of his descendants, becoming the very fibre of their existence, will presently appear. Thus the spirit of the time tended to develop that new race of Americans of which Thomas Lee may be esteemed the prototype.   The Virginian did not regard himself quite as the usual run of American: he was the citizen of an empire, not of a colony; there was a time, in the first Richard's day, when Virginia was another name for America, and when the land north of the Potomac, including even New England, was known as "North Virginia"; this spaciousness must have had much to do in forming the Virginia character, its feeling of superiority, even its "arrogance."   Perhaps the largeness of view explains the fact that this period of Thomas Lee — the first half of the eighteenth century — has passed into legend as the "Age of the Barons," as the "Golden Age."   It was then, we are told, that a few families gained supreme power in Virginia, acquired great riches, upheld a lofty style of living, became the breeders of statesmen, and played chief part in laying the foundation of the new republic.   In all such conceptions there is much idealization; yet, in its main motives, the traditional picture of eighteenth-century Virginia is true. The conspicuous families — the "barons" — are easily identified. The constant recurrence of the same names in the political body that was almost supreme — the Council — is a reliable index of power.   These are Ludwell, Nelson, Lee, Blair, Byrd, Wormeley, Page, Burwell, Fitzhugh, Harrison, Carter, Digges, Randolph, and a few others.   These families were both the richest in Virginia and the heads of its social system.   Their authority was increased by intermarriage.   The petty princes of pre-Napoleonic Germany were no more scrupulous about exclusive matrimonial alliances within their own lines than were these lords of eighteenth-century Virginia.   In most of the clans enumerated above, the Lees made frequent alliances.

The rise of the "barons" was contemporaneous with the development of another class which was far from baronial in character — those black helots who now become an overshadowing fact in Virginia life.   Again we should look back at that first Richard's estate on the York, with its planked dwelling and its small army of Anglo-Saxon workers — the humble English men and English women who laid the basis of Virginia's white population. In place of English domestic servants and laborers, the fields of

Stratford were now tilled by a mass of black men, most of them recently reclaimed from the African jungle. Paradise, the first Lee estate, sheltered, so far as records disclose, not a single negro, while Thomas Lee possessed about five hundred servitors of this kind. If we should seek the consequences of this dark invasion, a trip in almost any section of Tidewater would provide it. In these areas, a small proprietary class, recruited chiefly from graduated indented servants, had, in the latter half of the seventeenth century, independently of the great plantations, established a contented society. Now, however, the situation had materially changed. Where middle-class prosperity had formerly prevailed, evidences of poverty desolated the land. Houses were in disrepair, fields were overgrown with weeds; in place of thrifty settlers and their broods, a rather dilapidated folk seemed barely scraping livings from the soil. The fact is that this happy social order, the large company of white yeoman farmers who were giving Virginia that industrious middle class essential to the symmetrical state, had, by the time Thomas Lee reached his prime, all but disappeared.

It is absurd to suppose that these three circumstances — the rise of a powerful planter group, the virtual disappearance of a prosperous small farming contingent, and the influx, on a huge scale, of negro workers from Africa — were not interrelated. The one preëminent fact that distinguishes the Virginia of Thomas Lee from the Virginia of Richard I, and, to a great extent, of Richard II, was the growth of slavery. This was the institution that made the first half of the eighteenth century the most prosperous in Virginia history. Under this influence the misery that had racked the colony in the preceding generation changed to unprecedented wealth, and to the fine living that wealth frequently brings; but it was a prosperity limited to an upper class. To the political and industrial commotion that had marked so large a part of the second Richard's time an era of harmony and happiness succeeded. The cause was economic. The Navigation Laws of England had robbed Virginia of the world market for tobacco that had made the days of the first Richard Lee so prosperous. This caused a sudden drop in price that made tobacco, for several years, no longer a profitable crop. As always, the burden fell particularly upon the small producer, who had no reserves of capital to sustain him through the period of readjustment. The new situation resulted in his complete and irretrievable ruin. The owner of the great plantation, however, better equipped to stand the strain and so circumstanced as to be able to profit by new developments, not only weathered the storm but emerged far stronger than before.

In describing the demoralizing effect produced by the sudden clamping down of Navigation Laws, confining Virginia tobacco to a single market, where previously the world had been at its disposal, a comparison was suggested with the Western farmer of to-day, whose wretchedness has been brought about by causes producing similar effects. But imagine that the producer of Minnesota or Kansas could discover some means of so decreasing his labor costs that foodstuffs could be profitably sold in the world market even at the low prices prevailing in recent years. Obviously his troubles would vanish overnight and prosperity again enliven his scene. That is the way the plantation owner of early eighteenth-century Virginia solved his problem. He discovered a method of enormously reducing labor costs. Up to about 1700 the white indented servant had been the main source of labor supply. But he was expensive, uncertain, and impossible under the conditions of low-priced tobacco that now set in. The original purchase price was high: the maintenance of Anglo-Saxon required a greater outlay than that of black man; more important still, he served for only four years, while the negro served for life and usually left a brood of children who also became the master's possession. Professor Wertenbaker, in *The Planters of Colonial Virginia,* shows that the number of slaves increased from 6000 in 1700 to 30,000 in 1730 — out of a total population of 114,000. "In other words the slaves, who in 1670 had constituted but 5 per cent of the people, now comprised 26 per cent." And in thus lowering the cost of tobacco, the negro completely changed the status of the English dealer, enabling him to compete in the European market and ultimately to dominate it. Up to this time, Spanish-grown tobacco — largely from the West Indies — had been the chief European supply; being grown by slaves, its cost was low. England, now enjoying this same labor advantage, began exporting the Virginia weed to Spain itself, and presently the vastly enhanced crop from Virginia was pouring into the English market as through a funnel, and thence finding its path into every European country, giving the Virginia leaf a prestige which it still retains. The thing that made this possible was the great fleet of slave ships, sailing from Africa to Virginia ports. It made the favored planters rich, but had deplorable effects upon the middle-class white man's civilization that had gained such headway in the seventeenth century.

For only great planters could really profit by this African invasion. The multitudinous small agriculturists, scattered all over Tidewater, cultivating a few acres with their own hands, could make little use of slaves. Not only was the initial investment large, far beyond their pocketbooks, but the small tobacco farms offered no field for this kind of labor. Tobacco raising now became a large-scale operation, like American industry in the latter nineteenth and the twentieth century, and, as in the days of the manufacturing "trust," the "little fellow" was pushed to the wall. So long as high prices prevailed, this small-scale farmer raised his own food supply, while his little crop provided clothes and the other manufactured articles essential to a modest existence. But survival was impossible when his daily toil failed to produce a living wage. Thus the social crime of slavery was that it checked the growth of the white middle class which was coming to the front in Virginia, as in other colonies, even if it did not completely destroy it. Since white workers were no longer imported or came of their own free will, the material disappeared on which a middle class could be developed, and Virginia's increase in population henceforth came chiefly from the negro. Not only did white immigration cease, but the existing population, being unable to compete with low-priced negro labor, was forced to seek its living in other fields. Great numbers migrated to Northern colonies, strengthening their agricultural and town populations. Others left for non-slavery regions in the new sections of the South — in western Virginia, western Maryland, and North Carolina, where they developed into a strong slavery-hating, union-loving people, their descendants, by thousands, fighting in the Northern armies in the Civil War. Many remained in old

Virginia and fought a hard battle for existence against the constantly increasing army of blacks. In this struggle a small minority won, ultimately acquiring good-sized estates and becoming slave owners themselves, but the larger number, finding no employment on the farms, and reduced to ineptitude by the stigma cast on manual labor, — work fit only for negroes, — went to pieces, becoming hangers-on of the fringes of civilization.

The modern Virginian properly resents the expression "poor whites"; it seems to imply that the masses of present-day Virginia are descended from an inferior order of humankind. Any such inclusive generalization as this is never just. It is probably true that the division of Virginians into two classes — on one hand plantation magnates and on the other landless, worthless, half-starved, and inefficient dependents — can be pushed too far. Certainly when new lands were opened in the West, in the Shenandoah and beyond, a middle-class yeomanry, engaged in general agriculture, making little use of slaves, did develop, profoundly affecting the whole course of Virginia history and its society and institutions. In this region, a land entirely distinct from Tidewater Virginia, slavery did not exercise its blighting power. In old Virginia, however, the influence of the institution in making difficult the way of the small proprietor and discouraging the progress of a thrifty middle class cannot be exaggerated. At least that, as will appear, was the judgment of the Lees, and explains the hostility, from 1750 onward, this family consistently manifested against negro labor. Richard Henry Lee, in 1759, was no more strongly opposed to slavery — and on this ground of injustice to white men — than Robert Edward Lee in 1861.

Thus negro slavery concentrated wealth in a few hands, and with wealth, as is almost inevitably the case, went social and political prestige. The Virginia Council, a body of twelve men, all great planters, now became Virginia's ruler, and seats around the green baize table in the Williamsburg capitol were virtually hereditary in "baronial families." As a Byrd, a Nelson, a Wormeley, a Lee, passed to his fathers, the name of another member of the dominant caste as "one of the Principal men of the colony" was automatically submitted to the king, and as automatically received the royal sign manual. More important still, the Council, despite the formula of nomination by governor and approval by king, was practically self-perpetuating, for the governor, in making nominations, invariably accepted suggestions from that body.   Thus no outsider, no new rich, could gain admittance except by approval of those already entrenched in power. For the Council consolidated its monopoly in two ways — first by limiting the authority of the royal governor, and secondly that of the citizen.   The supreme control exercised by Governor Berkeley under the Restoration was not enjoyed by his successors. The four royal governors who followed this despot all attempted to rule Virginia in Berkeleian style, but all failed.   The fifty years from 1676 to 1722 was a time of incessant conflict between the representative of the king and the Council, and in each case the Council emerged as victor.   Alexander Spotswood is to-day one of Virginia's heroes; he was unquestionably the ablest royal governor ever sent from England, yet this executive became embroiled with the Council, and as a consequence was removed from office.   Examples of this kind were not lost on officials dispatched from England as nominal representatives of the king.   Most were deputies, the real governor remaining in England and drawing half the salary; they were impecunious politicians, to whom the emolument was the main inducement for crossing the seas; only by maintaining friendly relations with the real sources of authority could they keep their jobs; after 1722 quarrels between governors and Council ceased, for the big ancestral families had established a Roman peace, with themselves in supreme command. A few years after the death of Thomas Lee the royal governor, Francis Fauquier, was rebuked by the home government for approving a law obnoxious to the king.   It was a bad law, Governor Fauquier admitted; he had signed it because the Council told him to!

Similarly the Council became an imperium independent of the populace.   Its spirit of isolation and self-sufficiency set the members apart from their own people — the Virginia Commonalty — and made them an exclusive headquarters of power.   Now developed the conception that directed affairs until settlements beyond Tidewater introduced more democratic theories: that government was the exclusive prerogative of a few well-born families — of a few educated gentlemen, with abundant leisure, who had specifically trained themselves for the task. As many leaders of the Revolution served their political apprenticeship under this system, it looks as though, *prima facie,* much could be said for it; yet it had aspects less public-spirited. That councilors were constantly seeking their own advantage is true. This also its members regarded as their hereditary right. They monopolized most lucrative offices, acted, in the administration of justice, as ultimate court of appeal, and, after the head-right system perished, allocated public lands, assigning huge estates to themselves in most unblushing fashion.

One might expect that the House of Burgesses, nominally the popular branch of the Virginia legislature, might prove a check upon the "barons." Yet the fact is that, for the first half of the eighteenth century, the power of the feudal gentlemen extended to this body also. For, in that time, it could hardly be regarded as a popular assembly; rather it suggested the House of Commons in rotten-borough England, when great noblemen, themselves ensconced in the House of Lords, virtually had the naming of the men who sat in the lower chamber. In this same way the House of Burgesses in Virginia became a camping ground of younger sons, and of second-string aristocrats, such as the Washingtons. All during this period the head of the House of Lee sat in the Council, but a multitude of Lee cadets figured in the burgesses. While Thomas Lee was occupying the presidential chair, his nephew Henry, ancestor of Robert Edward Lee, was representing Prince William County in the less exalted chamber downstairs. Indeed, in this so-called popular branch again appears that succession of identical names which has been observed in the great senate house of privilege. The simple fact is that this "popular" chamber was not popular at all. The steady restriction of the suffrage had deprived the common man of participation in elections. The day when an "inhabitant" could vote in Virginia, or even a freeman or small property owner, had disappeared. After Bacon's suppression, laws were passed steadily limiting the franchise to "free holders" and "housekeepers," until, in 1736, the qualifications were permanently fixed to holders of one hundred acres of uncultivated land, or twenty-five acres of cultivated land, with a house on it. This shut out all but the most successful of those modest citizens who had withstood the onslaught of slavery. Under these circumstances the Virginia burgesses became an assembly largely of well-born men, many of ability and high public spirit; that body itself soon acquired a prestige second only to that of the Council, and membership in it was eagerly sought for. But the "popular" body really strengthened the great families. There is a tradition that, on the retirement of Sir William Gooch, governor, in 1749, a royal commission passed the great seal appointing Thomas Lee to his post, and that it reached Virginia after his death. The story is apocryphal, but it might just as well have been true, for, as president of the Council, acting governor, and commander in chief of Virginia's military forces, Lee exercised a power that was fairly regal.

What was the attitude of Thomas towards the institution of slavery that so enhanced the status of his caste? Probably not materially different from that of his New England compeer, for slavery entered the Northern region at the same time that it did the South, and had the rocky New England soil yielded a staple crop, cultivated profitably by black men, the system would unquestionably have flourished there as in the more genial clime. Let it not be supposed that, in the seventeenth or first half of the eighteenth century, either Puritan or Cavalier saw any inherent wickedness in taking profit from the sweat of negroes. In both regions he was regarded as little higher in the scale of civilization than a horse or an ox; in both the question was solemnly debated whether he was of human creation or belonged to a rather superior order of animal. That Thomas Lee accepted the plantation system, with its slaves, as part of nature's order, even divinely sanctioned, may be taken for granted. Certainly it vastly enhanced his prosperity, as it did the prosperity of all his social group, and assumed symbolic form in the houses that now sprung up on the Potomac, of which his own Stratford is the oldest and almost the only survivor. The planters selected the loftiest ridges for their "Halls" — like Stratford, on the "Cliffs" which had so enraptured the eyes of the youthful Thomas. They built them frequently in the shape of letters — Thomas adopting the letter "H." The interiors were frequently sumptuous; certainly the middle hall of Stratford is a noble apartment; family portraits hung on the walls; the furnishings were importations from London, and the grounds were laid out in gardens, box hedges, orangeries, and walks. The delightful social life that adorned these establishments has been frequently described. The finely garbed and beautiful women, the silver-buckled gentlemen, the four-horse coaches, house parties that lasted a week or more, weddings continuing almost as long, funerals that commonly ended in Homeric barbecues, horse meets, cockfights, fox hunts, dicing and card playing, gatherings at church and at muster and county court — all these details form a now familiar story. But the plantation had a more important significance. Its influence on American history, its part in changing Virginia from an outpost of British Toryism into a determined enemy of British rule, is its greatest contribution to American life. It is this plantation that, above all, differentiates Virginia from the Northern colonies. Nothing like it had ever been known before in America or elsewhere, and those philosophers who like to trace the influence of external circumstances in shaping life and character could find no better material than this unique institution. Even more analytical would be a study of the effect wrought on history by that peculiar plant which gave Virginia the economic groundwork of existence. Tobacco was Virginia and Virginia was tobacco; banish the weed and the colony would have shriveled up and died. John Rolfe figures in the American story chiefly as the husband of Pocahontas, a romantic rôle that, so far as the development of the continent is concerned, has not the slightest consequence; his greatness, as a historic force, was laid in an event whose result was not foreseen. It was when Rolfe, in 1612, planted the first Virginia tobacco garden that he took the step which was to direct the course of the North American Continent. Had it not been for tobacco, there probably could have been no Virginia at all, at least not at that time, for the struggling settlements would have had no crop to bring in a steady revenue and sustain existence.

The point was that tobacco made necessary the great plantation. It is a crop that constantly exhausts the earth; in those days fertilizers were practically unknown; the farmer cleared one patch of land, raised two or three crops, then abandoned it and moved to virgin soil. It was necessary, therefore, that great expanses be held in reserve, and so the plantation of one thousand, two thousand and more acres became the unit, as much so in Virginia as the small farm in New England. This fact influenced every department of life; it would be difficult to mention a phase of Virginia character, or of Virginia institutions, that is not traceable to it. Certainly the plantation caused the growth of slavery. Burke even asserted that the love of liberty for which Virginia became so celebrated was largely explained by the omnipresent black men. The Virginian, having constantly in view the miseries attending serfdom, — so ran the ingenious paradox, — placed a higher value on the free state than men who lacked his opportunities for observation! Probably that quality that has so charmed all commentators on Virginia society — its hospitality — is explained in large degree by the plantation. To settlers removed great distances from the nearest neighbor, living at best a desolate existence, the appearance of new human faces was naturally a matter for rejoicing; social "calls" and "receptions" of urban convention were impossible, for it frequently took several days, even long water trips against adverse winds, to make a journey, and protracted visits and houses full of guests were thus inevitable. Again, that single feature which so differentiated New England from the South, primary education and the district school, can be attributed, in part at least, to the same cause. In neighborly, compact settlements like those in the North, children could easily congregate in the little red school building, but this was hardly possible in a country where trips of ten and twenty miles — usually by water — would be a necessary preliminary to each day's session.

That, on the personal side, the plantation and slavery produced traits of character which the rest of the nation regarded as unpleasant is also true. The fact that the overlord possessed almost life and death power over droves of blacks — men who must tamely receive orders and could not answer back — tended to develop an overbearing manner. That the white population, outside of the dominant landholding class, — until a sturdy small proprietor element grew up in western Virginia, — were constantly sinking in the social and economic scale encouraged this spirit. No more conspicuous example of this type of Virginian could be asked for than Thomas's eldest son, and family head in the fourth generation, Philip Ludwell Lee, to whom most references in contemporary writings are disagreeable; for he was rough-mannered and arrogant, treating with equal disregard both negro and down-at-the-heel white man, and manifesting little public spirit in the face of epochal events.   On the other hand the plantation had an influence in developing fine qualities of service and patriotism, as well as courtly behavior and intellectual vigor — all qualities marked in Thomas's other sons, especially Thomas Ludwell, Richard Henry, and Francis Lightfoot.   The plantation may have stimulated haughtiness and pride, but at the same time it instilled a spirit of independence and gave leisure for the cultivation of mental graces and the study of deep concerns, notably of philosophy and government.   The Virginia planter, such as Thomas Lee, lived amid circumstances that made him free as air. His estate was a little principality of which he was ruler.   Let all the surrounding land sink into the sea, the plantation could still maintain a fairly satisfactory career, for it raised its own food, grew and spun and wove its own wool, made its own brick and lumber, had its own blacksmiths, tanners, shoemakers, and carpenters — contained within itself, that is, most of the elements essential to an integrated community.   The man who controlled this demesne, treated by retainers and friends as a superior being, elevated, as a birthright, to the highest offices of state, and accepted as the head of its social life, naturally became an "aristocrat," but he also became — at least the best of them did — a self-reliant, freedom-loving leader, not easily brooking restraint, even the restraint of kings.   All this was not an inheritance from baronial England, as the fanciful have imagined; it was an immediate consequence of the circumstances at hand, a development from within, loyal to itself, not to a monarchical régime three thousand miles distant.   In all history barons have been famous for breaking away from their liege sovereign and setting up for themselves, and to this extent the Virginia planters justified the title the romantic have given them.

No man better embodied these qualities in their highest aspect than Thomas Lee. In the latter part of his life, as president of the Council and acting governor, he was the head of the political and social oligarchy just described. Most loyal to his king, so far as acts were concerned, he evinced the tendencies and the spirit that were to play a leading part in establishing a new nation. How his love of the Western country foreshadowed the covered wagon and the forces that welded the discordant colonies into a conscious national will! When Thomas scaled the mountains, staked out a great country on the Ohio, and proclaimed his creed that the French must be excluded from the continent, the "President of Virginia" stood forth as one of the first Americans. When he advocated the bringing in of Germans and other foreign stocks to settle the Shenandoah and the banks of the Ohio he was similarly forecasting that march of immigrants into America's vacant lands that makes such a splendid chapter in history. His death took place before his most cherished schemes had reached fulfillment. Most of the Virginians who were to become builders of the new United States — such as Washington, Jefferson, Patrick Henry, George Mason — were living, but they were young men, or children, whose future even the most visionary prophet could not have predicted. When events, a dozen years after the death of Thomas, were to call these paladins to their destined tasks, they were to find co-workers in a group of brothers who, at the time of their father's death, were children at Stratford or schoolboys in England. When these brothers did their part in establishing independence and hastening national expansion, they were carrying into practice the new American spirit that was an inheritance from the first proprietor of Stratford.

PART II

THE SIX SONS OF STRATFORD

IV

A COLONIAL STATESMAN

I

THE building in which the six sons of Thomas Lee and Hannah Ludwell obtained their primary education is still in existence, a little red brick cabin, as sturdy and unpretentious as the New England district school. And daily proceedings here, two centuries ago, were quite as Spartan as in the more sombre Northern clime. The boys were taught not only reading and writing, but the "grammatical sciences" — that is, the languages, especially the ancient ones. The presiding genius was a Scottish clergyman, Mr. Craig — unquestioned master of the establishment, for the plantation tutor, in the eighteenth century, was a more dignified person, and held in greater esteem, than one would gather from tradition. Frequently, as in the present case, he was an educated gentleman, and, as such, commonly took his meals at the family table, acted as escort for the ladies to church and social functions, and had, and was expected to have, predominant influence in moulding his charges. His association with the boys was far more intimate than that of their parents; for "permissions" they came to him, not their father; he himself frequently accompanied them to cockfights and horse meets, and participated in their sports, not infrequently serving as antagonist in foot races, boxing contests, and the like. Mr. Craig had general supervision of their morals and deportment and even of their "correction" — that liberal use of the rod regarded as essential in any educational system. The smaller boys did not sleep in the "Big House," but in a bedroom over the school, and their daily routine was severe and industrious. The school bell rang at seven for "one round" of the classroom before breakfast; after this meal instruction began again at nine, and lasted until the dinner hour at two. Then it was again resumed, the day's work coming to an end at five. All this was accompanied by Bible readings, the catechism, and probably excursions in literature.

The value of such training depends upon the preceptor; and that the Reverend Mr. Craig proved a civilizing agent with the fourth generation of the Lees the sequel showed. Four of the sons — Philip Ludwell, Thomas Ludwell, Richard Henry, and Arthur — supplemented their Stratford education by several years in England, but Francis Lightfoot and William owed all their mental training to Mr. Craig. William, as a man, displayed solid, if not brilliant qualities, was well informed in history and general letters, while Francis Lightfoot was an outstanding Virginian for the charm of his conversation, his wit and even erudition — a convincing illustration of the results produced by the plantation school. The fact is not surprising, for the method used was one that has been approved from ancient to modern times. A teacher of learning and character, in constant friendly companionship with four or five boys, supervising their classroom exercises, directing their reading, filling their minds, at the most impressionable age, with thoughts and principles that remain lifelong possessions — it was the method of Mark Hopkins and one towards which the best educators of the present day are working as an ideal. The gratitude with which the Lees looked back, in afterlife, to their old tutor, Mr. Craig, indicates also that this training had another desirable quality: schooling had been a pleasing experience, something to be remembered with affection and delight.

After this preparatory training Richard Henry Lee spent several years at an academy in Wakefield, England, established by Queen Elizabeth in 1592, which had long been popular with Virginia boys. There he came under the supervision of the Vicar of Wakefield, the Reverend Benjamin Wilson, said to have been the original of Goldsmith's famous parson; whether or not this identification is historic, the fact that such an impression prevailed gives the quality of the man. Wakefield was an ancient city, with Roman associations, drenched in memories of the Wars of the Roses and Cromwellian incursions; it was also the seat of much noble ecclesiastical architecture, and thus, as a classic background, as a constant object lesson in British history, and as a reminder of the Middle Ages, presented a congenial abode for an actively-minded boy.   Here Richard Henry spent at least seven years, from his twelfth to his nineteenth, supplementing the traditional classic studies of the time with his own extensive reading.   In the latter years of his sojourn, the two elder brothers, Philip Ludwell and Thomas Ludwell, were studying law at the Inner Temple in London.   Not improbably Richard Henry would have followed them to the same great training ground of lawyers, or proceeded to one of the English universities, but the father's death, in 1750, called all three students back to Virginia.

Philip Ludwell, the oldest, born in 1726, and now therefore in his twenty-fifth year, found himself not only family head, master of Stratford, and heir of the most flourishing family estates, but, in association with Thomas, guardian of the younger brothers and supervisor of their education and future.   Philip Ludwell, in the family annals, remains a somewhat lonely figure, the link that joins the colonial Lees with the aggressive sons of revolution. In sympathies, he belongs to the pre-Revolutionary time; he was really the last of the descendants of Emigrant Richard, the last, that is, who embodied the old Virginia conceptions, loyalty to colony, to king, to eighteenth-century principles and tradition. Philip Ludwell died in 1775, at the age of forty-nine, on the eve of the Revolution, but from that convulsion he had held aloof, and is thus a figure isolated from his five patriotic brothers.   This is the rôle that might normally be expected from him.   As member of the Virginia Council, that inner circle of great planters, which, as already set forth, represented the royal power and actually ruled Virginia socially and politically, allegiance to the king was almost presumed.   That the Council had developed much independence, and that sympathy with the colonial cause, even in this body, was marked, the event disclosed; but Philip Ludwell Lee was apparently one of the members who chose to remain aloof from the prevailing disorders.

Certain traits of his character have been already indicated. He was never concerned with popular movements, not a man likely to sympathize with agitators, uninstructed in political

theories and colonial problems. Handsome, gay, the proprietor
of Stratford in its most animated period, dispenser of a hospitality as unrestricted as it was warm-hearted and lively, colonel
of the Westmoreland militia, devoted to all the outdoor sports
that were second nature in the Virginia of his time, Philip's talents were apparently social rather than philosophic, his rôle in
Virginia rather that of the beneficiary of established things than
of an image breaker of a new day. A few scraps of his surviving
letters display chiefly his interest in music; he was also something
of a versifier; a "monody" on his mother's death was published
in the *Gentleman's Magazine* of London, in 1751, and is at least
interesting as revealing the lofty veneration Hannah Ludwell
inspired in her sons, though its lugubrious imagery hardly accords
with Philip's temperament as disclosed in contemporary references. In Philip Fithian's diary, an invaluable compendium of
pre-Revolutionary manners, he makes several appearances, always
in some festive rôle. "Early in the morning came Philip Lee,
in a travelling chariot from Westmoreland. So soon as we rose
from supper the company formed into a semicircle around the
fire and Mr. Lee, by the voice of the company was chosen Pope
and Mr. Carter, Mr. Christian, Mrs. Carter, Mrs. Lee and the
rest of the company were appointed Friars in the Play called
'Break the Pope's Neck.' . . . Today stayed for a short time
Mr. Blain and Mr. Lee, who were going to one Mr. Lane's for
a christening which I understand is one of the chief times for
Diversion here. . . . About four Col. Philip Lee's chariot arrived, in which came four young misses to be ready for the dance
which happens here tomorrow."

Other contemporary data are not so pleasing. According to
these Philip embodied the less ingratiating side of the plantation
character: unseemly family pride, an overbearing attitude towards
inferiors, and a disdainful insistence on the privileges of rank.
"A strange mortal stalked into my house," writes the melancholic
George Fisher, in his reminiscences of his sad Virginia career.
"He had no servant with him, but an arrogant, hauty carriage
which in the opinion of most men is a necessary or inseparable
accomplishment in what they call a person of Note, would at once
indicate to you that in his own thoughts he was a person of no

mean Rank or Dignity. . . . He turned from me with an air of what they call a Gentleman." Westmoreland court records reveal even more serious defects. In these Philip's younger brothers are constantly suing for the cash payments provided for them in their father's will, suits that were continued even after Philip Ludwell's death, apparently without success. The relations between the second master of Stratford and the younger brothers present almost the only episode in Lee annals resembling a family feud.

All this, however, in 1750, was very much in the future, for the arrival of these three older brothers, Philip, Thomas, and Richard Henry, on their father's death, produced a startling effect upon the younger sons — Francis Lightfoot, aged sixteen, William, eleven, and Arthur, ten. With them the glories of Europe seemed transplanted to Westmoreland. Their English manners, their English clothes, their conversation, impressed these wondering striplings as the perfection of humankind. To talk like Philip and Richard Henry, to be the master of such infinite charm as Thomas — earth presented no loftier ideals for emulation. The younger brothers' future now became the chief responsibility of Philip and Thomas. The four older sons had been endowed, in their father's will, with landed estates, presumably ample to support them in dignified comfort, but the youngsters at the end of the family tree, William and Arthur, were left to make their own way. The jurisdiction of the guardians was complete. They were enjoined to rear their brothers "religiously and virtuously and, if necessary, bind them to any profession or trade, so that they may learn to get their living honestly." This reads like a cold thrusting adrift, suggesting the Elizabethan custom of transforming younger sons into artisans and shopkeepers! Francis Lightfoot offered no problem. Genial, smiling, debonair, humorous, handsome, and lovable, he was already approaching his seventeenth year, and for him the transition was easy from paternal Stratford and Parson Craig's academy to the tobacco plantation his father had appointed in Loudoun County. There Francis presently became a farmer in the best old Roman sense, cultivating not only his acres but his mind, nourishing not only his tobacco and his wheat but his friends, unassertively watching the course of events, now and then called, almost reluctantly, to play a modest but none the less effective rôle in public affairs. The future of William, too, seemed plainly indicated. In those days one member of a great plantation family — as already described — was commonly selected for establishment in London as merchant and tobacco trader; that William would eventually be translated to England was apparent.

Arthur was as definitely set apart for an intellectual career. When Thomas Lee suggested binding one of his sons to a "profession," not improbably he had the youngest in view. At that time medicine was a degraded occupation in Virginia. In the whole colony there were said to be less than half a dozen practitioners who rose above the degree of quacks. Thomas Lee desired that one of his sons should join this profession, and exemplify in it the highest European standard, and Arthur, even as a lad, showed mental qualities equal to the task. Quickminded, energetic, a glutton for books, enthralled not only by polite letters but by science, as keenly interested in botany as in Latin orators and statesmen, Arthur impressed his guardian brothers as one likely to elevate any profession. The Reverend Mr. Craig, in glowingly describing Arthur's endowments, may have touched upon a few disqualifications of temperament. The kind of excitable energy for which Arthur Lee was distinguished commonly produces a character captious, self-willed, imperious, impatient of control, determined in pursuing his own ambitions and fancies, and not especially deferential to the opinions of others. All these traits Arthur Lee displayed as a man, and naturally they must have marked him as a boy. But on one point there could be no question — he was a child of great intelligence and industry. Schooling at Eton, higher education at some British university, and travel in Europe were the plans Philip and Thomas regarded as adequately fulfilling their father's will. And so on a day in 1751, Arthur Lee, eleven years of age, embarked on one of those tobacco ships that served as the *Mauretanias* of the time — ships that were usually infested with fevers and distressingly uncomfortable at their best. Yet Arthur departed in a spirit of joy and anticipation. That eagerness which was perhaps his most conspicuous trait was fired by the prospect of life and studies in the "homeland." For more than ten years Arthur disappears from Virginia — and from the present narrative.

2

The most agreeable side of Philip Ludwell Lee is shown in his relations to Richard Henry, now for several years to be his inseparable companion. This attachment was based exclusively on affection; certainly Richard Henry's formidable studies did not attract the older brother, neither could he have had anything but an indulgent smile for the younger man's political convictions. Nevertheless there was something in the philosopher's mere presence which Philip found essential to contentment. In 1751, the date of the return from England, both brothers were unmarried; Stratford, with its walks and gardens and vineyards, made an ideal bachelor's hall, and here Philip and Richard started a life together that continued for nearly a decade. The lands left Richard Henry in Fauquier were leased to strangers whose rents provided for the moderate wants of their owner; all Richard's time could therefore be given to books and human companionship. In the latter avocation Richard Henry was by no means deficient. A somewhat forbidding character he seems in the perspective of history, possibly a little dour and humorless, a kind of New England Puritan placed incongruously on the banks of the Potomac. Yet life had gayer aspects in this existence at Stratford. The place, under his brother's hospitable rule, was the scene of parties, fox hunts, and the like; all this the young Richard Henry enjoyed, and such experiences proved a wholesome distraction from those sedentary pursuits to which his hours were unremittingly devoted.

If any American statesman ever had substantial preparation for his work, Richard Henry Lee was that man. He may be taken as a type that Virginia, probably to a greater extent than other colonies, produced in the ante-Revolutionary era. From his earliest days Richard Henry's career was definitely fixed. Business, even the routine of tobacco planter, — at which he was not successful, — had little interest. Even the profession of law did not attract him. For the third Stratford son only one occupation made any appeal. That was public life. That these great Potomac families were born with the sense of public service — what they usually described as "statesmanship" — has been already indicated. From his childhood such had been the future Richard Henry pictured for himself. It was something he owed, not only to his family, but to Virginia. It is thus worth while to pause and observe a type of citizen that has disappeared from America — and observe him with regret, for the type made great contributions to the Republic. Richard Henry belonged to the "leisure" class in the best sense of the word, which signifies a group born to the duty of government — able men with ingrained traditions and an intellectual background for public careers. Study and reflection are not too common qualities in a democratic order, and a constant hurly-burly, not leisured contemplation, seems to be the essential preliminary to statesmanship. This has not always been the case in America. There was a time when men inherited a sense of public responsibility, and prepared for legislative chambers as assiduously as they now prepare for medicine or law. At that time, too, the community was always ready to welcome such leadership, surrendering power as naturally as their leaders assumed it. Especially in Virginia, two hundred years ago, did there flourish a school of statesmanship of this mellow kind, and no career better portrays it than that of Richard Henry Lee.

We may profitably glance back into this forgotten era and observe this faithful inheritor of tradition, a tall and lithe figure, in his early twenties, comfortably ensconced in the hall of Stratford, or sitting at ease in the garden, book in hand, searching his favorite writers and occasionally pausing to make notes, for reading was no profitless pastime, but a serious task, the results of which were to be put down in written form. In the library of the University of Virginia is still preserved the notebook in which Richard Henry records his studies of his favorite thinkers on government, such writers as Montesquieu, John Locke, Pufendorf, and other laureates of the English Revolution. Imagine a young American of to-day studying such pundits in arduous apprenticeship for work in a legislative chamber! Early letters between Richard Henry and Arthur Lee frequently turn on constitutional questions, with extracts from French and Latin writers; these, in the original languages, would perhaps strike the present generation as pedantic, but they were second nature to the students of that time. This picture of Richard Henry is stimulating, for such a spectacle was not limited to Stratford; other Virginians of that time were spending hours the same way, deriving lessons that were subsequently to produce wide reverberation. "He thinks much; such men are dangerous. . . . He reads much" — this Shakespearean warning might well have been taken to heart by British statesmen of the time, as their eyes wandered towards the Potomac and the James. And Richard Henry's intellectual diversions showed the progress the Lees had been making in two generations. That mental fodder on which the second Richard had nourished his political and theological beliefs no longer encumbered the household. In 1729 a merciful fire reduced Mount Pleasant to ashes, and in this holocaust all the brimstone and divine-right literature of that period met appropriate sepulchre. In its place a new library had gradually taken form, to which Richard Henry was making daily additions.

The old Lees, Stuart adherents, would have been shocked at the transformation. Only one comfort would they have found: the classics still held preferred position, one Latin author in particular seeming to hold preëminence over the early builders of the Republic. Even Patrick Henry, whose book "larnin'" — to use his own pronunciation — was not extensive, read his Livy in translation once a year, much as his Presbyterian elders went annually through their Bibles, cover to cover. To modern Americans these statuesque heroes of Rome — Brutus, Cato, Cincinnatus, and the rest — look a little stodgy, but to our eighteenth-century forefathers they were flaming exemplars of everything desirable in citizenship. Not only did they serve as pen names for pamphlet literature, but their actions were taken as precedents and justifications in all crises. Even John Adams, when advocating, before the Continental Congress, the creation of an American navy, cited the precedent of the Carthaginians against Rome. Hardly a speech was made, or a letter to the newspapers written, that did not proclaim, at the masthead, a Virgilian extract or an Horatian tag. Consider the names with which the Lees of this generation burdened their children: Brutus, Augustus, Cassius, Portia, Cornelia, Octavia — "your Roman cousins," as William called them in a letter to a nephew. "We learn from antiquity that Solon, the great Athenian legislator" — so begins one of Richard Henry's few surviving speeches; when he warns the Virginia legislature on slavery, he points out the evils which it brought to Rome. Let the South beware lest another Spartacus arise!

English literature, too, especially Shakespeare and Milton, charmed Richard Henry, and let his insistence on the study of English be set down to his credit. The fault of eighteenth-century education, in Richard's view, was its failure to develop English studies alongside the universal classics. One who has handled the correspondence of this time, observing how scholars highly extolled for mastery of ancient tongues are illiterate in their own, will sympathize with this opinion. "A thorough knowledge of English" he prescribed as one of the items in the education of his son. In its use he trained himself carefully, as did his brothers, all of whom wrote their language neatly and — an almost unprecedented phenomenon of the eighteenth century — were painstaking about spelling, the use of capitals, punctuation, and similar niceties.

History and political science, however, claimed the larger part of Richard Henry's time, and, in particular, the English constitution was deeply pondered. As a result he became an expert on its guarantees and flexibilities, its political crises, parliamentary discussions, court decisions — the conflicts of social classes, the revolutions, the seatings and unseatings of kings that had gone to make that instrument. Even a portentous author like Grotius did not deter him; that teacher's justification of the United Provinces in their revolt from Spain was not lost on a mind troubled about the clouds rising between England and America. Indeed the right, even the obligation of revolution, under appropriate circumstances, was extolled in most of Richard's political studies. Among his favorite heroes was John Hampden — an authority much quoted by those Americans who afterward declined to pay taxes they had had no part in levying. Indeed no better introduction to the times presently to distract the colonies could be found than the respectable, but incendiary literature on which this young man was feeding his mind. Ralph Cudworth and Richard Hooker do not excite many readers of this present age, but they advocated religious toleration in a day when this doctrine was not liked, and they defined the theory of the "social compact" many years before the prize-winning essay of Rousseau. But the writer in whom Richard Henry most gloried was John Locke. No author affected colonial thinkers to the same extent. Occasionally an inventory of an eighteenth-century library on the Potomac comes to light, and invariably among the volumes listed are Locke's *Treatises on Government* and *Toleration*. That these works rested for many years on the Stratford shelves, and were patiently thumbed, is well known. The man was a popular author of the day, and not only in Virginia, for James Otis and John Adams in Massachusetts and Benjamin Franklin in Pennsylvania drank deeply at this fountain of sedition.

As for Jefferson, despite a tendency to trace his iconoclasm to French influence, the fact remains that his chief inspirer was Locke. One need only read the second paragraph of his Declaration to discover that. "Richard Henry Lee," Jefferson ruefully wrote John Adams in old age, "charged it as copied from Locke's treatise on government." That all men are created with equal rights; that they establish governments to obtain these rights; that all governments rest upon consent of the governed; that they can be dissolved when they fail to accomplish the purpose for which they were formed — such were the main outlines of Locke's philosophy, originally set forth to justify the "glorious revolution" of 1688, but found similarly applicable to American affairs a century afterward. And other lessons, not always favored by Richard Henry's co-workers, were derived from this English thinker. That one should not debase the currency, that paper money was a perilous adventure, that a nation, like a person, should pay its debts — these teachings, set immutably forth in Locke's economic writings, were lost on certain leaders of the Revolution, especially on that inflationist, Patrick Henry, and that advocate of repudiation, Thomas Jefferson; but Richard Henry Lee, true to his instruction, stood a bulwark of sound money and national honesty in difficult times. On the more

touchy problem of the relation of state and church the Virginian
remained a loyal disciple. Like Locke, Richard Henry was a
Christian believer and, again like Locke, insisted that the state
could properly encourage religion. But he also accepted his men-
tor's dictum that every man was entitled to his own belief, and
that the state should not establish one church and creed, but protect all.

3

A splendid preparation this, for a political career, especially of
the kind in which Richard Henry Lee was about to engage. Still,
the young man's earliest ambitions were not legislative, but military. In 1755, the year that witnessed Braddock's expedition to
the Alleghany, Richard Henry was twenty-three — almost exactly Washington's age, the two men having been born within a
month of each other; like Washington, Lee felt the impulse to
martial affairs. He marched with the Westmoreland militia and
made tender of his services to the haughty Briton. His reception was even more humiliating than Washington's, for Braddock,
taking one disdainful glance at the eager recruits, sent them
packing back to the tobacco fields. He made an even greater mistake, for he treated Richard Henry with personal obloquy, in this
way insulting the whole tribe of Lee. "Mr. Lee had walked down
to the shore," writes the family biographer, "with General Braddock and some of his officers, where a boat was in readiness to
convey them to the Commodore's ship. When his officers were
on board, although he saw Mr. Lee standing on the shore, General
Braddock ordered the men to push off; but the Commodore, afterwards the celebrated Admiral Keppel, observing this, sternly
ordered them to stop, and invited Mr. Lee into the boat in which
he accompanied them to the ship." Little episodes like this frequently have an important influence on history. The effect of
Braddock's behavior during the entire Alleghany campaign in
alienating American sympathy, especially that of Virginia, from
the British crown can hardly be exaggerated; he personalized the
feelings of many of his class toward colonials, and manifested, as
a soldier, the same attitude of scorn that Charles Townshend did

as a politician. The Lees of this generation were entirely human, themselves not lacking in arrogance and rancor; that they had plenty of reasons, founded on public policy, for their anti-British attitude, the sequel showed; yet this public insult entered deeply in their minds, and did its part in creating the hostility which is frequently a potent, if unconscious, motive in forming great decisions.

Richard Henry's rôle was not destined to be martial, but statesmanlike. The extent to which public work was a family responsibility appeared in every session of the Virginia Assembly from 1757 to 1774. That was a critical era in the story of Virginia; it was the period of the French and Indian War, the American phase of that world struggle Pitt was waging for the predominance of England and the destruction of its ancient enemy. In this vast contest Virginia, as well as the other American colonies, played a generous part, and the House of Burgesses, in which the youthful Richard Henry quickly became a leader, showed throughout a coöperative spirit. When the student of Stratford entered the capitol at Williamsburg, he must have felt at home. In 1757 and for several years following, it seemed a sanctuary largely peopled by the House of Lee. Both the burgesses from Westmoreland were Lees — Richard Henry and his cousin, also named Richard, that "Squire" of Lee Hall who figures so notably in family legend, as famous for unloquacity as Calvin Coolidge, also as persistent in officeholding; entering the House in 1757, he remained laconically at his post for nineteen years, until that noble chamber itself passed out of existence. Henry Lee, brother of the "Squire," had just taken his seat, coming from Leesylvania in Prince William, leaving there his young wife, Lucy Grymes, — that "lowland beauty" for whom Washington, according to a fable that dies hard, had vainly sighed, — and their oldest son, an infant one year old, destined to fame as "Light Horse Harry" of the Revolution. Richard Henry's two brothers, Francis Lightfoot, of Loudoun, and Thomas Ludwell, of Stafford, were also on hand, and three or four years later appeared John, raising the complement of Lees at Williamsburg to seven — for in the council chamber Philip Ludwell Lee had succeeded to the seat so long filled by his father. The predominance of Lees in this session is a fair illustration of the fact, set forth in the preceding chapter, that the House of Burgesses was largely the preserve of young sons of the big planter families.

But Williamsburg at this period was not entirely a Lee head-quarters. Though the House was merely a provincial chamber, it would be difficult to name any American legislature, before or since, that contained so many men of full stature. In addition to the Lees, the roster discloses such names as Washington, Pendleton, Harrison, Mason, Bland, Carter, Nicholas, Wythe — all prominent in the history of the next two decades. Three years after this session began, another young man, seventeen years old, joined the ranks, not as member, but as hanger-on, a red-haired and freckle-faced student of William and Mary who was accustomed to add variety to his college course by stealing into the communicating hall of the House and listening to debates; in this surreptitious fashion did Thomas Jefferson gain his first insight into the processes of government. Soon afterward came a shambling, rawboned, uncouth fisherman and hunter from Louisa County, that Patrick Henry whose flamboyant oratory eventually startled a continent into rebellion. In 1757, however, the house was not in a mood for wild demonstrations. The cleavage into what would to-day be called "left" and "right" had begun, but had not attained definite outline. Those serried ranks of aristocracy embodying "baronial" power were still unbroken, though here and there traces of the approaching democratic invasion were apparent. But the great men of the rivers still occupied strategic points. John Robinson, speaker, was almost as conservative as Lord Bute himself; he had a considerable following of fellow spirits on the plantations, who were presently to involve him in ruin. Even the group who, a few years afterward, were to lead in defiance to the king were at this time not members of the radical wing: George Wythe, finest legal mind in Virginia, as famous for learning as for having had Jefferson as favorite pupil; Harrison, a man of coarser strain, but substantial in mind, bulky in frame, having also those qualities of Rabelaisian joviality that lightened up many a lugubrious problem; George Mason, another Virginian who, like Richard Henry, combined bookishness and action, afterward author of the Virginia Bill of Rights and the Virginia Constitution; Richard Bland, influential pamphleteer and expounder, in Stamp Tax days, of the theory that the colonies were not dependencies of Britain, but self-reliant nations who merely happened to have the same king; and Peyton Randolph, afterward first president of the Continental Congress. This group were open-minded, prepared to listen to new ideas, but, at this time, mildly conservative, ready to howl down Patrick Henry for "treason" — as they did — when he loudly proclaimed certain resemblances between George III and Tarquin and Cæsar and Charles I. But, even before these agitations, there were signs of radicalism in the House of Burgesses. A new Virginia was evolving. Neither geographically nor psychically did Tidewater bound its confines. No longer was tobacco its only industry and slavery its one form of labor. In the Shenandoah and beyond a horde of new immigrants had found fruitful farms, mostly Scotch Irish, Presbyterians in religion, and cultivators of the soil, largely with their own brawn. These men and women were frankly plebeians; they had no awesome attitude towards the ancient order; they resented attempts to hold them in subjection and to exclude them from influence and political preferment; as a matter of fact they were yeomen of substantial type and had, in many cases, reached comparative wealth. They were beginning also to wedge their way into the legislative chamber; and the session of 1757, which marked Richard Henry's first appearance, contained a respectable segment who stood aggressively for a new and more democratic order.

Thus Richard Henry and his associate Lees had the choice of three allegiances — the unbending conservatism represented by Robinson and a waning group, the mild but open-minded traditionalists headed by Harrison and Wythe, and the aggressive radical sons of the middle section and the West, so far with no particularly defined leadership. To the astonishment of most Virginians, and possibly to their own, the Lees — as they would say in the House of Commons — crossed the gangway and joined the democratic contingent. Perhaps Richard Henry's reading had something to do with his new fantastic theories; perhaps the corruption of Virginia's hereditary nobles, already becoming a whispered scandal in the Tidewater, made him turn from his ancestral beliefs; at any rate, Lee had not long been a member when the new men from the Piedmont and the mountains discovered that he was one of themselves. Still the Lees retained their family influence, as was evidenced by the important committee assignments received and the prominence acquired in debate. Of them all Richard Henry was the most powerful. In those days, as already intimated, no popular characters could escape comparison with classic heroes: thus Francis Lightfoot Lee was dubbed the Atticus of the House, while Richard Henry found himself its Cicero. By this one is probably to understand that Francis was urbane, gentle, devoted equally to letters and to friendship, and that Richard was learned, thoughtful, conscientious, and at the same time possibly a little austere, not lacking in vanity, nor disinclined to champion unpopular causes.

There was even something in his appearance that suggested the sterner side of the Roman character. Just twenty-five years old, "tall and spare" in frame, as John Adams afterward described him, Lee's face was thin, clearly revealing the bony structure beneath; the high, receding brow, the ears, pressed tightly against the skull, the sharp yet pensive eyes, the slightly aquiline nose — in the prevailing enthusiasm for literary allusion, it is not strange that Richard Henry's contemporaries should envisage him as one of Plutarch's men. There was something in his posture when he spoke — the shoulders bending forward, the head inclining persuasively, as though determined to seize attention and drive home the argument — that suggested a meditative statesman. The man's gestures were so graceful that Edmund Pendleton accused him of practising before a mirror. But the one point chiefly emphasized was the voice. The "harmonious Richard Henry Lee" one commentator calls him, referring to the soft and musical timbre of his speech, its copious modulated flow, its clear-cut language and well-turned periods. Lee eventually became one of the greatest orators of his generation, but he was never a popular speaker — not a speaker, that is, most effective with the crowd. "The great orators here," wrote John Adams, referring to the Continental Congress, "are Lee, Hooper, and Patrick Henry," but the first never approached the quality of the "forest born Demosthenes," — Lord Byron is responsible for this analogy, —

the man who, according to another observer, "could make the blood run cold and the hair stand on end." Richard Henry's manner was more academic, yet he was not exclusively an orator of the lamp; he did prepare his most important addresses, but he had as well the gift of spontaneous argument, and his readiness in debate and quickness of retort made him a formidable opponent.

However just may be the comparison of Richard Henry with Cicero, in one respect at least it was far of the mark: plenty of the Roman's orations survive, but of his successor, living eighteen centuries afterward, only fragments are preserved. One can gauge his literary habits chiefly from his letters, which exist in abundance; so far as the man's sweep, in history, political doctrine, and general learning, is concerned, they quite fulfill contemporary opinion; they display similarly a solid grasp of the English idiom, an alertness for facts, and comprehension of the meaning of passing events. Yet anyone who searches the Journal of the Virginia House of Burgesses for tense situations or lively colloquies will waste his time. Such things colonial Virginians apparently regarded as unworthy of preservation; even of Patrick Henry's impassioned speech in his Stamp Tax resolves — familiar to every schoolboy for a hundred and fifty years — not a word appears in the Congressional Record of that time. Authorizations to build tobacco warehouses, to establish ferries or dock entails, are faithfully immortalized, but the great concerns of the day appear only in barest outline. Thus the picture of Richard Henry that glimmers in this grudging record only now and then approaches the heroic. That he was an active legislator is plain. His name runs constantly through the minutes; when important committees were appointed, Richard Henry Lee is usually found on the list, sometimes as chairman; of his speeches, however, — and the statement is true of all other members, — there is not even an abstract.

Yet one oration survives among his literary remains — a document that in itself would justify his fame as a farseeing statesman. Slavery was a dangerous topic in Virginia, then and afterward; on this institution the colony's prosperity was supposed to rest: this consideration, however, did not deter the youthful Lee. Whether the paragraphs surviving represent his finished speech, or merely its heads, on which he enlarged according to the inspiration of the moment, is not determined, yet these jottings contain more wisdom on a great theme than most of the pamphlets and books that followed, in an avalanche, in the next hundred years.

The resolution in question called upon the House "to lay so heavy a duty on the importation of slaves, as effectually to put an end to that iniquitous and disgraceful traffic within the colony of Virginia." The custom of forcibly transporting black men from Africa to the colonies revolted the most humane Americans North and South and formed one of their grievances against Great Britain, for British traders were the chief offenders; yet all efforts to end the business had failed. That Richard Henry should take a hostile stand need cause no surprise. His father, Thomas, had been a large slaveholder, but practically all his descendants showed little enthusiasm for the system. The forty slaves Richard Henry inherited gradually decreased in number, until, at his death, his property included only three or four chattels of this kind. Manumission of slaves was nothing unusual among the Lees or other Virginians of the eighteenth century; Washington, Patrick Henry, Jefferson, George Mason, and others have left written records evincing their detestation of the evil. That Richard Henry Lee should have taken his stand against the institution is therefore not remarkable: what is remarkable is the reason for his opposition. Up to that time slavery had impressed most thinkers as an ethical wrong, repugnant to Christian principles and to the new idealizations of liberty that were rapidly attaining favor. Jefferson, in his *Notes on Virginia,* assailed it as destructive of manners and morals; holding men in subjection and ruling them by force tended, he said, to brutalize the owner; "the most unremitting despotism on the one part, and degrading submission on the other," demoralized both master and man and had an especially deplorable influence on children in their formative period. Emotional Patrick Henry railed against slavery as incompatible with a religion "mild, humane, gentle and generous," and as contrary to the principles of liberty and humanity. In Madison's view it made ridiculous the political order which he so admired; "Republican theory" becomes "fallacious" "where slavery exists." Quotations could be reproduced without end from other distinguished

Southerners, all opposing slavery and the trade, in almost every case on the grounds set forth above.

Yet Richard Henry Lee, whose voice was lifted against this labor system in a Virginia legislative body long before the opinions of these distinguished men had become public property, attacked it on different grounds. He indeed assailed the African trade as barbarous and unchristian, but the points on which he laid chief emphasis were economic and prudential. Slavery, injurious as it may have been to the negro, was an even greater danger to the white. As he was gazing at the American colonies, one fact, evidently apparent as early as 1759, but more glaringly manifest in the nineteenth century, had given Richard pause. "And well am I persuaded, sir," he said, "that the importation of slaves into this colony has been, and will be attended, with effects dangerous, both to our political and moral interests. When it is observed that some of our neighboring colonies, though much later than ourselves in point of settlement, are now far before us in improvement, to what, sir, can we attribute this strange, this unhappy truth? The reason seems to be this: that with their whites they import arts and agriculture, whilst we, with our blacks, exclude both. Nature has not partially formed them with superior fertility of soil, nor do they enjoy more of the sun's cheering and enlivening influences; yet greatly have they outstripped us."

That was one of the profoundest observations from an American public man in the colonial period. In two sentences it epitomizes the history of the continent for the next hundred years. One should keep in mind the date of this address, 1759 — fifteen years before the Revolution, a century before the Civil War. The assertion must have been extremely unpalatable at the time, and rather surprises a reader of the present day. Virginia, in the middle of the eighteenth century, was conscious of no inferiority to the other colonies; in arts and humane advancement, in population, wealth, cultivated manners, and gracious existence, she regarded herself, with considerable justice, as in the van of American civilization. To be informed thus tartly, by a youthful scion of one of her proudest families, that all the time she was living in a fool's paradise and falling backward, while Pennsylvania, New York, and New England were outstripping her, must have come as a bewildering shock. This bold deliverance also exemplified that disposition in Richard Henry already indicated — what may be called his Puritanical strain, the habit of speaking unpleasant truths, of administering chastisement where it seemed demanded.

The ideas set forth in this speech never met with widespread agreement in the South. To understand the Southern attitude it is necessary to look a century ahead, for, in 1857, an antislavery book was published that enraged the South even more than *Uncle Tom's Cabin* — a work, indeed, that was a more eviscerating handling of slavery than that romantic classic. This book, like Richard Henry's speech in colonial days, was the work of a Southerner, Hinton Rowan Helper, of North Carolina; so fierce were the passions it aroused that Helper, for his personal safety, had to flee to New York, while his treatise, banned by good society, outlawed as an incendiary appeal to prejudice, was regarded by the South as entirely responsible for John Brown's raid at Harpers Ferry. Merely to be suspected of possessing a copy of Helper's *Impending Crisis* caused a man to be shunned by his neighbors and disqualified for public office. What was the thesis that so maddened the Southern states? Precisely the same as Richard Henry Lee's speech a century before. There it is, on the very first page of Helper's volume: "What we mean to do is simply this: to take a survey of the relative position and importance of the several states of the Confederacy [meaning the Federal government] from the adoption of the national Compact: and when, of two sections of the country starting under the same auspices, and with equal natural advantages, we find one rising to a degree of almost unexampled power and eminence, and the other sinking into a state of comparative imbecility and obscurity, it is our determination to trace out the causes which have led to the elevation of the former and the depression of the latter and to use our most earnest and honest endeavors to utterly extirpate whatever opposes the progress of any portion of the Union." Then follow four hundred pages of letterpress, — a boundless array of statistics and a wealth of argument, frequently ill-tempered and faulty in logic, — all pressing home the same point: that slavery is an evil, not necessarily on humanitarian and religious, but on economic grounds, an injury not so much to the black man as the white, everywhere the foe of progress. Richard Henry Lee, Potomac aristocrat, and Hinton Rowan Helper, North Carolinian hillbilly, are found, a hundred years apart, taking precisely the same stand on the greatest question of their time. There are probably few enlightened Southerners to-day who would differ with their diagnosis.

Richard Henry's Old Testament qualities, even a gift for prophecy, appear in the first sentence of this speech. "As the consequences we must make in the determination of this day's debate will greatly affect posterity, as well as ourselves, it surely merits our most serious attention." No argument is necessary to strengthen the truth of that forecast. It was one that the Lees, above all, were to bring to bitter fulfillment.

4

At the present time Richard Henry would probably be regarded, and stigmatized, as a "reformer," fearlessly laying bare the misdeeds of powerful men, and summoning a wicked generation to mend its ways. Though under thirty, already was manifest that Virginia "habit of command" — that imperiousness of temper, that quiet assumption of authority — which afterward, in the Continental Congress, was to arouse antagonism at the same time that it was to concentrate power in Richard's hands. Certainly the Virginia of that era needed something in the shape of a public scourge. The colony, from 1761 to 1766, presents a contradiction in behavior: on the one hand it was aflame with public spirit, and was performing a conspicuous, indeed a leading part in the cause that led to American independence; on the other, it was stewing in official corruption. "Tory" and "Whig" meant more than those who followed the king and those who opposed him; the terms signified as well the group who had been plundering the Virginia treasury for several years and those who were seeking to uproot the evil at its source. Both problems were traceable to the same cause — the Seven Years' War, out of which Britain had just emerged victorious. So much has been heard of the great cost of this struggle to the mother country that the expenditures of the colonies have been almost forgotten. To contemporary ears Virginia's expenditures of £500,000 do not seem especially large, but in modern money that is not far from $10,-000,000, and such a debt, for a community of about 150,000 white men, was by no means inconsiderable. This money had been raised by the issue of treasury notes — promises to pay; since taxes were levied for redemption, and since these obligations were promptly paid each year, the paper readily passed as current money. As the notes came in and were redeemed, they were to be burned, the duty of incineration devolving upon the treasurer, Mr. John Robinson.

At that time Robinson was the particular darling of Virginia. For nearly thirty years — since 1738 — he had held the office both of speaker of the House and of treasurer, and his administration of these duties, especially that of the speakership, had brought him fame and affection. Next to the governor, we are informed, he was "the highest model of elegance and fashion." "His reputation was great," writes Edmund Randolph, "for sound political knowledge and an acquaintance with sound parliamentary forms, — a benevolence which created friends and a sincerity which never lost one. When he presided the decorum of the House outshone that of the British House of Commons, even with Onslow at their head. When he propounded a question his comprehension and perspicacity brought it equally to the most humble and the most polished understanding. In the limited sphere of colonial politics he was a column. The thousand little flattering attentions which can be scattered from the chair, operated as a delicious incense." Robinson had evinced this spontaneous charm on an occasion that has become historic. In 1758 he was instructed by the House to extend its congratulations to their gallant fellow member, George Washington, who had just resumed his seat after the successful campaign at Fort Duquesne. Robinson performed this task so felicitously that the subject of his praise was much confused. Washington rose to make his acknowledgments, but blushed, stammered, and found it impossible to go on. "Sit down, Mr. Washington," said the speaker. "Your modesty is equal to your valor, and that surpasses the power of any language to express."

It was this affability and kindness that had made Robinson the hero of rich and poor, aristocrat and plebeian. His bearing, his quiet but none the less positive assumption of authority, his handsome impressive figure, his wealth and social eminence, had for a generation made him seem almost the embodiment of the state.   Popular as Robinson was, he had little sympathy with the new ideas that had already obtained representation at Williamsburg.   The planting oligarchy that had ruled Virginia for generations found in him its typical exemplar.   One needs only to read the letters of the governor, Francis Fauquier, to learn how serenely the speaker basked in royal favor.   In the troubles that were then exciting the colonies Robinson's allegiance was completely with the king.   "This event," wrote Fauquier, in a letter dated May 11, 1766, referring to the recent death of "our late worthy Speaker," "would have been a sensible loss at any time, but more particularly so now, as I had promised myself great assistance from him in the next session of the Assembly, to quiet the minds of the people and bring them to a just and proper sense of their duty."   The popular discontent to which the governor referred was that aroused by attempts to enforce the Stamp Tax. That Robinson should have been one of the few Virginians, even of his own class, to side with Parliament against Virginia in this dispute does not necessarily imply any deep political conviction, based on justice or precedent.   The speaker was simply obeying the instincts of his being; the royal cause, above everything else, was the cause of a gentleman — of that small group, in Virginia and elsewhere, that had been set apart from the populace, endowed, at birth, with rights and duties all its own.

This point should be emphasized, for it was probably this attitude, and not inherent villainy, that caused Robinson's downfall. The social group for whom his reputation was sacrificed had greatly degenerated from the character displayed in the time of Thomas Lee.   They were a fast-living lot, devoting most of the waking hours to unproductive pleasure.   The chief purpose in life was no longer the maintenance of their estates and service to the community, but a continuous round of excitement.   Under these circumstances the inevitable happened.   The times themselves were not propitious, for war had worked havoc with the tobacco trade, and heavy taxation had almost drained the colony of its wealth. Yet the glory of the Virginia planter must be maintained, and money for the purpose must be found. Many were members of the House of Burgesses and had naturally turned to their leader, the speaker, who, despite the prevailing distress, was still a rich man. Robinson began lending money from his own private purse, and when these resources came to an end discovered another way of relieving his friends and, at the same time, building up a political machine. Those treasury notes that were annually presented for redemption and destruction now became a general providence, for, instead of committing them to the flames, Robinson quietly handed them over to aristocrats in distress. The fact that securities were taken for the loan, and that, in the last resort, the defalcation could be made good from the treasurer's still ample fortune, helped to salve his conscience. That benefactor and beneficiaries in this sordid conspiracy would become hidebound political henchmen needs no demonstration; in this close community cynical observers, after the whole thing was laid bare, discovered one of the reasons for the great political power that Robinson had concentrated in his own person.

That their suave and gentle presiding deity had appropriated £105,000 — not far from $1,000,000 in modern money — in this way, involving many of the outstanding luminaries of Virginia, was not definitely known in the fall of 1764, but that certain irregularities were besmirching the treasury department was a matter of general gossip. For months these suspicions had formed the topic of discussion in ordinaries, in the Raleigh Tavern of Williamsburg, around the firesides of all Virginia homes. Yet any attempt to drive these rumors to their lair involved a problem. Who was there in Virginia sufficiently strong and influential to assail such great pillars of the state — to paint Speaker Robinson for what he probably was, a grafter on a scale so far unprecedented in America, and to face the gang of high-livers who were responsible for his crimes? Yet here was a task not uncongenial to that Virginia "reformer," Richard Henry Lee. No man of lower social rank could undertake the enterprise, yet that a man of Lee's standing should stand forth and assail his own social brethren was hardly to be expected. Lee, however, was not averse to unpopular courses, then or afterward. And here he seemed measurably to justify his identification with his Roman prototype. Though any comparison of Robinson with Catiline makes one smile, yet Lee, on a December day, 1764, stalked into the Senate of Williamsburg with a stride that was really Ciceronian, determined, with eloquence and tight-set jaw, to confront these despoilers of their country and lay bare the truth. His oration has not been handed down, but its incisiveness and power long remained a tradition in Virginian annals. His biographical grandson has preserved some of the atmosphere of the scene. Speaker Robinson, the object of attack, "fixt his eyes with a dark and terrible frown upon Mr. Lee. The members opposed to his motion turned their faces from him, with haughty and disdainful airs, but these things had no other effect than to animate Mr. Lee to strains of indignant eloquence. The most able and influential members of the House opposed his motion, yet he refuted with all force, all objections and seemed to gain strength and ardor, from the very means taken to defeat it."

This performance may inspire comparisons with one of the greatest dramas in Roman history, but on the whole it rather suggests happenings of more recent date in modern America. Richard Henry's procedure has a distinctly contemporary flavor: what he demanded was one of those legislative investigations that have become the commonest events in American life. "Resolved, that a committee be appointed to inquire into the state of the treasury": such was the motion on which his eloquence was expended. The committee so eloquently demanded was appointed, and Richard Henry became a member, — not chairman, however, no such error as that was made, — for his name appears next to the last in a list of eight. Most unexceptionable gentlemen were named to this inquisition: Mr. Edmund Pendleton, Mr. Dudley Digges, Mr. Archibald Cary; this, the greatest present concern of the state, could clearly be in no more respectable hands. The several volumes of detailed testimony that follow in the wake of such investigations to-day, however, do not clog the shelves of Virginia libraries. There is no record of subpœnaed witnesses, of expert accountants, or the vociferations of famous cross-examiners. Six months later, however, at a time when Richard Henry was absent from his legislative duties, Mr. Archibald Cary submitted a report.   Everything, it seemed, was all right in the treasurer's department.   There had been no defalcation, no improper use of Virginia's money.   By inference, the charges insinuated by Richard Henry Lee and his abettors were outrageous slanders.   A detailed statement of the treasurer's accounts was offered as complete justification.   In other words the investigating committee adorned the speaker with a coat of whitewash that would have done credit to many similar performances since in free America.   Speaker Robinson's triumph was superb, and Richard Henry's humiliation and disrepute correspondingly abject. About a year afterward, however, Mr. Robinson died, — his end undoubtedly hastened by the mental torments he must have undergone in recent years, — and then his abstractions from the public treasury became a great, uncontradicted scandal.   For the next ten years the energies of Virginia were largely devoted to recovering its lost money from the Robinson estate, and in this it was largely successful, his beautiful plantation on the Rappahannock, sold at auction, and other assets being converted to the public treasury.   Robinson's accomplices — the ostentatious planters whose needs had found in him their victim — escaped uninjured, not even their names having ever been made public.

This ultimate triumph had divergent consequences on Richard Henry's future.   His courage, honesty, and success added to his rapidly growing reputation and explained the standing attached to his name in the Virginia House of Burgesses from this time forward.   The experience made him more than ever an ally of the popular party; he and Patrick Henry, for the rest of their lives, were the spokesmen of the people, and constant associates in reform.   At the same time Lee became an object of hatred with his own class, and from now on the odium that falls to the leader who deserts the friends among whom he has been born was Richard Henry's portion.   This Robinson episode was one that the old rock-ribbed Virginia aristocrats never forgot; it followed Lee even in the larger national stage where his future was to lie. "Jealousies and divisions appeared among the delegates of no state more remarkably than those of Virginia," wrote John Adams in his diary, referring to the Continental Congress.   "Mr. Wythe told me that Thomas Lee, the elder brother of Richard Henry, was the delight of the eyes of Virginia and by far the most popular man they had; but Richard Henry was not. I asked the reason; for Mr. Lee appeared a scholar, a gentleman, a man of uncommon eloquence and an agreeable man. Mr. Wythe said this was all true, but Mr. Lee had, when he was very young, and when he first came into the House of Burgesses, moved and urged on an inquiry into the state of the treasury, which was found deficient in large sums, which had been lent by the treasurer to many of the most influential families of the country, who found themselves exposed, and had never forgiven Mr. Lee. This, he said, had made him so many enemies, that he never had recovered his reputation, but was still heartily hated by great numbers. These feelings among the Virginia delegates were a great injury to us. Mr. Samuel Adams and myself were very intimate with Mr. Lee, and he agreed perfectly with us in the great system of our policy, and by his means we kept a majority of the delegates of Virginia with us; but Harrison, Pendleton, and some others, showed their jealousy of this intimacy plainly enough at times."

V

SEDITION IN WESTMORELAND

I

OTHER matters, of even graver import than treasury defalcations, were stirring Virginia during these memorable years. In March 1764, Great Britain passed its Declaratory Act, asserting the right of Parliament to raise an internal revenue in the American colonies, and its intention of presently exercising that right. The British plan was to station 10,000 soldiers in the Northwest Territory recently ceded by France, and the contemplated levy on the transatlantic settlements was to pay, in part, the cost of that establishment. The garrisons in question were needed primarily to "protect" the colonists from Indian attacks; was it not just, therefore, that the people chiefly concerned should pay part of the cost of "protection"? Perhaps the Americans could devise some other method of raising their contributions; there was no British insistence on stamp duties; in case the provincial assemblies should vote the money themselves, the parliamentary exaction would not be enforced. Financial aid from America, however, to help the British exchequer bear the expense entailed by the new American empire, the Grenville ministry was determined to obtain.

The connection between the Northwest Territory and the American Revolution is thus apparent. Indeed, a certain school of historians insist that the crisis of 1776 can be interpreted properly only in terms of the Ohio and Mississippi valleys. In this broader view, the matters that traditionally serve as explanatory of that event — stamp acts, duties on tea, billeting of troops, smuggling of molasses, Boston massacres, boycotts, port bills, and the like — are merely surface incidentals; the really important thing is the long and tangled story of British blundering in the Mississippi country.   That all wars have two sets of causes, general and specific, recent events have emphasized.   The general are the underlying, constantly operating sources of irritation and misunderstanding — the steady and frequently subtle circumstances that breed resentment and develop the national moods ultimately resulting in violence.   The specific causes are those particular sensational events — the firing on a Fort Sumter, the murder of a dynastic heir at Sarajevo — which ignite long-smouldering trouble. That many fundamental incentives of discontent had been gradually estranging the American colonies from their transatlantic allegiance, and that, irrespective of particular reasons for taking up arms, separation, in the nature of the case, was inevitable — with this generalization there will probably be little disagreement. In both these sets of causes — the general and the specific — the Lees of Virginia were conspicuous actors; the Northwest country, as well as the Stamp Act and succeeding embroilments, forms the background of the family saga.

The cession, by France to England, of that vast expanse lying north of the Ohio and east of the Mississippi occasioned great rejoicing in all America: the usual bonfires lighted up the country from one end to the other, the usual sermons of thanksgiving occupied pulpits North and South, and the usual resolutions of congratulation issued from a dozen provincial assemblies to the feet of the new, youthful king.   In no part did the bonfires burn more brightly, and the sermons glow more devoutly, than in the Potomac region of Virginia, and no families hailed the news with more excited anticipation than the Washingtons, the Fitzhughs, and the Lees.   The latter especially saw in the event the fulfillment of their most cherished family tradition.   The solemn pronouncement of Thomas Lee — "the French are intruders into this America" — had been justified.   His efforts to make this country English-speaking — his treaty of Lancaster, his Ohio Company, the expedition of Christopher Gist, the highway across the Alleghanies, and the founding of the city of Cumberland — had now reached fruition.   How often must the sons of Stratford have heard their father discourse on this new region, prognosticate its future, foretell the fortunes to be made in its lands as well as the destiny it was to serve as the abode of millions of Americans! An interest in the undeveloped West was thus a part of their education, and that, as soon as opportunity arose, this interest should spring into activity was in accordance with family aspiration. For several years after the death of Thomas Lee, however, far Western matters had been marking time, waiting the result of the war which was to determine, among other things, whether this territory, fondly believed to be part of Virginia since its original charter, was to accomplish its fate under French or English control. In the military operations which decided this question in England's favor, Virginia had played an important part — a fact that was never forgotten in the fierce discussions of the next thirteen years. That the ancient colony had impoverished herself in this struggle, and accumulated a debt enormous in view of her scanty population, is another circumstance that Great Britain was likely to ignore, but which was always present in the consciousness of the Virginian taxpayer. All during the war the colony had been discussing the future of their Western country, should the peace treaty assign it to Britain, and, of all Virginians, none were more absorbed in this problem than the grandees of the Potomac.

This eagerness was not restricted to the great landlords; it was an emotion that excited the whole of Virginia. The "Ohio country" was almost a fabled land, and stories of its beauty and fertility were part of the training of every Virginia child. To the ordinary eye there was still plenty of available soil east of the mountains; most of it, however, was held by large grantees, and could not be purchased in fee. Western Virginia was becoming democratic; the impulse for independent ownership, and the higher political and social status that it implied, was growing more powerful every day; the husbandman was no longer content to remain merely a villein of a Fairfax, a Carter, a Fitzhugh, or of a Lee — he was determined to end his career as rent payer and to become an upstanding possessor of acres of his own. Not unnaturally, therefore, his eyes were turned longingly to this apparently endless domain. His ambition was not checked even during the war; thousands of squatters, although there was no certainty that this land would become British, had straggled into the present

Kentucky, Ohio, and Indiana, establishing claims before anything resembling a legal title could be acquired. Thousands of others had placed themselves on the border, ready to leap into the new country as soon as the question was determined. The formal alienation of this territory by France, February 1763, was accepted as a signal for invasion. One of the most inspiring scenes of nineteenth-century America was that endless procession of covered wagons making their way across the prairies, seeking permanent homes in the West; and something akin to this took place on the Virginia frontier in the years 1763–1776. Oxcarts crossing the Cumberland divide, loaded with household goods, farm implements, and families of children, entraining for the rich lands on both sides of the Ohio, were the commonest sights of the time; and mingled with these bona fide settlers went the hordes of speculators, wild rangers, freebooters, and the like, who inevitably accompany such migrations. Among them was a considerable array of soldiers — veterans of the recently ended war, who had been promised, as part payment of military service, tracts of four hundred and more acres per man. All these trail blazers were forced on by the same purpose — a dream that had been a living reality with Virginians since the earliest settlement on the James. "The lands belong to Virginia!" — this, some years later, became the rallying cry sounded by that great improviser of "slogans," Patrick Henry; for more than a century that had been gospel on the Potomac. The reports emanating from an occasional hardy pathfinder added fire to this enthusiasm. Millions of acres of river bottom, of productive meadows and grazing lands, of mountain woodlands, watered by an intricate pattern of rivers, brooks, and lakes — and all this the property of Virginia! The most fertile valleys in the world — such is the modern verdict on the Mississippi and the Ohio; just how rich they were the earliest immigrants did not know, but the tenacity with which Washington and his compeers maintained the Virginian contention, and the mania that assailed the popular mind for settlement, show that they had intimations of the future.

Previously certain hindrances had held this exaltation in check. The Indians, despite treaties and "presents," still stubbornly clung to their ancestral soil; Virginians, however, especially those who had passed through the recent war, with its frontier atrocities, scalpings, burnings of villages, and tortures of women and children, felt no tender compunction in encroaching on their fields. Since the earliest massacres on the James, the red man had never been popular in the Old Dominion. At one time an official reward was paid for Indian scalps, just as for wolves! The only enemies for whom Virginians had had any respect were the French, and now the ancient foe had surrendered all claims to the Northwest. The ink had hardly dried on the Treaty of 1763 when the westward pilgrimage began.

Presently, however, the pioneers discovered that there were other impediments than the French and the aborigines. These new obstructionists were comfortably seated in the cabinet room in Downing Street. The Bute ministry, as odious to colonists as to independent Britons, gave place, in April 1763, to the Grenville coalition, bringing in, as president of the Board of Trade, and thus chief supervisor of colonial policy, another politician whose name was to become hateful to America in the next fifteen years. Lord Hillsborough knew nothing of America or its aspirations, and cared nothing, but — under promptings, Americans believed, of his "boss," Lord Bute — quickly developed a suspicious and hostile attitude towards transatlantic pretensions. Washington was especially insistent that the 200,000 acres promised his soldiers in the French and Indian War should be surveyed and allotted; readers of his letters remember how long and how unavailingly he advanced their claims. This failure to keep a promise was merely one manifestation of the continuous British attitude towards the Western lands. Prevailing British ignorance of this country was colossal. "Large tracts of America were added by the last war to the American dominions," remarked Dr. Johnson, illustrating again his genius for going wrong on transatlantic questions, but they were "only the barren parts of the continent, the refuse of the earlier adventurers, which the French, who came last, had taken only as better than nothing."

That Britain should seriously debate, in the peace negotiations in Paris, whether they should annex Canada or the West Indian island of Guadeloupe indicates that Dr. Johnson's opinion merely reflected the misinformation on America then prevailing in high

quarters.   In the discussion that followed between Virginia and
the mother country there is ever present a mild amazement that
this stretch of useless solitude could stir such passions in the
colonial breast.   British statesmen advanced many objections to
settlement, not all of which were worthy.   There was land
enough east of the Alleghanies to satisfy settlers for centuries to
come!   This argument gained new point when it was discovered
that many of the foremost British public men of the time were
large holders of these Eastern lands, the disposal of which would
naturally be jeopardized by the release of the prairies west of the
mountains.   This group comprises several names — notably the
Earl of Dartmouth with 40,000 acres and Charles Townshend
with 20,000 — afterward conspicuous in British-American dif-
ferences.   But there were other reasons for opposition, based on
public policy.   The opening of these new lands, it was feared,
would start emigrations from Great Britain and Ireland, even
depopulate the mother country, and all the assertions of the promoters of their intention to settle the country with immigrants
from the continent of Europe did not quiet this apprehension.
Perhaps the strangest fear was that, in some way unexplained, a
great agricultural community in the West would stimulate American manufactures, thus contravening the fixed British policy of
prohibiting American growth on industrial lines.   Underlying all
was the danger — and this was justified — that an American
trans-Alleghany empire would result in a huge native population,
at an early date perhaps greater than that of England, and that
the inhabitants of such a region, far removed from Great Britain,
enormously rich, conscious of their power, would never submit to
domination from a small island three thousand miles away.

2

There was one section in which these British contentions, real
or assumed, failed to strike a responsive chord.   The Potomac
"barons" did not propose to sit idly by, while the land for which
they had spent themselves in seven years of warfare, and involved
their community deeply in poverty and debt, was handed over to
the traditional enemy.   On September 7, a group of planters who

resented most keenly the British attitude met at Belleview, in
Stafford County, the home of Thomas Ludwell Lee, discussed the
future of Virginia's Western domain, and organized the Mississippi Company, which presently appealed to Britain for a grant
of 2,500,000 acres, located north and south of the Ohio River at
its confluence with the Mississippi.   A few years ago the existing
documents on this and subsequent sessions were discovered, in the
London record office, among the papers of the Earl of Chatham.
All these ancient manuscripts are in the handwriting of William
Lee, Secretary.   They disclose the extent to which the Lee family
was the head and front of the undertaking.   The original Lee
members, besides William, were Richard Henry, Francis Lightfoot, and Thomas Ludwell; at a subsequent meeting Arthur Lee
was elected an associate.   All the sons of Stratford, therefore,
participated, with the exception of the oldest, Philip Ludwell Lee,
an abstention of the family head that was significant.   As a member of the Virginia Council, presumably a loyal adviser of the king,
Philip could hardly participate in an organization known to be
unpopular in the British court.   But there were plenty of other
dignitaries to add weight to the enterprise.   Among them were
the Washingtons, George and his brothers, John Augustine and
Samuel; the Fitzhughs, William and Henry; and others of similar
standing, "all men," in the words of William Lee, "of such influence and fortune as are likely to insure success."

Thus in main it was a Lee-Washington-Fitzhugh operation.
In plan and personnel, it seemed almost identical with the Ohio
Company projected fifteen years before by President Thomas Lee,
though the proportions were vastly larger.   Thomas, in 1748, had
asked for a mere 500,000 acres in the region of the Alleghany and
the Ohio, but his sons now projected an undertaking a thousand
miles to the west, with a principality of 2,500,000 acres, embracing
tracts now included in western Kentucky, Illinois, and Indiana.
The transaction reminds one of that old London Company of
1606, organized to plant the English flag and establish English
trade in the Western World.   Like its progenitor, its motives
were mixed — the extension of Virginia's power and glory, the
inauguration of a new American empire, and also the enrichment
of its promoters.   Like the old London Company, it was a joint

stock enterprise, and each shareholder, adopting the Elizabethan terminology of its predecessor, was known as an "adventurer." That there were Indians blocking the way, presumably with an ancient title to the estate, was true; but this had been equally true of the Virginia on which John Smith and his associates had encroached — and the Powhatans of the Mississippi and the Wabash had even less claim upon their forbearance than had those who had displayed an ugly front to the early Virginia pioneers.   Undoubtedly the Lees had discovered, long before their nineteenth-century brethren, that "higher law" under which it was ordained that the Anglo-Saxon was to inherit the earth, and William Lee's letters and minutes of meetings indicate that a particularly desirable bit of the planet had been now set aside for this superior tribe.   "Many reasons have contributed to the choice of this place," he writes; "the goodness of navigation from thence to the Gulph of Mexico, the fineness of the climate, it being in about 38° North latitude, the country level, and the soil, from unquestionable intelligence, as fertile as any on the globe."   In one respect the new company represented an advance in Virginia's development. Land was to be sold, on easy payments and in small lots, to veritable settlers; the promoters had in view a plan not unlike the homestead laws of the nineteenth century.   The trans-Ohio country was not to become a proprietary, but a democratic society.

The Lee-Washington-Fitzhugh appeal fell on unresponsive ears. Before their petition reached the throne, the British ministry had already taken the step that destroyed the Mississippi plans, not only of this coterie, but of several others working to the same end. On October 7, a month after the meeting at Thomas Ludwell Lee's, came the great Hillsborough ukase, framed hastily not only to propitiate the Indians, but to throttle at their birth all colonization schemes.   This proclamation drew a somewhat indefinite line, separating the lands open to settlement from those in which the white man was no longer to venture.   The watershed separating the rivers that fell into the Atlantic from those flowing into the Gulf of Mexico was to be the boundary; roughly this meant that the white men were to confine their activities to the country east of the Alleghanies, while territory west of that landmark, and north of the Ohio, was to be reserved for the Indians.   Canada, it is true, was still made available to American immigrants, as was all the territory south of the Ohio, including that known as west and east Florida. But that agricultural paradise, the Northwest, was taken from the energetic white men and transferred to its aboriginal people. Not only was all future settlement prohibited, but such "seating" as had already taken place was to be undone. The army of buckskin pioneers, gathered at the passes, were ordered to pack up their goods and return home; the thousands of log-cabin squatters who had established their families in the forbidden country were commanded to abandon their carefully selected clearings and start life anew in old Virginia. Any land purchases made from the Indians were now declared invalid, and any future acquisitions from the same source were made illegal. All transactions in this region were in future to be under jurisdiction of agents appointed by England; neither Virginia nor the other colonies were to enjoy any prerogatives of this kind.

Not only did the purport of this decree enrage the colonists, but its language was frequently undiplomatic, even insulting. Possibly the sharp dealing that had marked colonial transactions with the native tribes could not be defended, but it was a little unpleasant to be rebuked in an official state paper. Minor dissatisfaction on this score, however, disappeared in face of the consternation aroused by the plan of making the Ohio and Mississippi valleys — the land of that Middle West which figures so largely in the present America — an Indian hunting ground and forcing future colonial development to take place in Canada and the Floridas. The Northern region was then regarded as a land of ice and snow, and the Floridas spelled swamps, malarial miasmas, and unproductive soil. The possession that had been Virginia's pride since the earliest days, which in itself largely explains that sense of leadership in America which Virginians looked upon as their birthright — to deprive the Old Dominion of this, by a stroke of the pen, and deliver it to an enemy whom Virginia despised, — this was a specimen of British statecraft that put the loyalty of this oldest colony to a strain almost more severe than it could survive. It was the harmonious coöperation of Virginia and Massachusetts that led to the Declaration of Independence. British policy, 1774–1776, was largely devoted to separating these, the greatest colonies; had that policy succeeded, there would have been no Revolution — at least no successful Revolution. It is interesting to speculate whether, except for Britain's stupidity in attempting to deprive Virginia of her imperial inheritance in the West, the Old Dominion would so eagerly have joined hands with Massachusetts in hostility to the crown.

It was well enough to denounce the Washingtons and Lees and Fitzhughs and other Virginia families foremost in Northwestern affairs as "speculators" and swindlers of the natives — as this proclamation did, almost in so many words; the fact remains that they were thinking of more than their private interest, and had the future of America in mind. In the letters of Richard Henry Lee, "the backs of our lands," as he described this Virginian empire, were an ever-present consideration; no American statesman was more insistent that, after the surrender at Yorktown, its cession should be a foremost article in the treaty; nor was any American more solicitous for its development on national lines. In the incoherent situation that followed the peace the voice of the Lees was one of the first raised for transferring the Northwest from Virginia to the Federal government, for future expansion into great, free states of the Union; and, in the document making this cession, the signature of Arthur Lee appears as agent for Virginia. The land companies in which the Lees and other distinguished Americans played so conspicuous a part also served a genuine historic purpose; they focused Continental attention upon this country, made widely known its limitless resources, educated the American mind to regard it as its own, and to rest content with no rearrangement of sovereignty in America that did not allot this territory to the new nation.

To just what extent the Hillsborough Proclamation was an incentive to revolution historians are not agreed. That British statecraft, in its handling of this problem, from 1763 to the separation, displayed itself in its crudest and least understanding phase is apparent. Whenever British leaders touched the Northwest, it was only to commit a new blunder and anger Americans again. The long chapter of ignorance and tactlessness culminated, in 1774, in the Quebec Act — a piece of legislation which, as the final crown to other grievances, annexed the whole country, as far south as the Ohio River, to the Province of Quebec. It is absurd to suppose that behavior of this sort did not stimulate American independence. It certainly acted as one of those forces, always irritatingly at work, estranging loyalty and affection and emphasizing the ever-growing conviction that Britain was unfitted to control the destinies of the Western World. Setting up an artificial barrier in the West, which shut Virginia from the land she had immemorially regarded as her own, and limiting her growth to a comparatively narrow area on the Atlantic Coast, would inevitably have sown the seeds of hostility. If it did not anger her to rebellion, it helped to produce the mood that made rebellion possible. Virginia's grievance found its way into the Declaration of Independence, written by a Virginian who was a zealous champion of Virginia's estate in the West. George III, wrote Jefferson, cataloguing American complaints against that monarch, "has endeavored to prevent the population of these states: for that purpose obstructing the laws for naturalization of foreigners, refusing to pass others to encourage migration hither, and raising the conditions of new appropriation of lands."

The able historian of the Mississippi Valley, Clarence Walworth Alvord, who has gone deeper into the matter than any other writer, sums up the matter well: "Tories were few in number in Virginia, when you compare their number with those in Pennsylvania and New York. Here is something to think about. Have you ever wondered why the men of Virginia, both those of property and those prominent in politics, almost unanimously took sides with the patriotic cause and thereby made it a success? Why was it that Virginia furnished the leaders of the Revolution, men like Henry, Washington, and Jefferson, whose adherence to the side of the colonies meant the difference between success and failure? Why was it that such men were to be discovered almost solely in the Old Dominion? Their counterparts in the other colonies, save in Massachusetts, risked life and property by adhering to the cause of the British Empire. The problem is a complex one and cannot be given a simple answer. No one force will account for the cross currents of the political life in Virginia; but it is certain that the wiggle-woggle of the Imperial policy concerning the opening of the West, followed as it was by the final decision to erect a boundary for Virginia in the West, stirred up a popular discon-

tent, particularly among the members of that class which led public opinion, the planters. In the make-up of Virginia popular
psychology the anger at the Imperial plans for the West is an important component."

3

There has been much argument as to who first sounded the
alarm against the British decision to tax America; certainly one
of the earliest to detect the significance of the Declaratory Act and
its historic consequences was Richard Henry Lee. A letter written May 31, 1764, about two months after the Declaratory Act,
and a year before the Stamp Act, contains an outline of the
grounds on which America subsequently based its resistance, and
also, what is even more remarkable, an intimation as to the inevitable outcome. For Parliament — said Lee, in effect — to
reach over three thousand miles of ocean and levy a direct *ad
hominem* tax on Americans was unprecedented and a violation of
the British Constitution; if persisted in, it would lead to American independence. The letter was written to a friend in England,
unquestionably an Englishman, though his identity is unknown.
"Many late determinations of the great, on your side of the water,"
wrote Richard Henry, "seem to prove a resolution to oppress
North America with the iron hand of power, unrestrained by any
sentiment drawn from reason, the liberty of mankind, or the
genius of their own government. 'T is said the House of Commons readily resolved that it had 'a right to tax the subject here,
without the consent of his representative'; and that, in consequence of this, they had proceeded to levy on us a considerable
annual sum, for the support of a body of troops to be kept up in
this quarter. Can it be supposed that those brave adventurous
Britons, who originally conquered and settled these countries,
through great dangers to themselves and benefit to the mother
country, meant thereby to deprive themselves of the blessings of
that free government, of which they were members and to which
they had an unquestionable right? or can it be imagined that those
they left behind them in Britain, regarded these worthy adventurers, by whose distress and enterprise they saw their country so
much enlarged in territory and increased in wealth, as aliens to

their society and meriting to be enslaved by their superior power? No, my dear sir, neither one nor the other of these can be true, because reason, justice and the particular nature of the British constitution, nay, of all government, cry out against such opinions! Surely no reasonable being would, at the apparent hazard of his life, quit liberty for slavery; nor could it be just in the benefitted, to pay their benefactors with chains instead of the most grateful acknowledgments. And as certain it is that the free possession of property, the right to be governed by our own representatives and the illegality of taxation without consent are such essential principles of the British constitution, that it is a matter of wonder how men, who have almost imbibed them in their mother's milk, whose very atmosphere is charged with them, should be of opinion that the people of America were to be taxed without consulting their representatives?"

In the next twelve years both Great Britain and America re-sounded with argument on the rights and wrongs of colonial tax-ation; a vast literature of pamphlets accumulated on both sides of the Atlantic; yet the discussions on the American side advanced few points not incorporated or foreshadowed in this hastily writ-ten paragraph. The subsequent arguments rested on two grounds, those based on the British Constitution and those based on the writings of political philosophers; the first precise, — taxation founded on representation, — the second more abstract — the natural rights of man, the social compact, the state of nature, and the like. All these conceptions entered into Richard Henry's protest. In another respect this private communication was a far look into the future. Few of the patriots of the next ten years advocated any step so radical as separation from England. Prac-tically all the leaders — James Otis, John Adams, Benjamin Franklin, George Washington, Thomas Jefferson — were con-stantly pledging their loyalty to the British crown, and deprecat-ing any suggestion of independence. Yet Richard Henry Lee, as soon as the news of the contemplated action reached Virginia, insisted that such would be the outcome, if Britain persisted in her programme. "After all, my dear friend," he writes in this same letter, "the ways of heaven are inscrutable; and frequently, the most unlooked-for events have arisen from seemingly the most inadequate causes. Possibly this step of the mother country, though intended to oppress and keep us low, in order to secure our dependence, may be subversive of this end. Poverty and oppression, among those whose minds are filled with ideas of British liberty, may introduce a virtuous industry, with a train of generous and manly sentiments, which when in future they become supported by numbers, may produce a fatal resentment of parental care being converted into tyrannical usurpation."

It was an apprehensive and deliberative group of legislators who arrived at Williamsburg in November 1764. New York and Massachusetts had already passed on the Declaratory Act, sending in the first of those colonial manifestoes which subsequently, in a unanimous stream, proceeded from America to the seats of high authority in Great Britain. As soon as the Virginia House of Burgesses assembled it adopted similar measures, going even further than other colonies in forwarding to the House of Commons not a petition but a "remonstrance." Though there are contemporary accounts of the prevailing excitement, of the "flame" that swept from one part of the colony to the other, the behavior of the burgesses themselves was most orderly and respectful. The situation was one clearly justifying the use of that immemorial privilege of Englishmen, the right of petition, and the committee appointed to draw up these papers was formed of the most respectable elements in Virginia — Peyton Randolph, Richard Henry Lee, Benjamin Harrison, Richard Bland, and others of like standing. The first two petitions, to the king and the House of Lords, were written by Lee. No document phrased with greater dignity ever issued from the Virginia legislature. The arguments rested on those constitutional grounds which subsequently became so familiar; they formed an elaboration of the ideas set forth in the letter quoted above. Stress was laid upon the fact that Virginians were Englishmen; that, encouraged by their king, they had built up a flourishing state in the wilderness, bringing all the rights and privileges which, as Englishmen, their forefathers had enjoyed on their native soil; that the most prized and most ancient of these was taxation only by their own consent. His Majesty was deftly informed that, in proposing to ignore this bulwark of English freedom, he was doing something that none of his predecessors on the throne of England had ever attempted to do. There was tactful reference to the great commerce which England enjoyed with her transatlantic possessions; was not this commerce — such was the implication, though it was not precisely set forth in this memorial, as it was subsequently in thousands of places — sufficient compensation to the mother country for the protection the colonies were entitled to receive from the British army and navy? The question of expediency was also raised. His Majesty and their Lordships were informed that Virginia was unable to bear the new burdens; its finances were in disorder; and the threatened stamp duties would drain the colony of such small amounts of specie as still remained within her borders. The "hard times" through which the colony was passing, an aftermath of the recent war, and accentuated by the demoralized condition of the tobacco market, were insisted on. In such restrained language as this did Virginia "approach the throne with humble confidence," and while it is true that Lee's address to the House of Lords was somewhat stiffer in tone, and that to the Commons — which Lee did not write, its authorship being usually attributed to George Wythe — even more outspoken, there was not a word in the memorials suggesting disobedience or anything except the most subservient loyalty to the king's "sacred person."

The effect produced in official quarters, however, was far from satisfactory. The royal governor, Francis Fauquier, declared the memorials "warm and indecent," prorogued the burgesses, and sent them abruptly back to their plantations. Protests of Virginia and of other colonies were not received in England; Americans were informed that the age-long right of petition did not apply to money bills. Great Britain, it was added, had little interest in reasons why the suggested taxes should not be levied, but would be glad to learn what form of tax would be more acceptable. The one result of Richard Henry's rhetoric, and that of other memorialists, had evidently been to fortify the British policy of a colonial revenue, and on February 27, 1765, Parliament adopted fifty-five resolutions requiring Americans to affix stamps of varying denominations on "every skin or piece of vellum or parchment, or sheet or piece of paper" recording legal or business transactions

— invoices, wills, certificates of birth, marriage, or death, ship clearances, transfers of real estate, surveys, court proceedings, and dozens of other matters.   The act was to go into effect on November 1 following; after that date no ship whose clearance papers should be unstamped would be legally at sea; no court proceeding, unstamped, would have any force; no couple whose marriage certificate should not be similarly ornamented would be man and wife; in fact all business in the colonies, unless so certified, would come to an end.   To defy the Stamp Act meant social and economic dissolution.

This interim — from March 22 to November 1 — proved to be an active one in the life of Richard Henry Lee.   It marked the transition from the judicial temper displayed in his memorials to a fairly impassioned state of hostility.   No longer the calm philosopher, he became a fiery "son of liberty."   The modern scholarly and minute student of the American Revolution will hardly approve Richard Henry Lee; and in turn those American academic investigators who have been so busy, in recent years, discovering reasons why the colonies were wrong in this famous altercation and Great Britain right would have been regarded by Richard as traitors little less reprehensible than Grenville.

At times one wonders whether this eagerness for rewriting American history and reversing established judgments has not been slightly overdone.   The practice is probably a revulsion from Bancroft and other "patriotic" historians, reënforced by the contemporary passion for "truth," "impartiality," and "human interest."   The arguments against the traditional American position are familiar enough.   Great Britain, after the Seven Years' War, conducted partly in the interest of the colonies, found herself burdened with a debt of £140,000,000.   Should not the colonies, in whose interest this military establishment was created, stand at least a part of the expense?   There are other considerations involved, but that, in main, represents the case of British statesmen one hundred and fifty years ago, and of their American apologists to-day.   The matter has been argued with great plausibility and skill and, at times, almost with conviction; but there is no occasion for rehearsing the contention in this place.   The fact is that the dispute involves a problem which was in a state of chaos in 1765, and which has not been adjusted yet. Probably Disraeli came nearer than any British statesman to putting his finger on the crux of the matter when he declared that the whole conception of colonies was fallacious; when they are young and weak, they are an unproductive burden to the mother country; when they become ripe and strong, they set up in business for themselves. The very conception of colony, as entertained by British statesmen a hundred and fifty years ago, contravenes human nature itself. The supposition that three million people were to regulate their agriculture, industries, and trade in the way that would most contribute to the fortune of six million people three thousand miles away — that was the great absurdity in eighteenth-century statesmanship.

The misconception made ultimate separation inevitable. Of this the matter of levying direct taxes on what was essentially a foreign population was a single phase. The principle was one that could not be admitted. Richard Henry Lee hit the nail on the head. "They may take from me one shilling in the pound," he said, for colonial protection, "but what security have I for the other nineteen?" Once grant that Parliament possessed this power and there was no limit to which it could be pushed. That the colonies should contribute to the cost of their "protection" — to the stationing of troops against Indian raids and French machinations — seems, on this simple statement of the problem, reasonable enough; but without going into all the numerous details that modify the contention, it is sufficient to observe that Britain, after wrestling with the difficulty for more than a hundred years, with Canada, Australia, South Africa, and New Zealand, has given it up as a bad job. Should Great Britain attempt to assess a stamp tax on Canada to-day, to help support the British fleet, — maintained, among other reasons, for the protection of that and all the Dominions, — the disturbance of 1765 would seem a summer's breeze compared with the uprisings that would start north of us. It may also be recalled that the most scholarly English historians do not agree with this modern school of American writers. Perhaps the ablest discussion of the causes of the American Revolution are the 170 pages devoted to that subject by the great historian of England in the eighteenth century, William

E. H. Lecky.   The subject is canvassed there with an exhaustiveness, an impartiality, a knowledge, and a genius for lucid exposition that make it a masterpiece of historical writing.   While
recognizing the dialectical niceties elaborated to justify this form
of imposition, the fact remains, says Mr. Lecky, that the Grenville
measure infringed upon "a principle which the English race both
at home and abroad have always regarded with a peculiar jealousy. . . .   That no people can be legitimately taxed except by
themselves or their representatives lay at the very root of the English conception of political liberty. . . .   The principle which led
Hampden to refuse to pay twenty shillings of ship money was sub-
stantially the same as that which inspired the resistance to the
Stamp Act."   Whether or not the Stamp Act was unconstitutional, the fact remained that it represented the exercise of a
power which Parliament had never before used.   No tax had
been levied on Wales until its incorporation into the British system and until it had been given representation in Parliament.
Even in Ireland no measure like this had ever been attempted.

On this subject Richard Henry Lee never had any qualms,
theoretical or practical.   This student of Bolingbroke and Montesquieu presently blossomed out as a "give me liberty or give me
death" patriot.   In his attitude there seem to have been two
phases.   In 1764, when the legislation loomed merely as a threat,
Lee's opposition was reasoned, based strictly on legal grounds;
this was the mood of his letter of May 21, already quoted, and his
protests to king and lords.   The actual passage of the Stamp Act
completely changed his state of mind.   The fiercest hostility now
took the place of respectful disquisition.   The famous coterie of
Virginia grandees, — Peyton Randolph, Benjamin Harrison,
George Wythe, and the rest, — though intellectually opposed to
the measure, still regarded themselves as loyal Britons.   Ultimately all these leaders became Whigs; in 1765, however, they had
not reached this degree of emancipation.   But Richard Henry
Lee, as soon as the king had given royal assent, shifted to the side
of the extremists, and with Patrick Henry, who from this time
was his confidential friend and correspondent, became leader of
the radicals.   And no patriot of those days assailed the new legislation in more unmeasured terms.   In Richard Henry's letters

George III is always the "Tyrant" — with capital letters; his minions are "Tyrant's tools," "foes to human kind," and "Devils of Despotism," while the American cause is "the greatest and most virtuous that the sun ever shone upon." Nor was there anything phlegmatic about Arthur Lee's literary style. "But know, my Lord, and tremble! The murmurs of an incensed people are just, they are universal, they must, they will reach the throne!" That Britain was transforming Americans into "slaves," who were "groaning" under British "chains" — on this point the impetuous youthful Lee had no question.

4

In the whirlwind of resentment that swept the colonies from June 1765, to November, Virginia furnished the main inspiration. The opposition in all the colonies, North and South, assumed two forms. There were tense but orderly public meetings, newspaper discussions, legislative "resolves," pamphlets, sermons, and the like. There were also the tumultuous performances of the mob, "Liberty trees," hangings in effigy, and attacks on the persons and homes of especially obnoxious "Tories." These disturbances reached the height when those opprobrious functionaries, the distributors of stamps, landed on American soil. As a propitiatory gesture, the British government had selected Americans for this duty; and late in October ships were known to be approaching the most important ports, bringing these agents, armed with the stamps and stamped paper, for sale to their anticipating countrymen. Practically all these emissaries were men of standing in their respective colonies; this high repute, indeed, had been a qualification for appointment; all had accepted their posts in the utmost good faith, entirely unconscious — in that day of slow communication — of the state of American opinion. Of the warm reception that had been prepared for them and their stamps in all sections of the country they were innocently unsuspecting, and the rough handling they received in all parts of the land is an enlivening but not a particularly creditable episode of the Revolution.

Virginia had its outbreaks as well as Massachusetts and Rhode Island; in one respect, however, the land of the cavaliers presented a contrast to its neighbors.   In other colonies the mobs were composed "of people of the meaner sort," led by roughs long accustomed to this manner of inciting public sentiment, while in Virginia the champions of disorder were derived from the cream of society.   In the Old Dominion the stamp distributor was Colonel George Mercer, member of a distinguished family, himself for years a popular idol, a hero of the Seven Years' War, and Washington's colleague for several sessions as member for Frederick in the House of Burgesses.   Colonel Mercer had spent the three years preceding the Stamp Act in England as agent for the Lees' Ohio Company; in his absence on a visit to Ireland his friends in England had secured his appointment as stamp distributor in Virginia, thinking they were handing out a rich plum.   Colonel Mercer had accepted the post as a public duty, entirely unaware that, in doing so, he had transformed himself into a public enemy. He regarded it as "an office as genteel as profitable."   Francis Fauquier, royal governor of Virginia, wrote a description to the Lords of Trade of Mercer's reception that forms one of the liveliest official documents in colonial annals.   How, on news of Mercer's arrival the citizens of Williamsburg "one and all" advanced in his direction; how they stopped the king's representative in front of the capitol, and demanded that he abandon the unpopular mission; how Fauquier inserted his own form between the swelling throng and its objective, and thus protected him from assault; how he escorted Mercer to his home, respect for his office restraining the multitude, "who did not molest us, though there was some little murmurs"; how Mercer, next day, conciliated his friends and transformed himself into a public hero by throwing up his place and depositing all the stamps on shipboard — this story Fauquier tells with vividness, touching it up with a sardonic reflection: "This concourse of people I should call a mob, did I not know that it was chiefly, if not altogether composed of gentlemen of property in the colony, some of them at the heads of their respective counties, and the merchants of the county, whether English, Scotch or Virginia, for few absented themselves."

And in those other expressions of public opinion — the mock trials, hangings in effigy, and the like — the solid elements of Virginia also served as leaders.   The outrageous demonstrations in Boston — the marches of the populace, the limp effigy of Stamp Distributor Oliver, the lootings of private houses, the destruction of Governor Hutchinson's mansion, finest in the colony, and his priceless library — always figure in histories of the Revolution. The captain of this riot was Ebenezer Mackintosh, a cordwainer, or shoemaker, who for years, as leader of the South End gang, had been one of the most disorderly characters in town. For contrast in leadership one may turn to Westmoreland County, Virginia, on a late day in September, a few weeks before Colonel Mercer had reached Williamsburg. The account is taken from the *Maryland Gazette,* October 17, 1765. Here, in a location not far from the county courthouse, came a solemn parade of negroes, dressed in "John Wilkes" costumes, escorting a hangman's cart in which were seated two effigies — to the "acclamation and applause of a large concourse of people, of all ranks and denominations." One of the images bore on its breast a placard, "I am G——e G——e" (hardly an adequate disguise for the British statesman, George Grenville), "the infamous projector of American slavery." His companion was similarly labeled, "I am G——e M——r, C—l——r of St—— for Virginia" — which abbreviation was sufficiently indicative of George Mercer, the stamp collector then sailing towards his port. In one hand this latter official bore an inscription, "Money is our God," and in the other a motto, "Slavery I love." Then followed an array of mock sheriffs, bailiffs, jailers, and hangmen. Directly behind the Mercer simulacrum walked the tall and dignified figure of Richard Henry Lee — no effigy in this case, but the flesh-and-blood gentleman himself. His function was to hear the last confession and to read the "dying speech" of the culprit. It was commonly published at the time, and not denied, that Richard Henry was himself the author of Mercer's "dying words"; the Vergilian touch at the close and the Homeric distich of "Mr. Pope" lend reasonableness to this accusation. "With parricidal hands," — such were the words which were put into the mouth of this rag-baby Mercer, and which Richard Henry read with his usual accomplished oratory, — "I have endeavored to fasten chains of slavery on this, my native country, though, like the tenderest and best of mothers, she has long fostered and powerfully supported me. But it was the inordinate love of gold which led me astray from honor, virtue and patriotism. As I am about to suffer the punishment so great an offender deserves I hope my fate will instruct tyranny and avarice that Virginia determines to be free.

"*Quid non mortalia pectora cogis,*
—— *auri sacra fames?* [1]

"Jove fixed it certain that whatever day
Makes man a slave, takes half his worth away."

The sequel to this demonstration was rather unfortunate for Richard Henry Lee — one, indeed, that was almost crushing. The Mercer family was naturally enraged, and proceeded to turn savagely on its perpetrator. The gentleman in whose honor the ceremony had been staged presently sailed for England, where he died many years afterward, but his father and brother presently acquired certain documents which they used pretty effectively against their Westmoreland traducer. They charged that Richard Henry Lee had himself been an applicant for the post of stamp distributor in Virginia, and that his patriotic enthusiasm and his anger against Colonel Mercer were purely the result of his failure to secure the post. The first part of this charge was true, though the second did not necessarily follow. Richard Henry's reply and justification appeared in a letter dated July 25, 1766, addressed to the editor of the *Virginia Gazette*. That he had applied for the appointment, the writer admitted, was the fact: at the time he had not given the matter sufficient consideration; as soon as the full purport had dawned, he had written again, withdrawing the application, and then proceeded to oppose taxation with all his power. The explanation was not candid, and the episode is not a brilliant chapter in Lee's career. His life throughout displays two qualities: one that of rendering great, unselfish services to his country; the other that of the politician, with an eye for office, and especially for the enhancement of his family. His activities in the Stamp Act troubles seem to illustrate both characteristics. The chief interest of the episode is that it brings out the vacillating state of American public opinion at the time toward the mother

[1] "What do you not force the hearts of men to do, O cursed hunger for gold?"

country. Lee was not the only distinguished American involved in such an application. Benjamin Franklin moved for two jobs of stamp collector, not for himself, but for his friends, Jared Ingersoll, of Connecticut, and John Hughes, of Pennsylvania, nor did Franklin reverse his attitude, as did Lee, for his office-seeking was successful — most unfortunately for the gentlemen concerned, their receptions in their respective states being about as agreeable as that of Mercer in Virginia and Oliver in Massachusetts.

5

For sixty years one of the proudest memorials of Stratford was a yellow paper, signed by more than a hundred names well known in the Northern Neck, including a liberal contingent of Lees. This document, always known as the Westmoreland Resolutions, now reposes in the Historical Society of Virginia. It has frequently been compared to the Declaration of Independence, and certainly, in the defiance hurled at British authority, it is far more seditious than that momentous rescript. Like the Declaration of 1776, the Westmoreland Resolutions bound together a group of citizens in a solemn compact; and the end in view was not dissimilar. The Westmoreland "Associators," by their signatures to this paper, formed themselves into a body for the purpose of opposing the Stamp Act, "at every hazard and paying no regard to danger or to death." The first paragraph is almost a battle cry of rebellion. It pledges allegiance to "our lawful sovereign, George the Third," and agrees to abide by his laws and keep the peace "so far as is consistent with the preservation of our rights and liberty" — a rather generous reservation, especially as the Westmoreland patriots proposed themselves to decide when such inconsistencies arose. The literary style is that of Richard Henry Lee in his most fiery mood; here is a determined soul, who has abandoned deferential phrases, quite another person from the suppliant who, in his address to the king two years before, approached his "sacred majesty . . . with humble confidence" and "dutiful loyalty." Now the whole spirit is exacting, even contemptuous.

The chief purpose of the Westmoreland Association was to breathe destruction on anyone who facilitated the enforcement of the Stamp Act, either as vendor or as user of stamps. It was an anti-Stamp Act organization without fear or favor. The members bound themselves, by solemn oath, to "exert every faculty to prevent the execution of the Stamp Act, in every instance whatever, in the colony of Virginia; and every abandoned wretch, who shall be so lost to virtue and public good, as wickedly to contribute to introduce the said act in this colony, by using stamp paper, or by any other means, will, with the utmost expedition, be convinced that immediate danger and disgrace shall attend his prostitute purpose." At the first sign of such an intention, the fiery cross was to be uplifted. "Immediate notice shall be given to as many of this association as possible, and every individual so informed shall, with expedition, repair to some place of meeting, to be appointed as near the scene of action as may be." Just what means of persuasion were to be used against Stamp Act devotees is not specified — the language of the resolutions, however, intimates that it would not be gentle. Supposing the constituted authorities should interfere to prevent the "Associators" from taking the law into their hands? "In that case we do most solemnly bind ourselves, at the risk of our lives and fortunes, to restore such an associator to his liberty and to protect him in the enjoyment of his property."

The first name appended to this association was that of its author, Richard Henry Lee; other Lees added their autographs — Thomas Ludwell, Francis Lightfoot, Richard (the "Squire"), John, and William. Most of the great families on the Northern Neck were represented by at least one signer, including four Washingtons. The association indicates again that the leaders of disorder in Virginia, unlike those in the other colonies, came from the top rungs of the social ladder. For this proclamation was certainly an incentive to riot. The Westmoreland company was a group of private citizens, who assumed the prerogative of setting aside the law and of inflicting punishment. It was an eighteenth-century Ku Klux Klan, and the one instance handed down of its *modus operandi* duplicates almost precisely the workings of that supposedly modern organization. The story is told by Richard Henry Lee, II, grandson of its progenitor. "A person, whose name need not be mentioned, had not only declared his intentions to use stamp paper, but had accepted the office of stamp collector. When Mr. Lee was informed of these circumstances, according to the fourth article of the Association, he gave notice to as many members of it as he could, and summoned his company of horses. They proceeded to the residence of the Stamp Collector and required him to bring out his commission, and all the paper he had in his house and deliver it to them; and also to bind himself, by an oath, neither directly nor indirectly to promote the sale or use of stamp paper. The Collector expostulated, hesitated and at length refused. A stout and fierce looking man of the troop advanced at this moment to him and with a stern look and penetrating voice addressed him, 'Swear!' The terrified Collector pronounced the oath, and brought out his commission and stamp paper, which were solemnly burned in his presence."

How modern all that sounds! It was lynch law, pure and simple. This solemn covenant was signed February 27, 1766. A month later Parliament repealed the Stamp Act, so the situation that had inspired the association no longer prevailed. That it performed its part in alienating Virginia from the mother country can be taken for granted. The seeds of disaffection had been sown; a new sensitiveness to oppression and a new readiness to resent further attacks on colonial "liberties" had been instilled in the heart of every Virginian. That segment of Virginia that should have been foremost in protecting royal pretension — the landed aristocracy — had been estranged, and, as it appeared, for all time.

VI

ARTHUR LEE — PATRIOT AND PAMPHLETEER

I

FROM this time forth the influence of the Lees on American history was exercised from two centres, three thousand miles apart — from the Potomac region of Virginia, and from the capital of the English race in England itself. While Richard Henry and Francis Lightfoot, on American soil, were teaching Americans their rights, two younger brothers, William and Arthur Lee, were putting courage into provincial hearts from their vantage ground in London. Perhaps it was the vigorous mentality of the youngest of the Lees, Arthur, that was particularly felt in the deliberations of America, for his letters, depicting English statesmen and their varying attitudes on the colonial crisis, were falling into influential hands in Boston, New York, Philadelphia, as well as in his native region. Arthur's career had well prepared him for mediation of this kind: in almost everything except devotion to the American cause he was an Englishman. Born in 1740, he passed the greater part of his life, until 1781, in England and on the Continent. Sent to Eton as a boy of ten, he spent six years at this ancient English school, acquiring that classical training, that love of outdoor life, that fondness for country houses, that disdain of all peoples not of English blood, which constituted the eighteenth-century English gentleman. Yet Arthur's childhood experiences at Stratford remained vitally persistent, and when difficulties arose between the mother country and his native land, the old fires again burst into flame, with the result that few men, from 1765 to 1776, made more stimulating contributions to the American discussion.

Arthur, after leaving Eton, paid a flying visit to his American relatives before proceeding to one of the English universities. His adviser was that elder brother whom, above all other men, he revered, Richard Henry Lee.   Richard had fondly planned that the youngest of the Lees, regarded by the whole family as also the most brilliant, should take up residence at Oxford or Cambridge, ultimately qualifying for a medical degree.   For Arthur, unlike most Lees, had no patrimony, no tobacco-growing land from which he could expect to derive a leisurely income; he must earn his own bread, and medical practice seemed the most promising and gentlemanly trade at hand.   It was with this idea that, in the latter part of 1760, Arthur again sailed for England.   His letters home were interesting from the first.   He reached London in December 1760 — a momentous time for England and, as events proved, for America as well.   A spectacle partly of grief, partly of rejoicing, burst upon the young Virginian, then in his twentieth year.   "On our arrival here we found this great city in deep mourning for the loss of his late gracious Majesty, King George II.   His death, which happened in the beginning of October, as the great Julius is reported to have wished his might be, was sudden; the large artery in his heart burst, and in an instant he was no more.   This moment saw him in perfect health, powerful and much beloved; stript of his all, he was in the next numbered with the undistinguished dead — so frail is human grandeur and all sublunary joys.   The general grief occasioned by this melancholy event was soon allayed by the welcome accession of his grandson, George III.   Never did a King ascend the throne with a more universal applause.   Each heart and voice was for him and every tongue was busied in his praise.   A perfect harmony subsists between his ministers, at the head of whom William Pitt still holds the foremost place in worth and eminence.   The young King has committed but one error since his succession; instead of permitting the ladies who come to court to kiss his hand, he salutes them himself.   Pleased with his royal touch they flock in such numbers to his court that he is like to suffer for his gallantry in being kissed to death, — an effectual way this to win the hearts of the ladies and consequently of the men, for who can help loving such a polite, genteel, good-natured young King?"

Who indeed?   Certainly not this stripling from Virginia, who could hardly be expected to envision, in this Prince Charming, then in his twenty-second year, the madman who was presently to split the British Empire in two, and against whom Arthur himself was to wage ferocious combat.   But there were other places in London that delighted Lee almost as much as the British court. One in particular has exercised a more powerful influence on the English-speaking mind.   It says much for the attractiveness of the youthful Arthur Lee that, in whatever place he might find himself, he almost naturally became a part of its interesting society: thus three days after landing in London he was engaged in conversation with the man who, as a personality and literary giant, was the sensation of the day.   Arthur's letter gives a memorable picture of Samuel Johnson when he was still "Mr." — the Johnson of the pre-Boswell epoch, fairly in his early fame. "Last night I was in company with Mr. Johnson, author of the English Dictionary.   His outward appearance is very droll and uncouth.   The too assiduous cultivation of his mind seems to have caused a very great neglect of his body; but for this his friends are very amply rewarded in the enjoyment of a mind most eloquently polished, enlightened and refined; possessed as he is of an inexhaustible fund of remarks, a copious flow of words, expressions strong, nervous, pathetic and exalted; add to this an acquaintance with almost any subject that can be proposed; an intelligent mind cannot fail of receiving the most agreeable information and entertainment in his conversation.   He proposes soon to publish a new edition of Shakespeare, a work which he says has employed him many years."

When Richard Henry started Arthur in the direction of Oxford, he failed to take into account this overbearing genius of literary London.   "Mr." Johnson promptly set his foot against an English university.   Oxford and Cambridge were no places for medical study!   There students were not permitted to "enter upon Physic" until a seven years' apprenticeship had qualified them for the degree of Master of Arts.   The Scotch were far more thrifty — and, in his usual vein, Samuel found in this greater economy of time another opportunity for one of his favorite thrusts.

"Sir," he boomed to Arthur, "Scotch education is like a house

built to last a man's lifetime only; the English is like a Palace or
Fortress intended to last for many ages. The first build lightly,
the last lay a very strong and firm foundation before they begin
to work."

Then remorselessly pushing the argument, the lexicographer
went on. "If you have a large fortune and time enough to spare,
go to either of these. If you would choose immediately to enter
upon Physic and to attain sufficient knowledge therein to carry
you through life, at a small expense and in a short time, by all
means go to Edinburgh or Leyden."

Other friends who were consulted agreed with Samuel, the
result being that in a few weeks Arthur found himself ensconced
in the greatest medical school of Great Britain, listening to the
lectures of Cullen, Monro, Hope, and other luminaries, still
famous names in the healing art. But Lee's studies were more
than medical. Already an excellent classicist, Arthur added
mathematics, philosophy, and history to his mental furniture, as
well as a large amount of systematic reading, a favorite field
being political science. Though the young Virginian was graduated, in due course, with high honors, his thesis, on the "Peruvian
Bark," all writ in choice Latin, being "decreed" to be published
by the university, it is not unlikely that the real profit gained from
this British residence lay in different fields. From the first the
study of "physic" was a duty, but other things in Edinburgh entranced Arthur far more. The Scotch themselves he did not
like; indeed the scurrilous comments on this pertinacious race
that appear in Arthur's letters would have recommended him
cordially to his friend, "Mr." Johnson. Hatred of the Scotch
was a fashion of the day, expressing, among other things, the
hostility and jealousy aroused by the unpopular Scotch advisers
who surrounded the young king. "Nothing can be more disagreeable to me than this town and the manners of the people
in it"; the Scotch are "an uncivil, unsocial people, utterly strangers
to politeness." Yet with certain Scotsmen Arthur entered into
friendly forgathering. One of his most interesting letters describes a day's visit with Adam Smith — not yet author of the
Wealth of Nations, but famous for his "theory of moral sentiments." Lee and his "agreeable companion," as he describes

Smith, were both interested in the "new husbandry," a plan for increasing the yield of the soil; they made together a trip to a farmer who was putting the theory into practice, apparently with good effects.   That the Virginian did not lack for friends is apparent; "Arthur Lee," writes Boswell in his *Life of Johnson,* "was an old companion of mine when he studied physic at Edinburgh."   Perhaps his greatest consolation was the interesting group of Americans then pursuing medical studies with him at the university — William Shippen, of Philadelphia, who presently married Arthur's sister Alice and became chief surgeon in the Revolutionary army and ultimately one of the founders of the Medical School of the University of Pennsylvania, Theodorick Bland, afterward conspicuous in Virginia public life, and John Berkenhout, an easy-going vagabond whose friendship, acquired in Edinburgh at this time, was subsequently to prove something of an embarrassment.

Yet it is not likely that either friendships or medical science furnished the main satisfactions of Arthur's existence.   He might grind away conscientiously at his anatomy and botany, — a favorite study, — but England and English public life were the things that really captivated his spirit.   He confesses, in letters to Richard Henry, that he views a return to Virginia with dread and his reasons for this aversion are worth recording.   The "chains" being forged on the American colony by British "tyrants" augured ill for its attractions as a place of residence, and that social institution which had formed the subject of Richard Henry's first oration at Williamsburg Arthur also held in abhorrence.   "The extreme aversion I have to slavery, and to the abominable objects of it with you, the blacks, with the lamentable state of dependence in which I perceive America must, for many years, be held by Britain, make me dread a return to America notwithstanding I am drawn to it by the strongest ties of family affection and patriotic love."   Arthur had set forth in even harsher terms his dislike of slavery in his first literary undertaking, a pamphlet written in such intervals as he could find from the dissecting room.   This was a broadside leveled at none other than his distinguished host, Adam Smith, whose *Moral Sentiments* contained a rather absurd and ill-informed attack upon Virginia and its treatment of slaves. In due course there appeared, in London, a pamphlet, *In Vindication of the Continental colonies against the aspersions of the author of the Moral Sentiments.* Arthur's championship of the Virginian character is a little labored, but his own ideas of slavery are significant. He detests the system as cordially as Adam Smith himself, or as his brothers, and assails Great Britain with a vehemence that was subsequently to be echoed throughout the colonies for introducing the slave trade and opposing all efforts made by Virginia and other American provinces for its extinction. Slavery is "absolutely suppressive of all the nobler exercise of the human mind." Like Richard Henry Lee, he scores the institution chiefly as the enemy of progress. It is "unfavorable to trade and manufactures, which have ever flourished in free states. Commerce especially flees from oppression and rests only under the wing of liberty. If slavery then be necessarily an enemy to arts and sciences, good policy would surely direct us to suppress it."

This was the kind of thing Arthur Lee temperamentally loved; polemical writing, discussion of public events, association with men who were directing history, even participation in these proceedings himself. He was what someone has called a "viewy person," and we can readily picture him holding forth in Edinburgh with Boswell, Ford, Cardross, and David Hume himself, then the great pundit in Edinburgh society, on the British political crisis. For British politics were now shaping themselves in new directions, and new constitutional ideas, in which America was much concerned, were gaining the upper hand. That airy, sentimental young sovereign whom Arthur pictured so delightfully in his first letter from London was now appearing in less pleasing aspects, and, from the darling of the ladies, was becoming almost a sinister character. Yet the question which, above all, excited this young Virginian was causing hardly a ripple in Great Britain. Arthur was constantly receiving letters from Virginia, telling of the fiery opposition and the public disturbances caused by the Stamp Act; yet in all this England apparently did not have the slightest interest. One to-day can turn back to the London newspapers and magazines of 1763–1765 and find few traces of the arguments that were rocking America end to end.

"I remember," Arthur Lee wrote many years afterward, "to have heard some considerable members say, in the lobby, during the debates upon the repeal of the Stamp Act, that though they were in the House when it first passed, yet they did not pay so much attention to the reading as to hear what the bill contained." A measure destined to start the course of history on entirely new lines was practically unknown to the British masses until the latter part of 1765, a year and a half after it had been first proposed. Not that the British populace was indifferent to America; the fact is that they were vastly interested and that America was the source of great pride. Had it not witnessed the recent triumph of British arms; had it not been the force by which Pitt had destroyed the ancient Gallic foe? But local political problems were occupying the minds of British leaders; John Wilkes, *North Briton No. 45,* and the *Essay on Woman* proved far more entertaining than America's aversion to being taxed — in itself not an unfamiliar human phenomenon. In due time, however, driblets of the hostility began to percolate British consciousness and letters eventually brought to astonished ears stories of riots in Boston and high proceedings in Williamsburg and Westmoreland. Englishmen now learned that Americans were agitating great constitutional questions, were quoting Hampden and the heroes of the "glorious Revolution," and that something closely resembling a mutiny was confronting them in these colonies that had witnessed the exploits of Amherst and Wolfe.

Arthur obtained his medical degree in September 1764, yet, instead of returning to Virginia, he lingered for a time in Edinburgh, spent a year traveling in Germany and Holland, finally reaching London in 1766, on the eve of historic events. That America had no intention of submitting tamely to the new taxation had now been made sufficiently clear, and British merchants suffering from a diminution in colonial trade were foremost in demanding repeal. The Grenville ministry had collapsed, and a new one, headed by Rockingham, in which Pitt was an influential force, had determined to wipe the obnoxious measure from the books. One of the most familiar sights in the lobby and gallery of the House of Commons during this session was the recently graduated medico from Virginia, and momentous speeches then making history in the two houses of Parliament had no more attentive listener.   Perhaps it was Arthur's presence on the ground, perhaps it was his genius for feeling out public sentiment and analyzing political motives, perhaps it was that distrust of his fellow man which was afterwards alleged to be his predominating trait — the fact remains that these evidences of parliamentary repentance did not arouse his enthusiasm.   Arthur's native colony, on receiving news of repeal, lighted its bonfires, Williamsburg celebrated the occasion with one of its most brilliant balls, and the assembly voted a statue to George III in honor of the British recantation.   But Arthur's pessimistic spirit remained aloof from all gratitude and rejoicings.   This repeal, he insisted, in conversation and in letters to friends, was not the conclusion of the matter.   He was present at the debates that preceded the vote, and listened to Pitt's orations with an emotion that remained with him all his life.   "Never," he wrote, "were the power and fascination of eloquence more strongly exemplified."   Yet these very forensic masterpieces in a way made stronger Arthur's distrust. They nobly advocated repeal, and advocated it on grounds of justice, but the House, in adopting this great statesman's recommendation, studiously disregarded the arguments he had advanced. The fierceness with which Pitt turned on Grenville aroused the same admiration in Arthur's breast that it has in millions of American schoolboys who have been declaiming the speech for a hundred and fifty years.   "I rejoice that America has resisted. Three millions of people, so dead to all the feelings of liberty, as voluntarily to submit to be slaves, would be fit instruments to make slaves of all the rest."   And Pitt's final solution similarly stirred his American listener.   "Upon the whole I will beg leave to tell the house what is my opinion.   It is that the Stamp Act be repealed, absolutely, totally and immediately.   That the reason for the repeal be assigned, because it was founded on an erroneous principle."

That was the point — the argument on which America had rested its case; the act was un-English, unconstitutional, contrary to a thousand years of English history.   But that was precisely the contention Parliament refused to entertain.   Repeal the Stamp Act — certainly; it was "bad for business," and English

merchants were clamoring for relief; but never repudiate the principle involved; this was the ministerial attitude, and this persuaded
Arthur Lee that the struggle between Britain and her colonies had
only begun.   Another speaker in this debate, Robert Nugent, set
forth the doctrine which Parliament adopted with acclaim.   This
gentleman had insisted on the right to assess an internal revenue
on Americans — and this right, he proclaimed, must never be surrendered.   Repeal the Stamp Act, if you will, as a matter of grace
and expediency, and as a measure that was injurious to England
and to English trade, but never proclaim, as Pitt had insisted,
that the underlying principle was "erroneous."   "A peppercorn,
in acknowledgment of the right, is of more value than millions
without it."   When Parliament, in rescinding the act, added a
clause asserting its right "to bind the colonies in all cases whatever," it accepted this "peppercorn" theory of the British Constitution and aroused misgivings in the breast of Arthur Lee which
all the frenzied rejoicings in the colonies could not alleviate.
"Though the obnoxious act was repealed," he afterward wrote,
"yet I was persuaded that the spirit which dictated it and was still
resting near the throne, was not changed."

2

"Having industriously gathered the healing balms of Europe
and Asia," Arthur wrote Richard Henry, "I return, with all the
united power of medicine to heal the sick, relieve the miserable and
quell the tyranny of death."   In accordance with this heroic programme the youngest of the Lees, in the latter part of 1766, found
himself installed in Williamsburg, determined to make the best of
what rapidly became an uncongenial career.   Arthur must have
been an incongruous figure from the first.   His English bearing
was necessarily exotic in his new homespun environment.   Despite his hostility to recent British policy and to conspicuous British statesmen, love for England was something that he made no
effort to conceal.   Only a sense of family responsibility and the
exhortation of Richard Henry had persuaded Arthur to abandon
the prospect of an English practice and take his chances with life
in what was still the wilderness.   "I cannot help wishing to settle

in England," he had written Richard Henry, "the Eden of the world and the land of liberty and independence, to me the most valuable of all blessings, since I know not a more bitter ingredient than dependence that can enter the cup of life." "America," the stern elder brother replied, — and to Arthur, Richard Henry's word was almost law, — "has a parent's claim to her descendants, and a right to insist that they shall not fix in any place where, by so doing, they may add strength to cruel and tyrannical oppression."

The young man who responded to this claim of country and family was a striking and handsome figure, a valuable addition to Virginia life both on personal and on professional grounds. Arthur was destined to become an historic character — one with whom American writers have not dealt overgently; it is pleasant therefore to view him in this early time, before controversy had obscured his genuine qualities. Tall, erect, firmly built, even dashing, bearing traces of that Eton cricket field traditionally regarded as the training ground of statesmen, with manners usually described in those days as "elegant" — here indeed was a contrast to the more ponderous quality of a Richard Henry, and the more gracious, domestic attributes of a Francis Lightfoot. Arthur's portrait, painted by Charles Wilson Peale, evinces again the persistent traits of Hannah Ludwell — the delicate oval face, great light blue brooding eyes, thin lips, pointed chin, head proudly poised, and thrown back with a slightly defiant air, much like his mother's. It is a fair outward representation of the nature, complex and even mystifying, that makes Arthur the most interesting, if not the most commendable, of the Lees. But not until he spoke did the man's unusual qualities come to the front. The conversational powers that had first attracted Samuel Johnson, and afterward the brilliant circles of Bath and Edinburgh, similarly charmed the less sophisticated surroundings of Virginia. But Arthur not only charmed, he frequently irritated. Rapid in cerebration, lightning-like in retort, not overtactful, even to his elders, mentally and physically restless, probably somewhat neurotic, Arthur was always a centre of activity, intellectual sensation, and frequently of disturbance.

Perhaps the impression of superiority which his mere presence conveyed was arrogance, but at least it had a more substantial basis, for, young as he was, Arthur Lee was one of the most learned Americans of his day; "much reading," he wrote at this time, "has produced in me the effect of age." He spoke fluent French and had a working knowledge of Italian and Spanish; his mind had been nourished, from childhood, on the finest literature of all peoples and was profoundly versed in history and government. About his nature there was nothing sluggish or non-committal; supreme egotism, a hopeless deficiency in humor, the most generous capacity for hatred, an ambition of heroic proportions — these qualities and more Arthur Lee possessed, yet they did not always display themselves in unworthy purposes. If fanatical, Arthur's fanaticism took the shape of devotion to his country; if impatient and overbearing, his determination to advance American interests was commonly the spring of action; if headstrong, his eagerness for getting immediate results was usually the explanation; if keen on advancing his own career, it was that, like most egocentric men, he identified his own success with the success of the matter at issue; if suspicious of others, — the charge most frequently made against Arthur Lee, — that may have been a serious crime once, but is so no longer, for it is every day becoming more apparent that grounds in plenty existed for his suspicion. That he was of fundamentally unhappy temperament he recognized himself. In a letter to a favorite nephew Arthur set forth his poor opinion of the world, quoting Hamlet, — " 'T is an unweeded garden," and so forth, — and there was something in his own nature that suggests the Dane. Arthur too was introspective and melancholic, given to philosophizing, spasmodically energetic, pensively thoughtful, attached to friends, loving everything that was fine and beautiful, determined to set a disjointed world to rights, lacking practical sense but always pursuing ideals; and, again like Hamlet, his life, from birth to death, was a series of disappointments and frustrations.

This hesitant attitude towards the human race appears in Arthur Lee's political beliefs, already well formed in 1766. To the present age they seem little less than the acme of snobbishness, but in Arthur's view they represented a genuine political and social creed. He had little confidence in the masses, though not without

interest in them.   The world never held a more uncompromising
advocate of liberty, and, at the same time, one who had less faith
in democracy.   A republican of Roman type, Arthur had no
patience with popular rule.   Intellectually he was an exquisite, —
sensitive, fastidious, — and his political opinions were attuned to
this spirit of exclusiveness.   That the populace had the gift of
government, that universal suffrage was the cure for public ills,
that all men, irrespective of birth or training, could be entrusted
with high office — these widely accepted tenets of the modern
world would have been regarded by Arthur as a flaunting of nature.   The system which the Lees had upheld in Virginia now for
four generations, in his view, approached perfection.   Of that
system he was the extreme spokesman; his insistence on the right
of birth explains, more than any other cause, the trouble in which
he became enmeshed.   A contented, industrious, intelligent, and
well-behaved commonalty, ruled honestly and capably by a few
high-born, educated ancestral families, responsive to public obligation — such was the Virginian scheme of things, and better the
wit of man had not devised.   Arthur Lee, that is, was a high
Whig — a hater of tyranny, injustice, and intolerance, an enemy
of predominant royal pretension, a believer in the supremacy of
lawmaking chambers and in the sovereignty of brains and character.   In his last days, surveying his wide experience with governments and public men, Arthur put his ultimate convictions in
writing; the passage is as characteristic of his beliefs as of his literary style, and as representative of his early convictions as of his
mature judgment.   "The science of government is no trifling matter.   It requires education and experience, it requires the habit of
great worlds and great men, it requires the leisure which independent fortune gives and the elevation of mind which birth and rank
impart.   Without these you might as well attempt to make Sèvres
china out of common earth as statesmen and politicians out of
men bred and born in the sordid occurrences of common life."
Alexander Hamilton and Arthur Lee would have had much in
common; yet both men, despite this aversion to mass rule, were
undeviating champions of liberty and American independence.

Arthur himself had already experienced what he expressively
calls "the habit of great worlds and great men" — a fact that

renders incongruous his career as country doctor in Virginia. According to tradition he soon acquired a satisfactory practice in Williamsburg and the surrounding country; it is also the tradition that the occupation proved distasteful.   His interest in medicine, it presently appeared, had been exclusively scientific; the human body as a mechanism had proved a fascinating subject, but mixing pills and driving around tobacco plantations, in all seasons and hours, proved far less entertaining.   The diseases of the body politic were far more absorbing than those of his ailing patients. Williamsburg, in which he had settled, was a fertile field for the study of both; one almost wonders whether Arthur selected it with malice prepense.   That first winter, 1766–1767, was tranquil enough, stirred only occasionally by felicitations over the celebrated "repeal," but in the spring of '67 the cauldron began to boil again.   The philosophic Lee proved to have been an excellent prophet; the misgivings he had felt, when listening to Chatham's and Camden's speeches in Parliament, that British plans for colonial taxation had merely been scotched, not killed, were soon justified.   The Rockingham ministry quickly expired and the new Grafton cabinet, in which that evil genius of American affairs, Charles Townshend, held almost dominant influence, promptly moved to obtain, not only its "peppercorn," but a substantial American revenue.   The blow fell even earlier than Arthur had expected.   That the new bill levied import duties on paper, glass, paints, and tea was bad enough.   Even more vicious was the way in which these taxes were to be expended.   They were to pay, so far as the returns permitted, the cost of maintaining the British establishment in the colonies: the salaries of those governors who represented the king's authority, of those admiralty judges who were to have jurisdiction — without the aid of juries — over the enforcement of the new acts, and of a multitude of other royal retainers.   That the king proposed to pay certain charges formerly falling on colonial taxpayers may seem a strange pretext for quarrel, but to Arthur Lee and other gentlemen experienced in the mentality then controlling British affairs, these provisions meant one thing only: they strengthened the suspicion, already widely held, that Britain had in view a complete reorganization of colonial relationship; the fear was general that colonial charters were to be annulled, colonial boundaries possibly changed, and the rights America had enjoyed from the day of settlement abrogated — in a word, that the colonies were no longer to live placidly as self-governing independent units of the British Empire, but to be absorbed into the closest possible connection with the crown. The payment of official salaries out of royal revenues was, Arthur insisted, merely the first step in a deliberately contemplated scheme for the suppression of American liberties.

All this was vastly more important than the daily round of a physician's life. The new British ministry suddenly altered the course of Virginia's highly educated practitioner; it exercised, indeed, an influence on Lee's career not unlike that wielded on the course of a famous Massachusetts patriot who was to become one of his closest friends and co-workers. All biographers like to picture Samuel Adams's failure as a business man; the gentleman who made a mess of his father's brewery and who had difficulty in providing for the wants of his family felt no hesitation in reading lessons to the rulers of the British Empire! Arthur Lee now abandoned his consulting office as blithely as had the Massachusetts patriot his countingroom, when the larger affairs of the political world sounded the clarion. The real explanation in both cases was probably the same. The two men, before they were anything else, were men of affairs, with whom the humdrum matter of earning a living was not life's absorbing interest; Arthur and Samuel were fundamentally agitators, controversialists, leaders in public discussion, performers on the political stage. That was the rôle for which they had been sent into this world, and now, according to nature, they began to function. Williamsburg was just the environment for which Arthur's spirit yearned. All the anti-Stamp Act demonstrations of the year before sprang suddenly into new life. The statue of George III, recently voted by Virginia, quickly passed into forgetfulness — into permanent oblivion, as it proved; the House of Burgesses rang again with denunciation of British policy; "resolves," from the gifted pens of native lawmakers, began to fall at the feet of the British throne; the voice of Richard Henry Lee took on new melodious volume; and the more strident notes of Patrick Henry began to electrify the Atlantic seaboard.

America, from North to South, now rained pamphlets, gazettes, handbills, sermons, and other forms of exciting discussion, one book in particular, still a classic of American political literature, going, like a flame, all over the land.   On December 2, 1767, the first of a series of articles, brief but packed with learning and argument, appeared in the *Pennsylvania Chronicle*. Though modestly signed "A Pennsylvania Farmer," the fact soon became known that the author was that distinguished lawyer, John Dickinson, of Philadelphia.   Born of a rich and scholarly Pennsylvania family, educated at the Middle Temple in London, quickly reaching, on settling in practice, an eminent position at the bar, Dickinson was also a gentleman of infinite charm, of compelling presence, of achievement in letters as well as in law, a man famous similarly for discretion and poise, impartiality of judgment, and the utmost restraint in action and the spoken word. All these traits were illustrated in his "Farmer's Letters."   The writer's reputation would have given an argument from his pen authority that the more acrimonious publicists could not attain, and the fact that now, in language as dignified and calm as it was fine in diction, he submitted the new proposals to constitutional dissection, showing that they were contradictory to the age-long rights of Englishmen and a violation of British legal principles of six centuries standing, made his interpretation the evangel of a new nation.   The ease with which Dickinson swept aside Charles Townshend's favorite argument won especial admiration.   The Americans objected to a stamp act, said the brilliant Englishman, because it was new, an innovation, an internal tax; very well, why not then an external tax, one levied on imported articles, a kind of customs impost which they had willingly paid for a hundred and fifty years?   Dickinson's exposition was devoted to destroying this fallacy.   What made these levies unconstitutional, he declared, was the intention that lay behind them — the idea of collecting a revenue without the consent of the colonial assemblies; previous customs duties had been assessed not for taxation but for the regulation of trade.   The difference, he showed, was profound; it was the manifest purpose of taxation, without the consent of the persons taxed, that made the new proposal so monstrous.   Readers of Dickinson missed certain arguments that had done pretty effective — and perhaps wearisome — service with other authorities, notably Richard Henry Lee and Samuel Adams. He apparently cared nothing for that "state of nature" and "natural right to life, liberty and property" so dear to these debaters, as well as to Thomas Jefferson in his Declaration. He rested his powerful thesis on law and the British Constitution, and, instead of quoting Locke and Algernon Sidney, Dickinson quoted Magna Charta, the Bill of Rights, and reviewed all those parliamentary acts and historic proceedings which had made the constitution a great protecting wall against taking the subject's money without his consent.

Dickinson made many admirers in the colonies, and in England itself, for the *Farmer's Letters,* republished in London, met almost as great an acclaim as in America, but no hero-worshiper attained quite the degree of exaltation of Arthur Lee. From now on the "Pennsylvania Farmer," whose friendship was quickly made, became an object of adoration, and from incense Arthur quickly turned to emulation. Pen and ink now became his consolation; instead of prescriptions and medical works, his physician's desk was transformed into a litter of scribbled paper. The *Monitor's Letters,* which presently flowed from Arthur's pen, were written as a companion piece or supplement to the Pennsylvanian's master stroke. Their style, it is true, fell short of the stately English and Olympian calm of their prototype, and the content was not so profound a presentation of judicial principles; Arthur's pamphlet was a fierce philippic, in which Americans were pictured as "slaves" and George III and his ministers as "tyrants." One statesmanlike note Arthur did strike — a note that became the saving inspiration of American action for the next ten years. The Latin motto adorning his title-page was *"Divide et Impera,"* inserted, not as a recommendation, but as a warning. There was the policy, said Arthur, of the British government, the rule that for ages had guided the Hapsburgs and other enemies of freedom. "Divide and rule"; already was the British king applying this method to solving his American problem, already was he attempting to separate one colony from another, that he might destroy them one by one! Arthur's brochure was thus a plea for "union"; let the colonies organize as one power and use their

united strength against the enemy. It was a warning which
Arthur and his brother sounded from this time forward, and thus
this early appearance of the Lees on the Revolutionary stage is as
upholders of a united country. Dickinson was clearly pleased by
the work of his Virginia disciple, and the two productions, the
Farmer's Letters and the *Monitor's Letters,* were issued as a single
volume by Rind in Williamsburg, with an introduction by Richard
Henry Lee. For good measure "The Liberty Song," which
Dickinson had written as a more popular definition of his doctrines, and which was presently sung in roaring chorus from
Maine to Georgia, was inserted. "My worthy friend," wrote
Dickinson in a letter, "Dr. Arthur Lee, a gentleman of distinguished family, abilities and patriotism, in Virginia, composed
eight lines" of this song — though just what lines they were must
remain a literary mystery. Yet one of its most impressive stanzas
is devoted to Arthur's favorite idea of colonial coöperation, and
it is highly probable that this excellent sentiment represents
Arthur's contribution to the rollicking ballad which presently became the "Marseillaise" of insurgent America. Probably, therefore, the following lines may be attributed to Arthur's pen: —

> Then join hand in hand, brave Americans all,
> By *uniting* We stand, by *dividing* We fall;
> IN SO RIGHTEOUS A CAUSE, let us hope to succeed,
> For heaven approves of each generous deed, —
>   In FREEDOM we 're born . . .

3

But printer's ink, even in such distinguished company, did not
satisfy Arthur Lee. He aspired to labor in a wider field. Why
should he expend his energies in Virginia? Could he not serve
his country better in a land he knew far more intimately than his
native soil — in England itself? There he had many friends,
most of them sympathizers with the American cause; why not, in
modern phrase, transform himself into a kind of "liaison officer"
between English Whigs and their American co-workers? No
agency could more potently serve the colonies at this time than
such an intermediary. Had modern methods of communication

existed in 1763–1776 it is altogether unlikely that the American Revolution would have taken place. Three thousand miles of water separated the parties to the dispute; there were no cables or wireless or telephones, not even swift steamers; letters ordinarily took from six to eight weeks crossing the ocean; there was no omnipresent press, instantaneously sending news and opinions; thus there was no adequate means of transmitting points of view and interpreting all phases of the discussion. The plan now evolving in Arthur's mind represented a slight effort to bridge this deficiency: it was his ambition to serve as an interpreter between the leading actors on both sides of the drama. "In the course of a few months," he afterwards wrote, reviewing this episode in his career, "it was manifest that the people of this continent did not propose to be finessed out of their liberties; and as I knew that the British cabinet was determined to enforce rather than abandon the usurpation, I was persuaded that a very serious contest was approaching. To prepare for that was the next object in my mind. The most effectual way to accomplish this, it seemed to me, was to form a correspondence with leading patriotic men in each colony. I wrote myself to London, where the acquaintance I had would enable me to obtain speedy and accurate information of the real designs of the British ministry, which being communicated to leading men in the several colonies, might enable them to harmonize on one system of opposition, since on this harmony the success of their opposition would depend. In pursuance to this plan I went to Maryland, to Philadelphia and New York. The men I had in contemplation were Mr. Daniel Dulany, who had written some able pieces, Mr. John Dickinson, who was the author of the celebrated *Farmer's Letters* and the leader of the Livingston party in New York, who is at present Governor of New Jersey." [1]

Arthur's first approach proved disappointing. This visit to Mr. Daniel Dulany, of Maryland, was not auspicious. Mr. Dulany was one of the most respected men in the colonies. "A Maryland lawyer," writes Woodrow Wilson, "had turned from leading the bar of a province to set up the true theory of the constitution of an empire with the dignity, the moderation, the power,

---

[1] William Livingston (1723–1790), an influential member of the Continental Congress.

the incommunicable grace of a great thinker and genuine man of letters." Mr. Dulany's fame, in two continents, rested upon a single pamphlet, *Considerations on the Propriety of Taxing the Colonies,* which was held to have destroyed the constitutional argument for the Stamp Act, just as Mr. Dickinson's *Farmer's Letters,* two years afterward, had shattered the legal justification for external taxes. Mr. Dulany's reasoning, finespun and learned, had impressed England even more profoundly than America; for here was a colonial jurist who seemed to comprehend British law and precedent more intimately than British authorities themselves! Mr. Dulany's paper, on the constitutional side, furnished Chatham the basis for that stupendous speech against the Stamp Act, in the House of Lords, to which Arthur Lee had been an entranced listener. Not unnaturally, therefore, he approached Mr. Dulany with all the fire of his nature, expecting to enlist his sympathies as a matter of course. Possibly this eagerness, in a stripling, offended the dignity of Maryland's leading citizen, then nearing his fiftieth year; perhaps Mr. Dulany had no faith in the proposal; the more probable fact is that he did not wish to be associated with a movement which smacked of disloyalty. Despite his hostility to parliamentary encroachment, Mr. Dulany was an upholder of the British connection, it subsequently becoming the sad fate of this great lawyer to part with his fellow Americans on the issue of independence, to join the ranks of the Tories, to suffer trial for "treason," and to sacrifice wealth and position. Not unlikely this loyalty was aroused by Arthur's eagerness; in this young man was manifest the spirit that was ultimately to cause the rupture he so dreaded! Whatever the reason, Arthur's reception was unfriendly. "I found Mr. Dulany so cold and distant," he wrote, "that it seemed in vain to attempt anything with him. . . . Mr. Livingston, of New York, was absent from the city in the country lamenting the death of a child, so that I did not see him." His interview with John Dickinson, however, left nothing to be desired. He was just the kind of man — genial, cultured, and human — to sympathize with an idealist like Arthur Lee. The young man's proposals similarly fell into his mood, for Dickinson was not a believer in the more robustious methods of arguing with England, — not for him hangings-in-effigy, tar-and-featherings, or subsequent throwings-overboard of tea, — but in precisely that scheme of information and persuasion which Arthur's propaganda committee implied.

"Mr. Dickinson received me with friendship and the contemplated correspondence took place. The time I was to sail for England approached; I could not therefore proceed further eastward. Embarking with one of my brothers, we arrived safe in London."

VII

"JUNIUS AMERICANUS"

I

THE brother who accompanied Arthur in the latter part of 1768 was William, his senior by a year, a Lee who has so far figured little in the family story, but who hereafter will be one of its most active and conspicuous participants. Arthur and William, closely linked because of their ages and their joint activity in the diplomacy of the Revolution, were little alike, either in temperament or in character. Their physical exterior fitly portrayed these divergences; Arthur, tawny-headed and thin-featured, bore little resemblance to the swarthy and tight-jawed William; Arthur, the romantic, the imaginative, the tilter at windmills, had similarly little in common with William, the most realistic, hard-fisted, and, in practical affairs, the ablest of his generation. They had one strong bond of sympathy, however, in their childhood, for it had been a difficult and unhappy time with both. Probably followers of the new psychology would find great significance in this fact. Of those "mental wounds" and "shocks" which, inflicted in man's tenderest years, are pictured as indelibly fixing character in mature life, both the younger Lees had had abundant experience. William and Arthur were the ugly ducklings of Stratford, and, unhappy to relate, the person held responsible for a disregarded childhood was their mother — that Hannah Ludwell whose qualities in other ways proved so splendid an inheritance. The authority for this statement is the family biographer, the second Richard Henry Lee. "Arthur was the youngest son," he writes, "and, according to the customs of the day, in regard to younger sons, was left until an advanced period of boyhood, with the children of his father's slaves, to partake of their fare and to participate in their hardy sports and toil." Their Spartan mother, "one of the high toned aristocracy of the day, confined all her care and attention to her daughters and her eldest son, who was to be the head of the family, and gave up her younger sons, when boys, to be fed, in great measure, by their own enterprise and exertions, without which they might have wanted the necessaries of life." This same discrimination appeared in their father's will, which made the oldest boy, Philip Ludwell, heir to Stratford and other plantations, gave excellent estates to Thomas, Richard Henry, and Francis Lightfoot, but not an acre to William or Arthur, each of whom was dismissed with a legacy of a thousand pounds. William's education was similarly overlooked, much as his father's had been, despite the fact that he was a child of vigorous intellect, and, like his father, he supplied the deficiency by literary exertions of his own. Thus no career as lawyer, as physician, as lord of tobacco plantation, was marked out for William; no part in the public life of Virginia was assigned him; instead, he was cast adrift when barely in his teens to earn a living by manual toil.

His oldest brother, as has been already related, treated William — and Arthur also — harshly and unfairly. That paltry inheritance apportioned as his preparation for life was never paid. Necessarily an adolescence of this sort made harder a spirit that was naturally aloof, brooding, determined, and not particularly social. William's bitterness in his letters is directed at his older brother, against whom his reproaches occasionally became savage. "You know my necessities for money" — this is one of many outbreaks of the kind — "and certainly to be twelve years out of my pittance which my father left me, without even common interest for it, while you have been indulging in affluence and I, procuring my bread with the sweat of my brow, is surely bad enough and it is time to put an end to it."

Sardonic as he was, grim, lacking small talk and facile compliment, unsentimental in his feeling towards humankind, still William had a compelling quality. Not easy of access, he possessed dignity and breeding; unschooled in a university sense, he was a man of ample education, a reader of hard books, as glib at quoting Montesquieu as Arthur and Richard Henry themselves; and, as letter writer, master of a style terse and determined like himself, his zest in public matters making this vast correspondence a precious authority on early American annals. Still William lacked the personal grace and nimble intellect of his younger brother and found his field in the countinghouse rather than in the drawing-room. His gift for details, even minutiæ, his insistence on economies, his talent for close bargaining, and his bluntness in conversation also set him apart from the typical Virginia gentleman; but he had other qualities that went with the character — a splendid scorn of lying and deceit, and a pride of ancestry even surpassing that of his tribe, for, like Arthur, William regarded the Potomac Brahmins as a class especially created for high emprise. "You were born," he writes to a young man of this sacred order recently arrived in England, "to act in a sphere above the common herd, and to do this with propriety you should take care not to imbibe the principles, motives and manners of the lower classes of mankind, which are totally incompatible with a gentleman." One may object to the high mightiness of the Lees, but certainly the attitude came to them by nature, not affectation, and the frankness of its expression left nothing to be desired.

It is easy to dislike William Lee, and many of his time did dislike him, as have historians since; yet there is something about this distant tobacco merchant that stirs one's admiration. That he was unsocial, in a promiscuous sense, — one who ploughed his lonely furrow, — is true; "partnerships," he significantly wrote, after one unhappy experience of the kind, "I dislike"; that he was subject to violent outbreaks of temper and was remorseless in his antagonisms — this also is on the surface; yet there are important counterbalancing virtues. The man's crystal intelligence shines in his every act and word. His native ability is evidenced by his business success. The confidence he inspired in the common run of men is proved by his substantial political career in London.

He came to England in 1768, not to engage in political disputation or diplomacy, but because Virginia had proved a sterile ground and he was forced to earn his living elsewhere. Every generation of his family, since the first Richard, had had a representative in London on the Virginia Exchange, to handle tobacco and general merchandise for the Virginia planters. This business had undergone few changes since the earliest settlements on the James.

William Lee in 1769 found himself established at 33 Tower Hill, conducting the tobacco trade along essentially the same lines as his Great-grandfather Richard in 1650. His headquarters served both as residence and as countinghouse; every spring he chartered a ship, sent it to the Potomac and the Rappahannock, where it collected hogsheads of tobacco and, full loaded, proceeded to London. William sold this tobacco to such customers as he could find, charging a 25 per cent commission; the proceeds were not sent home, but invested in articles of luxury and use then required on a tobacco farm. After disposing of the tobacco and receiving payment, William would visit the London shops, buying clothes, shoes, hats, garments for slaves, farm utensils, furniture, wines and delicacies of all kinds — everything that the planter needed to maintain his state. Similarly William's wife was called upon to shop for the planter's "lady" and to select all the necessities and furbelows — gowns, jewels, millinery of all kinds — on which the Potomac chatelaine had set her heart. The whole business was thus most simple and neighborly. Obviously only Potomac grandees themselves were fitted for such a task. A knowledge of the customers and their tastes was essential, and this was obtained only by years of social intercourse; thus William would know exactly the kind of small clothes and silver plate and precious wines desired by his neighbor of Mount Airy, while his spouse could tell at a glance whether a particular stomacher or bolt of seersucker, or brooch or party slippers or furs, accorded with the likings of her grace of Nomini Hall. Tobacco trading was an art of the aristocracy; the common man, not having this precise knowledge, could make no headway. William in his letters refers scornfully to "woolen drapers," tobacco evidently representing in his mind a caste thousands of degrees above this plebeian trade. Success depended largely on the merchant's wife, and William had chosen his most judiciously. Intermarriage in this clan had now become almost a commonplace, and a few months after reaching England William joined fortunes with his first cousin, Hannah Phillipa Ludwell, daughter of his mother's brother, Phillip Ludwell — fourth bearer of that famous name and the last male member of the gens. This family had now been long domiciled in Bow, near London, where the Ludwell

WILLIAM LEE, 1739–1795

FRANCIS LIGHTFOOT LEE, 1734–1797

From Paintings in the Westmoreland Courthouse
Montross, Virginia

vault in Bow Church still contains many representatives of the race, including the wife of William Lee. The marriage at St. Clement Danes in the Strand formed the basis of William's delightful domestic life and provided a dignified background for the mercantile success and high political honors that presently came his way.

Arthur, devoted to his brother and cousin sister-in-law, spent many days at Tower Hill, his letters occasionally bearing that address; and at other times he wandered over England, to Bath and Bristol Wells, thinking perhaps to establish himself in medical practice, but without result. Suddenly, in 1770, he abruptly changed his course of life; bidding farewell to medicine, at the age of thirty, he decided to turn to an entirely new profession. Now he took up a studious existence in the Middle Temple, where his brothers Philip and Thomas had prepared for the law, and where the two Americans whom he so admired, John Dickinson and Daniel Dulany, had absorbed that knowledge of the British Constitution which made them such formidable antagonists to Mansfield and Townshend. Probably a desire to qualify for great legal disputation was among the motives for embarking in this field. This was the most charming period in Arthur's not particularly happy life. His four years' residence at No. 2 Garden Court, Middle Temple, — a delightful retreat which exists to-day practically unchanged, a tablet marking the rooms occupied, a century and a half ago, by Arthur Lee, — was the time that he most fondly looked back to in his later days — one cannot say old age, for Arthur was not destined to reach anything resembling superannuation. "I was placed in chambers in the Temple," he wrote in his journal, "which looked into a delightful little garden on the Thames, to which I had the key. I would go in and out at all times and have what company I pleased, without being questioned or molested. I was near the Royal Society, of which I was a fellow, where every week whatever was new and ingenious in literature was communicated. Not far from me was the hall of Arts and Agriculture, of which I was an honorary member, and where I had access to all the new devices in Art, Agriculture and Mechanics. The play house and the opera were equally convenient, where I could select the opportunity of seeing the best tragedies and comedies represented and of hearing the most exquisite Italian music.   I was a subscriber to Bach's and Abel's concerts, where the most masterly performers in the world (Bach, Abel, Fishar, Tassot, Ponto and Crosdal) played to a most polite and fashionable audience, in one of the most elegant concert rooms in the world.   In the field of politics, from the politician in the cider cellar to the peer in his palace, I had access and influence.   At the Bill of Rights,[1] the City of London, the East India house, and with the opposition in both houses I was of some consideration.   Among my particular friends, to whom I always had access, were Lord Shelburne, Col. Barré, Sergeant Glynn and several others.   I was so well with several of the nobility and gentry that I could spend all my leisure time at their country seats. At Bath I had a very extensive acquaintance, and there is not in the world a more agreeable place to one so circumstanced.   As one of the law I enjoyed the protection and distinction of that body, with the prospect of rising to place and profit, which all of that body, who have even moderate abilities, enjoy.   So circumstanced, nothing but the peculiar and extraordinary crisis of the times prevented me from being entirely happy, and pursuing the fortune which sat with golden plumes within my reach.   But everything was absorbed in the great contest which I saw fast approaching and which soon called upon me to quit London and take an open part in the Revolution."

This certainly reveals a variety of interests — science, literature, music, the theatre, social enlightenment, notable friends; but the leading concern of Arthur's life from 1769 to 1775 — even more important than the law — was politics.   That six years certainly witnessed transcendent events in the history of his country; it was the era in which America became a nation, and in all the controversies of the time Arthur Lee was an active agent. The wisdom with which he chose his friends is apparent.   Not all the forces powerful in British affairs supported royal attempts to subdue colonial ambitions.   The merchants and freemen of London bitterly opposed the king and his friends, and many of the

---

[1] This was the name given to the Association formed to defend John Wilkes and his principles.   See page 166.

most striking figures in English public life were strong on the American side. It is observed, from the list of associates enumerated in this extract, that Arthur gravitated toward this pro-American group. All the men he names were fighting British policies with the zeal of the Lees themselves. The Colonel Barré mentioned was the gallant veteran of Wolfe's attack on Quebec, — his cheek bore a heavy scar witnessing the fact, — one of the few members of the House of Commons to speak against the Stamp Act, his famous characterization, on this occasion, of America's patriots as "Sons of Liberty" having been adopted as title by patriotic organizations in the colonies.[1] Mr. Dunning, afterward Lord Ashburton, was forging his way to leadership of the English bar; his sympathies were shown when he resigned as solicitor general of the Grafton administration that he might oppose the prevailing policies. Sergeant Glynn, ally of John Wilkes, was constantly fighting the American battle, and another close friend, not specified in this list, was one of the most spectacular characters in British life, usually referred to as "the celebrated Mrs. Macaulay," a pioneer in the field of feminism, author of a seven-volume history of England, a book that was a panegyric of republicanism. The American colonies never had a more energetic champion than this lady, who, despite her oddities, was a woman of intellect, a predecessor of the famous Englishwomen of the nineteenth century.

Probably of all Englishmen the friend most sympathetic to Arthur Lee was the Earl of Shelburne, a cabinet member who championed America in every crisis. Bonds of friendship existed between these two men on personal grounds. Both were young — Shelburne only three years Arthur's senior; both had a passion for books and learning; Shelburne, afterward the first Marquess of Lansdowne, was a collector of manuscripts and historic materials, the founder of that Lansdowne library which is one of the literary glories of England. Temperamentally the two had something in common, for the young English statesman had the habit of acid portraiture, and an occasional irascibility of temper not unknown to the American. Both men also had

[1] It was in honor of Wilkes and Barré that a well-known Pennsylvania city was named.

common ideals.   To both the British Empire was the great fact in modern history, and Arthur, at this time, wished for his country no more exalted future than that it might remain one of its component parts on self-respecting terms.   In 1783 it became Shelburne's duty, as Prime Minister of Great Britain, to sponsor the treaty that alienated the former American colonies from the one-time mother country; it was the most painful duty he ever had to perform.   And no Englishman, from the first, had worked more earnestly to prevent this consummation.   How modern Shelburne was, and how devoted to honorable British-American coöperation, is apparent in the correspondence with his American friend.   For a hundred and fifty years a packet of Arthur Lee's letters has been reposing in the archives of Bowood, Wiltshire, offset by a packet of Lord Lansdowne's to Arthur Lee, in Harvard University.   Both collections furnish revelations of the two men, and of the hopes they entertained for the friendly relations of their two countries.   One of Arthur's, dated July 3, 1769, has particular interest, for it refers to a plan then meditated by Shelburne for creating a better understanding between Great Britain and the estranged colonies.   This was to select from the most upstanding students of Harvard, Yale, William and Mary, and the other five American colleges, scholars for education in one of the English universities: in this way had Lord Shelburne anticipated, by more than a century, the plan of Cecil Rhodes for drawing the two nations together.

That Shelburne should have originated such a programme in that unidealistic age, at a time when most Englishmen of his caste were daily heaping insults on America, shows how far he stood above the statesmen of his day.   Just when Arthur Lee and Shelburne became friends cannot be said; the earliest reference obtainable is an entry in the journal of Lady Shelburne, for January 12, 1766: "At our breakfast came Dr. Leigh,[1] an American." This was on the eve of the repeal of the Stamp Tax, so that the association began at an early day.   Besides his personal qualities, Arthur was a desirable ally in the cause — not for any influence (which the young man at that time did not have) but for furnishing information on America, for transmitting, from Richard

[1] The variation in spelling was common at the time.

Henry Lee and others, correct conceptions of the American stand-point. To what extent Arthur influenced the British statesman is undetermined; one fact is important, however, and that is that Shelburne's policy was a perfect counterpart of Arthur's. In the Virginian's eyes that Declaratory Act in the repeal, insisting on Britain's right to "bind the colonies in all cases whatsoever," was England's fatal mistake; it was the crux of the whole problem. This was an advanced opinion, but it was the standpoint of Shelburne also. Thus both men stood for the modern British conception of the empire; that the Dominions should remain units in the British Commonwealth, owing allegiance to the same king, but that they should be independent of parliamentary control. Thus when Britain, repealing the Stamp Act, inserted a clause proclaiming a constitutional right to levy directly on the colonies, it made reconciliation impossible, and precluded the organization of the British Empire on a just and lasting basis. The Bowood estate, with its familiar spirits, Colonel Barré, Dr. Price, Dr. Priestley, and others, was for many years the shrine of this school of thinking. "It is with much pleasure that I can assure you," Arthur writes Richard Henry, December 3, 1769, "that Lords Shelburne, Chatham and Camden are determined to unite once more in supporting America against the present weak and wicked administration. I am at present at Lord Shelburne's, in the country, and you may depend on what I say concerning our friends."

An entirely different character, but of similar political principles, was the man who had put London in an uproar, and of whose circle Arthur became an intimate member. That year, 1769, was indeed a fateful date in British and American history: John Wilkes had recently returned from exile in Paris, to be elected almost unanimously Member from Middlesex. The disturbances attending that event had reached their height when Arthur appeared on the scene. He was an indignant witness of Wilkes's repeated attempts to gain admission to the House of Commons against the royal veto, and not improbably the riots, the threatening mobs, the violent discussion in press and Commons, the scourgings of Junius, added a pleasant excitement to Arthur's life. There was probably much in this "libeler of his

King and blasphemer of his God," as Chatham called the ousted Member for Middlesex, that Arthur would not have found especially to his taste; but profligate, spendthrift, and general harumscarum that he was, Wilkes manifested one virtue which atoned for all superficial defects — he was a friend of America, the enemy of America's enemies, and in Arthur's eyes, as in those of most enlightened Englishmen, such as Shelburne and Barré, the name of Wilkes has come to symbolize English liberty. America had closely followed Wilkes's career, and by 1769 looked upon him as a brother. For years he had been a favorite toast at meetings of the Sons of Liberty; many Americans smoked their tobacco through "Wilkes and Liberty" pipes, and Richard Henry Lee, in his demonstrations against Mercer, had dressed his negroes in "Jack Wilkes" costumes — flaming red coats, cocked hats, and high shiny boots. Wilkes was one of the rages of the times.

Two months after Arthur's arrival was organized "The Supporters of the Bill of Rights," with the idealistic purpose of spreading the doctrines inherent in Magna Charta, and the more practical one of paying off the debts of their tempestuous defender, Wilkes. Into both these objects Arthur entered, taking upon himself the American department, enlisting American members — such men as Samuel and John Adams, Joseph Warren, his brothers Richard Henry and Francis Lightfoot — who not only did their duty in a political sense, but also contributed to the ransom. In due course, under Arthur's promptings, a ship sailed from the Potomac bearing a consignment of tobacco, the gift made by Virginian adherents to the good cause. Arthur was a frequent visitor to the prison where Wilkes lived in luxury — at the expense of his sympathizers — and from which he directed a campaign against the foe.

Arthur Lee and John Wilkes, indeed, became almost inseparable companions, the pen of the American being frequently used in drawing up papers for the Bill of Rights. The Virginian liked to take prominent Americans in London to visit the satanic demagogue; Dr. Benjamin Rush has left in his diary an account of such a visit. "While I was in Britain Mr. Wilkes was the object of universal attention. The nation was divided into his friends and enemies according as they espoused or opposed the measures of

the government. Mr. Wilkes was expiating some political offense in Newgate while I was in London. My curiosity was
excited to see the man that had so universally agitated and divided
a nation. Arthur Lee, of Virginia, who knew him intimately,
invited me to accompany him to a dinner which he had prepared
in prison for a number of his friends. The company consisted
of fourteen or fifteen gentlemen and the conversation was interesting and agreeable. Mr. Wilkes abounded in anecdotes and
sallies of wit. He was perfectly well-bred. Not an unchaste
word or oath escaped his lips. I was more surprised at this as he
had been represented a monster of immorality."

Who does not recall the dinner given by Dilly, the publisher, to
Wilkes and the man who, of all in the world, probably detested
him most heartily — Dr. Samuel Johnson? It is one of the
most entertaining episodes in Boswell's *Life*.

"Who is that gentleman?" Johnson whispered to Dilly, as he
came in, apparently not recognizing, or feigning not to, the young
man whom fifteen years before he had persuaded to "enter on
Physic" at Edinburgh.

"Mr. Arthur Lee."

"Too, too, too," said Johnson under his breath — "which,"
adds Boswell, "was one of his habitual mutterings. Mr. Arthur
Lee could not but be very obnoxious to Johnson, for he was not
only a *patriot* but an *American*" — meaning that he was both a
Wilkite and a revolutionary colonial.

It was Arthur Lee's remark, at this dinner, about certain
Scotch people who had taken possession of a part of America that
led to a long and most uncomplimentary discussion of that unpopular people, occupying a page of the *Life*. William Lee's
characteristic comment, "Poor old England is lost," set Johnson
off again on a favorite topic: "Sir, it is not so much to be la-
mented that old England is lost as that the Scotch have found it!"
The next day Johnson wrote Mrs. Thrale about the dinner. "I
dined yesterday in the Poultry with Mr. Alderman Wilkes and Mr.
Alderman Lee and Counsellor Lee, his brother. There sat you the
while, so sober, with your W——'s and your H——'s and my
aunt and her turn-spit; and when they are gone, you think per-

chance on Johnson, what is he doing?   What should he be doing?
He is breaking jokes with Jack Wilkes upon the Scots.   Such,
madam, are the vicissitudes of things."

2

This dinner party took place May 15, 1776, when Britain and
her colonies were at war, a year after Lexington and Concord;
not improbably Dr. Johnson's disapproving "Too, too, too!" was
reminiscent of the part Arthur Lee had taken in the public discussions which preceded those events.   Arthur's writings, for the
period 1770–1775, had aroused popular attention.   He took as
his model that sledge-hammer craftsman then the day's literary
marvel, and even took his name, thus becoming Junius Americanus, a signature that appeared frequently in the *Gazeteer*.   These
outgivings, afterward collected in a widely circulated volume,
pictured colonial problems as merely one phase of the general
crisis precipitated by the autocratic tendencies of George III.
Royal usurpation in the colonies, manifested in Stamp Acts, duties
on paints, paper, and tea, quartering of troops amid a peace-time
population, proroguing of provincial legislatures — behavior of
this sort, said the American Junius, was merely another evidence
of that determination to concentrate all power in royal hands
which was also manifest in the suppression of popular liberties in
England.   "Jacobitism," Junius Americanus called it, and he
pointedly showed that the king's chief instruments — Bute, Hillsborough, Mansfield — were Scots, formerly sympathetic to the
Stuart claims; indeed that the first was himself, illegitimately, of
Stuart descent.   This "arbitrary thane," as Arthur calls the
Scottish leader, formed the principal quarry of the attack.   "This
indicates subversion of liberty in both countries, springing from
the same source.   I am therefore earnest in recommending to the
free people of this country to cultivate the friendship of the
Americans, who are pursuing the same sacred course of freedom,
with the same virtuous determination to succeed, and to persist
in the attempt.   The cause is common, let us be united in the attempt, the Liberties of both countries are embarked in the same
bottom, the same storm that sinks the one, will overwhelm the

other. . . . The people of England and of America, united in their efforts, will vindicate the Liberties from every attempt of a despotic Stuart [that is, Lord Bute] and maintain them inviolate to the latest posterity."

The attitude was statesmanlike and is now generally accepted by modern historians, such as Trevelyan; in 1770, however, the date of Junius Americanus, the interpretation was novel, but proved a powerful one in enlisting English allies. Arthur took great satisfaction in his literary device. "It is a chance," he wrote Richard Henry, "whether you ever meet with a series of letters signed *Junius Americanus,* in which the enemies of America are chiefly attacked, though to make what was written in defense of the colonies acceptable it was necessary to give now and then a stroke to the characters obnoxious here. It is desirable to make a signature popular; when that is affected I shall be able to write for America under it with success, which it is otherwise difficult to accomplish." One man who did not enjoy the letters was Sir Francis Bernard, the very unpopular governor of Massachusetts, then in London to defend himself against his constituents, who were demanding his recall; a series of Americanus letters was especially leveled at Bernard, and his protests were loud but unavailing, though the Massachusetts Council, then under the domination of Hutchinson, formally censored the volume. One who did enjoy the letters was the veritable Junius, the great unknown. "My American namesake," he wrote Wilkes, "is plainly a man of abilities. You may assure Mr. Lee, that, to my heart and understanding, the names of Americans and Englishmen are synonymous."

Other publications followed the Junius. In the *Correspondence of the Late John Wilkes* (1805) appears this statement: "At the commencement of America's contest, this Mr. Lee wrote a tract of much ability, entitled *An Appeal to the Justice and interest of the People of Great Britain in the present disputes with America.* Dilly declined to print it, because he thought that the sale would not be sufficient to defray the mechanical expense, upon which Dr. Franklin sent it to Mr. Almon who accepted it. There were many thousands of it circulated, both in England and America. It was the best tract on the subject at that time." The essay

went rapidly through four editions and was quickly followed by
*A Speech Intended to have been delivered in the House of Com-
mons in support of a Petition of the Continental Congress* and by
a *Second Appeal.* A new Arthur Lee emerges in these documents: it is the scholar of law who had spent four years at Inns
of Court; the thesis is set forth with all the learning and dignity
of a Dickinson himself; and the whole tone is sober and thoughtful. In his Junius letters Arthur jibes freely at Hillsborough,
the Duke of Grafton, Lord Bute, and Sir Francis Bernard; but
times are now more serious — England and her colonies are on
the brink of war; these later Arthur Lee pamphlets represent his
final effort to do his part in healing the breach; his love for the
real England was as active as ever, and, as he expressed it, "the
first wish of my heart is that America may be free; the second is
that we may forever be united to England." He ends the presentation with his favorite admonition, drowned this time by the
guns of Bunker Hill: "May the liberties of England be immortal
— but may Englishmen ever remember, that the same arbitrary
spirit which prompts an invasion of the constitution in America,
will not long leave that of England unattacked, and that the same
corrupt servility in their members will make them the instruments
of the crown in all its attempts."

3

Arthur's greatest service to the cause, however, was not his
pamphleteering, but his correspondence, for the six years preceding hostilities, with many of the leaders in America. The object
he had in mind, in sailing for England, was never lost sight of.
The correspondence with John Dickinson began almost immediately on arrival, Arthur's first letter being dated December 21,
1768. Unfortunately his contributions have disappeared, but
many of Mr. Dickinson's survive, suggesting in every line the
writer of the *Farmer's Letters.* They also indicate the main lines
of Arthur's discourse. The idea constantly pushed by him at
this time, as it had been in his Williamsburg writings, was that
colonial salvation lay in one thing — union — and that only
Americans and their friends in England could be depended on for

success. "From the justice of Great Britain nothing is to be expected; from her fears and interests everything." This was the unvarying theme also of Arthur's letters to his brother Richard Henry, to Thomas Cushing, Speaker of the Massachusetts House, and to Dr. Joseph Warren, another New Englander for whom the Lees always had the deepest affection — evidenced to-day by the name "Warrenton," given to the Virginia city that was founded through the efforts of Richard Henry Lee on the land bequeathed him by his father.

The most valuable of Arthur's pre-Revolutionary correspondents, however, was Samuel Adams. One of the most charming phases of the great Samuel's character was his interest in young men. His eye was ever searching the field for youthful spirits whose hearts could be enlisted in the cause. "Samuel Adams, to my certain knowledge," wrote his kinsman John, "from 1758 to 1775, that is, for seventeen years, made it his constant rule to watch the rise of every brilliant genius, to seek his acquaintance, to court his friendship, to cultivate his natural feelings in favor of his native country, to warn him against the hostile designs of Great Britain and to fix his affections and reflections on the side of his native country."

Inevitably Samuel would discover the apt young Virginian, the associate in London of all British statesmen affecting the American cause, already a celebrated pamphleteer. But there was another reason for Samuel's inclination to Arthur. Massachusetts was getting more deeply involved in the quarrel with England than any other colony, and the rage of the North administration was focusing on the port of Boston. Already a British military force was established in the seditious town and a British fleet was practically blockading the harbor. British strategy was occupied in isolating the cantankerous Puritans from the other colonies, and the lukewarm spirit manifested by New York and Pennsylvania was an ominous sign that this plan might succeed. Already Massachusetts patriots were alarmed lest they might find themselves engaged alone in a military struggle with the most powerful nation in the world. In this gloomy prospect the attitude of Virginia put new enthusiasm into the New England leaders. "This is a glorious day!" shouted Samuel Adams when there came into his hands the resolutions adopted by the Virginia House of Burgesses in 1768 endorsing the Massachusetts course and extending its sympathy. From this time on Samuel began assiduously to cultivate the Lees, and now was founded that close friendship and coöperation of the Lee and Adams families that influenced so powerfully the course of American history. In 1770 the death of Dennys De Berdt left vacant the post of Massachusetts agent in London — the agent being a kind of colonial ambassador to the mother country, an office not particularly important in normal times, but of the utmost consequence now. Samuel Adams nominated Arthur Lee for this place and carried one-third the House with him in the vote. The great fame and mature experience of Benjamin Franklin, however, then resident in London, proved too strong; the philosopher was chosen, with Arthur Lee as his assistant and successor in case of death or removal from London. Samuel was disgruntled over Franklin's victory, for he distrusted the Pennsylvanian, regarded him as not sufficiently incensed against England and altogether too much disposed to an unsatisfactory reconciliation.

Samuel Adams now solicited Arthur as a correspondent, sending his request through Stephen Sayre, recently partner with William Lee in the tobacco trade. The interchange of letters continued uninterruptedly for thirteen years, and, though the two men did not meet until 1781, the feeling of Samuel towards his young friend was always affectionate, almost paternal. The lonely watchman of Massachusetts's freedom found his greatest solace in the eloquent missives received from the Middle Temple, his eagerness, almost impatience, being constantly apparent. Every ship from London Samuel scanned in hopes of a word from Arthur. "I am disappointed if I do not receive a letter by every vessel that arrives here," he writes almost plaintively. The disappointment was natural, for Arthur Lee's letters, as Adams afterwards said, furnished the best insight obtained during this time into the state of feeling in England and the attitude of British statesmen. The testimony to their value that was afterward borne by John Adams, who subsequently himself became a correspondent of Arthur Lee's, is sufficient. From 1770 "to the year 1774 Arthur Lee held a constant correspondence with several of the gentlemen who stood foremost in the Massachusetts Bay against the innovations and illegal encroachments of Great Britain. From September, 1774, to November, 1777, I had the honor to be in Congress and the opportunity of seeing his letters to Congress, to their committees and to individual members. Through the whole of both those periods he communicated the most constant and certain intelligence which was received from any individual within my knowledge."

Even now, if we put together Arthur's letters to Samuel Adams and to his brother, Richard Henry Lee,[1] we can fairly vision all the actors in the drama and feel all the vibrations of an exciting time. The way Arthur kept his correspondents informed of the personal qualities of British statesmen was especially valuable in that time when exploitation of great characters in press and books was not so common as now. Arthur had the gift of throwing off brief characterizations. Charles Townshend was "an overgrown, opinionated schoolboy"; Lord Bute — "from so impure a fountain no good can be expected"; and George III, "with whom revenge is a virtue." His rapid summation of the Grafton ministry, as the Chatham combination was known after 1767, gives his method; "Grafton is the Premier, profligate, arbitrary and contemptible; Weymouth, abandoned to gaming and drinking, totally involved but extremely clever; North, Gower and Bristol — nothing; Hillsborough or Pownal, arbitrary, opinionated, subtle and severe." King George's statement, in his speech of 1768, that he had "no wish but that of reigning in the hearts and affections of his people" rouses the Virginian's scorn. "There is not an action of his reign, some few treacherous ones excepted," he writes Samuel Adams, "but what manifest it to be his sole wish to be the tyrant of his people. To assert a thing therefore so notoriously false and flattering, argues such a turpitude of mind as ought to doom its possessor to a suspension between heaven and earth, as unworthy of a place in either."

Beware of Lord Hillsborough! Arthur knew him well, for he constantly discussed American matters with him and had taken

[1] Many are published in *The Life of Arthur Lee* (1829) by his grandnephew, R. H. Lee, and in *The Life and Public Services of Samuel Adams* (1865) by William V. Wells. Others are still in manuscript in the Samuel Adams papers, New York Public Library.

his measure. His mildness is all craft — a deliberate plan to lull Americans into slavery. "Lord Hillsborough takes great pains to persuade and assure your countrymen" — again Arthur is addressing Samuel Adams — "that as long as they continue quiet nothing will be done to their prejudice. As treachery and imposition is his forte, there is most danger when his professions are warmest. Besides, as he certainly intended mischief, he is more strongly induced to exercise these arts in order to quiet the alarm which such an intention going forth would necessarily produce. He possesses too perverse a spirit that thinks he is doing nothing if he is not doing mischief." Arthur's opinion of Lord North was even more destructive. "The character of North" as that disastrous administration came in, "and the consideration of what surprising things he has effected toward enslaving his own country, makes me, I own, tremble for ours. Plausible, deep and treacherous, like his master he has no passion to divert him — no pursuits of pleasure to draw him from the accursed design of deliberately destroying the liberties of his country. A perfect adept in the arts of corruption, and indefatigable in the application of them, he effects great ends by means almost magical, because they are unseen."

And underlying every thought of Arthur Lee's was his love of America and confidence in her future. "To one who adores liberty and the noble virtues of which it is the parent," he wrote Samuel Adams, December 24, 1772, "there is some consolation in seeing, while we lament the fate of British liberty, the rise of that of America. Yes, my friend, like a young Phœnix she will rise full plumed and glorious from her mother's ashes. The numbers who are daily emigrating from this country, and the multitudes that in any public calamity will resort to us, must in a little time lay the most permanent foundation of populousness and power. America, in her turn, will be the imperial mistress of the world." How is such an outcome to be achieved? It all lay in one word: union. Let all the colonies rush to the support of Boston; let there come together a colonial congress, for only in united action could there be safety. "American liberty must be entirely of American fabric. . . . My Lord Chatham and my Lord Shelburne remain faithful to the cause of this country and America.

But I would wish my countrymen to remember that salvation cometh not from the East nor from the West, but from themselves. The Scripture tells us that to put our trust in princes and in great men is futile and certainly we were never so respectable here as when we seemed to be on the eve of appealing to God." [1] And so, as the year 1774 drew near, Arthur's incessant injunction to Adams and his co-workers was that all the colonies should combine, and present a united front for the struggle which every day seemed more inevitable.

[1] The "appeal to Heaven" or "to God" was a favorite expression of the time for "war."

PART III

NEW ENGLAND AND VIRGINIA IN THE REVOLUTION

VIII

THE "LEE–ADAMS JUNTO"

I

An impression prevails to-day that the United States of America declared its independence of Great Britain on July 4, 1776. The fact is commonly overlooked that, two days before this historic decision, — on July 2, — the revolting colonies, in general congress assembled, adopted the following resolution: —

That these united colonies are, and of right ought to be, free and independent states; that they are absolved from all allegiance to the British crown, and that all political connection between them, and the state of Great Britain, is, and ought to be, totally dissolved.

Nothing could be more explicit than that. So far as a pronouncement of the Continental Congress could effect a separation from the one-time mother country, this resolution accomplished that result. After such a proceeding the Jeffersonian Declaration, adopted — but not signed — two days subsequently, seems almost superfluous. Yet so overwhelming is the force of Jefferson's rhetoric that it has fixed, quite unhistorically, the date of the great American holiday. The purpose of the Jefferson document was not to proclaim a new nation; that proclamation had been made, two days previously; its purpose, as set forth in the first sentence, was "to declare the causes which impelled to the separation"; the final paragraph, again asserting American independence, merely repeats the resolution already adopted, using, indeed, the very words.

At least one member of the Continental Congress entertained no doubt that America had taken this momentous step on July 2. The following day John Adams wrote jubilantly to the ever-faithful Abigail: "Yesterday the greatest question was decided that was ever debated in America; and a greater perhaps never was nor will be decided among men. . . . The second day of July, 1776, will be the most memorable epoch in the history of America. It ought to be commemorated, as a day of deliverance by solemn acts of devotion to God Almighty. It ought to be solemnized, with pomp and parade, with shows, games, sports, guns, bells, bonfires and illuminations, from one end of this continent to the other, from this time forward, forevermore."

America adopted the Adams programme of commemoration almost in detail, amending it only by changing the date from July 2 to July 4. That change must be accepted as a tribute to literature. Had Jefferson compiled a dull and uninspiring list of grievances, his declaration would have quickly passed into oblivion, and to-day we should be observing July 2 as the national festival. His stately cadences, the dignity of his reasoning and expression, the unassailable logic — as it seemed — of his presentation, immediately became the mental possession of every American; after that parchment had once issued from Philadelphia, the birthday of the United States had been immutably determined.

Richard Henry Lee introduced the resolution that established American independence and John Adams seconded it. This association in the final act epitomizes and personalizes the story of American independence. British policy, for several years preceding the Continental Congress, had aimed to isolate New England from the other colonies; it had particularly sought to separate Massachusetts and Virginia, the two most powerful American commonwealths, and the most determined leaders in revolution. That Richard Henry Lee should have introduced the resolution of independence and that John Adams should have seconded it indicates how lamentably this had failed. The joint appearance of Cavalier and Puritan strategy pictures as well the combination that, from the first assembling of Congress, had worked in unison to this ultimate triumph. It is hardly too much to say that the American union was the work of these two, the most ancient of British communities in America. Certainly without the New England delegates, under the guidance and the counsels of the Adamses, and the Virginia representation, under the generalship of the tribe of Lee, both working harmoniously and unremittingly, from the beginning, for one definite end, the American nation would not have come into existence at that time. When Carter Braxton, a Virginia delegate, out of sympathy with the result, attributed independence to "the wise men of the East and some from the South," he accurately summarized that achievement.

2

America had never witnessed anything like the coming together of the First Continental Congress in September 1774. It was not the first grand council in the history of the colonies, but it was the first that really represented anything resembling sincere cooperation, the first that included in its membership the highest type of American character and talent. That each section should send its finest men was inevitable, for it was a gathering which Americans had anticipated for ten years. To the Lees and the Adamses in particular Congress was a dream come true. From 1763 the Virginia brothers and their sympathetic partners in New England had insisted that only the united efforts of all, the presentation of a solid front to Britain, could successfully confute the increasing encroachments of the king. Arthur Lee's pamphlets, his letters to Richard Henry, to Samuel Adams, to John Dickinson, had constantly harped upon this string, and Patrick Henry's first speech in Carpenter's Hall, with its eloquent refrain, "We are no longer Virginians, no longer New Englanders, we are Americans," embodied a new political conception in American history. The group of fifty-five men who met to give direction to this modern doctrine enhanced its dignity and impressiveness. It is doubtful if any of America's subsequent Congresses matched in worth and ability this initial gathering. All colonies were represented, except Georgia, and all had sent their picked men. Those from Massachusetts and Virginia naturally became the chief objects of attention, for these two commonwealths had taken the lead in opposing parliamentary pretensions.

In personal bearing the leaders from the Old Dominion easily bore the palm. The short, rotund, and undistinguished figures of John and Samuel Adams seemed rather unimposing when placed beside the majesty of a Washington, the venerable dignity of a Peyton Randolph, the clean-cut, scholarly presence of a Richard Henry Lee, or even the more plebeian, rather shambling simplicity of a Patrick Henry, this time no longer garbed in leather breeches, but in subdued gray, looking, as one observer remarked, very much like a Presbyterian parson. This superiority in personal distinction the New England members freely acknowledged. Two New England delegates, Silas Deane and John Adams, had a talent for recording impressions, and both, in diaries and letters to their wives, have left enduring sketches of their Virginian colleagues. "Mr. Randolph," wrote Deane, "our worthy President, may be rising sixty, of noble appearance, and presides with dignity. . . . Mr. Pendleton is a lawyer of eminence, of easy and cheerful countenance, polite in address, and elegant if not eloquent in style and elocution. Mr. Henry is also a lawyer and the completest speaker I have ever heard. If his future speeches are equal to the examples he has hitherto given us, they will be worth preserving, but in a letter I can give you no idea of the music of his voice or the high wrought yet natural elegance of his style and manner. Col. Lee is said to be his rival in eloquence and in Virginia and to the southward they are styled the Demosthenes and Cicero of America. God grant they may not, like them, plead in vain for the liberties of their country! These last gentlemen are now in full life, perhaps near fifty and have made the constitution and history of Great Britain and America their capital study ever since the late troubles between them have arisen."

Again: "Our President [Peyton Randolph] seems designed by nature for the business; of an open, affable and majestic deportment, large in size though not out of proportion, he commands respect and esteem by his very aspect. . . . You may tell your friends that I have never met, nor scarcely had an idea of meeting, with men of such firmness, sensibility, spirit and thorough knowledge of the interests of America, as the gentlemen from the southern provinces appear to be. May New England go hand in hand with them!" "Randolph is a large, well-looking man," wrote

John Adams. "Lee is a tall, spare man; Bland a learned, bookish man. These gentlemen from Virginia appear to be the most spirited and consistent of any."

Richard Henry seemed to be an object of particular interest. Still young, in his forty-second year, his reddish hair was yet unstreaked; his slim figure, more than six feet high, had lost nothing of its grace; his voice, as ever, was soft and insinuating; only his left hand showed signs of decrepitude. Richard Henry had recently lost the fingers of this in an accident, and the gesticulating member, swathed in a black handkerchief, quickly became one of the characteristic features of the assemblage. Lee's grace of utterance, now practised for sixteen years in the House of Burgesses, had reached almost perfection at this critical moment. "The fine powers of language," wrote St. George Tucker, describing him, "united with that harmonious voice, made me sometimes think that I was listening to some being inspired with more than mortal powers of embellishment." Yet the ten years that had preceded Philadelphia, rich as they had proved in Lee's public career, had known their hardships — hardships perhaps reflected in his slightly haggard cast of countenance. Established as a planter at his modest Chantilly estate, on the Potomac, only three miles from Stratford, Richard Henry had not been oversuccessful; ill-health had haunted his days; and the death of his first wife, Ann Aylett, in 1768, had been a serious affliction. To domestic troubles and adverse fortune the political interest which now consumed most of his time had probably been a boon. Certainly Richard Henry's spirit had not softened towards the mother country. The sufferings of Massachusetts and its audacious stand against "tyranny" had more and more aroused his sympathy for that colony. The dour and almost Puritanical phase of his nature had become more marked. Day by day he seemed more like an Adams and less like a Virginia aristocrat. There was not an act of this Northern colony that he did not approve. He rejoiced as gleefully as Sam Adams when the tea was thrown overboard. At the same time he withdrew, in sympathy, from the opinions of the James River mandarins; his great-grandfather and grandfather, the two first Richards, would have been horrified to note the extent to which their descendant and namesake was abandoning their conceptions of divine right and turning to the democratic "leveling" of the masses. This admiration for New England was something Richard Henry never outgrew. It remained with him to his dying day. "For my part," he wrote several years after the first Congress, "I must cease to live before I cease to love these proud Patriots with whom I early toiled in the vineyard of liberty."

That Richard Henry's attitude towards the great prevailing question — Reconciliation with England or non-Reconciliation — would closely approximate that of the Adams clan was therefore to be expected. While he did not come to Philadelphia with his mind closed to accommodation, the early feeling of tenderness towards the British connection no longer ruled his spirit. From 1768, when the ministry began its policy of repression against Boston, Richard Henry's attitude underwent a startling transformation. The acts that converted Samuel Adams into an outspoken champion of independence similarly hardened Richard Henry's heart against Great Britain and the possibility of separation was something that he was entirely willing to contemplate. This feeling reflected the change that was taking place in Virginia itself. Perhaps it would be more accurate to say that new forces were gaining ground in the Old Dominion. The planters' stock, the James River group, — men like Peyton Randolph, Benjamin Harrison, Edmund Pendleton, all of whom were delegates to Philadelphia in 1774, — still found it impossible to regard themselves in any other light than as subjects of the British crown; the suggestion of a division of the British Empire was to them a horror; they clung to their allegiance on grounds not only of sentiment but of prudence. The democratic movement was gaining headway in Virginia, especially in the new Western country, but it was a development these great landholders strongly disapproved, and the British connection, with its royal governors, its royal Council, its monarchical ceremonial and its recognition of definite social classes, seemed a bulwark against this rising tide. New England, with its town meetings, district schools, Congregational churches, independent farmers, and rustic manners, — so the Virginia grandees regarded them, — its idealization of the common man, was not admired; and New England

seemed to be the leader for independence. That Samuel Adams
to whom the Lees became so devoted appeared to Harrison,
Pendleton, and Randolph as a rather uncouth creature, down at the
heel both socially and financially, a man who might well shout for
separation since he had nothing to lose; but men of great estates
and lofty rank must necessarily take their future, and that of their
families, into consideration. With most of these elder statesmen
Lee was personally unpopular. His extreme championship of
colonial prerogatives seemed a betrayal of his class; besides, the
sores produced by Lee's attack on the Robinson group who had
been plundering the public treasury ten years before were still
unhealed. That Harrison and Carter Braxton — a member of
the Continental Congress of 1775–1776 and a strong upholder
of the British connection — had been supporters of Robinson was
a matter of general knowledge, and this was in itself sufficient
explanation for their intense hatred of Richard Henry Lee.

All these Virginian adherents of Britain were outspokenly
opposed to Stamp Acts, duties on tea, Boston Port Bills, and the
other anti-colonial measures which had led to the Continental
Congress, but their purpose was reform, reconciliation, not a
resort to drastic measures such as war and independence. They
honestly hoped that his "gracious Majesty" would see a new light
and withdraw his unpopular acts, but were not breathing fire and
slaughter. Meanwhile, a small inner ring in Virginia had been
quietly at work for the preceding five years — a group whom
Jefferson, anticipating modern political terminology, referred to
as "forward men." In the House of Burgesses, the old conservative crowd still outwardly maintained supremacy, but in
1773, five or six "insurgents," to adopt another modern phrase,
began sedulously working in the other direction. Jefferson, in
his *Autobiography*, mentions the following as members: Richard
Henry Lee, Francis Lightfoot Lee, Patrick Henry, Dabney Carr,
and himself. The aim was to usurp that control over Virginian
action which the conservatives had wielded for several years and
to enforce a "progressive policy." Concretely, the programme
was to place Virginia emphatically on the side of Massachusetts
in its struggles with the king. The insurgents operated somewhat surreptitiously, but to definite effect. The meeting place

was a private room in the Raleigh Tavern at Williamsburg; here they would "cook up" — the expression is Jefferson's own — resolutions and policies, most of which subsequently became legislation of the House of Burgesses. The "Resolves" of March 1773 against transporting Americans to England for alleged offenses committed on American soil were wangled through the House by this little association. On the passage of the Boston Port Bill, Virginia set aside June 1, the day the measure was to go into effect, as a day of "humiliation, fasting and prayer"; this also emanated from the private room in the Raleigh Tavern, and, as Jefferson afterward admitted, was merely a scheme to publicize the issue and arouse the masses, who, in truth, were becoming a little "lethargic" over their wrongs. A more revolutionary document, written by Jefferson under the same inspiration, failed to meet approval. This took the flat stand that the British Parliament had no constitutional right to legislate for America; that the relation of the colonies to George III was precisely the same as that of the Kingdom of Hanover; he was their lawful sovereign, with all that that implied, but America was completely independent of Parliament — as independent as was Hanover itself. Parliament, in repealing the Stamp Act, had asserted its right "to bind the colonies in all matters whatever"; this Williamsburg Doctrine of 1774 insisted that it had no right to bind them in any case whatever. Thus was the new day bringing a new point of view! It will be observed that the back-room insurgents were thinking far ahead of their time and were rapidly approaching a state in which the word "independence" would have no terrors. It was a word which one of the "cabal," Patrick Henry, did not hesitate to use as early as 1774, almost as frequently and as loudly as Samuel Adams himself, and Richard Henry Lee was under suspicion of revolving the idea in his mind in a not unfriendly spirit.

The Lees, Jefferson, and Patrick Henry became members of the Continental Congress; Dabney Carr died in 1773. Patrick Henry and Richard Henry Lee appeared at the first session. Patrick Henry was the first speaker to address that body; Richard Henry Lee the second. Their speeches were significant of the new day. There is one infallible rule by which the conservatives and radicals on this great issue can be separated. Both groups were opposed to British policy, but the grounds of their opposition at once fixed them as "stand-patters" in the British connection, or "progressives." The old-timers argued against British exactions on constitutional grounds — such restrictions violated the age-long rights of Englishmen; the radicals controverted them on the grounds of "natural rights" — rights, that is, that are inherent in men as men, God-given to them at birth. One side appealed to Magna Charta and a long array of constitutional precedents, while the others fell back upon those old favorite philosophers, Locke, Harrington, and the rest. Richard Henry Lee's first speech, like Patrick Henry's, showed how far he had gone on the advanced side. The sentiments amounted almost to red revolution, for the colonies, Richard Henry declared, were "in a state of nature." That is, British authority had expired, three million Americans were without government, and had no standing except Mr. Locke's "right to life, liberty and property" — the last word subsequently expanded by Jefferson into "pursuit of happiness" — and thus must reconstruct their society on that basis. This sufficiently discloses Richard Henry's attitude towards British pretensions in 1774. John Adams also pictures him as in defiant mood. Although not adamant on the question of "independency," Lee was extremely advanced in his conditions for "Reconciliation." Every parliamentary measure affecting the colonies adopted since 1763 must be erased from the statute book. Especially must that Quebec Bill, annexing all territory north of the Ohio and east of the Mississippi to Canada, and establishing "Popery" as a state religion, be repealed. That insult to the Virginian empire rankled as keenly as standing armies and Boston port bills.

Such a counsel of perfection delighted the New England delegates, but made little impression elsewhere. Just what were the sentiments of John Adams, at this moment, on independence are not precisely recorded; his eagerness for such action a few months subsequently, however, makes it probable that in September 1774 the conception, if not enthusiastically welcome, was at least not obnoxious. He afterward declared that, for many years preceding 1774, he had regarded separation as certain, deplorable as it might be, and that, when Congress assembled, he nourished no illusions that a peaceful understanding could be accomplished. At this particular moment, however, the important Adams was not John; Samuel was then the New Englander on whom all eyes were fastened. To the "insurgent" Virginian he was the polar star. And on this question of separation from England Samuel was not merely acquiescent; he was fanatical. Independence had become as predominant a faith in his days as that Puritan religion which had made him what he was — a strict moralist and Sabbatarian, an intense nature that unerringly followed the inner light, a man tireless, unchanging, and unselfish in the pursuit of an ideal. Nothing mattered, fortune, position, fame, except one thing — the establishment of a free and independent American nation. The sincerity of Samuel's nature impressed all beholders then as it does to-day. Even those who reprobated him the most still found the elder Adams an object of fascinating interest; he was the one American, for example, who chiefly dominated the mind of George III, and no transatlantic voyager could be admitted to the royal presence without being closely questioned on this illustrious rebel. "The grand Incendiary" — such was the way in which loyalists referred to Samuel; it was a tribute to his power and singleness of aim. "He eats little, drinks little, sleeps little, thinks much and is most decisive and indefatigable in the pursuit of his objects," wrote his archenemy, Joseph Galloway, and the summation is not inadequate.

Samuel, indeed, was the great anchorite of the cause. While cousin John was munching dried sprats and consuming punch with gentlemen from Delaware and Maryland, and Richard Henry Lee was tossing off bumper after bumper of Burgundy with John Dickinson and other companionable Quakers, becoming, as John Adams wrote, "very high," Samuel could usually be found in his modest lodgings at Mrs. Yard's, writing letters and instructions to his fellow schemers in Boston, transmitting and receiving information by his private "express," Paul Revere. He was a wire-puller in an exalted political game. Samuel Adams had two great talents that effectively supported his emotional fervor: few Americans have ever equaled his skill as a manipulator of "faction," and as a controversialist and

pamphleteer hardly anyone approached him.   Certainly no others
were so persuasive and prolific.   Samuel is one American political writer whose "complete works" can never be assembled; they
are scattered in dozens of newspapers and gazettes, under twenty
or thirty signatures, — Vindex, Valerius Poplicola, Sincerus,
Candidus, to mention only a few that have been identified, —
and they would fill, if collected in volumes, a fair-sized library.
And they had a quality that influenced not only his native province,
but a continent, including those sections in Virginia whose representatives so eagerly awaited the author.   Despite his inflammatory opinions, Samuel's writings were calm, persuasive, dignified, and cutting, — "every dip of his pen," wrote John Adams,
who vastly admired his kinsman, "stung like a horned snake," —
for Samuel, contrary to present impressions, was a man of education, a graduate of Harvard, deeply read and by no means, despite
his humble manner of life, without culture.   Richard Henry Lee,
now his correspondent for several years, was somewhat taken by
surprise at first meeting, for he had heard much of Samuel's
poverty — the chief grievance Harrison and other patricians held
against him — and was hardly prepared for the suave and even
ornate gentleman who greeted him.   He was a man of medium
height, stocky in frame but as erect as a New England pine,
showing no signs of advancing years except a slight tremulousness
of hand and voice, with a blond, clear complexion and kindly but
piercing blue eyes; his attire, a new black cocked hat, sombre-
colored and expensive coat, silk black breeches, silk white stockings, glistening shoes with silver buckles, and heavy gold-headed
cane, almost put to shame the more commonplace garments of a
Randolph or a Lee.   Richard Henry, who did not know that
Samuel's Boston admirers had clubbed and purchased raiment
suitable to the new Congressional dignity, as well as advanced the
modest stipend Massachusetts allowed its representatives, was
possibly a little disappointed at finding his plain-living Puritan
so out of character.

But the two immediately became the closest cronies.   It was an
association that angered and alarmed the conservatives.   One of
the bitterest now summed up the leadership that presently took the
Continental Congress in hand: "Adams with his crew and the

haughty sultans of the South juggled the whole conclave of delegates." Indeed, in this first Continental Congress, there were few representatives disposed to assume a valiant stand against Great Britain, except the New England forces, led by the two Adamses, and the Lee-Henry contingent from Virginia. With the exception of a few scattered "patriotic" souls, — such as Samuel Chase of Maryland, Cæsar Rodney of Delaware, and Christopher Gadsden of South Carolina, — the Adams-Lee combination was confronted by a pretty solid wall of opposition. New York was irreconcilably on the king's side. James Duane was almost as extreme as Joseph Galloway, of Pennsylvania, in opposing New England-Virginia plans, and John Jay, who eight years afterward served as a member of the peace commission that alienated America from the British crown, and who became the first Chief Justice of the United States Supreme Court, was, in 1774, antagonistic to any action that might lead to rupture. "I cannot think that Government is at an end," was an expression constantly on his lips. New Jersey, under the lead of its Tory governor, William Franklin, illegitimate son of the great Benjamin, was working hand-in-glove with Galloway on the British side. The "pro-British" leader who commanded greatest authority was John Dickinson, the "Pennsylvania Farmer," former ideal of Arthur and the other Lees. The fact that a man whose writings against British policy had stirred the continent, and whose "Liberty Song" had fired hundreds of thousands of American hearts, should now counsel moderation in itself indicates that hostility to stamp acts and port bills did not in itself imply a desire for the disruption of the British Empire.

If living to-day, John Dickinson would probably be described as a "mugwump." Born to wealth, always accustomed to luxury and good breeding, finding his companions, from earliest childhood, among the educated denizens of fine country houses, Dickinson had that slightly distant and superior air, that habit of judicially balancing all sides of a question, that distrust of the masses, that confidence in intellect, all combined with a sincere desire to give his best, which make up a well-known type in modern American politics. John Adams, who disliked Dickinson intensely, — a sentiment most cordially reciprocated, — applied to him certain destructive adjectives: "very modest, delicate and timid"; but admiration for "the Farmer," in his new aspect, could hardly be expected from New England, for had not Dickinson advised Massachusetts to settle its quarrel with England by paying for the tea thrown into Boston Harbor? That extremely unpopular suggestion gives the key to Dickinson's attitude in Congress. Afterward, when suffering obloquy for his course, Dickinson issued a long and labored "vindication" of his career from 1774 to 1776. He assigns many reasons for his disbelief in American independence, at that time — the country's immaturity, its unpreparedness for war and its lack of foreign alliances. The real fact is that the gentleman who so ceremoniously called upon his fellow delegates in a fine coach drawn "by four beautiful horses" could not bring himself to sever relations with a country to which he was so proud to belong as England. The idea was repellent to his inmost nature, and the fact that he had himself sown much of the dissatisfaction that ultimately made separation inevitable did not alter this deep-lying emotion. Nor was Dickinson alone in his aversion to measures that would promote such a calamity. Probably a large majority of the First Continental Congress sympathized with him. Even Washington, in October 1774, on the eve of adjournment, sought an interview with Richard Henry Lee and John Adams to obtain assurances that their policy was not aimed at "independency" — an assurance that was given, and sincerely enough, for both men entertained hopes that the measures just adopted would preserve the British-American *status quo*. The episode illustrates not only the spirit of loyalty to king upheld by a large group, but the prevalent belief that the most dangerous enemies of Britain were the Virginia and Massachusetts leaders.

3

Practically all the acts of this first Congress bear evidence of the Adams-Lee association. The boycott of British goods was Richard Henry's pet measure for bringing Great Britain to terms. "Lee is absolutely certain that the same ship which carried home the resolution will bring back the redress," wrote John Adams, who, though he supported the scheme, did not share his friends' optimism. Both John and Samuel Adams and Richard Henry Lee served on the committee to draw up a Declaration of Rights; the document submitted was fiercely contested, point by point, by the die-hards; again that famous contention on "natural rights" versus the constitution raised its head, Lee and the Adamses, as usual, championing the philosophic contention, while "Mr. Galloway and Mr. Duane were for excluding the law of nature." John Adams wrote the most difficult article, on the jurisdiction of Parliament, and ultimately, after three weeks of acrid debate, licked the whole paper into shape — a *pronunciamento* which, in every paragraph, foreshadows the Declaration of Independence. But meanwhile a more revolutionary proposal — really an inflammatory one — was receiving attention. Again the Adamses — especially Samuel — and Richard Henry Lee were the moving spirits. After reading the Suffolk Resolves, it is difficult to maintain that there was no rebellious spirit in the first Congress. The hand of Samuel Adams appears in every line, though the responsible author was his intimate friend, Joseph Warren. This manifesto had been adopted by a meeting of Suffolk County, Massachusetts, — which included Boston and several large Massachusetts towns, — and was so revolutionary that the opposition described it as a declaration of war. Parliament had no jurisdiction whatever over the American colonies — such was the main contention; all Massachusetts was summoned to enlist its militia to full quota, to hold weekly drills, and to keep in constant preparedness for eventualities. Warren gave a copy to Paul Revere, who, at breakneck speed, brought the paper to Samuel Adams in Philadelphia. Despite ferocious conservative opposition, Congress endorsed this proclamation, adding insult to injury by publishing the action broadcast, thus making an exception to its rule of secrecy. It was the way in which all America placed itself on the side of Massachusetts. To John Adams it was another "epocha," and on the same day he wrote in his diary: "This was one of the happiest days of my life. In Congress we had generous sentiments and manly eloquence. This day convinced me that America will support Massachusetts or perish with her." At the same time was passed a resolution calling upon all the colonies for contributions "for supplying the necessities and alleviating the distresses of our brethren at Boston." The manuscript copy of this resolution exists in the handwriting of Richard Henry Lee.

One might suppose that the colonies, by this time, would have wearied of memorials, addresses, and petitions to the king, as methods of obtaining their rights. For ten years an unending rhetorical stream of this kind had flowed from America to the exalted seat of authority, without producing the slightest effect. Occasionally His Majesty would receive the essays "graciously"; more frequently they were never suffered to reach their destination, and seldom had they been deemed worthy of acknowledgment or reply. In reviewing the vast petitionary literature that preceded the break, one recalls the voluminous correspondence — the "notes" — that, in more recent days, America addressed to the German government, before the outbreak of war. In both cases the result was the same. Still the conservative force which, after all, controlled the First Continental Congress had not lost faith in epistolary methods of persuasion. So now another "whining petition," as John Adams called it, was regarded as in order — a last attempt to move the hitherto immovable. Richard Henry Lee, of all men, was appointed chairman, which meant that to him would fall the duty of composition. For three days, so important was the measure regarded, Congress debated on points to be incorporated. This debate significantly brought out the Virginian's sardonic state of mind. The excuse for colonial taxation, it will be recalled, was to raise money to "protect" the colonies, specifically to station an army of 10,000 in the Northwest Territory acquired from France in 1763. Richard Henry now proposed that the colonies, in their petition to the king, declare their willingness to provide such "protection" themselves. His resolution was to this effect: "The Congress do most earnestly recommend to the several colonies that a militia be forthwith appointed and well disciplined and that it be well provided with ammunition and proper arms." Naturally this suggestion made the loyalists squirm. Richard Henry's grim sense of humor must have enjoyed their mental gyrations. At this time Britain and America were on the brink of war; minutemen were organizing

North and South; and not unnaturally a suspicion prevailed that the resolution was only one item in that "preparedness" which the Virginian was now everywhere advocating. His conservative opponents at once saw the point, and inserted amendments that robbed the measure of all its "teeth." The manuscript of the unemasculated recommendation, among the Lee papers, carries this endorsement, in which all deceit is removed: "A motion made in Congress by R. H. Lee to apprize the public of danger, and of the necessity of putting the colonies in a state of defense. A majority had not the spirit to adopt it." Foolish majority! As a few months demonstrated, when the colonies, without trained men, or arms or ammunition, or supplies of any kind, found themselves face to face with the experienced soldiers of Great Britain.

How far apart radicals and conservatives were drifting appeared again when Richard Henry brought in the rough draft of his petition — a draft that was rough in more senses than one. The reading produced little less than consternation. In literary style it formed a complete departure from those lucubrations in which the colonies had previously "prostrated themselves before the Throne." This tentative petition exists to-day, in Richard Henry's handwriting, in the library of the University of Virginia, and a reading of it explains the amazement and protests it aroused. It is the effort of a weary and disillusioned man. Lee had composed so many papers of this sort in ten years that his ennui and "asperity" — this was the word Dickinson applied to his draft — are easily understood. After the usual initiatory assurances of devotion to His "gracious Majesty," the author descants on the "brave and loyal people of Massachusetts Bay," — these same people at the moment being the particular objects of royal detestation, — informs George III that the "glory and prosperity of Great Britain" are owing largely to the American colonies, — so far as foreign trade was concerned, and all that successful trade implied, this was true, — and then, in no gentle, diplomatic fashion, instances the "unexampled oppression" America had endured throughout His Majesty's reign. But the harshest shafts are reserved for the peroration. The king's "Tory councillors" — these are Lee's precise words — are pilloried, as well as their "violent and unconstitutional councils." They are, the memorialist proceeds, undermining the principles of the "Revolution" — that is, the revolution of 1688, which established parliamentary supremacy and placed William and Mary on the throne — and are a constant danger to the Hanoverian dynasty. The petition even threatens war. "The machinations of such men . . . shall never succeed if they can be prevented by the fullest exertion of the lives and fortunes of your Majesty's loyal and affectionate subjects in North America." Who are these men? The irate Virginian names the king's most intimate confidants, and in this petition goes so far as to demand their dismissal from royal favor! "Our apprehension of danger can never cease so long as the unwise and destructive councils of Lords Bute, Mansfield and North are suffered to approach the throne."

Clearly, Congress made a mistake when it selected Richard Henry Lee as chief petitioner to the king, and the mistake was speedily rectified. That John Adams chuckled as the incendiary phrases fell upon astonished Congressmen, most of whom had come to Philadelphia in the search for reconciliation, may well be imagined, and probably Richard Henry did not expect his draft to meet acceptance. The usually stilted minutes of the Continental Congress on this occasion possess genuine eloquence. "The address to the King, being brought in, was read, and after some debate, ordered, that the same be recommitted, and that Mr. J. Dickinson be added to the Committee." Clearly Mr. Dickinson was selected for the purpose of "editing" or "revising" the composition of the impatient tobacco planter, a duty he performed in the same way that countless editors have performed it since; he threw this fine Virginia rhetoric into the waste-paper basket and wrote an entirely new petition. It was a masterpiece of its kind, interweaving many of Lee's less acrimonious points, but doing so in language urbane, even obsequious; the eulogy passed upon the Dickinson dissertation and other American state papers by Lord Chatham has often been quoted. Unfortunately it was not similarly appreciated by the monarch to whom it was addressed. It fell to Arthur Lee and Franklin to present this petition at the British court. The parchment was delivered to Lord Dartmouth, Secretary for the Colonies, who in due course informed Lee that His Majesty had received it "very graciously" and was pleased that it was so "decent and respectful." A few days afterward Arthur paid a visit in the country to Lord Chatham, in the course of which there was much talk of the petition. "He approves it exceedingly," wrote Arthur to Richard Henry. "His words were, 'the whole of your countrymen's conduct has manifested such wisdom, moderation and manliness of character, as would have done honor to Greece and Rome in their best days. *Laudari a laudato* [1] should make us cautious that we support the character by a manly perseverance in those measures that support it.' His opinion is that a solemn settlement of the question, by a renunciation of the right to tax on one part, and an acknowledgment of supremacy on the other, might be made. My object is to unite the heads of opposition upon one uniform ground, which, with the present popularity of our cause, will I think enforce a complete abolition of these pernicious measures. . . . The inconsistency of this plan is no objection to the probability of it, for these men have long been disciplined to turn and turn and turn again. But you may learn from it that there is little cordiality in the relief to be given and that we are to hold a jealous eye over the measures of men whose minds are actuated against us by the bitterest rancor and revenge. . . . Let no hasty gleam of hope go forth which may tend to make men remiss in their exertions or relax in the terms they demand."

The subsequent fate of the document seems to have been checkered. By "graciously" receiving it the king's interest apparently ended, and Dickinson's fine essay was left to shift for itself. Dickinson afterward ruefully recorded that his petition and other similar revolutionary exhibits ultimately found their way to the House of Commons, where they were finally discovered "bundled up in a mass" and labeled "American papers."

4

The situation that confronted Congress in its second session, in May 1775, was quite different from the one that prevailed in 1774. Great Britain and her American colonies, to all practical purposes, were now at war. Lexington and Concord had been

[1] To be praised by a man who is himself praised.

From the Independence Hall Collection

JOHN DICKINSON, 1732–1808

RICHARD HENRY LEE, 1732–1794

From Portraits by Charles Wilson Peale

fought a month before the delegates assembled; Bunker Hill, Ticonderoga, and the invasion of Canada took place soon after that body started its deliberations.   Events like these, one might think, put an entirely new face on the question of *Reconciliation* vs. *Independence*.   The Second Continental Congress, however, at least in the early months, was more pacific than its predecessor. The outbreak of hostilities, far from solidifying American sentiment against separation from Great Britain, seemed to have had a contrary effect.   The truth is that these warlike demonstrations abruptly brought the colonies face to face with the most appalling decision in their history.   Disunion had previously been a more or less academic question; but now it became a reality.   Bunker Hill made Americans appreciate, as they had not appreciated before, the imminence of division, and they recoiled before the impending change.   The crisis served only to incite the conservatives to new attempts at accommodation.   To them war with England — then actually being waged — did not signify "Independency," but merely a method of bringing Great Britain to terms and securing colonial rights.

There were some realistic souls, indeed, who saw the inevitable issue.   The New England-Virginia junto overcame any doubts they may have held.   Samuel Adams, an enthusiast for independence since 1768, threw off all disguise, preached it in conversation, and presently assumed an active position in Congress.   John Adams, who had looked regretfully on separation, abandoned all hesitation and showed only anger and scorn at colleagues still inclined to temporizing.   Richard Henry Lee was now keen for an open pronouncement.   Virginia was also suffering from British depredations, for Lord Dunmore, royal governor, was ravaging the eastern country and inciting negroes against their masters; the New England and Virginian leaders, therefore, now found themselves closer comrades even than in 1774.   The delegation from the "ancient Dominion" had considerably changed.   An important accession was Francis Lightfoot Lee, whose geniality and charm, and unswerving devotion to the cause, had at once made him a brother to the Adams clan.   "Lee is a brother of Dr. Arthur," observant John confided to his diary, "and of our old friend Richard Henry, sensible and patriotic, as the rest of the family." The anti-Lee and anti-New England contingent in the Virginia delegation, however, was still strong. Carter Braxton, a new arrival, was, as already said, extremely hostile. It was not only independence he and his sympathizers feared, but the consequences of independence. Secession from the king, they believed, — and rightly enough, — could result in but one thing, and that was republicanism, a system they despised. Nothing seemed to them so abhorrent as the thing they called the "levelling system of New England," and the possibility of Virginia being converted into a country of small landholding democrats, with town meetings, selectmen, and psalm-singing Congregationalists and Presbyterians, — for such was the nightmare their imagination called forth, — vastly cooled their desire for an independent America. It is said that the Virginia patricians had sent the fiery Braxton, already eminent as a foe of Yankeedom, to Philadelphia to forestall such a calamity. "I am satisfied," Braxton wrote home, "that the Eastern colonies do not mean to have a Reconciliation. Two of the New England colonies[1] enjoy a government purely democratical, the nature and principal of which, both civil and religious, are so totally incompatible with monarchy that they have ever lived in a restless state under it. . . . I am convinced the assertion of independence is not far off." Yet the sentiments of other Virginians were sympathetic to New England and its anti-British aims. There is no evidence that George Washington ever spoke in Congress, — except when he was voted command of the Continental army, — but he appeared at this second session clothed in military uniform — more significantly eloquent than a hundred Patrick Henry speeches. George Wythe, lawyer and scholar, was ready for all eventualities; even the word "independence" did not startle him. But there was one new delegate from Virginia destined to plunge a deeper sword into the old Virginian system than all the New Englanders extant; this was a sandy-haired young man of thirty-three, already famous as a penman of resolutions, protests, "views," and the like, the Thomas Jefferson who, a few years before, had organized the "forward" men of the House of Burgesses into an anti-British bloc.

[1] Connecticut and Rhode Island.

The Declaration of Independence is something so immemorially American that few realize to-day the terrific battle it caused in the Congress of 1775–1776. The achievement was the work of this Virginia-New England coalition. Practically all the rest of America, with an occasional oasis of independence, was still for reconciliation, though, with the exception of one man, the leadership for peace was not particularly able — certainly not brilliant on the floor. That man was John Dickinson, who, for several months, carried the middle states and at times part of the lower South in the hollow of his hand. Dickinson came to the second Congress a greater enemy of the Adams-Lee crowd than ever. The outbreak of hostilities had had the same effect upon him and the Quaker-Proprietary interest that it had exerted upon the stalwarts of New York and New Jersey. England and America on the brink of war! John Adams gives a picture of Dickinson in May 1775 which reflects his state of mind. "He is a shadow; tall but slender as a reed; one would think, at first sight, that he could not live a month; yet upon a more attentive inspection, looks as if the springs of life were strong enough to last many years." That this spectre was still full of fire Adams and his Virginia partisans were quickly to discover. In the interval between the two Congresses greater pressure than ever had been exerted on Dickinson. That Dickinson was sincere in his devotion to the British connection his bitterest enemies never denied; the fact is also true that all the strongest motives affecting human action — property, professional standing, social relationships, family and friends — were now brought to bear to enhance his zeal for the royal cause. His marriage, in 1770, to the daughter of one of the richest and most distinguished Quaker families had created an environment hardly sympathetic to radical opinions.

The plain New Englanders who were entertained at Dickinson's beautiful and sumptuous country estate, with its gardens and vineyards, its comprehensive library and its majestic view of the Delaware, did not feel themselves in a setting congenial to democracy. The difficulty of the situation in Pennsylvania, as in Maryland, was the proprietary interest. In the one the Penns, in the other the Baltimores, as lords of the country, were necessarily royalists, for, with the disappearance of the king, their domains would pass from their control. The Pennsylvanians selected for the Second Continental Congress were thus more royalist than the first. Franklin[1] indeed, now a delegate, had for years been combating the proprietary family, but certain new members — Thomas Willing, James Wilson, Robert Morris, and Andrew Allen — were outspoken foes to separation. With this combination Dickinson had long been a sympathetic coöperator, and in the struggle between the colony and the Penn family he had championed the Penns, thus becoming a lifelong rival to Franklin, who had espoused the popular side. Dickinson's early manifestation of sympathy for the American cause had aroused apprehension in the family circle. His mother and wife kept warning of the danger of pushing the question to extremes. "You'll be hanged, Johnny," his mother would exclaim, and pressure from his wife, heiress of Fairhill, was even more insistent. So great was Dickinson's reputation, however, and so deep the affection and respect felt for him by Congress, that his influence on the assembling of the new session was profound — in the early weeks, indeed, sufficient to forestall the plans of the New England and Virginia delegates. The three most powerful men in that revised body were Dickinson, John Adams, and Richard Henry Lee, and Dickinson proved, in the early period, more powerful than his old-time friends.

Massachusetts and Virginia came to Philadelphia with well-defined plans. The safety of America, they declared, lay in a resort to arms. Such being the case, any further negotiation with Great Britain was not only mistaken but dangerous. In warfare time is the important matter; further correspondence would mean delay in military preparation, the lulling of the public conscience into a sense of false security, and would thus spell defeat. The vigorous prosecution of the prevailing war, the creation of a navy and the outfitting of privateers, the formation of independent state governments, the union of these governments into a confederacy, a declaration of independence, the making of alliances with foreign powers, particularly France and Spain — this was the effective programme on which the Adamses and the

---

[1] Franklin did not become a delegate until the second session of the Continental Congress. He had just returned from a long sojourn in England.

Lees united.   And this was the programme that the opposition, under the lead of Dickinson, successfully circumvented — for a time.   One important consideration told in their favor.   A colonial combination against Great Britain, to be successful, must be practically unanimous.   A majority, even a large one, would not suffice.   But in the summer of 1775 no majority, to say nothing of unanimity, was at the disposal of the radicals.   Dickinson "controlled" not only the five middle colonies, — New York, Pennsylvania, New Jersey, Delaware, and Maryland, — but, on an issue such as separation from Great Britain, the three lower Southern commonwealths, North Carolina, South Carolina, and Georgia.   All these sections were willing to fight the mother country in order to obtain redress of grievances, but to "sever the political bonds" was another matter.   Philadelphia became a hotbed of intrigue in the effort to keep these lower "doubtful states," as they would be called to-day, faithful to the royal mother.   Many of the delegates had brought their "ladies" to Quakertown, and these became the object of social attentions. There were teas, dinners, parties, and trips to great estates in the country.   Dickinson's early victory clearly rested upon personal grounds and ingrained loyalties, and certainly his programme showed no genius, no originality, and practically no promise of success.   Against the robust policy of the Lee and Adams group, their plan of open opposition to Great Britain, culminating in a declaration of independence, Dickinson could only bring forward his familiar proposal, — already tried with no success, — a second petition to the king!   His fine literary effort of the previous year had been kicked from one official servant to another, yet he insisted on trying his hand again.   Only the fact that Dickinson, with straight face, suggested this feeble step saved it from general ridicule.   The suggestion made the radicals rage and groan. In letters and in his diary John Adams gave vent to his disgust: "This measure of imbecility," he called it, "will find many admirers among the ladies and fine gentlemen" — perhaps the irascible Yankee was thinking of the parties and dinners — "but it is not to my taste.   Prettiness, juvenilities, and much less puerilities — become not a great assembly like this, the representation of a great people."

Bad blood was brewing between the New Englanders and the

Quaker spokesman.   One day John Sullivan, a witty Irishman from New Hampshire, was making a speech, holding the proposed second Dickinson petition up to laughter.   The angry Pennsylvanian, who could not stand this kind of debate, rushed out into the yard, where Adams was taking his ease.

"What is the reason, Mr. Adams," this usually restrained gentleman shouted, in what Adams afterward described as a "violent passion," "that you New England men oppose our measures of reconciliation?   There now is Sullivan, in a long harangue, following you in a determined opposition to our Petition to the King.   Look ye!   If you don't concur with us in our pacific system, a number of us will break off from you in New England and we will carry on the opposition ourselves in our own way."

Though shocked at Dickinson's rudeness, Adams made a cool reply.   The two men never spoke to each other again.   A few days afterward Adams wrote his celebrated letter to James Warren, which was intercepted and published by the British. In this he referred to Dickinson as a "certain great fortune and piddling genius whose fame has been trumpeted so loudly," and who "has given a silly cast to our whole doings" — that is, by his petition.   This publication reached Philadelphia and was gleefully passed from delegate to delegate.   Mr. Adams, in his diary, has made an inimitable record of the sequel.   "Walking to the State House, this morning, I met Mr. Dickinson, on foot, in Chestnut Street.   We met and passed near enough to touch elbows.   He passed without moving his hat or head or hand.   I bowed and pulled off my hat.   He passed haughtily by. The cause of his offense is the letter, no doubt, which Gage has printed in Draper's paper.   I shall, for the future, pass him in the same manner; but I was determined to make my bow, that I might know his temper.   We are not to be on speaking terms nor bowing terms for the time to come."

This gives a fair idea of the personal feelings aroused by the proposal to assume a stiff attitude to England.   Personal hostility, too, was venting itself on Richard Henry Lee.   His relations with John Jay, Dickinson's ablest ally, were becoming strained.   The fact that Arthur Lee had written a letter from London, describing Jay as a "suspicious character," — suspicious, that is, in his lukewarmness towards independence, — and that its contents had been whispered from delegate to delegate, did not improve relations between the New Yorker and Richard Henry. "These gentlemen," wrote Jefferson, after describing one unimportant altercation, "had had some sparrings in debate before, and continued ever very hostile to each other." By the latter part of the year Jay advanced more formidably upon the adversary. The Adams-Lee alliance was beginning to make progress, the influence of their ideas was spreading, and a plan for driving a wedge between New England and Virginia, of separating their leaders and thus breaking the united front, appeared to be the indicated strategy. In the fall two committees had been appointed: one the Committee on Commerce, organized to procure the importation of war munitions; the other a Committee on Secret Correspondence, the title subsequently changed to that of the Committee on Foreign Affairs, its business being to consider relations with European countries and to obtain, if possible, recognition and even alliances. Of course, this latter committee had mainly in view France and Spain. The mere statement of the purposes of these committees indicates their importance. They were, indeed, the most radical steps Congress had so far taken, and the two ends aimed at — the procurement of war munitions and negotiation of treaties with foreign governments — would naturally make them of the utmost concern to advocates of independence. Yet this "forward" group was ignored in forming the committees. It is significant of the power exercised by Jay, Dickinson, and their allies that such an exclusion had been accomplished. Most members appointed belonged, incongruously enough, to the "cold element," the crowd not working for independence; many were Tories of extreme types. The only Virginian appointed was Harrison, notoriously hostile to independence. New York and Pennsylvania, most fiercely opposed to an independent America, held control. As previously all important committees had included members from all sections of America, embodying all schools of opinion, this pointed discrimination aroused little less than a sensation. Its meaning was too clear: adherents of the

British connection had evidently obtained control of Congress, and from now on, the manœuvre seemed to say, not so much would be heard of the New England and Virginia firebrands. Yet the way of repentance was laid open to one of the outcasts. A day or two after this slight had been inflicted, John Adams received a visit from John Jay. The purpose of the call was evidently to explain why Adams had been ignored. The ingratiating New Yorker, then only twenty-nine, began the conversation in the most diplomatic manner — appealing to Adams in his vulnerable spot, his vanity. Adams's character, he said, stood very high in Congress and there was only one thing that prevented him from being universally acknowledged the foremost man in it. And what was that?

"There is a great division in the House," answered Jay, "and two men have effected it, Samuel Adams and Richard Henry Lee. As you are known to be very intimate with these gentlemen, many others are jealous of you."

At this the Adams backbone, not famous for its resiliency, stiffened at once. He had no claim, he replied, to be regarded as the first man in Congress; if such a valid title existed, he would decline to assert it. However, he had thought it very strange that no Massachusetts man had been placed upon the Secret Committee of Correspondence, and had attributed "the omission" to some "secret intrigue out of doors." "I am a friend and very much attached to Mr. Lee and Mr. Adams, because I know them to be able men and inflexible to the cause of their country."

And then in one icy sentence the Massachusetts statesman extinguished the hopes which had clearly inspired Mr. Jay's visit: —

"I cannot therefore become cool in my friendship for them, for the sake of any distinctions that Congress can bestow."

Adams, as a parting shot, informed Mr. Jay that the considerations that had led to the composition of the committees were apparent. He thought that commercial projects and private speculations had something to do in the choice of members. This is probably what he meant by "a secret intrigue out of doors" — that is, outside the walls of Congress. But the overwhelming motive was "the great division in the House on the subject of Independence and the mode of carrying on the war."

And so Jay's embassy failed. Its only result was to draw the Lee and the Adams family closer together. "Mr. Jay and I," writes Adams, "parted good friends and have continued such without interruption to this day."

Despite Adams's brave defiance, the middle colonies clearly held the upper hand — far more than the balance of power. Dickinson wrote his new petition, as polished in style and as loyal in sentiment as its many predecessors, and entrusted it to the hands of Richard Penn, of Pennsylvania, about to sail to England. However, His Majesty refused to receive the appeal; instead he issued a proclamation declaring the colonies in a state "of open and avowed rebellion," and, as such, out of the royal protection. It would seem that a douche of cold water like this would discourage the most obsequious souls; it did not have that effect, however, upon the Dickinson cohorts, who were apparently only spurred to new endeavors for reconciliation. Nor did they lack resourcefulness. In one respect — and in one respect only — the Continental Congress resembled that distinctive American institution, the Presidential Convention, with the exception that issues, not candidates for office, were the great matters in question. The alignment of the colonies on independence — their division into three groups, those definitely against, those definitely for, and those "doubtful," and therefore objects of persuasion from both sides — has a familiar sound. Unfortunately materials are not available for a detailed picture of this first great American essay in political struggle and wire pulling; the *Journals* of Congress, which give only the skeleton of proceedings, bear little resemblance to the garrulous *Congressional Record* of modern times; yet, from the scattered correspondence of members and from their reminiscences in after years, it is plain that these pioneers in a fruitful field hit upon an effective and favorite device not unknown to the present generation. That is the practice of "instructing" delegates. After the failure of the royal petition and other schemes of accommodation and delay, the pro-British leadership began to tie the hands of the colonial delegations in this fashion. Practically all the assemblies in which anti-independence was strong passed resolutions forbidding their representatives to vote for any motions that in the slightest degree savored of separation. North Carolina set the example in November 1775. South Carolina followed suit, and Georgia had already adopted an even more effective method of veto — its delegates appeared in Philadelphia so few times, and so irregularly, that its indifference to independence, if not its hostility, was made plain. New York had refused to approve the proceedings of the first session, and its merchants repudiated the non-importation and exportation agreements. Pennsylvania took the same stand, New Jersey, Delaware, and Maryland promptly following the example. Poor Virginia and New England! In February 1776, they found themselves isolated, their leaders fighting a lone hand; with such great commonwealths as New York and Pennsylvania joined to their neighbors and the lower South, only the most optimistic souls could anticipate success. Congress, if another modern comparison may be permitted, was definitely deadlocked, and the jubilation of the "Proprietary Gentlemen" was unrestrained. Even the recalcitrant members from the "Antient Dominion" set up a rejoicing. The violent Carter Braxton was shaking his fist at New Englanders — "I hate their government — I hate their religion — I hate their levelling" — and Jefferson, in a letter to a friend, referred to "the extreme, imprudent and inimical conduct of his lady."

Yet the humiliation of New England and Virginia was not so complete as it might seem. Most of the country, in its official aspect, was apparently solidified against them, yet there were distinct forces working in their favor. The Assemblies had voted against independence, but to what extent did these bodies represent public opinion? The new year — the great year 1776 — brought many indications that the masses, even of the colonies apparently most wedded to the British connection, such as New York, Pennsylvania, and Maryland, were not entirely reconciled to these official acts. In Pennsylvania and Maryland, parties of long standing had been fighting the proprietary governments, and the same forces which had been struggling against these dominant aristocracies now took stand against "instructions" to their delegates; the anti-proprietary forces were numerous and influential, the leader being Benjamin Franklin. Even in New York the "mob," as Duane and Livingston called the great proletariat, was extremely hostile to the action of its legislature. One could pass in review the colonies recorded as opposing the proposed declaration and find, in all cases, a large minority, and, in most, probably a good majority of the agricultural and working classes, in a state of anger at the false position in which they had been placed. Several happenings now put new life into this, as yet, inarticulate public opinion.

His Majesty, as usual, came to the support of the Virginia-New England irreconcilables. The contemptuous treatment of Dickinson's last petition, combined with the denunciation of the colonies as "open and avowed rebels," and the virtual reading them out of the British Empire, made countless adherents to the patriotic cause. John Adams was joyful. The king himself, he exclaimed, has declared America independent; why should the colonies hesitate to follow the royal example? Thomas Paine's *Common Sense,* published in January of the new year, had an incalculable influence in turning the people from Great Britain. The logic of the situation was unavoidable. New England insisted that America had been independent since the battle of Lexington; a vote by Congress would only recognize the reality; besides, there was no chance of foreign recognition and assistance without a declaration. Why should France recognize America if America refused to recognize herself? The argument was a powerful one.

These and other influences had produced such changes in public sentiment that the Lees and the Adamses decided to play their greatest card. The one place where a victory would bring widespread success was Pennsylvania, and there the proprietary crowd was making its final battle for life. The Penns and their large following had a weighty stake in the event; this family, said Franklin, were the greatest landowners known to history; their farm, which they managed as a farm, making the largest possible revenue and paying the smallest possible taxes, comprised 35,000,000 acres! Pennsylvania's change from proprietary colony to a state independent of the British crown meant that this vast territory would pass from private to public control. A resolution introduced on May 10 ultimately accomplished this result. It called upon all colonies to adopt state governments independent of the British crown. "It was brought before the committee of the whole house," wrote John Adams to James Warren, "in concert between Mr. R. H. Lee and me." To dissolve at a stroke all existing American colonial governments — to make them return, as Adams and Lee would say, "to a state of nature" — would seem a heroic measure, possibly not within the powers of Congress; the *coup d'état* was justified, however, by success. At a stroke, the elaborate paternal systems that had ruled Pennsylvania and Maryland since settlement fell in ruins. The excitement of the enemy was intense. Livingston, of New Jersey, confided his emotions to Jay. "It has occasioned great alarm here and the cautious folk are very fearful of its being attended with many ill consequences next week when the Assembly are to meet." And Duane wrote to the same correspondent: "The resolution was first passed and then a committee was appointed to fit it with a preamble. Compare them with each other and it will probably lead you into reflections which I dare not point out." John Adams had his customary outbreak of epistolary rejoicing. "This day the Congress has passed the most important resolution that ever was taken in America." The reason for his happiness came out in the debate. While this was in progress Duane, still an unreconciled Tory, called out to Adams: —

"It is a machine for the fabrication of Independence."

Adams turned towards the adversary with his most gracious smile: —

"I think it is Independence itself."

5

Matters were developing most favorably now for the patriotic party. On this very May 15, North Carolina instructed its delegates to vote for independence — thus withdrawing previous enactments of a contrary import; South Carolina had already fallen into line, and, on May 20, Button Gwinnett and Ly-

man Hall arrived from Georgia with powers to take such
action on the great question as the welfare of all the colonies
seemed to require. New Jersey in June dismissed its loyalist
governor, William Franklin, and selected a new batch of delegates, instructing them for independence. But the really decisive step had been taken by Virginia. Harrison and his allies,
in February, according to John Adams, were still attempting
to hold Virginia for the king. Adams's references to this distinguished citizen are most uncomplimentary. "Harrison was
still counted among the cold party. This was an indolent, luxurious, heavy gentleman, of no use in Congress or Committee, but
a great embarrassment to both. He was reported to be a kind of
nexus utriusque mundi, a corner stone in which the two walls of
party met in Virginia. He was descended from one of the most
ancient wealthy and respectable families in the ancient dominion
and seemed to be set up in opposition to Richard Henry Lee."
All Harrison's machinations, however, availed nothing. Virginia had for several months been in a state of upheaval against
Great Britain. County conventions everywhere were passing
resolutions for independence. Two Lees were active in this
provincial disturbance, Richard of Lee Hall, that "Squire" who
figures picturesquely in family annals, and Thomas Ludwell Lee,
brother of Richard Henry. Richard Henry in a letter to General Charles Lee [1] now spoke the decisive word: "You ask why
we hesitate in Congress. I'll tell you, my friend, because we
are heavily clogged with instructions from these shameful Proprietary people and this will continue till Virginia sets the example of taking up government and sending peremptory orders
to their delegates to pursue the most effectual measures for the
Security of America."

This letter was written April 22, about three weeks before the
decisive blow had been struck against the "Proprietary people";
on the very day that "epochal" resolution passed, Virginia, in
convention assembled, acted on the suggestion in Richard Henry's letter. The body was of distinguished membership. Ed-

[1] This Charles Lee, whose subsequent career was so odious, must not be
identified with the Virginia Lees. He was not an American, but an Englishman, in no way related to the Virginia family.

mund Pendleton was president, and Patrick Henry added his oratory to the universal fervor. The far-reaching resolution, introduced by Thomas Nelson, commanded Virginia's delegates in Philadephia to move at once for three things: a declaration of independence, a confederation of the thirteen independent states, and foreign alliances. The passage of this measure was followed by one of those celebrations in which Virginia delighted: Williamsburg was illuminated almost as gayly as on the repeal of the Stamp Act; a special subscription was passed to purchase grog for the soldiers, and toasts were drunk, accompanied by the discharge of firearms, to "American Independence," to the "Grand Congress of the United States and their respective legislatures," and to "General Washington." Richard Henry Lee was notified of the pleasant command now laid upon him, in a letter from his brother, Thomas Ludwell Lee: "Enclosed you have some printed resolves which passed our convention to the infinite joy of the people here. The preamble is not to be admired in point of composition nor has the resolve for Independency that peremptory and decided air which I could wish. However, such as they are, the exultation was extreme. The British flag was immediately struck at the Capitol and a Continental hoisted in its room." And Squire Richard sent an expansive — for him — notification to John Adams.

6

In this way Richard Henry Lee's great moment came. The Resolution of Independence, printed at the beginning of this chapter, now exists, in Richard Henry's handwriting, as one of the treasures of the Library of Congress; presumably the phrasing — subsequently incorporated in Jefferson's Declaration — was his own. These eight or ten lines made the American colonies the free and independent nation that we know to-day. It naturally was a solemn moment when the tall and handsome Virginian rose to offer this pronouncement. Unfortunately, however, the materials do not exist with which the scene may be reconstructed. Tradition has had much to say of the beauty and nobility of Lee's oration, but not a phrase or a word has been preserved.   The same is true of the seconders, John Adams and George Wythe.   Though these authentic speeches are lost, one can supply the deficiency by reading the history of the American Revolution written by the Italian, Charles Botta.   So great a theme, the romantic Italian believed, demanded the method of Thucydides, so, like the Greek historian, he composed speeches for his heroes and generals.   His most ambitious efforts are the orations put into the mouths of Lee and Dickinson, who pro and con each other in best Periclean and Alcibiadean style.   But evidently Lee's hearers needed no Attic oratory to stir them to conviction. As a matter of policy a final vote was postponed for three weeks to give the proprietary colonies, which were still wrangling over the subject of independence, time to reach a decision.   When that period had expired, their attitude — excepting that of New York, which remained on the king's side until the Declaration — was fixed.   All the twelve other colonies cast votes for independence.   In Maryland, Pennsylvania, and Delaware popular sentiment had won; the authority of the proprietaries had been overthrown, and the colonies that, in early June, seemed opposed to the step now joined the almost unanimous procession.

Meantime, on June 11, a committee of five had been appointed to draw up the Declaration — the document that would explain "to a candid world" the reasons for separation.   It was then the practice of parliamentary bodies, as it is to-day, to appoint the mover of a resolution chairman of the committee selected to carry it into effect.   In accordance with this time-honored procedure, Richard Henry Lee should have become the author of the Declaration of Independence.   However, when the vote was counted Lee's name did not appear as chairman; he had not even been chosen a member of the committee.   The persons selected for this work were Thomas Jefferson, John Adams, Benjamin Franklin, Roger Sherman, and R. R. Livingston.   The Lee family rankled under this slight for a hundred years.   To an ambitious man ·like Richard Henry, the disappointment must have been crushing, though he stood the blow manfully, his letters of this time betraying no repining.   According to one family tradition, Richard Henry missed this chance at immortality because he had hastened to the bedside of his wife, at

Chantilly, said to have been alarmingly ill. But there is plenty of evidence that this was not the case. That he left Philadelphia to serve as delegate at the Virginia Constitutional Convention is evident from a passage in a letter from Williamsburg to General Charles Lee, of June 29: "The desire of being here at the formation of our new government brought me from Philadelphia the 13th of this month."

Had Lee been appointed chairman of the Committee on the Declaration, however, there is little doubt that he would have remained in Congress. Just what went on in the inner circles of those exciting days will never be known; but that a fierce struggle took place over the chairmanship of this committee is plain. The Harrison-Braxton wing in the Virginia contingent hated Richard Henry Lee, for reasons most creditable to Lee himself; his action in the Robinson scandal, already mentioned, was sufficient explanation. Lee's whole policy since then — his friendly attitude toward political equality, his association with Patrick Henry, Jefferson, and other "levelers," his alliance with John Adams and company for independence and confederacy — still further alienated the overlords of the James. Not unnaturally they organized to keep Lee off this committee. Their favorite choice for the chairmanship sent shivers down John Adams's spine: this was Benjamin Harrison himself — a suggestion so startling to the radicals that they were only too glad to drop Lee and turn to another man! It is a little difficult at the present day to realize that Thomas Jefferson, as author of the Declaration of Independence, was a "compromise candidate," but such seems to have been the fact. John Adams told the story in one succinct sentence: "Jefferson was chairman because he had most votes and he had most votes because we united on him to the exclusion of R. H. Lee, in order to keep out Harrison."

Jefferson had been a member of Congress for about a year, but had attended sessions only intermittently, and had taken no part in discussion. He had thus aroused no antagonisms, and was precisely the kind of candidate upon whom rival factions could unite. But, above that, he had one superb qualification: he was the ablest writer in Congress, his pamphlets had given him international fame, and one in particular, his *Summary*

View, had produced the profoundest impression in Philadelphia. John Adams reports that, in pressing Jefferson to retire, take his pen, and write the Declaration, he gave, as his main reason: "Because you are ten times a better writer than I am." The same comparison could be made with Richard Henry Lee. Certainly America has had no cause to regret that the Declaration fell to Jefferson, and not to his fellow Virginian. The event did not ripple the friendship between the two men. On July 8, Jefferson sent Lee a copy of his paper as originally written, before being subjected to certain excisions by Congress in committee of the whole. Lee, in his answer, signed himself "your affectionate friend," and commiserated on the changes made in this draft. The most important passage disapproved was Jefferson's denunciation of the slave trade, and it is to this that Lee referred. "I wish sincerely, as well for the honor of Congress, as for that of the states, that the manuscript had not been mangled as it is. However, the *Thing* in its nature is so good, that no cookery can spoil the dish for the palates of Freemen."

All members of the Virginia group signed the Declaration — even Harrison and Carter Braxton. In this the last two showed the distance, in character, that separated them from John Dickinson. The doughty Quaker, consistent to the end, did not append his signature to a paper that violated his conscience. He suffered greatly at the time for this, but posterity has given him that honor owing to all men who, at the risk of ruin, insist on upholding their convictions. Especial tribute should be paid Dickinson, for, unlike others of his Philadelphia circle, he did not "go over" to the king, but, after his countrymen had made their decision, accepted their verdict loyally, took arms in defense of the American cause, became its staunch champion for seven difficult years, and subsequently rendered conspicuous service to the new nation, especially at the critical time when it came to adopt the Constitution.

IX

FIGARO AND "LE SIEUR LEE"

I

THE influence of the Lee and Adams families extended far beyond the borders of America. Eight months before the Declaration their policies had reached London and Paris and were profoundly affecting European diplomacy. In November 1775, Congress chose its Committee on Secret Correspondence for the purpose of sounding foreign governments and obtaining foreign aid. This body, presently transformed into the Committee on Foreign Affairs, was the beginning of the American State Department. It selected, as its secret agent in London, Arthur Lee, who thus became the first diplomatic representative of the American nation. Not that Arthur was emblazoned to the world as an American ambassador. He was embarking on a ticklish business, in which silence was the main necessity. That French genius subsequently associated with Arthur Lee catalogued as indispensable talents for delicate negotiation "a head, a heart, arms and no tongue," and Benjamin Franklin's instructions to Lee on his mission in England emphasized the same points. "It would be agreeable to Congress to know the disposition of foreign powers toward us and we hope this object will engage your attention. We need not hint that *great circumspection and impenetrable secrecy* [1] are necessary. The Congress rely on your zeal and abilities to serve them and will readily compensate you for whatever trouble and expense a compliance with their desire may occasion. We remit you for the present £200. Whenever you think the importance of your despatches may require it we desire you to send an express boat

[1] The italics are Franklin's.

with them from England, for which service your agreement with
the owner there shall be fulfilled by us here."

Arthur's real task, as he understood, was to obtain the sympathy
and coöperation of the Bourbon governments of France and
Spain in the transatlantic rebellion. This might seem quite a
responsibility to place on a man of thirty-four. What possible
interest could the two great autocracies of Europe, both of them
possessing colonies that might readily emulate the example of
successful revolution, have in giving this enterprise their blessing
and helping it with materials of warfare? Merely to state the
problem would seem to show its absurdity. Sons of Liberty,
Revolution, Republicanism — how could these ideas appeal to
powers that for centuries had upheld and practised absolutism in
government? The spirit of Machiavelli was an active force in
European politics, however, and, according to his teachings, any
means were justified that served the purpose of the state. Americans are still too much inclined to look upon their Revolution as
an isolated event, peculiar to America; the fact is that, soon after
the struggle began, it became involved in European politics —
in European eyes it represented merely one phase of the Old
World battle for power. Certain chivalric Frenchmen might
join their fortunes to the colonial armies, in a zeal for liberty and
adventure; the minds directing French and Spanish policy, however, saw in the uprising an opportunity of realizing ambitions
in no way identified with freedom and democracy.

The new French king, Louis XVI, was nephew of the Spanish
monarch, Charles III; for fifteen years, since 1761, these two
branches of the House of Bourbon had been united in the celebrated "Family Compact," as important an influence in the
European politics of the day as was the Triple Alliance before
1914. This Family Compact existed for one purpose: the main-
spring was jealousy and hatred of England, and the object in view
was the humiliation of the ancient foe and her destruction as the
dictator of Europe. Spain had reasons enough for an anti-
British attitude, — the traditional inheritance of hostility, based
on antagonistic character and ideals, on memories of the Armada,
the War of the Spanish Succession, England's possession of
Gibraltar, the defeats, with consequent loss of territory, in the

Seven Years' War, — but the fires of hatred burned with even greater intensity in France. The humiliation she had suffered in 1763, at the hands of Great Britain, can be paralleled only by the indignities heaped upon the Gauls by Germany in 1871. William Pitt, in the eighteenth century, and Bismarck, in the nineteenth, afford many resemblances in their temper towards France: both hated the ancient foe; both were determined to eliminate her as a first-class power; and both, one with the impregnable British fleet, the other with the unconquerable German army, accomplished their purpose — at least for a time. In 1763, as in 1871, France emerged from a ruthless war prostrate and seemingly stripped of all hope for the future; in both crises, however, France accepted the inevitable with a soul burning for *revanche* and reëstablishment as the great Continental nation. The outlook, however, in 1763, was not encouraging. So far as European alliances and resources were concerned, there seemed little chance of regaining the prestige enjoyed under Louis XIV. England's wealth and sea domination precluded any hopes in that direction. But the outbreak of troubles between Britain and her American colonies opened a new vista. In no place did the Stamp Act of 1765 arouse such delight as in France; in no place did its repeal of 1766 spread such gloom. England's fatuousness in starting troubles anew in 1767, the storm that rapidly ensued, the Continental Congress — all these events put new heart in French statesmen. From 1765 to 1776, the French government kept a small army of spies in the American colonies to observe the rising tide of animosity toward the mother country; French archives to-day are full of their optimistic reports.

Why did France identify her own resurgence with the separation of England from its colonial empire? Her Foreign Ministers, first Choiseul and afterward Vergennes, believed that England's wealth, and consequently her power, depended upon this new Britain growing up overseas. Strip Albion of her vigorous children, these statesmen argued, and the haughty foe would sink into a minor kingdom, stranded in the North Sea, while France would ascend to new glory on her ruins. French and Spanish statesmen were not the only ones who held these views; the most enlightened English leaders entertained the same opinion. This was certainly the conviction of Pitt and largely explains his heroic efforts to preserve America for the British crown. It was the strength derived from the colonies, he said, in the speech on the repeal of the Stamp Act, that enabled England to wage the Seven Years' War and to emerge from it with Europe at her feet. At that time British foreign trade amounted to £4,000,000 a year, three fourths of which was with America; these figures look small to-day, but in the period before the great industrial age they were really huge; no other nation had any source of economic strength comparable with it. From this trade had developed the great British merchant marine, and from this, in turn, that mighty British navy, now the unquestioned mistress of the seas. By 1775 this transatlantic trade had grown to £7,000,000, and with the amazingly rapid increase in the American population no one could foresee its limits; so long as the American colonies remained a part of Britain, Choiseul and Vergennes believed, there was no hope of displacing her; France and most of Europe must remain under the British heel. It is therefore apparent why the independence of America seemed to these despairing statesmen like a new era, and why monarchical distaste for rebels and republicanism was not sufficient reason for thrusting aside the opportunity heaven had placed in royal hands. In the pending dispute France did not aim at territory — not even Canada and other American possessions of which she had been recently ravished. She wanted one thing, and one thing only: American independence, the absolute separation of Great Britain from her possessions overseas.

This is one reason why the Declaration of Independence was a consummate act of statesmanship, for that gave France and her associates the argument they needed for assisting the cause. Even before the Declaration Congress had taken a step that virtually implied the same thing. Here again the statesmanlike strategy of that Continental Congress appears in high light. Up to the First Continental Congress, Great Britain had enjoyed a monopoly of the American trade. Under that mercantile system which still held economists spellbound, all American products went to England, in British ships; and Americans could purchase manufactures and other supplies in no country except Great Britain and British possessions. But Congress changed all that: by its embargo on British trade it closed all American ports to English ships, thus ending the monopoly which, Chatham maintained, was the source of England's commercial ascendancy; and in April 1776 it opened American ports to other nations. Here was another consideration in the eyes of French statesmen for American independence; obviously this new system of free trade could not endure if the colonies were suppressed. It is therefore evident that when the Secret Committee, on November 30, 1775, selected Arthur Lee as a confidential negotiator and sounder-out of Bourbon propensities, it did not leave his hands empty of persuasive arguments. Not only was the atmosphere of Europe friendly to colonial success, but he presently had material advantages to dangle before the covetous eyes of Europe.

2

By this time both of the brothers Lee had attained established positions in London. The sacrifice they were called upon to make for the colonial cause had been a serious one. Arthur, called to the bar in April 1775, had quickly become identified with important cases, and had before him an eminent and lucrative career. In March 1775, Benjamin Franklin, Agent for Massachusetts, sailed home; his important office, for which Arthur had been acting as deputy for several years, now became his own. In the prevailing situation, this post was one of great dignity, for the Massachusetts agent served virtually as ambassador between Congress and the British court. William Lee had also prospered. Not only had he become one of the successful tobacco traders in London, but he had entered on a unique political career. From 1773 to 1774 he served as one of the two sheriffs of London; and in May 1775 he was elected alderman for Aldgate ward, in succession to John Shakspeare. That an American, a citizen of one of Britain's most rebellious colonies, should have been chosen to this high post, a month after the battle of Lexington, not only indicates the popular respect entertained for the new incumbent, but displays the incongruous state of popular opinion at the time towards America. No American had ever before been an alderman of London; one must not associate the honor with the rather dubious estimation the title inspires to-day in American cities; an alderman of London, in the time of George III, was one of the great men of the City, with his chains and robes, his official coach, his public banquets, his duties as magistrate and lawgiver, and his position as leader of the Livery — that is, the freemen, the voters — of his ward. The office was for life and, as the body was a small one, the likelihood was strong that the incumbent, if he lived long enough, would become Lord Mayor. Neither was William Lee called upon to abandon his American opinions on reaching this office; indeed, probably these convictions had much to do with his election. This ancient city had no admiration for the home policy of George III, nor for his attitude towards the colonies, and had recently chosen as Lord Mayor that John Wilkes who was such a riotous enemy of both. One of William Lee's first official acts as alderman was to accompany Wilkes when he made his unwelcome approach to the throne, to present the protest of the Lord Mayor and aldermen against the American policy; that petition, incidentally, had been written by Arthur Lee, and when, a few months afterwards, a letter arrived from Philadelphia expressing the thanks of Congress, this address proved to be the work of Richard Henry Lee. It was not until many years afterward that the two brothers, comparing notes, discovered the part each other had played in this correspondence! All this shows that William Lee had to make no compromise with his conscience in entering his honorable office. In his speech accepting the aldermanship, he boldly set forth his attitude, and his sentiments were received with cheers by his constituents: "As an American I declare it my wish that the union between Great Britain and the colonies may be reëstablished and remain forever, but that constitutional liberty may be the sacred bond of that union." This view was then held by most Americans, even of the forward type, such as Richard Henry Lee, John Adams, Thomas Jefferson, Franklin, Washington, and most of the rest; it was also the view of the party with which the Lees in London were identified. Both Arthur and William, as years went on, had become closer to Wilkes, at the same time maintaining their association with the Chatham-Shelburne group, whose political programme differed little from that of their more obstreperous colleague.

But the Lees probably found more than political satisfaction in the Wilkes environment. Arthur especially, while he enjoyed the more sedate companionship in the country of Shelburne and Chatham, also liked to join in the animated society that gathered in the Mansion House, under the genial hospitality of the immortal demagogue. A French writer described these evening parties as *soupers libertins;* unquestionably they had a free, Bohemian character quite new to that solemn establishment. Wilkes assembled not only the writers, actors, men about town, and politicians of London, but the most enlivening visitors from overseas. One of these was Count Lauraguais, a French nobleman and millionaire, famous not only for his wit, his diplomatic escapades, his many comedies and tragedies, — most of them, alas! unacted, — but for his association with Sophie Arnould, the great French opera singer, as celebrated for her artistry on the stage as for the depravity of her life. His epigrams, which frequently appeared in collected editions, explained the visits of Lauraguais to London at this time; his sojourns were compulsory, for Lauraguais's bright sayings, usually directed at the mighty characters of the court, caused him to be exiled five times. What more charming place of rustication could he find than the supper parties of John Wilkes? But Lauraguais, like his host, compensated his lighter traits with more solid qualities, for science, medicine, and the law occupied his soberer moments, his attainments in chemistry making him an intimate of Lavoisier and co-worker in his experiments. Another enthusiasm that was reaching fever heat in this year 1775 was the American Revolution; in this Lauraguais saw the fulfillment of his political ideas, and its leaders he heralded as reincarnations of virtues long since lost to mankind. Other famous forgatherers at Wilkes's were Gudin, author of a history of France in thirty-eight volumes, — a work for which the poor man never found a publisher, and which reposes to-day, in all its unread immensity, in the Bibliothèque Nationale, — and that most astonishing character of an astonishing age, the Chevalier D'Éon

— or Chevalière, for the speculation on this person's sex was as widespread as that concerning his occupation in England. At certain periods of D'Éon's life he — for there is no mystery to-day about his sex — appeared in woman's garb, "smoking, drinking and swearing like a German trooper," as one observer remarked, and the fact which rendered this disguise especially strange was that it was assumed at the command of the French king, who would not let the man appear in France otherwise garbed. It was D'Éon's activities that brought to London, and immediately to the Wilkes coterie, another Frenchman who became the bosom friend of Arthur Lee. The association rested on practical as well as sympathetic grounds. This new recruit labored under one serious disqualification: of the English language he knew only one solitary word — that "Goddam" which, he said, was constantly echoing in his ears, and which, he protested, must be the foundation of English speech. This observation, introduced into the traveler's most famous play, created a new species of the human race, the "Goddams" — a word which, in France, now became the accepted name for Englishmen. Manifestly a man with so restricted a vocabulary, especially as he had so much to say, incessant conversation being the rule of his being, would join hands with an acquaintance who spoke such excellent French as Arthur Lee. The discovery was quickly made that the two new friends had more in common than a means of communicating ideas; their ideas on most outstanding subjects, above all the one that was filling Arthur's time, were invariably in agreement.

This new arrival bore a name — not his by birth — which is one of the glories of French literature; his two most celebrated plays, *The Barber of Seville* and *The Marriage of Figaro,* still hold their place in classic French repertoire, and, embellished by the music of Rossini and Mozart, are performed constantly to-day in all the opera houses of the world. Pierre Augustin Caron de Beaumarchais was now in his forty-third year; in that comparatively brief time he had crowded all the excitements, public disputations, transitions in fortune, duels, imprisonments, exiles, and sentimental adventures that made up the career of so many French characters in the latter part of the eighteenth century —

the age that produced Cagliostro, Mesmer, the Cardinal de Rohan, and Voltaire. In variety of life and trade the man bears a strong resemblance to that gentleman of endless resource and many occupations, his own Figaro. Watchmaker, musician, song writer, dramatist, author of memorials that set all France in an uproar, courtier, man of fashion, financier, industrial promoter, publisher, shipowner, filibusterer, secret agent of French kings and their mistresses, pamphleteer: all these trades Beaumarchais had followed, and, in addition, had spent more than one term in jail, had had to meet whispered accusations of poisoning three wives, — here there was a little slip, for he had had only two, and the charge, even in this amended form, was never regarded seriously by French public opinion, — and had actually been convicted of forgery and of attempting to bribe a French judge, through his wife, into a favorable verdict. The comparison to Figaro is well made, for life to Beaumarchais, before it was anything else, was *bon théâtre,* and its every transaction was a scene in a play; he was always the actor, and in every episode, even the most trivial, the leading man. Beaumarchais, said Henri Martin, "loved everything — renown, money, philosophy, pleasure, and, above all, noise." It was his genius for self-exploitation that gave the man his start, for Beaumarchais did not begin life in circumstances presaging so romantic a career. Born the son of a watchmaker, Augustin Caron — for such was his baptismal name — had little schooling; apprenticed as a boy of thirteen to his father's trade, he was presently expelled from the family hearth for his scapegrace life, but, restored on the promise of reform, quickly lifted the ancestral firm to eminence by the invention of a new escapement — a contraption that made possible the production of watches of minute size. Soon these dainty timepieces were the rage of Paris and were adorning the bracelets of Madame de Pompadour and dangling on the necklaces of other court beauties. When a rival watchmaker began infringing this discovery, Caron set up a howl that echoed from one end of Paris to another; he quickly made it the occasion of his first *coup* of advertisement, succeeding in having his claims passed on, not by the courts, but by the learned Academy of Sciences, which, after protracted hearings, decided in the young

CHARLES GRAVIER, COMTE DE VERGENNES

PIERRE AUGUSTIN CARON DE BEAUMARCHAIS

*Portrait by J. M. Nattier, Courtesy of
Frick Art Reference Library*

man's favor.   As a result, Caron became *horloger du roi,* and a person of interest to the court.   The triumph likewise made him the friend of a lady of rank and fortune, several years his senior, whom he married on her husband's timely death; her influence secured a position as comptroller of the royal pantry, and presently the youthful Caron, having abandoned his trade, appeared in magnificent vesture, bearing the plate containing the king's meat, which he was also permitted to place before His Majesty.

The post was not a menial one, but was usually reserved for a member of the aristocracy; in order to qualify, Monsieur Caron purchased — with his wife's money — a title of nobility, deriving his style from one of her family's more obscure estates, adding to his name that de Beaumarchais which he was destined to make immortal.   When a haughty court noble twitted Caron upon his sudden elevation, the youngster replied: "I know I am an aristocrat, for I have the parchment conferring nobility and a receipt for the money it cost me."   There was no stopping a man like that, and Beaumarchais, with his instinct for showmanship, soon justified his new station.   He had one advantage that easily made the court, especially its feminine side, forget his plebeian origin: his exterior was most handsome; he was tall, slender, erect, with manners not eclipsed by peers of the realm.   His talent for repartee, for brilliant conversation, for composing these *séguedilles* and couplets that were the fashion of the day, for his skill on several musical instruments, especially the harp and the flute, made him the favorite of every woman and the object of jealous detestation to most courtiers.   To those four sedate ladies, neglected daughters of Louis XV, known to history as Mesdames, Beaumarchais proved a solace; if he deserves no other praise, the brief period of brightness he brought into their lives is an item on the credit side.

But Beaumarchais was more than a hanger-on of courts; he was a man of intellect, profoundly interested in human institutions, a commentator, both in his plays and in his more formal writings, on the sordid aspects of the time.   The raciest man of a racy epoch, his pen was courageously to uncover the social and political abuses of contemporary France and do its part in destroying that court in whose favor, as a young man, he so proudly basked. At the moment of his appearance at the Wilkes *soupers libertins,* however, his fortune was in decline. The greatest dramatist of his day was an outcast before the law: the French Parliament had issued against him its decree of *blâme;* had pronounced him *infâme* and deprived him of French citizenship and all civil rights. The Goezman case — too long and complicated for consideration in this place — had caused this terrible sentence; it was the one in which Beaumarchais had been accused of forgery and attempted bribery of the court. At the same time the disgrace had been a triumph; for, unable to secure any advocate to plead his cause, Beaumarchais undertook his own defense, and produced those *Memorials* assailing, with magnificent vituperation, the very Parliament which was trying him, exposing its venality and injustice — orations which did not save the man from punishment, but which made him the hero of France. "All Paris," Beaumarchais afterward wrote, "left their cards at my door the day following my conviction." In the hope of regaining the favor of Louis XV, and the reversal of his ostracism, Beaumarchais entered royal employment. His duties were not dignified or even, in normal conditions, self-respecting, but they had great consequences for the new United States of America; they brought the author of *Figaro* to London, to the Wilkes circle, and to the group plotting the American Revolution. A notorious blackmailer named Morande had written the biography of Madame du Barry, under the rather unpleasing title, *Mémoires secrètes d'une fille publique.* Beaumarchais was sent to England by the king to purchase this scamp's silence, acquire his manuscript and all printed copies of the book. He succeeded so adroitly in this mission that the classic has vanished from literature; not a copy is in existence to-day. Probably Beaumarchais would have received his reward — restoration to civil rights — except for one thing: Louis XV died immediately on his return from the victorious quest.

But *Figaro* promptly entered into similar engagements with Louis XVI. Now followed his most famous embassy, the one that brought him into association with Arthur Lee and the American cause. This concerned that same Chevalier D'Éon — or Chevalière — who had long been an ornament of the Wilkes

entourage. This man for years had been a thorn in the side
of the French court. For he also had literary gifts: in addition
to an extensive correspondence, his published memoirs filled seven
good-sized volumes. But his epistolary works were what especially interested French statesmen. Precisely what this "dyna-
mite" — as one would call it to-day — consisted of is not known,
but it was clearly of a highly explosive character. D'Éon was
a more important person than the others with whom Beaumarchais had dealt, for he was a nobleman who had held high posts
in the diplomatic service, especially in Russia. His letter file
was full of state secrets; if made public, so it was said, war would
ensue between England and France and half the courts of Europe
would fly at one another's throats. It was in May 1775 that
Beaumarchais appeared in London on this delicate business.
For eight months he kept running back and forth from Paris,
the final treaty with D'Éon not being arrived at until Christmas.
However, these visits presently assumed another interest, which
lifted Beaumarchais to a new plane and brought him, among
other things, the quashing of the *blâme* of "infamy" and restoration of all rights as French citizen. From the job of queller
of blackmailers and the status of political outcast Beaumarchais
was transformed into secret intermediary between France and
those revolting colonies of whose existence French ministers were
supposed to be diplomatically unconscious. It was the greatest
rôle in Beaumarchais's histrionic career — and he made the most
of it.

3

Beaumarchais came to London in August 1775, with two distinct missions. One was to complete the difficult negotiations
with D'Éon; the other was to renew an old friendship with Lord
Rochford, British Foreign Secretary. Many years before, in
Spain, Rochford, then British ambassador to His Catholic Majesty, and Beaumarchais, then spending several months in Madrid
on a personal mission, — a mission that ultimately provided him
with the Spanish background of his most successful plays, —
became boon companions; both men were excellent musicians

and used to while away many hours singing duets. Vergennes now hoped to turn his harmonious association to state account; he encouraged Beaumarchais to resume his duets with the Foreign Secretary, in the expectation that so charming a companionship would have practical results. Rochford, the French minister believed, was not especially keen mentally, and might easily fall victim to Beaumarchais's musicianship and let drop an occasional state secret. At that time Vergennes had formed no plan for aiding America; it was a matter in which Beaumarchais apparently had little interest; but accurate information on the state of affairs in Great Britain would be useful to France. Beaumarchais succeeded to the extent of reëstablishing relations with Rochford; the reports he sent home, however, indicate that his efforts as an observer were not especially to the point. On September 21 he addressed a letter to the king, conspicuous for its inaccuracy and misinformation. England is pictured as on the verge of revolution; in a few months most members of the cabinet will lose their heads, while the king is to be deposed and driven from the country. England is facing ruin — if her enemies only have the sense to take advantage of her miseries. The Americans have 80,000 men in full arms and the British forces in Boston are slowly starving. The colonies are already lost and civil war is soon to deluge Britain.

There is nothing in this letter about giving aid to the Americans, — who, in fact, seem already to have won their liberties without European assistance, — and nothing about the political motives which made such action excellent statesmanship for France. The man who wrote it was far at sea about the British-American imbroglio, to say nothing about the domestic situation in England. The French historian of the participation of France in the American Revolution, Henri Doniol, declares that this memorial is so foolish as not to deserve reprinting; clearly at this time Beaumarchais had not formed any conception of the part in that great proceeding that was to be taken by France. Three months afterward, however, on December 7, 1775, Beaumarchais again writes the king, in very different spirit; the project of French assistance to the Americans had evidently taken form, the purpose of this memorial being to remove certain scruples that still paralyzed the royal will. In it Beaumarchais gives the youthful Louis XVI a preliminary lesson in the technique of Machiavelli: it is even commendable to break a treaty if such violation of faith will promote the welfare of France! It is a strange, one might almost say impudent, communication; Beaumarchais at this time was officially an outcast, with no rights of citizenship; yet his letter is almost peremptory in tone, instructing the king on his royal duties, comparing his present spirit most unfavorably with that of Louis XIV, even that of Louis XV. Encouraged, perhaps, by royal acquiescence, Beaumarchais continued his course. The important document in this correspondence is the famous memorial of February 29, 1776, addressed *au roi seul*. This is one of the great state papers of history — great, at least, in its consequences, for it is the presentation that drew the family of Bourbon into the American cause. The very first sentence discloses a philosophic insight hardly to be expected from the gay and volatile Figaro. "Sire — The famous quarrel between America and England, soon to divide the world and change the European system, makes it necessary for each power carefully to examine in what way this event of separation can effect it and either be an advantage or a destructive influence." And the examination follows — eloquently phrased, always pitched in dramatic form, for this was the big scene in the life of Beaumarchais. The memorial was a plea for French secret aid to the colonies, and the argument was based on precisely those grounds most likely to prove irresistible to the French government.

It is evident that, between the composition of the ridiculous letter of September 21 and the mature reasoning of February 29, 1776, Beaumarchais's mind had undergone a change; he had received a sound education in the pending British-American difficulty. Who had been his instructor? The question is unnecessary; only one man could have fulfilled that rôle. Only one man in London was qualified and authorized to discuss American policy with an emissary of the French king; that was the gentleman whom Beaumarchais called "Le Sieur Lee, secret representative of the colonies in London." The six months preceding February 29, 1776, Beaumarchais had spent in London, with occasional trips to Paris; that he passed much time with Arthur Lee his correspondence clearly indicates. Arthur's chambers in the Middle Temple served as one meeting place; a third party to the conversations was Lauraguais, as keen a promoter of American interests as Arthur himself. Arthur was an animated talker, full of ideas, impulsive in persuasion, and in Beaumarchais's correspondence we can almost feel him constantly at the Frenchman's elbow, now cajoling, now pleading, now demanding. That insistence, even that arrogance, which Arthur's colleagues in Paris subsequently found so irritating evidently served their purpose when used on the impressionable Figaro. The indomitable man did not even hesitate to employ threats, and the noble art of bluffing was not to him unknown. This is no exaggeration, for Arthur appears in all these lights in the memorial that worked so powerfully on the king. For the letter is really a little drama, in which the main performers are Arthur Lee and Beaumarchais. It was a collaboration, Arthur furnishing the ideas, Beaumarchais the rhetoric — and splendid rhetoric it was. M. Doniol, who inspected the complete correspondence in the French archives, makes the same point — the memorial, he says, was written by Beaumarchais "in concert" with Lee. So alive was the dramatist's genius that this document, supposed to be a solemn state paper, had a title, like a play: "War or Peace." The most interesting part of the dialogue is placed in the mouth of Arthur Lee. Arthur is portrayed as weary of French procrastination and the scruples of the king; after several months of discussion, of writings back and forth, he turns almost ferociously on Beaumarchais with demands for what to-day would be called a showdown. The time has come when the impatient American resorts to threats: let France beware, for if the aid solicited is not forthcoming, her position in the future world economy will be a sad one! Says Figaro: —

"On the other hand le sieur L. (M. de Vergennes will give your majesty his name), secret deputy of the colonies in London, completely discouraged by the failure of the efforts he has made through me to obtain assistance from the French Minister in the shape of powder and munitions of war, said to me to-day: 'I ask you for the last time, has France definitely decided to refuse us all help and to become, because of this unbelievable torpor, the dupe of England and laughing stock of all Europe? Oblige me by replying positively; I await your final answer so that I may give mine. *We offer France, as reward for its secret aid, a secret treaty of commerce. This treaty will give France, for a certain number of years after peace is established, all the advantages of that commerce with which for a century America has enriched England. This trade will pass to France, and in addition, we agree to guarantee French possessions to the full extent of our power.*[1] Do you not wish this?' "

There is a vast amount of guile and statesmanship in these few sentences. The transfer of America's commerce and trade to France, and the guarantee of her sugar islands in the West Indies — clearly America had plenty to offer in exchange for French consideration. That trade, as related above, was regarded by French statesmen — and by British — as the foundation of England's power. And there is a particular ominousness in Lee's remark, "I await your final answer so that I may give mine." Lord Shelburne, Arthur's friend and leader of the opposition, had recently proposed a settlement of colonial troubles on the basis of erasing from the statute book all colonial legislation passed after 1763. Had this proposal been made at this time — four months before the Declaration of Independence — the chances were strong that it would have been accepted, and that the country known as the United States would to-day be a dominion of the British Empire. Probably Arthur Lee, even though he was secret agent of Congress, did not have complete authority to commit his country, but his power was sufficient for diplomatic purposes — the assumption of authority, when such assumption would gain an advantage, was a device Arthur never hesitated to avail himself of. Here again he was a Lee. Beaumarchais quotes him as follows: —

"I need ask of Lord Shelburne only the time it takes for a ship to sail to America and return — a ship which will inform congress of England's proposals; and I can tell you now what resolution congress will adopt in the matter. It will immediately issue a public proclamation in which all the nations of the

[1] Italics in original.

world will be offered, in order to obtain their help, the terms which I today offer you secretly. And to revenge itself on France and force her to make a public declaration in their interest which will commit France absolutely, they will send into your ports the first ships they capture from the English: then in whatever direction you turn, this war which you are seeking to avoid and which you so greatly fear, will become inevitable. For either you will receive our prizes in your ports or you will refuse to do so. If you receive them a break is certain with England: if you reject them, at that moment congress will accept the conditions offered by the mother country. The Americans in anger will join all their forces to those of England and fall upon your islands and prove to you that the splendid precautions that you have taken to guard your possessions will be precisely those by which you will be forever deprived of them."

This threat looks like rather high talk; yet the fact is that nothing Lee could have said would so have assailed France on the raw. Americans to-day are vaguely aware of certain French islands in the West Indies, especially Martinique and Guadeloupe; but they are not regarded as important. No one can visualize the positions these outposts of empire held in the France of the eighteenth century. Commerce in those days involved mainly certain indispensable staples — tobacco, rice, indigo, sugar; and the sugar of its leeward islands was the greatest article in French trade. Of them all Guadeloupe was the largest and richest. It was sugar of Guadeloupe, converted into molasses, and smuggled into New England ports, — in violation of English law prohibiting trade with other than English islands, — which caused that Molasses Act of 1733, New England's first grievance against the British government. That Guadeloupe was regarded as an asset of imperial consequence the peace negotiations of 1763 made clear. In the Seven Years' War, England had captured both Canada and Gaudeloupe; the problem now confronting Britain was whether she should keep the barren wilderness to the north or add this teeming sugar country to the Empire — for the possibility of keeping both was not practical statesmanship. Popular opinion, and it seems at times Pitt himself, inclined to Guadeloupe; a memorial of Franklin's, in favor of the Canadian country, is said to have exercised almost decisive influence and saved Britain from a ghastly mistake. But that Britain still covetously regarded the great sugar islands France well knew, and that she could seize them at a moment's notice, once relieved of her colonial troubles, was as plain as daylight. Arthur Lee's threat, therefore, was no idle one and it gave Beaumarchais one of the most effective arguments for assistance.

"Go to France, Monsieur," Lee continued, in this historic interview, "go to France and display there this picture of affairs. I am going to shut myself up in the country until your return —I do this so that I may not be forced to give an answer [to Lord Shelburne] until I have received yours. Tell your ministers that I am prepared to follow you, if necessary, in order to confirm in Paris this statement of the case. Tell them also *that I have just learned that congress has sent two deputies to the court of Madrid with the same purpose in view, and that I can add, for your benefit, that they have received a very satisfactory answer.*[1] Can the French Council today have the glorious privilege of alone being blind to the glory of the King and the interests of his kingdom?"

Here then Arthur Lee seems to have risen to the stage of an ultimatum. The British were considering an offer of peace which conceded all the points Americans, especially the Washingtons, the Lees, and the Franklins, had been contending for. Arthur now gave the French king a few moments to think the matter over. That Beaumarchais took the matter seriously is evident from his comment to the king on Lee's proposal: —

"There, Sire, is the terrible and impressive picture of our position. Your Majesty sincerely wishes peace! The way in which you can preserve it, Sire, I shall now set forth in this memoir."

The French dilemma, as Beaumarchais now presents it in categorical form, has a strange sound to-day, but it furnished the final argument that led to French assistance. It resembles certain reasons advanced to persuade the United States, in 1917, to intervene in the European struggle. Either England, wrote

[1] Italics in the original.

Figaro, would crush the colonies or America would succeed in winning its independence. In the first contingency hated Albion would emerge so powerful that all Europe would be at its feet, and the seizure of the French West Indies would be the task of a summer's day. If defeated, with the loss of those colonies that made up the nation's wealth, Great Britain would seek "compensation" elsewhere; in this case the French West Indies would represent a slight recompense for her loss. This was the idea Arthur Lee had been instilling into the Frenchman's mind for nearly a year. And how could France avoid the calamity? Again we hear the voice of the Lee-Adams junto. Neither the Massachusetts nor the Virginia statesmen at this time desired an alliance with France. The letters of Richard Henry Lee reiterate a conviction that American independence must be her own achievement; Arthur's constant promptings to Samuel Adams — "American liberty must be of American fabric" — insist on the same determination. John Adams's unfriendly attitude to French intervention at this early stage is no secret. But France had certain things that the insurgent colonies absolutely needed. Before the Continental Congress Adams was pointing out the part that France could play. No political connection, no military expedition; but saltpetre, cannon, stands of arms! Massachusetts had dearly learned the importance of such accessories. Twice, at Bunker Hill, Massachusetts farmers had sent the British redcoats reeling; they would have done so the third and the fourth time, except for one thing — the two attacks had exhausted their ammunition. The ordinary materials of war were so scarce in Washington's army, then before Boston, that Franklin, in all seriousness, advised that the soldiers be armed with bows and arrows. What the revolutionists desired of France at this moment was not recognition and an alliance, but war supplies. What were the demands being made upon the French by Le Sieur Lee at this final interview? Beaumarchais mentions them specifically: "Powder and other munitions" — to be supplied in secret, roundabout fashion.

And this latter point was the rub. Louis XVI was a gentlemanly sovereign, keenly conscious of the fine honor that should direct the relationships of kings; the idea of surreptitiously arm-ing for rebellion the subjects of a monarch with whom he was openly on terms of friendship was revolting. The thing simply was not done. Royal etiquette forbade it. Besides, there was the hesitation of Spain. Charles III, king of that nation, was Louis's uncle; the two countries had been linked in closest alliance fifteen years; there was no man for whom the French king had such reverence, and whose advice meant so much, as the occupant of the Spanish throne. This was the real reason for the hesitation of Vergennes that made Figaro and Le Sieur Lee so impatient. So long as Charles refused to associate Spain with the plots of Paris and Beaumarchais, the French king remained obdurate. Even the urgings of his queen, Marie Antoinette, who was partial to the *braves américains,* did not resolve his scruples. All the finespun arguments of Beaumarchais did not bend this young sovereign usually regarded as so weak and pliable; the respectful casuistries of Vergennes had not caused his royal master to deviate from his duty; time was pressing, Britain was known to be massing large forces for transportation to America, yet majesty was inviolate. Probably only one person in Europe could have led Louis XVI to behave in the underhanded manner desired; if Charles of Spain would only take his stand! The springs of history are frequently trivial and capricious; who would have imagined that Arthur Lee, all unconsciously, would have been the means of easing the conscience of royal France? Arthur undoubtedly died never knowing the part he had played; not until M. Doniol published his documents, in 1888, did the facts about this little comedy come to light.

In Arthur's vehement tirade to Beaumarchais, quoted above, he referred to two emissaries sent by Congress to the Spanish court — not without success. Whether Arthur, in saying this, was himself a little *rusé,* or was merely reporting unverified rumor, is not apparent. Vergennes, however, regarded the intelligence as of such importance that he immediately communicated it to Grimaldi, Prime Minister of Spain. Was Le Sieur Lee's statement true? Had American envoys already obtained assistance from His Catholic Majesty? Grimaldi immediately replied: No, it was not true. "No one has asked us to furnish help to the revolting colonies, consequently we have not given any." This *démenti,* however, was not the important part of the letter. Spain had given no help, Grimaldi went on, but she was entirely willing to do so. In one cynical sentence, Grimaldi sets forth the attitude Spain pursued then and afterward toward this international question. The "formula," as the diplomats say, was sharp and concise. "Certainly it is to our advantage that the rebellion of these peoples be supported. We ought to wish that they and the English reciprocally exhaust each other!" Spain hated both England and the colonies; England on historic grounds, also for the dispute then pending between the two countries over Portugal; the colonies because their determination to seize the Mississippi River, then a Spanish monopoly, was already manifest; the more England and her colonies gouged and enfeebled each other, the better for Spain. Was there anything dishonorable in giving secret aid? Not at all; this was only what England had done on every available occasion. When Spain was at war with Morocco, wrote Grimaldi, England had furnished arms of all kinds to the natives. She had done the same in the war with Algiers. She had even, complained Grimaldi, reached over into the Pacific, and surreptitiously furnished arms to the Moors to assail "our people in the Philippines." "Right and interest should thus persuade us to assist the English colonists; *voilà la maxime.*" The only question was how it was to be done. It must be so managed that, if discovered, it could be immediately disavowed! The Spanish Premier was willing to leave these details to the French; they managed such things so much better in France! "But the King is ready," wrote Grimaldi, "and offers to share, within reason, in the expense. . . . His Majesty commands me to tell you that he submits the matter entirely to the decision of the King, his nephew."

And so Arthur's remark had had the effect, quite unforeseen, of smoking out the Spanish and obtaining considerable subsidies for the American cause. It may be assumed that Vergennes lost no time in placing this communication before his royal master. It was precisely the argument he had been looking for. Incidentally Grimaldi's letter shows that the first definite commitment of secret aid to the colonies came from the Spanish court and not from the French. Grimaldi's revelation that Great Britain had set the example of secretly assisting subjects revolting against their liege lords helped to quiet the king in his ethical struggle. Vergennes could have given him another illustration; in the recent revolution of Corsica, perfidious England had kept Paoli well supplied with powder and firearms.

Meanwhile Arthur Lee kept up his importunities; he, Beaumarchais, and Lauraguais were constant companions. M. Doniol says that the two Frenchmen were completely dominated by Arthur and his accounts of American progress; "seduced" (*séduit*) is the word the French historian uses. Beaumarchais's letters to Vergennes tell the same story. Their interviews, he says, lasted from morning to night. And the plea was always the same: "We need arms. . . . We need powder. . . . Above all, we need engineers. . . . It is only you who can help us; only you who have an interest in helping us."

"But that last article is a great difficulty," Figaro would reply. "We cannot send men without giving them a commission. Besides, men talk and that compromises us. Dumb help is dumb."

"Oh, well," Arthur would respond, "give us money and we will get engineers from Spain, Sweden, Italy. And you will not be compromised."

Arthur's constant demands were clearly not unwelcome. "The patriotism of these men," wrote Beaumarchais to Vergennes, "revives my own. It even seems that the precarious and dangerous situation in which I see myself, because of the suspicions and the severe inquisition which is made of everything I undertake, renders my zeal more ardent!" Perhaps thinking that a little of this spirit might help at headquarters, both Beaumarchais and Lauraguais wrote Vergennes, suggesting that Lee come to Paris and present the American case. It was a suggestion the French statesman put aside — as well he might. The essence of his plan was secrecy, and to be caught in consultation with the agent of Congress would hardly promote his purpose. Arthur's every step was being followed by British spies; his mail commonly found its way to the British Foreign Office; a meeting between him and Vergennes would lead to serious representations and perhaps make the whole thing a fiasco.

In fact Vergennes needed no persuasion. For months he had

been a convert to the plan of surreptitious aid, and every day was bringing stronger pressure on the king. The Beaumarchais letter of February 29, 1776, decided His Majesty; and Grimaldi's message, reaching Paris about a month later, removed all scruples. About this time also Bonvouloir, who had been sent to Philadelphia as an observer, returned to France; he gave most optimistic reports — rather more optimistic than the situation justified — of American success, and of the determined spirit of *le conseil privé*, as he called the Secret Committee of Congress. Events now began to move rapidly. On May 2 Vergennes wrote his famous letter to Louis, telling of his plans to forward 1,000,-000 livres to Beaumarchais for aid to the Americans. His authorization, said the Foreign Minister, would not be in his own handwriting; the document would be copied by his fifteen-year-old son, which would furnish as complete a disguise as one could ask. This historic paper now reposes in the archives of France; at the bottom appears one word, *"Bon,"* written in the hand of Louis XVI, King of France, his monosyllabic approval of one of the most fateful enterprises on which the Bourbon dynasty ever embarked. Two days afterward Vergennes wrote the royal treasurer, instructing him to place aside 1,000,000 livres and hold it subject to his orders. On June 10 this money was transferred to Beaumarchais, that gentleman's receipt for the amount subsequently becoming one of the most celebrated documents in Franco-American diplomacy. On June 27, Spain, in most roundabout fashion, duplicated the French subsidy, placing this money also in the hands of the French dramatist. Thus about $400,000 was appointed for the purchase of munitions at a time when the new American government most sorely needed them.

Meanwhile, on an early day in May, — the precise date cannot be determined, — a momentous scene took place in Arthur Lee's rooms at No. 2 Garden Court, Middle Temple. The participants were Arthur himself, Beaumarchais, and the inseparable third member of the trio, the Comte de Lauraguais. The purpose of the meeting was to inform Arthur Lee, official agent of the Continental Congress, — the only agent Congress had in Europe at the time, — that the French government was prepared to aid the new United Colonies to the extent of £200,000 sterling.

At least that is the figure appearing in all official documents bearing on the subject — a fivefold exaggeration of the first subsidy; whether the mistake was the result of Beaumarchais's exaltation, or his visioning of the not distant future, or whether it was caused by the fact that the details of the interview were not reduced to writing, but transmitted by word of mouth, cannot be decided at this late day. For Arthur Lee made no written report to Congress. He was too experienced a gentleman to do anything so foolish as that. This message of Beaumarchais was the greatest diplomatic secret of the time. Its disclosure might have meant war between England and France. Certainly France, if Arthur had put his news on paper, and the letter should have found its way into the hands of British agents, would have ceased all negotiations with the colonies. Congress, in entrusting this diplomatic post to Arthur, had insisted on "impenetrable secrecy." Moreover, Congress had sent Arthur an emissary for the transmission of messages; this was Thomas Story, a kind of international Paul Revere, who left America in December 1775, with instructions to get in touch with the agent of Congress. Mr. Story's experience, immediately on landing in England, in itself was a sufficient warning as to the danger of transmitting the written word. The efficiency of the British Secret Service, even in this early stage, was a matter of wonder and admiration. The purpose of Thomas Story's transatlantic migration the English perfectly understood; he was stopped by agents of the government, searched, and relieved of a letter to Arthur Lee from M. Dumas of The Hague. This happened in April 1776; certainly, after this experience, Arthur would have been an idiot had he entrusted to Story, a month afterward, a written report to Congress, telling all about the meeting of the triumvirate at No. 2 Garden Court, and the promised subsidy from France!

Arthur Lee therefore sent a verbal message to the Secret Committee, presently metamorphosed into the Committee of Foreign Affairs, with Richard Henry Lee as an additional member. On October 1, 1776, Thomas Story arrived in Philadelphia and delivered his message as follows: "On my leaving London, Arthur Lee, Esq., requested me to inform the committee of correspondence that he had several conferences with the French Ambassador, who had communicated the same to the French Court; that in consequence thereof, the Duke [*sic*] of Vergennes had sent a gentleman to Arthur Lee, who informed him that the French court could not think of entering into a war with England, but that they would assist America by sending from Holland this fall £200,000 sterling worth of arms and ammunition to Saint Eustatius, Martinique, or Cape François; that application was to be made to the governors or commandants of those places, by inquiring for Monsieur Hortalez and that, on persons properly authorized applying, the above articles would be delivered to them." This paragraph represented Mr. Story's recollection of a message entrusted to him six months before by Arthur Lee; it contains one or two inaccuracies, such as the sudden elevation of Vergennes from Comte to Duke, and the amount of money involved; but in its essentials it was an accurate repetition of what Beaumarchais had told Arthur in early May, and outlined the programme that was subsequently put into effect.

At the time Mr. Story reached Philadelphia, only two members of the Secret Committee, Benjamin Franklin and Robert Morris, were in town. These wise gentlemen at once adopted Lee's policy of secrecy. They made a memorandum, and placed it in their most inaccessible files — the document is now included in the Diplomatic Correspondence of the Revolution;[1] but they decided not to make the information known to Congress. The paper solemnly drawn up, explaining the reasons for this reticence, — subsequently formally approved by the signatures of Richard Henry Lee and William Hooper, new members, — shows that the distrust and dissensions of that storm year, 1776, had not subsided. New York, now in possession of the British and their Tory sympathizers, was a danger point; should the news "get to the ear of our enemies at New York they would undoubtedly take measures to intercept the supplies and thereby deprive us not only of those succors but others expected by the same route." "We find, by fatal experience, the Congress consists of too many members to keep secrets" — and here Franklin and Morris instance one case of a serious leak. The committee had

[1] See Wharton, Vol. II, pp. 151–52.

already made arrangements to receive the supplies at "Martinico," and thought it wise to keep the whole matter from Congress until safe delivery had been made.

In the early part of 1777 three ships, the *Amphitrite,* the *Seine,* and the *Mercure,* sailed from Havre, bearing war supplies for the American army, purchased with this subsidy of two million livres furnished by France and Spain. Probably no supplies of ammunition ever produced such historic results. For these were the arms, effectively used by the farmers of New England and northern New York, that won the battle of Saratoga in September 1777. This is only another way of saying that they won American independence. Only when one considers this fact can the magnitude of Arthur Lee's achievement be measured. Among the myths that have grown up about the Revolutionary War is that this French aid was first obtained by Silas Deane and Benjamin Franklin. But both French and Spanish governments had given their pledges and made their cash payments, and preparations for shipping the supplies had begun six weeks before Deane and six months before Franklin had set foot in France. The American diplomatic pioneer whose constant and frequently intemperate promptings exercised such a powerful influence on Beaumarchais, and through him on Vergennes and the French king, was the secret agent of the Continental Congress in London, Arthur Lee.

X

"MILITIA DIPLOMATS" AT LARGE

I

THE Declaration of Independence put a new face upon American negotiations with European powers. Until July 4 — or July 2 — there had been no independent nation; all the time that Arthur Lee had spent intriguing with Beaumarchais, his country was still nominally acknowledging British sovereignty: and naturally colonies had no claim to diplomatic standing. In March 1776, Congress appointed Silas Deane "business agent" at Paris, but Deane, like Lee, and for the same reason, was not entrusted with formal diplomatic powers, though both men were expected to sound out the foreign chancelleries and obtain such general sympathy and aid as their adroitness might accomplish. The Declaration, however, — at least this was the American pretension, — transformed thirteen dependent provinces into so many independent sovereign states; their relationship to foreign powers now became a matter of legitimate importance, and something in the nature of a diplomatic corps became essential. Certain leaders in Congress, even then, regarded American diplomatic envoys as hardly desirable. What could such emissaries accomplish? To send ministers to the great capitals of Europe, with no assurance that they would be hospitably received, — gentlemen who would trudge wearily from door to door, only to have them more or less politely slammed in their faces, — such adventures, it was urged, were unnecessarily foolish and humiliating. "Militia diplomacy," John Adams called such representation, evidently having in mind its amateur and volunteer character, as contrasted with the efficiency of a regular establishment. To Franklin the proposal seemed revolting. "I have not yet changed the opinion

I gave in Congress," Franklin wrote Arthur Lee, March 21, 1777, "that a virgin state should preserve its virgin character and not go about suitering for alliances, but wait in decent dignity for the applications of others. I was overruled; perhaps for the best." That Arthur did not agree is evident from a romantic proposal he made to Franklin; this was that the United States should send an embassy to the Emperor of China; an appeal from the youngest republic to the oldest despotism evidently fired his historic imagination, and even Franklin, he records, did not regard the suggestion as utterly preposterous.

At the time Franklin wrote the protest quoted above he was himself a "militia diplomat," head of the American Commission in Paris, and Arthur Lee was sojourning in Vitoria, Spain, engaged in one of the amateur excursions of which the philosopher so disapproved. However, the "militia" character of outposts at France and Spain did not utterly besmirch the "virgin" purity of the new United States. Both these nations had already made half-shamefaced approaches to America; their subsidies, amounting, at the time of Franklin's letter, to 4,000,000 livres, the cannon, mortars, and powder that were being stealthily removed at nighttime from His Most Christian Majesty's arsenals, whence they were transported to French harbors and loaded on ships that presently cleared for parts unknown — gifts like these might make the most maidenly country suspect that she was an object of interest to distinguished "suiters." The love affair was an illicit one, yet it manifestly gave promise of becoming something ultimately more regular and aboveboard. When, in October 1776, the American Commission to France was appointed, with Franklin as head, and Silas Deane and Arthur Lee as his associates, Poor Richard evidently saw no reason for not accepting. At his first meeting with Arthur, however, he expressed his surprise that his former deputy in the Massachusetts agency should surrender an excellent position in London and identify his lot with Revolutionists.

"You are making a great sacrifice," said the prudent Franklin. "Your employment here is only temporary. When this war is over you will be left without establishment. You will be proscribed in England."

Lee thanked him for his consideration, but he was determined to go on.

That the embassy to France rested on more substantial grounds than contemplated missions to other powers presently appeared, for the three men were cordially received by Vergennes, the Foreign Minister, assured the protection of France, and promised a new gift of 2,000,000 livres — which was duly handed over in installments. That Franco-American friendship still continued on a back-alley basis, the stipulations surrounding this subsidy made clear. "Such was the King's generosity," the commissioners wrote Congress, "he exacted no condition or promise of repayment. He only required that we should not speak to any-one of our having received their aid." At the first meeting with Vergennes Arthur especially was most cordially greeted. The charges subsequently made that the Frenchman, from the start, distrusted the Virginian, as too closely allied with British statesmen, are evidently unfounded.

"Yes," he said, with a smile, as he welcomed Arthur, "I have heard much of Dr. Lee." Figaro's correspondence of the preceding months was clearly still in mind.

And now the question arose of approaching that other power which had made friendly gestures in the direction of America. Besides being one of the commissioners to France, Franklin found himself slightly embarrassed with similar credentials to Spain. The season was midwinter; Franklin was now in his seventieth year; his letters at this time are full of references to his increasing feebleness. Would not Lee undertake this journey in his stead? Arthur demurred. He had no authority from Congress to visit the court of Madrid; certainly his usefulness in that capacity, doubtful at best, would be handicapped by this fact. Franklin insisted. He would write Congress, resigning the post to Madrid, and ask for Arthur Lee's appointment; meanwhile, in view of pressing circumstances, he thought the commissioners had power to make this change. In fact, after Arthur returned from Spain, a commission arrived appointing him to that post.

"I am really unable, through age," Franklin wrote Arthur, "to bear the fatigue and inconvenience of such a journey."

Arthur Lee left a written record of his experiences — still in manuscript form; this indicates, on every page, that Franklin's apprehensions were well founded. In this journal one catches glimpses of the sturdy Virginian, crossing the Pyrenees in his slow-going chaise, his servant following on horseback, traveling night and day, snatching such sleep as was possible in the jolting conveyance or in the shelter provided by that unprogressive country. There were no inns, even of rudimentary sort; now and then this primitive ambassador of a primitive nation found lodging in the second story of some barn, the ground floor having been preëmpted by horses, cows, hens, swine, rats, and other friendly companions. Arthur, always famous for his complaints, was not sparing of them on this occasion. The backwardness of the country and the dirtiness of the people made him groan. The noble Castilian, as a human being, he rated lower than the American Indian, and further than this dispraise could not go, for the average Virginian's estimate of the red man was something unspeakable. "There is no accommodation for travelers," he wrote, "or the least attention shown them but by the fleas and other vermin who pay their compliments in troops." The natives, however, "are alert enough at demanding your money for their dirt and at picking and stealing."

When the American reached Burgos, halfway to Madrid, another shock awaited him; the Spanish ambassador in Paris had given a passport to the Spanish capital, and letters of introduction to important officials there, so the possibility that the voyage might be interrupted had never risen. But here was an impassioned plea from the Marquis Grimaldi not to advance beyond Burgos; that gentleman himself was on his way to the historic city and the negotiations must wait his arrival. Arthur did not appreciate the fact at the moment, but his peregrinations had caused little less than a panic in the Spanish court. Spain was at war with Portugal over an obscure boundary dispute in La Plata, South America; England was Portugal's historic ally, and was displaying much interest in this dispute; that she might take a hand in the fray and send her mighty navy crashing on Spanish ports was a momentary fear in Madrid. The presence of Arthur Lee in the capital would probably give British statesmen the excuse for which they seemed to be searching. Besides, the Declaration of Independence, which had increased French enthusiasm for the American cause, had had the contrary effect in Spain. Spanish statesmen feared — and developments justified their suspicions — that an independent republic in North America would in due course be followed by similar political sovereignties in South America, with the result that the great Spanish Empire would materially shrink. Spain cared nothing for John Locke and "the state of nature"; the minister who sent this peremptory message to the bland Virginian, innocently approaching his capital, was that same Grimaldi who had written the letter to Vergennes, envisaging in the War of Independence a kind of cockfight, in which, he said, it was to be hoped that both contestants would destroy each other. He was willing to give money to the Americans for this purpose, but for no other. Spain never recognized the United States until after the peace of 1783; in the combinations then forming, the "colonies" — as Spain denominated the thirteen states, up to the Peace of Paris — could be utilized as one of the military powers to hold the British lion while the land of chivalry ran away with certain coveted booty, — above all, Gibraltar, — but that represented the utmost extent of Spanish coöperation.

There was nothing of this in Grimaldi's manner when the two men met at Burgos. His greetings lacked nothing in Latin warmth and sympathy. The whole Spanish court was afire with zeal for the noble Americans! Underneath all this fervor, however, another emotion was distinctly perceptive — a desperate wish that the representative of Congress speedily remove himself from Spanish soil. There were personal reasons involved, for Grimaldi's tenure of office was precarious; he had recently been elevated from Marquis to Duke, a promotion that usually heralded a statesman's sequestration to private life; in fact soon after this meeting with Arthur Lee, Grimaldi did retire, for good, to Naples, his native land; and Arthur's appearance at Madrid would probably have resulted in bringing about this dismissal even earlier. As these considerations seeped into the American's consciousness, he decided to turn them to diplomatic advantage. The trip to Madrid was not really essential, from the

Revolutionary standpoint. Neither did Lee or his co-workers especially care at this time for recognition and a treaty with Spain. But this land that impressed the Potomac grandee so unfavorably could still be useful to the cause. It had large supplies of that powder and of those muskets which keep constantly coming to the front as the prime necessities of transatlantic revolution. It even had considerable supplies of cash; at this very moment one of those *flotas* that annually brought tribute from South America was crossing the ocean with treasure to the extent of $40,000,000. All these things the ragged Continentals sorely needed. They were far more important in American eyes than the international courtesies implied in recognition. True enough, when Grimaldi asked Señor Lee in what way Spain could best assist the Americans, there came murmurs of "recognition," but when the Duke replied that "this was not the moment," the talk cheerfully passed to more tangible forms of friendship. "You should consider in what way we can help without committing ourselves," suggested Grimaldi — meaning without getting caught. First Arthur quieted certain fears that were being circulated by the wicked English. The Yankees, British emissaries insisted, were preparing to attack Spanish possessions in South America and the West Indies. Lee gave Grimaldi the most solemn assurances of Congress that no such schemes were entertained. Grimaldi bowed in best Spanish style.

"The Spanish court is persuaded," he replied, "that their dominions are in much less danger from a commercial Republic than from an ambitious monarch."

Even at that moment, he added, Franco-Spanish plans were aiding the United States. Both the French and the Spanish fleet had been disposed in ways that would prevent Britain from concentrating a large navy in American waters; it would be too busy at home! France was preparing to move large land forces into Brittany and Normandy, the vantage points for an invasion of England. Perhaps, before the autumn, Spain would have sufficiently "chastised" Portugal; then that might be the "moment" for intervention on behalf of America!

And now another of those experts in illicit traffic who contributed so largely to American success steps on the scene, for

Grimaldi had brought a merchant of Bilbao, a son of the great mercantile house of Gardoqui — a firm that was already well known in Great Britain and America, and which, as Grantham, British minister at Madrid, presently wrote to the Foreign Office, was showing great partiality for America. Gardoqui, indeed, fulfilled a rôle for Spain not dissimilar to that which Beaumarchais was performing for France. He was a very different character, however, for he was a solid, matter-of-fact man of business; a gentleman, greatly admired by Americans, who afterward served Spain as minister to the finally recognized United States. The first time Gardoqui came into association with the nation with which his career was to be so intimately identified was at this meeting of Grimaldi and Lee in March 1777. He came, at the instructions of the Catholic king, to discuss with Arthur the details of that aid which Charles III was only too anxious to give. At Grimaldi's request Lee furnished Gardoqui a list of the materials then most needed. It was a queer assortment: "large artillery, large anchors, coarse linens and cloths, white and yellow metal buttons, needles and sewing thread, stockings, shoes and hats, tent cloth, sail cloth and cordage, gun locks, gunpowder, muskets, bayonets, tin, copper, lead and 'white iron.'" Both Grimaldi and Gardoqui promised Lee that shiploads of these articles would be presently embarked from Bilbao. Besides there were 3000 tons of powder at New Orleans; the Americans could have this any time they sent for it. At Havana also large supplies of war material were at the disposition of Congress. They could be obtained for the asking! Arthur then suggested a new subject: the United States was building ships of war in Holland, for preying upon British commerce; a credit in Amsterdam to pay for these vessels would be most acceptable. America was also obtaining loans in Europe — or at least she hoped to do so; a credit to assist in meeting interest payments would lubricate these negotiations. At this Grimaldi hesitated; it was a new idea; he would go back to Madrid and consult the king, and meet Señor Lee at Vitoria on the twelfth of March. Only one promise was exacted: Arthur must not go to Madrid! British spies were everywhere; Arthur's presence would at once be reported to London, and such a step would infuriate England and probably ruin the whole plot.

So Arthur Lee philosophically spent a few quiet days at Burgos whiling away his time writing reports of his success to the Secret Committee and a memorial to the Spanish king. The latter Arthur composed in Spanish; it set forth the American situation and the reasons why Spain should accede to the republican cause. It is quite reminiscent of the letters which Beaumarchais had written in coöperation with Arthur to Vergennes and Louis XVI. Those same threatening arguments were again pressed into service. Spain also had great sugar islands in the West Indies — Cuba, Porto Rico, and many smaller possessions. These dependencies gave her reasons in plenty for wishing the Americans well. If England subdued the colonies, writes Arthur to the king, rehearsing the familiar, and apparently always impressive, argument, she would at once pounce on the Pearl of the Antilles; if she should lose her American domain, the Spanish West Indies would be taken as "compensation." And again the time-honored warning appears: should America and Britain be reunited, all Europe could not resist them. "America," Arthur admonished the king, "has been felt like Hercules in his cradle. Great Britain knit again to such growing strength would reign the irresistible though hated arbiter of Europe. This then is the moment in which Spain and France may clip her wings and pinion her forever." No record exists of the emotion of His Catholic Majesty on reading this pronunciamento, but Grimaldi, returning to Vitoria for the promised rendezvous, brought royal assurances that all Lee's proposals — except recognition of independence — would be acceded to. M. Gardoqui would, from time to time, ship war materials from Bilbao to a colonial destination. The large supplies at New Orleans and Havana could now be regarded as American property. Spanish ports would be opened for the reception and sale of American prizes. A credit would be established in Amsterdam for American use. At this point the practical American interrupted the king's mouthpiece.

"What amount will that credit be?" he asked.

This point had not been settled, but, said Grimaldi, it would be paid in installments.

Another comforting fact was adduced by the minister. No payment for these advances would be expected — they were to be regarded as free gifts. This, like a similar stipulation made by France, looks like philanthropy, but it was also statecraft. Both nations wished surreptitiously to aid America in its excellent work of harassing England, but desired no contracts and no agreements in return. Lending money and munitions on promise of reimbursement would amount almost to the recognition of the insurgents as a sister nation; the deal might easily rise to plague them; after the aid had been once extended, the Bourbon princes wished to have the whole thing sink into forgetfulness. They were simply willing to gamble small sums and count them among their war expenditures against the ancestral foe. They looked on America just as England had looked on the Bey of Algiers, or on Paoli in his struggle against France — as a warlike person whom it was worth while to supply with arms so that he might weaken an enemy power.

Grimaldi exacted only one favor from Arthur — he must immediately get out of Spain! And here was another case in which Arthur's "suspicious" nature proved an asset to his country. All these Spanish promises seemed almost too good to be true; perhaps they were only promises, to be forgotten as soon as he had transported himself across the Pyrenees! So Arthur quietly sat himself in Vitoria, determined not to leave until Grimaldi's pleasant gifts had made fair progress towards fulfillment, evidently reasoning that his mere presence on Spanish soil would make the traditionally procrastinating Spaniard show signs of action. He even — it would seem half maliciously — suggested that he might go to Bilbao, to assist Gardoqui in embarking the promised war supplies. On this Grimaldi had another attack of nerves. Anything so conspicuous as that would mean immediate war with England! Then Arthur wrote one of his complaining letters to the king, protesting against the royal veto on a trip to Madrid; it was not just, Arthur said, that after getting almost within eyesight of the forbidden city he should be excluded from the precincts; such an affront, published broadcast, would injure the prestige of an infant nation! In his journal Lee inscribes his motives for behavior of this sort; he really cared nothing about inspecting the glories of Madrid and the Spanish court; his purpose was to act as gadfly, — though he does not use this word, — holding over Spain the threat of a continued residence until the war materials were "settled." Considering that he had "no direct authority to go to, or credentials for Madrid," Arthur wrote, — in his diary he always refers to himself in the third person, — "he did not think it prudent to push that part any further, or employ it any otherwise than as a means of accelerating the aids he wished. . . . He thought Spain might advance more liberally in order to pacify and get him away." Humor was never an outstanding point in Arthur Lee, but his situation in Spain seems to have stimulated a faint sparkle. And for once the Castilian temperament did move expeditiously. That procession of munitions which steadily advanced, in the next two years, from Bilbao to American battlefields now set in. And presently Arthur Lee, satisfied that the end had been gained, ascended his creaky chaise, once more braved the mud of Pyrenean roads, and, in early April, again reached Paris. Soon after arrival, his fondest wishes were realized. The first cash subsidy, of 400,-000 livres, came to the American Commission. How personal the transaction had been appeared from the fact that these bills were made payable to Arthur Lee.

2

Arthur's next adventure in militia diplomacy has engaged the pen of Thomas Carlyle; it forms the subject of an inaccurate chapter in his *History of Frederick the Great*. This expedition had certain qualities of confusion and bleak humor which naturally appealed to that sardonic genius.

That the Americans should approach the Hohenzollern was to be expected. Frederick the Great hated England and its king, and any injury they might suffer, from any source, afforded him gleeful satisfaction. With rebels he had no more sympathy than had the courts of France and Spain; but, like those courts, he knew that rebels whose activities weakened the enemy might serve the royal purpose. The position of Frederick, however, was quite different from that of his Bourbon confreres. Prussia was a military, not a naval power; she had no colonies in the West Indies or elsewhere, not much of a mercantile marine, and very little commerce. Prussia therefore was not greatly interested, from a material standpoint, in the outcome of the struggle. The humiliation of Great Britain, on general grounds, would be welcomed, but advantages in trade and possessions, which France and Spain might anticipate, held forth little promise to the Prussian court. Therefore any attempt to win Prussia to the American side and to obtain from Berlin the money and supplies that had been wangled out of the Bourbons — this was about the most discouraging mission that militia diplomacy had yet presented to its devotee.

Arthur Lee left Paris on May 15, traveling in an English post chaise, painted a deep green, embellished with his initials in cipher — the nearest approach to diplomatic insignia that it was safe to use. With him, as companion and secretary, went Stephen Sayre, an entertaining character who, years before, had been William Lee's partner in London; a man of many adventures, the most exciting of which had been his arrest and confinement in the Tower, on the charge of plotting to kidnap George III. As Sayre and Arthur wheeled out of Paris that May morning, 1777, Sayre told his friend that, after Berlin, he intended to assail Petersburg to try his powers on Empress Catherine. Her interest in handsome men, said Sayre, was well known, and not unlikely she might satisfy her curiosity in an American cavalier. Arthur was not so gay. The route to Berlin was uncomfortable and circuitous. So many of the German states were in alliance with Great Britain, selling their peasants to King George as soldiers in America, that this American embassy was forced to make the trip in most roundabout fashion. Their four-wheeled carriage, drawn by two horses, went first to Strasbourg, Alsace, then to Munich, then to Vienna, and finally, by way of Prague and Dresden, to Berlin. The roads were almost as bad as those on the Spanish expedition; and the reception from official quarters, while polite, was more disheartening. Baron von Schulenburg, Frederick's chief minister, was courtesy itself; he promptly returned Arthur's call, invited him to dinner, and offered the hospitality of Berlin and its protection. The king had not the slightest objection to the envoys' presence in Berlin, — unofficially, — and any purchases they might make from German merchants, even for war purposes, would not be interfered with. Schulenburg and other high-placed Germans were most affable; the king, they assured Arthur, would like to see the Americans win their independence and was most desirous of obtaining all military news favorable to the colonies. And there the matter ended. His Majesty could not receive the envoys, for that would be an unfriendly act towards Great Britain, a nation with which he was on terms of amity; neither could he make loans or supply munitions — for the same reason. Arthur did stir up the faintest ripple of interest on the subject of establishing trade between the colonies and Prussia: he wrote one of his memorials, — this time in French, Frederick's favorite language, — enlarging his ideas on the subject. Nothing tangible resulted, and Lee and Sayre were forced to spend their time visiting manufacturers, inquiring about tent cloth and linen, — closely followed by English spies, — when an event suddenly took place which has made this trip one of the most famous on the lighter side of diplomatic history.

The English minister at the court of Frederick the Great was a scion of the House of Minto, Mr. Hugh Elliot, then twenty-five years old — an age that naturally inspired adventurous deeds. Arthur's projected visit to Berlin was no secret to Elliot. Dr. Edward Bancroft, a venerable American who occupied the dual position of Silas Deane's secretary and paid informer for the British government, had seen to that. Mr. Elliot's legation was situated not far from Baron Schulenburg's house; every time Arthur Lee's chariot drew up before the mansion His Excellency had a perfect view; and naturally these evidences of friendly association of Frederick's chief minister with the arch American rebel proved exasperating. To learn what took place in confabulations of this sort was one of the things for which Elliot had been sent to Berlin, and presently the less delectable side of the diplomatic trade began to function. A German servant in the British Legation was taken into Elliot's confidence; he, in turn, made friends with several retainers in the Hotel Corzica, where Arthur lodged, "gaining" (that is, bribing) them. How did the American emissaries pass their time? Lee, it was reported, spent many hours, especially in the evening, with his pen; in particular he was accustomed to make nightly entries in a journal, evidently an abstract of his proceedings — the same journal which forms the basis of our knowledge of his voyagings in Spain and Germany. "I would give two thousand ducats," exclaimed Elliot, in the hearing of servants, "for that journal!" Presently he and the German lackey completed plans. The diary was kept in a *portefeuille,* with other papers, in a locked bureau; Arthur's room was also kept constantly locked, but the making of duplicate keys was a simple matter. On the afternoon of June 26 Elliot's trusty spies reported that both Mr. Lee and Mr. Sayre had left for the country to dine with friends; on such expeditions they usually returned about eight in the evening. Mr. Elliot's German servant immediately made his way to the back of Arthur's hotel, climbed up to the window, in most burglarious fashion, entered the room, unlocked the bureau, seized the portfolio, and rushed with it to the British Legation. It was four o'clock: the minister was entertaining several guests, all of high rank, at dinner — such was the dinner hour in those days; all these gentlemen instantaneously dropped their knives and forks, seized goose quills and paper, and began furiously copying the American's documents.

While these writing implements, in the hands of members of the British aristocracy, were transcribing the stolen matter, the British minister blandly sauntered over to Arthur's hotel, on the pretext of visiting a friend. About eight o'clock Arthur Lee and Stephen Sayre came in. Mr. Elliot greeted them pleasantly, and in a few moments all four men were engaged in conversation. The British minister was delighted, he said, to meet travelers who spoke his language; it was a rare experience; the talk, ingeniously prolonged, lasted for two hours — thereby giving the lightning-like scribes, a short distance away, just that much more time for their labors. At ten Arthur rose; he must be excused, he said, for he had some writing to do! That is, he must make the customary entry in his journal. A minute or two afterward, sounds of tumult were heard from the general direction of the Virginian's room. In the hubbub such words as "thieves! robbers! police!" struck the Englishman's ear. In a few moments Arthur himself appeared, in a high state of mental disorder and, seizing the landlord, rushed from the hotel, shouting that his papers had been stolen and that he was to lay an information before the authorities. His disappearance gave Elliot another opportunity; the minister sped to his own mansion, grabbed the papers from the noble scribblers, — whose work was practically finished, — disguised himself (the statement is made on the authority of an official British document), and hastened back to Lee's hotel. Soon the servants, gathered in the public room, heard a knock, and a smothered voice through the loophole: "Here are the papers of your American." The landlady went to the door, and presently returned with the *portefeuille* in her hands. "No one was there," she said, "but I found these on the step." The story was not accurate, for the landlady was in the plot, having been "gained." In reality, on opening the door she had been confronted by the "disguised" British minister, who handed her the parcel and then sprinted home. When Arthur and Sayre returned, with officers of police, his precious papers were surrendered. Copies, however, were soon on their way to the Colonial Office in London. All of these documents repose to-day in the Public Record Office.

Many of the most hardened diplomats of the day — a day not especially squeamish in method — thought this proceeding a little beneath the dignity of the British Empire. Even that great practitioner of realistic statecraft, Frederick the Great, was disgusted. In a letter to the Prussian minister at London, the king relates the episode, with the following comment — dropping into the language of Figaro: "What a worthy pupil of Bute! What an incomparable man is your goddam Elliot! In truth Englishmen should blush with shame for sending such ministers to foreign courts." But Elliot fared better with his own royal master. He was reprimanded, of course, for "excessive zeal," but a few months following this letter came another, from Lord Suffolk, Colonial Secretary, conveying his congratulations, and enclosing a draft from the king of £1000, as a reward for this service. Elliot also continued in the diplomatic department, where he had a brilliant if somewhat erratic career.

"This astonishing mass of papers," writes Carlyle, relating the incident, "is still extant in England; — the outside of them I have seen, by no means the inside, had I wished it; — but am able to say, from other sources, which are open to all the world, that seldom had a supreme council board procured for itself, by improper or proper ways, a discovery of less value." This is only one of many misstatements in Carlyle's account. The present generation can see the inside as well as the outside of the packages. They contain information that must have been of great importance to the British government. Arthur's journal itself was a mine of secrets. It tells all about the reception of the American commissioners by Vergennes, of the French promises of supplies, and of the 2,000,000 livres additional subsidy, of Arthur's negotiations with Grimaldi in Spain, of the Spanish plans and aid, and many matters of similar consequence. That British spies in Paris had reported many of these proceedings is true, but Arthur Lee's portfolio must have been invaluable as corroborative evidence and as giving precisely the light the British service needed as to the reliability of its agents. Indeed, as one surveys this packet, the tip of £1000 which Hugh Elliot received from King George seems an inadequate reward. Only one event was necessary to crown this tragi-comedy. Many years afterward, when the United States had become a free nation and was on terms of amity with Great Britain, the post of minister to Washington fell vacant. Hugh Elliot, now in mature years and a distinguished member of the British corps, was suggested. However, official Washington's memory was still active, and information was conveyed to London that Mr. Elliot was not acceptable.

3

Pro domo sua was not the armorial motto of the Lees, but they were never averse to advancing family fortunes. That leadership in so momentous a crisis as the Revolution was one of the purposes for which the sons of Stratford had been trained accorded with family tradition. A weak spot in American representation in France was the seaport of Nantes, the vantage point for privateering operations against British shipping and for shipment of war supplies to America. Robert Morris, at that time a member of the Secret Committee of Congress, had dispatched his half-brother, Thomas, on this mission — a most undesirable appointment, for the young man was unstable in habits and inexperienced in business. It is now no secret that "Tom" had been placed in this important post for two reasons: to relieve the Morris family of a baffling personal problem and to have an outlook that might promote the interests of the mercantile house of Morris, Willing and Company. But the young man's almost incessant intemperance and inattention to business made necessary the appointment of a successor, or at least an associate. Arthur, in February 1779, wrote Richard Henry Lee that their brother, the alderman of London, was just the man for agent at Nantes, in place of the "sot," as he pleasantly denominated Thomas Morris, "a man who would not get a month's employment in any countinghouse in Europe. . . . The alderman in London, from his knowledge, his industry and his integrity would make the best controller of your commerce." Evidently Richard Henry acted promptly on the suggestion — which, on its merits, was an excellent one, for William Lee was on the ground, and had had ten years' experience in American commerce. In the latter part of April a letter arrived from Silas Deane informing Lee of his commission and asking him to repair to Paris. In this way another of the family of Lee joined the cavalcade of militia diplomats.

William Lee's attempt to serve his country as commercial agent; his trouble with the bibulous Morris, set forth with despairing and lengthy detail in his letters; his conflict with Franklin and Deane, who insisted, despite Lee's appointment by Congress, in supplanting him and appointing Franklin's nephew, Jonathan Williams; his charges, probably true, that American affairs in French seaports were turned to the personal advantage of a group of profiteers — all this forms a long and wearisome story which it is hardly worth while to embark on in this place. The pushing forward of Jonathan Williams, a young man of twenty-two, with no business experience, — "clerk of a London bake-shop" Arthur Lee called him, — solely because of his relationship to Franklin, was an impropriety, but one of Franklin's weaknesses was the habit of providing for relatives. The appointment of Morris had been even worse, but that young gentleman solved a difficult problem, soon after Lee's arrival, by dying as a culmination to one of his sprees. In December 1777, William Lee was saved from an awkward predicament by a new and unexpected honor; he was appointed commissioner to the courts of Berlin and Vienna, and instructed to proceed to these capitals, obtain recognition of American independence, and negotiate treaties of commerce. Such important duties probably seemed to William more worthy of his talents than residences at Nantes with all its sordid squabblings and transparent crookedness, yet William Lee's diplomatic career proved a rather barren one. No greater task could have been inflicted on a man than that of obtaining recognition of rebellious colonies, at this particular moment, from the Hohenzollerns and Hapsburgs. At one time, indeed, it looked as though something might be done at Berlin. Arthur Lee on December 18 had received a letter from Schulenburg volunteering the news that Frederick would "not be the last power to acknowledge your independence, but you must feel yourself that it is not natural that he should be the first, and that France, whose commercial and political interests are more immediately connected with yours, should set the example." What changes a military triumph can bring — especially in a militaristic nation! The surrender at Saratoga had changed the whole face of American affairs in Europe. After news of this event reached Versailles, France rushed to the American Commission, expressing its eagerness to join hands with the noble victors. And Prussia, judging from the letter to Arthur Lee, was inspired by the same desire to join the apparently winning side. Since the condition which Frederick had stipulated — recognition by France — as an essential preliminary seemed on the brink of fulfillment, William had some reason to anticipate a diplomatic success. Probably the fact that the Emperor of Austria was brother to Marie Antoinette, Queen of

France and now America's ally, had inspired faint hopes of favorable reception in Vienna — an optimism that led likewise to the appointment of Ralph Izard to another of her brothers, the Grand Duke of Tuscany. Whether Frederick the Great would have redeemed his promise to Arthur Lee, — for so Schulenburg's letter was interpreted, — had conditions remained favorable, cannot be fathomed; but at the moment in question the matter was not a practical one. Storm clouds were then gathering in Central Europe. The recent death of the Elector of Bavaria had raised quarrels as to the succession to that crown. Both Prussia and Austria claimed it, and were preparing to assert their claims by war — a war that presently broke out. This complication naturally made William Lee's credentials to those courts so much waste paper, for both Prussia and Austria desired Great Britain's assistance — at least her neutrality — in the pending hostilities, and neither cared to acquire England's enmity by friendly association with rebellious colonies. William Lee went to Vienna, but was not received. Word came that no encouragement could be looked for at Berlin, so that capital was not visited. William returned to Frankfort, an advantageous point from which to wait until a changed European situation should present a more opportune moment for his task, but that moment did not arrive.

The one episode in which William really influenced the war reads like a chapter from the writings of Diedrich Knickerbocker. Since the Declaration of Independence America had been casting eyes in the direction of Holland. The attraction was both sentimental and practical; the long struggle of the United Provinces against Spain Americans had taken to themselves as an inspiring example; the fact that Holland was a rich country, with large stores of gold always at hand for investment in foreign loans, and that her carrying trade made her England's most formidable rival, stimulated eagerness in the United States for an alliance. As soon as treaties with France had been signed, therefore, Franklin and his associates in Paris began flirting with The Hague. But insuperable difficulties arose. The Prince of Orange, stadtholder, was closely related to the British royal family and was an intimate friend of George III; however much the Dutch people may have inclined to favor the Americans and new ideals of freedom, their ruler's political opinions did not greatly differ from those of the British king.   Moreover, Dutch trade and extensive Dutch colonial possessions could be too easily assailed by the mistress of the seas.   Thus Franklin obtained no encouragement.   William Lee, sojourning at Frankfort and having plenty of time on his hands, decided to approach the problem from a different angle.   It is true that his commission from Congress accredited him only to the courts of Vienna and Berlin; but it is also true that he was a Lee, self-sufficient and independent.   As William wrote to Richard Henry, audacity in statecraft is unforgivable — unless it succeeds; should he present Congress with a *fait accompli* in the shape of a treaty of friendship and trade with Holland, the mere detail that he possessed no authority to negotiate would be overlooked.   After all, was he not a militia diplomat — a kind of Revolutionary Colonel House, with a roving commission to visit European capitals, extracting such scraps of consolation and advantage as possible from the confused political fortunes of the Continent?

Though the royal ruler of their High Mightinesses, the United Provinces, opposed American pretensions, the headquarters of Dutch wealth and financial power entertained a friendly disposition.   The city of Amsterdam paid five sixths of the taxes and, in all except the routine of administration, controlled the destinies of the country.   The burgomasters of Amsterdam wished to follow the French example and knit their country to the rising nation across the Atlantic.   Powerful as the burgomasters were, they technically had no more authority to conduct diplomatic negotiations for the central government than had William Lee for the thirteen United States.   Imagine, in the recent war, the Board of Aldermen of New York, representing, as it unquestionably did, a mighty city, engaged in diplomatic negotiations with an unauthorized private citizen from the French Republic!   That was what happened in the case of William Lee and the burgomasters of Amsterdam.   Necessarily the matter had to be proceeded with most gingerly.   Britain must not know; above all the intriguing Prince of Orange must be kept in the dark.   The burgomasters quietly instructed the Grand Pensioner, Engelbert van Berckel, to enter upon the task; he, in turn, appointed a Dutch merchant, Jean de Neufville, to begin a correspondence with William Lee — whom, it afterwards appeared, he mistook for Arthur.   To the Virginian, whiling away his idle hours in Frankfort, waiting the end of Austro-Prussian hostilities to resume his frustrated approaches, the proposal for a meeting with the deputy of the burgomasters must have been a positive boon. The session took place at the city so famous for its treaties, Aix-la-Chapelle; the discussions were neither difficult nor prolonged, for William had brought a copy of the agreements recently signed with France, and these, with a few improvisations of himself and Neufville, served as the new convention.   This document is still preserved in American diplomatic archives, and can be read, in all its thirty-six fine-print articles, in Wharton's *Revolutionary Diplomatic Correspondence of the United States.* It is most professional and solemn in appearance, precise in its arrangements for the association of the two countries, breathing friendship in every line.   Indeed, the time came when the amateur treaty of Aix-la-Chapelle reached almost accredited standing, for when John Adams, several years afterward, as first American minister to Holland, drew up a document of amity and commerce, he found the way all prepared; the Lee-Neufville treaty served as foundation for the agreement then formally negotiated.

But it served a more immediate end in the Revolutionary conflict.   The purpose of these transactions at Aix was to align Holland among the foes of Britain, an aggregation which was now rapidly assuming European proportions, and the astonishing part of the story is that it actually brought about that result. Not in a way, however, that the friendly burgomasters and William Lee had foreseen.   William went to Paris and presented the treaty to Franklin, hoping to have it formally adopted, but made little progress.   It is quite apparent from the curt note of acknowledgment that his meddling was resented.   The three commissioners at Paris, he was informed, were the proper persons to make treaties with those powers to whom Congress had dispatched no specific ministers.   Let William, therefore, concern himself with Berlin and Vienna; the Dutch lay without his province. Neither did Congress, to which body William transmitted a copy, dignify the paper with much attention. Two years passed with no approving echoes from responsible quarters, and then Henry Laurens, ex-president of Congress, was dispatched to Holland to obtain a ten-million-dollar loan. Mr. Laurens's unprotected ship got no further than the Newfoundland Banks, for a heavily armed British frigate, cruising about for just such opportunities as this, hailed within shooting distance. In such crises both British and American ships took the utmost precautions with official papers. It was the custom to keep them in a bag, heavily weighted with lead, which was thrown overboard as soon as it appeared that capture was certain. Mr. Laurens had much dangerous baggage of this kind, which, dropped from the side of the ship, disappeared beneath the waves as the British approached. One bag, however, proved recalcitrant and refused to sink. The enemy lowered a rowboat; a long boat hook was projected in the direction of the floating sack, which, in due time, was triumphantly deposited on the British warship. It contained many papers, which the British government, after the war, most handsomely bound in eight finely tooled volumes and returned to Mr. Laurens; these precious relics can now be consulted in the Historical Society of South Carolina, Mr. Laurens's native state. In the midst of all this recovered incunabula was a copy of the treaty William Lee had made with the burgomasters of Amsterdam. How it got there no one has ever discovered; it was certainly out of place; probably Mr. Laurens had received it as president of Congress, and in the hurry of departure it had been indiscriminately bundled in with other papers.

But the manuscript, when deposited in the British Foreign Office, proved exceedingly interesting to British statesmen. At that moment Britain and Holland were scarcely on speaking terms. The Dutch had refused to aid England in the war with France, thus, England claimed, violating a solemn engagement; they were on the verge of joining Catherine of Russia's armed neutrality, which was virtually a league of North Europe against Great Britain; they had permitted John Paul Jones to take refuge in the *Texel* after his battle with the *Serapis;* Americans were using their West Indian island of St. Eustatius as an *entrepôt* for smuggling munitions; a Dutch ship — and this was the bitterest insult of all — had been the first to salute the new flag of the United States of America.   Besides, the Dutch were pesky rivals to Britain in the carrying trade, and thus entitled to destruction on general principles.   And so the British, when the opportune boat hook fished William Lee's treaty out of the watery Atlantic, were in an ugly anti-Holland mood and seeking a good excuse for a declaration of war.   "Oh ho!" exclaimed the Foreign Office (in effect) ; "so these Dutchmen have been negotiating a secret treaty with the Yankees!"   All explanations were of no avail.   Here was precisely the *casus belli* the situation required. Presently The Hague received a severe visit from the British ambassador; at least he assumed the air of severity.   Disavowal was demanded of the Lee-van Berckel-Neufville treaty, and the punishment of the Grand Pensionary.   The Dutch government promptly repudiated the treaty, and honestly enough, for it had played no part in that volunteer negotiation, but refused to punish van Berckel.   What had he been guilty of, except a harmless summer diversion of make-believe diplomacy?   Then Britain issued its thunderbolt of war, mentioning, among the causes of its declaration, the following: "They have concluded a secret treaty with our Rebel subjects."

And so William Lee, in rather indirect fashion, had added another ally — or at least "associate" — to the American cause. As for Mr. Laurens, that unlucky gentleman was taken prisoner to London and deposited in the Tower, where he languished for sixteen distressing months, sputtering imprecations against everything British, and inditing a volume, in imitation of Gibbon's *Decline and Fall,* comparing the impending fate of England with that of the Roman Empire.   Finally, on the last day of December, 1781, Mr. Laurens was exchanged for Lord Cornwallis, whom Yorktown had made prisoner of war in American hands, an act that was interpreted on both sides of the ocean as sure sign that England intended to acknowledge American independence.

XI

THE FRANKLIN–LEE FEUD

I

Up to August 1777, Arthur Lee's career as American diplomatic agent had been successful. His association with Beaumarchais in 1775–1776 had resulted in large war supplies from France and Spain. His winter trip to Burgos, in 1777, had brought money and munitions at a time when Washington's army tragically needed them. If his adventurous sojourn in Berlin had accomplished nothing so ponderable, it had elicited from Frederick the Great a promise to recognize American independence whenever France should set the precedent. Perhaps Arthur imagined that these accomplishments would enhance his popularity with his colleagues in Paris; if so he was doomed to disappointment. Few diplomats have ever met so chilly a reception as the junior member of the mission received on his return to France. Just preceding Arthur's departure for Berlin, Franklin had been installed, by M. Le Ray de Chaumont, in a beautiful mansion at Passy, the establishment that, for the next eight years, served as the American Embassy in France. The structure was large, luxurious, roomy enough to provide quarters for an extensive force. Franklin had invited Arthur Lee to make his home in this elaborate castle, formerly the Hotel de Valentinois, and comfortable apartments had been set aside for the militia diplomat on his return from Berlin.

Lee at once reported to Passy, expecting to bestow himself in this congenial lodging. But another tenant had slipped into his place. The rooms that had been renovated for the proud Virginian were now adorned by the short and portly figure of the Connecticut Yankee, Silas Deane, whose familiar manners, general

air of accommodation to surroundings, and distant, even super-
cilious attitude towards the intruding, questioning Lee presented
the picture of a gentleman very much at home.   Dr. Franklin
proffered no explanation for this change in domiciliary plans, but
his grandson, William Temple Franklin, now serving as secretary, informed the returned ambassador that Deane had moved
in at his grandfather's request.   Thus shoved aside, the bewil-
dered and unquestionably very angry gentleman from the Potomac turned house-hunter, finally, with the assistance of M. Grand,
banker to the commission in Paris, settling in a fine mansion at
Chaillot, another suburb about three miles from Passy.   Thus
to the ever-watchful eye of Frenchmen and the still more watchful eye of the British ambassador, the American diplomatic triumvirate offered a spectacle of disunion — the two older members serenely placed in mediæval splendor at Passy, and the junior
associate isolated at Chaillot.   The situation was one that appealed
to the irreverent humor of the French.   Their first emotion was
one of astonishment, then scandal, then mockery.   Even the
Comte de Lauraguais, always loyal to Arthur Lee, could not
withhold his joke.   "Monsieur Lee," he wrote Maurepas, Prime
Minister, "much resents his exile to Chaillot, where he sees only
Gérard and a few girls."

This process of elbowing Arthur out of any share in the
Paris embassy had been under way even before his trip to Berlin.
That Berlin negotiation, though probably Lee did not comprehend the fact at the time, had been part of the general programme.
Useless as a brief stay in the Prussian capital might be, so far
as the interests of America were concerned, it would still serve
a useful purpose in separating the negotiator from the close corporation at Passy.   "Lee will not leave Paris till towards the
end of the week," wrote Edward Bancroft to his fellow spy,
Paul Wentworth, April 24, 1777.   "Til he is gone they deal
only in generals.   They don't like him nor his connections on
your side of the water."   And later: "A. Lee and Carmichael
set out again for Berlin.   There is really some business, but the
absence of Lee is the chief object."   Even while sojourning in
Spain, Arthur had been conscious of a lack of interest from
his colleagues.   Long detailed letters which he had written from

Spanish cities remained unanswered. On his return from Germany no account of what had happened in his absence was given
him. Franklin and Deane held frequent consultations on important matters — consultations to which Arthur was not invited
and on the results of which he was not informed. Critical decisions were taken without seeking the opinion of the junior
commissioner. To such records of proceedings as were made
Lee had no access. His standing in the commission was precisely
the same as that of Franklin and Deane, — all three were acting
under identical appointment from Congress, — yet official communications, addressed to the French government, frequently
bore only two signatures; and even requisitions on French bank-
ers sometimes lacked the name of Lee. Of incoming mail, addressed to the American Commission, the Virginian seldom caught
a glimpse, for Franklin usually opened these letters and passed
them on to Deane — practically never to Lee. All Arthur's attempts to establish working relations were rebuffed. Two out
of three, Franklin once replied to these protests, made a majority!

Arthur returned from Berlin, eager for toil and full of ideas,
but all his suggestions were ignored. That the American Embassy was in a state of disorder a preliminary inspection showed:
no books were being kept, no accounts preserved, although millions of livres were being spent; all kinds of nondescript characters had free access to the building, and apparently shared the
confidence of Franklin and Deane, but Arthur Lee's suggestions
for something resembling a businesslike routine met a hostile
reception. Despite this discouragement, the Virginian frequently
forced his presence on his colleagues, addressing them at length
and proposing reforms. His reports of these interviews, recorded
in his journal, always have the same conclusion: "I received
no answer." Franklin especially was irritating for his silent
treatment. "No attention was paid to what I said, which was
almost invariably the case." Even Arthur's not too active sense
of humor was occasionally aroused; after making a long statement to the senior commissioner on a subject of great importance,
he thus writes down the result: "Dr. Franklin in return entertained me with some very agreeable philosophical conversation."
Occasionally Arthur, discouraged by personal disregard, would

ARTHUR LEE, 1740–1792

Portrait by Charles Wilson Peale

send his ideas in writing; his letters were frequently unanswered, but now and then — something which enraged the Virginian fairly beyond control — a noncommittal verbal message would be sent by a servant. Franklin angered his not-too-even-tempered associate by benign neglect, a lack of interest in Lee's existence and proposals, a failure to keep appointments; but with Deane the causes of disagreement were more exasperating. That Deane and Bancroft — a precious rascal whose villainies will be presently set forth — were constantly abusing him to Franklin quickly came to Arthur's ears. "In short" — the extract is from Arthur's journal — "Mr. Lee on his return had the most authentic information from Mr. Grieve that two of the secretaries, who are lodged and fed in Mr. Deane's house, Mr. Carmichael and Dr. Bancroft, had employed themselves, in his absence, in villifying Mr. Lee, both in print and in conversation and in extolling Mr. Deane." Attacks on Lee began appearing in the London press — attacks which he attributed, probably justly, to the connivance of the enemy at Franklin's headquarters.

That there were faults in plenty on Arthur's side his best friends deplored. Of all these friends none was more honest and loyal than John Adams, and perhaps no better introduction to Arthur's career in Paris can be obtained than the references in the Adams diary. "Our old incidental agent [that is, of Massachusetts] is an honest man," wrote Adams, "faithful and zealous in our cause. But there is an acrimony in his temper, there is a jealousy, there is an obstinacy, and a want of candor at times, and an affectation of secrecy, the fruit of jealousy, which renders him disagreeable often to his friends, makes him enemies and gives them infinite advantages over him. That he has had great provocations I have never doubted. . . . Virtue is not always amiable, integrity is sometimes ruined by prejudices and by passions. There are two men in the world [Lee and Izard] who are men of honor and integrity, I believe, but whose prejudices and violent temper would raise quarrels in the Elysian fields, if not in heaven." And Adams thus sets down a conversation with Grand, French banker for the United States in the Revolution: "I said, coolly, that Mr. Lee was an honest man and that all suggestions of improper correspondence with England were groundless; that my brother Lee was not of the sweet-est disposition, perhaps, but he was honest.   Mr. Grand replied: *Il est soupçonneux, il n'a de confiance en personne, il croit que tout le monde est* ——.[1]   I can't remember the precise word.   I believe this is a just observation.   He has confidence in nobody, he believes all men selfish, and no man honest or sincere.   This I fear is his creed from what I have heard him say. . . .   Mr. McCreery insinuates to me that the Lees are selfish and that this was a family misfortune.   What shall I say?   What shall I think?"   These are the judgments of a candid and an admir-ing friend.   They are the words of a man who worked in closest companionship for eight years not only with Arthur, but with the whole Lee family.

It is doubtful whether any modern appraisement can deal more justly than Adams with one of the most perplexing characters, as well as one of the most interesting, in the Revolutionary scene. That family had much to do with Arthur's attitude is evident. One thinks again of his ancestors, those two Philip Ludwells who kept Virginia embroiled so many years — years that also marked their incessant struggles for the public good.   That "sel-fishness" about which Adams questions himself was really fam-ily pride — an inheritance of that baronial conception in Virginia which implanted in the consciousness of certain families a belief in their right, even their duty, to rule; and doubtless this sense of family obligation largely explains Arthur Lee.   One who fails to grasp this feeling can only faintly understand Arthur's emotions when, returning to Passy from Berlin, he found a Con-necticut Yankee calmly installed in apartments originally set aside for himself.   Silas Deane, son of a blacksmith, country school-teacher, tradesman, undistinguished in person and uncouth in manner, preferred to him, a Potomac Lee, descendant of a line of Virginia councilors, schooled at Eton and Edinburgh, famous pamphleteer, friend of Chatham, Burke, Shelburne, the sought-for guest of country houses and rising member of the English bar!   "The sending persons over here," Arthur wrote Count Sars-field, "who were neither bred or born gentlemen in such respect-

---

[1] "He is suspicious, he has faith in nobody, he believes that everybody is ——."

able [1] characters was either a great folly or a great contempt of those to whom they were sent." All references to Arthur at the time insist on these same traits: "haughtiness," "pride," "the most insolent creature living," "Lee can be compared to nothing but a proud woman" — such are a few of the comments passed upon him by contemporaries.

Probably the characteristic that most strikes a generation given to psychology is the man's egotism — an egotism that sometimes assumed monstrous proportions. Posterity can forgive this abnormality when exercised against such a person as Silas Deane, but that a great man like Benjamin Franklin should become its object has damaged Arthur's fame. One need not regard Poor Richard as an examplar of all virtues, public and private — for certainly he was a practical soul, not enamored of the ideal; the fact still remains that from 1777 to 1783 he was one of the greatest assets to the American cause. This was not so much for his achievements as for his personality. French aid to America was the accomplishment, not of men, but of events, the logical outcome of eighteenth-century statesmanship; yet the mere presence in France of a man who made the whole French nation, nobleman and peasant, America's friend was a fact of incalculable value. The French regarded Franklin not only as the greatest American, but as one of the three or four leading men of the time. His pictures and busts, issued in endless profusion, sold by the hundreds of thousands; he could not appear in public without having his footsteps dogged by most respectful crowds; at the theatre and opera his ovations equaled those lavished on the aged Voltaire — indeed, one of the great moments of the time was when Franklin and Voltaire embraced on the stage of the Théâtre-Français to the wild applause of the French public. The greatest French houses and most distinguished French hostesses were constantly quarreling for the favor of his presence. *Le grand Franklin* seemed to embody all those virtues which French philosophers had been preaching about for a score of years. The man of nature, uncontaminated by vices of civilization, who was already stirring the French imagination and was ultimately to

[1] This is eighteenth-century English. He means men filling such important positions.

spur France to revolution, was symbolized by this placid figure, dressed in plain gray and pointed fur cap — always smiling, always witty, always holding in reserve great intellectual power. Bonhomme Richard's inventions, his lightning rods, his bifocal spectacles, his stove, his kite, his learned discourses before the Academy of Sciences, his pithy and common-sense writings, many of which had already appeared in French translations, his infinite curiosity in everything, human and divine, the stand that he had taken in England for the American cause — all these matters made the Philadelphian, in French eyes, an ideal champion of a young forest Republic attempting to free itself from European shackles. If the chief business of an ambassador is to make his country loved by the one to which he is accredited, probably no other envoy in history ever achieved Franklin's success.

Whether Franklin deserved all this acclaim is not the point; the fact is that he received it, and thus became a force in promoting the American cause almost as powerful as Washington's army. All this was lost on Arthur Lee. He disliked Franklin, regarded his performances as overpraised, indeed believed that he was a positive deterrent to American success. Franklin's removal from Paris became the dearest purpose of Arthur's life. More than this, he insisted that he himself be installed in Franklin's place. "I have this year," he writes Samuel Adams on October 4, 1777, "been at the several courts of Spain, Vienna, and Berlin and I find this of France is the great wheel that moves them all. Here therefore the most activity is requisite; and if it should ever be a question in Congress about my destination, I shall be most obliged to you for remembering that I should prefer being at the Court of France." And on the same day, to his brother, Richard Henry Lee: "My idea therefore of adapting characters and places is this: Dr. Franklin to Vienna, as the first, most respectable and quiet; Mr. Deane to Holland; and the Alderman [that is, his brother, William Lee] to Berlin, as the commercial department; Mr. Izard where he is; Mr. Jenings at Madrid. . . . France remains the centre of political activity and here therefore I should choose to be employed."

No man ever wrote more unfortunate letters than these. They

were penned on the eve of one of the great days of the Revolution — the day that France joined the United States in alliance against England. Had Congress adopted Arthur's rearrangements, France would never have accepted the Virginian as representative and the progress of the alliance might have been interrupted. These proposals and subsequent troubles with Franklin have injured Arthur's reputation almost beyond repair. It was outbursts of this kind, as John Adams sadly noted, which gave advantage to Arthur's foes and have embittered against him so many American historians and biographers. They have also obscured a truth that only in recent years has become apparent — that, in much of the criticism Lee hurled against his Passy colleagues, the facts were on his side. Had his protests been harkened to, probably the American Revolution would not have lasted seven exhausting years, for the things that made matters so difficult were, above all, disloyalty and treason. Lee's wrath against Franklin and Deane was not all jealousy and ancestral pride, but based on patriotic motives. Arthur insisted that the Basse-Cour of Le Ray de Chaumont at Passy was a nest of spies and traitors, who, under the very nose of Franklin, were betraying the American cause and every day bringing it closer to disaster. The reason that he was ignored, Arthur insisted, — the reason all means were taken to keep him out of the secrets of the embassy, — was plain enough; things were going on that would not bear the light of day, and his elimination was desired because his presence would make impossible schemes that endangered his country. Whether this was an accurate explanation of Arthur Lee's unpopularity with his colleagues is a question that may be reasonably discussed. That he was right in denouncing Franklin's headquarters as a seat of espionage in the interest of Britain is something that can be substantiated by documentary evidence.

2

Franklin and Lee were not strangers when they came together in Paris in that Christmas season of 1776. Since 1765 both had been almost continuous residents of London, and since

1770 both had served in the Massachusetts agency. At first appearance it would seem that the men should have been sympathetic friends. Their tastes and interests were identical: books, science, British and American public affairs, above all Britain's policy towards their native land. Their friendships likewise lay in similar fields; that political coterie known as the "Opposition" — opposition to encroaching royal prerogative, to "King's friends," to stamp acts, port bills, and other items in the anti-American programme — claimed the allegiance both of Franklin and of Lee. Such bodies as the Royal Society, such leaders in the new science as Dr. Price, Sir William Jones, and Joseph Priestley, frequently offered the two men a common meeting ground. Yet in these early days in London the basis for the historic Lee-Franklin feud was laid. On one hand we have the austere and humorless Lee, lacking in the lighter graces, sombrely earnest and crusading in his approach to all problems, and on the other the gay and worldly Franklin, capable, at times, of rising to high points of public spirit, yet, in the main, content to make the most of the world as he found it — on personal grounds the men were not overcongenial; yet there were other reasons for disagreement. Franklin's early behavior in American matters had displeased his associate. To Arthur the philosopher seemed painfully slow in accepting the logical consequences of the dispute. While Lee was publishing his pamphlets, assailing "administration" and abusing Lord Hillsborough in best Junius strain, Franklin was not only assiduously courting that statesman, but indulging in dreams of a new British-American empire, its several units to have a common king and common purposes, but each to enjoy a large measure of self-government. Nothing in this conception was obnoxious to American patriots, not even to the Lees, but Franklin, in Arthur's view, seemed so devoted to his British citizenship as to be somewhat tepid in opposition to pending measures of oppression. Thus the Philadelphian began to occupy a conspicuous place in his famous catalogue of "suspects," men who blew hot and cold in patriotic zeal. That personal ambitions played their part it would be absurd to deny. Arthur was to succeed to the Massachusetts agency on Franklin's retirement, but the elder statesman's persistence in hanging on to this office (and its emoluments) led to many ill-natured comments by his impatient junior. "Dr. Franklin frequently assures me," Arthur wrote Samuel Adams, June 11, 1773, "that he shall sail for Philadelphia in a few weeks; but I believe he will not quit us till he is gathered to his fathers."

But the reasons for hostility lay much deeper. Franklin's chief activity in London was the thing that brought the men into disagreement. The matter has historic consequences, for Franklin's career in London, from 1765 to 1775, is closely related to subsequent proceedings in France, and unless this situation is understood, the strange developments at Passy cannot be explained. Again the story of the Lees, and of Revolutionary diplomacy, finds its background in the Northwest Territory of America. At first nothing could seem more remote from Versailles than the plains and forests stretching north of the Ohio, yet from the point of view of both interest and "psychology" they developed a close connection. For in the London days preceding the war Lee and Franklin devoted much time to these "back lands" of Virginia. When Arthur reached London in 1768, he came not only as prospective student at Inns of Court, but as resident agent for the Mississippi Company, that plan for developing the Northwest which, as already described, was organized in 1763 by the Lees, Washingtons, Fitzhughs, and other conspicuous men of north Virginia, most of them leading advocates of the colonial cause. So far as obtaining favor in "government" was concerned, the enterprise had fared badly, and in consequence the original plans had been changed. Instead of seeking 5,000,000 acres at the confluence of the Ohio and Mississippi, the promoters had restored the plans of Thomas Lee and his Ohio Company, and now asked a grant of 2,500,000 acres at the Ohio and the Alleghany. Arthur had been appointed London agent for the purpose of obtaining this grant. He made many approaches and filed several petitions, but with most discouraging results. The fact is that the Lees and the Washingtons were not great favorites of the North administration. That Arthur should leave the supper table of John Wilkes and the country house of Lord Shelburne and then appear in the anterooms of the Colonial Office, seeking a tract of these proportions, struck the political bosses of the day as a new specimen of colonial impudence. That Arthur should publish violent diatribes against Hillsborough one day and the following appear in his chambers, Ohio petition in hand — what could be expected next from this eccentric Virginian? Thus the revamped Ohio Company could expect little from "administration." Arthur's letters contain many references to his approaches and failures. Nothing could be done, he informs the Virginia aspirants over and over again, until Lord North should retire from office.

Ostensibly official disapproval rested on grounds of British policy; the Northwest, by the ordinance of 1763, had been reserved for red men, and no colonization of the white brother was to be permitted in future. But new developments disclosed that this attitude was insincere. All the time that Arthur Lee was cooling his heels in official waiting rooms and vainly inditing petitions to the king, another group of Americans were working to more effective purpose. While the Lee-Washington company was invariably cold-shouldered in Downing Street, a new organization, the Grand Ohio Company, with far more ambitious plans, was apparently making rapid headway. Arthur Lee's organization asked a patent of 200,000 acres near the Ohio and Alleghany, — present site of Pittsburgh, — while this new combination were seeking a tract of 20,000,000 acres, covering an area that comprises the eastern half of the present state of Kentucky, all of West Virginia, and generous slices of eastern Ohio and western Pennsylvania. To cap the insult, this proposed alienation included all the land that the Washington-Lee-Fitzhugh associates had staked out for their own.

To-day one can hardly conceive the passions such a scheme would arouse in the breast of the Virginia planter. It was a chapter in Virginia gospel that all the Northwest Territory was included in the original Virginia charter. Virginia was not then the comparatively restricted state that we know to-day; it included all the expanse north of the Ohio River and east of the Mississippi. The Lees were especially outraged, for the Treaty of Lancaster, negotiated by Thomas Lee with the Six Nations in 1744, was regarded as having bound the aboriginal proprietors into acquiescence with the royal parchments that apportioned this region to the Old Dominion. That "foreigners" should seek to appropriate this inheritance was bad enough; the particular gentlemen who were crowding Virginians from their cherished domain made the affront unendurable. Pennsylvanians, especially Philadelphia Quakers, had never aroused much enthusiasm south of the Potomac, and the apparently favored grantees were, for the most part, men who had championed the cause of Great Britain in the controversy with the American colonies. One of the most powerful Quaker families of Philadelphia, the Whartons, were especially active, Samuel Wharton, from 1768 to 1778, being resident in London, alert in advancing this land scheme. Another leader was that Joseph Galloway, arch-Tory of the First Continental Congress, who, on outbreak of war, fled to the more congenial clime of England. Other American Tories were Sir William Johnson, famous as the big white chief of the Mohawk Indians; William Franklin, Benjamin's illegitimate son, loyalist governor of New Jersey, and, after the Declaration of Independence, an exile from his native country. Dr. Edward Bancroft, born and reared in Massachusetts, but a resident of England and sympathetic with its aims, was another member. Next to Samuel Wharton, the American most concerned with the Grand Ohio Company was Benjamin Franklin, hardly a Tory indeed, and in all crises an American patriot, especially after 1775, but a man conspicuous, during the intervening period, as a conciliatory influence between Mother England and her unruly children. Not unnaturally a man like Arthur Lee, constitutionally keen for unworthy motives, and jealous of Virginia's great position in America, attributed what he regarded as Franklin's too friendly association with the Lord North administration as inspired by ambitions to push Pennsylvania's colonization programme.

Another name appears in the list of shareholders, afterward familiar to students of the Revolution — that Frenchman, Ray de Chaumont, proprietor of the Hotel de Valentinois at Passy, in which, on the outbreak of hostilities, he settled the American Commission. Indeed, while the Lee Ohio Company was a provincial affair, embracing a few Potomac families, its rival was international in scope, and in this the Walpole-Wharton-Franklin company showed their superiority, at least in a political sense. Samuel Wharton was one of the most skillful wirepullers of the time. "He was," says Professor Alvord, historian of the Mississippi Valley, "an excellent type of the pushing eighteenth-century business man, who had received in Pennsylvania politics a thorough training in the art of uniting influential men in support of national enterprises. He was now to employ his genius in a larger field and was to discover that the motives and methods of politicians in the old world did not differ from those which he had been long familiar with in the new; and that an appeal to self interest was as potent in securing influence in the mother country as in the colony." Even Lord Hillsborough felt the impact of Wharton's power. At first his lordship seemed to favor the Franklin land scheme; then suddenly he turned against it; the result — a result usually attributed to Wharton — was Hillsborough's resignation from the ministry and retirement to private life. The distribution of shares in regions where they would do the most good was this Quaker's simple formula for securing his ends. Many of the most powerful names in England appeared on his roster. Nearly all were "government men," leaders of the political forces then seeking to coerce America; not only this, but nearly all were close to the throne, so that the Grand Ohio Company, in its English branch, was almost a court affair. The Earl of Hertford, Court Chamberlain, an intimate of George III, was a large shareholder; others were John Robinson, ally of Lord North, undersecretary of the treasury in North's administration, in charge of the ministerial corruption fund; Grey Cooper, joint secretary of the treasury; Robert Wood, secretary to Lord Weymouth. Thomas Walpole, nephew of the great Sir Robert, London merchant and member of Parliament, was so active that the concern was commonly known as the Walpole Company. The identification with royalty appears in the name Vandalia, finally decided on. The first idea was to name the new colony Charlotta, after the royal consort, a name already considerably overdone on the American map. About this time a worthy scholar discovered that the Queen of England was descended from the ancient royal family of the Vandals, and the Wharton-Franklin-Walpole empire therefore presently emerged as Vandalia, a title which the cynical regarded as appropriate in another connotation.

Arthur Lee's letters during this period make rather sad reading. Disappointed hopes, jealousy of successful rivals, hatred of Philadelphia and its Quakers, outraged pride as a Virginian, hostility to a British administration which was both "robbing" his country of its lands and suppressing its liberties — all these motives, personal and patriotic, made him denounce the Vandalia crowd as rapacious despoilers of America. Arthur at times reminds one of Roosevelt I; like the mighty Theodore, he was inclined to regard those whose opinions and purposes differed from his own as enemies of society, and, again like the rough rider, he had a talent for vituperation that never spared the great and influential. And, in eviscerating Franklin and his associates in this Vandalia colony, Arthur never hesitates to use short and ugly words. Thus one is almost appalled to observe the venerated Franklin, in Arthur's correspondence, described as "a ministerial tool," a "land monger," the perpetrator of a "job," and the originator of a "villainous fraud." In fact Arthur sums up the whole coalition in one characteristic sentence: "Take my word for it, there is not a sett of greater knaves under the sun."

3

And now let us make the transition from Vandalia to Passy. As already intimated, the connection is not difficult to establish. At least to Arthur Lee, when he returned from his Spanish trip, the association between the proposed empire in Virginia's "back lands" and the seat of American authority in France was immediately apparent. Especially was the fact that Franklin and his companions had found lodgment in the Basse-Cour of M. Le Ray de Chaumont, French partner in Vandalia matters, something not to be overlooked. Subsequent information disclosed that, in one shape or another, many of the biggest men in Vandalia speculations had established friendly relations with the American Embassy. Arthur Lee's vexation was great when it appeared that Chaumont, Dr. Bancroft, the Whartons, Thomas Walpole, and other persons whom he regarded as obnoxious characters, stood on much better footing at Passy than he himself, the officially accredited representative of Congress.   Startling was the disclosure that Edward Bancroft was serving as private secretary to Silas Deane, was living in the Chaumont mansion, had constant access to all its secrets and was chief confidential man to Franklin.   Bancroft was a shrewd and clever gentleman, — Arthur had learned this in London, — but his agility in thus gaining access to American counsels was something of a surprise. Yet the fact had been accomplished simply enough; Bancroft had not wormed himself into the ambassadorial circle, but had been invited in.   Benjamin Franklin had written Deane's instructions, on his original appointment as representative in France, and these instructions had contained the following paragraph: "You will endeavor to procure a meeting with Mr. Bancroft, by writing a letter to him, under cover to Mr. Griffiths, at Turnham Green, near London, and desiring him to come over to you in France and Holland, on the score of old acquaintance.   From him you may obtain a good deal of information of what is now going forward in England and settling a mode of continuing a correspondence.   It may be well to remit a small bill to remit his expenses in coming to you.   You will also endeavor to correspond with Mr. Arthur Lee, agent of the colonies in London."   At the date of this letter, March 3, 1776, neither Franklin nor Lee was an American commissioner; Deane was the sole American representative in France.   Franklin's instructions to Deane to get in touch with Arthur Lee were ignored; and, when Arthur came to Paris in August, Deane wrote to Vergennes, virtually warning that statesman against the man who was presently to be his colleague, thus first implanting in the Frenchman's mind that suspicion which made Lee's career in Paris so difficult.   Deane's first act, in landing at Bordeaux, was to follow Franklin's instructions concerning Bancroft, who came over to Paris, spent several weeks with Deane, learned all about American affairs and American aspirations, accompanied Deane on his visits to Vergennes, and acted in general as good angel.   Two records exist of those first weeks of the American effort at Versailles, both historic documents of priceless value.   Deane wrote a long and highly entertaining account of his experiences, describing the encouragement extended

by the French court, the aid already promised and on its way —
all of which was about the most confidential and dangerous information then concealed in Europe. Deane sent this in the most
secret manner to the Committee of Congress, where naturally it
raised high hopes. Edward Bancroft wrote his story of the same
events, just as detailed, just as accurate, just as entertaining as
Deane's. But Bancroft sent his lucubration to Lord Suffolk,
head of the British Secret Intelligence during the American Revolution.

Of course neither Franklin nor Deane knew anything of Bancroft's literary exercises; in subsequent months Bancroft grew
increasingly indispensable to Deane, who informed him of all the
conversations with Vergennes, took his advice on all delicate
matters, and finally persuaded him to settle in Passy as personal
secretary. And there the astonished Lee found him — astonished because Arthur and William already possessed what they
regarded as irrefragable proof of Bancroft's double character.
Arthur informed Franklin, in his forthright way, that Bancroft
was a spy in the pay of the British government. He not only
made the accusation but submitted evidence. Bancroft, William
Lee had discovered, was closeted with the Privy Council on his
trips to London. What could such confabulations mean? But
the only effect on Franklin of Arthur's charges was to embitter
him. His backbone stiffened at the accusations. Amiable as
he was to most men, to Arthur, from this time forth, his manner
became little less than savage. Edward Bancroft, his long-time
friend, his assistant in literary and scientific pursuits, his co-
worker in Vandalia enterprises, to be accused, by this Virginia
upstart, as the paid betrayer of his inmost secrets! The indignation against Lee felt by the philosopher has been pretty generally
echoed by his biographers — at least all those who antedate 1889.
For Bancroft is a curious figure, in the history not only of
espionage, but of literature. Naturally Franklin's biographers
have found Arthur Lee's accusation against Bancroft something
of a stumblingblock, especially those biographers who wrote in
the time when glorification of one's hero, and corresponding
abuse of his detractors, was a fixed rule of the biographical art.
To admit that Bancroft was a spy, writes Francis Wharton,

"would involve grave imputations on at least the sagacity and the vigilance of Franklin" — hence the labored efforts of all Franklin chroniclers, including himself, to prove that the Lee imputations were slander.

That scholar who so mangled Washington's correspondence, — and almost everything else on which he got his hands, — Jared Sparks, led the procession; then came James Parton, one of whose counts against the "marplot" Lee was his "suspicion" of this good Dr. Bancroft, whom Parton regards as a devotee of the American cause. For Parton there is some mitigation; his Life of Franklin — in the main an excellent book, most readable at the present time — was composed during the Civil War, when Lees were not popular with Northern writers; Parton, indeed, portrays Arthur as a shining example of the arrogant, defiant person produced by the "plantation system." But Francis Wharton, who, as late as 1889, published his *Revolutionary Diplomatic Correspondence,* in five volumes, did not have the same excuse, though he also had reasons for disliking the Lees — a hostility that crops out constantly in his volumes. Francis Wharton was grandnephew to Samuel and Thomas Wharton, associates of Franklin in Vandalia, whom the Lees had assailed with the same virulence they lavished on Bancroft, and it is not unlikely that this Revolutionary antagonism, handed down two generations, may have had some influence in barbing his pen. Family feuds, especially among Virginians and Philadelphians, usually persist through the years! At any rate, Wharton's volumes are a glorification of Franklin and a vilification of the Lees. To make his case complete, Dr. Wharton devotes a chapter, of twenty pages, to Dr. Bancroft, Franklin's confidant; every available bit of evidence is scraped together to show that the suspicions entertained by the Lees of this gentleman were unfounded and to prove that he was a loyal American patriot.

Dr. Wharton's chapter on Bancroft is one of the most unfortunate bits of special pleading in all the curiosities of literature. The year selected for publication — 1889 — makes it almost a tragedy. For at this same time the famous American scholar resident in London, F. B. Stevens, began issuing his Facsimilies of the Auckland manuscripts, and other documents, then reposing in European archives. Lord Auckland, as the Honorable William Eden, was assistant to Lord Suffolk in charge of British Secret Service during the American Revolutionary War, and his papers, thus finally released by the British government to Mr. Stevens, are the reports he received from British secret agents in the course of duty. They now consist of twenty-five huge volumes, known to students of American history as the Stevens Facsimiles, and are available in most important American libraries. No one can understand the secret workings of the Revolution without a generous examination of these mighty tomes. The first impression is one of admiration at the completeness and accuracy of British Intelligence; a quality that evidently persists, for the spy system of Great Britain in the recent war was similarly exhaustive. From 1776 to 1781 it is not too much to say that the British Foreign Office was far better informed of American activities than was Congress itself. Franklin's embassy at Passy, it now appears, was almost a branch office of the British Secret Service. Not a thing happened there that did not instantaneously find its way to Downing Street and Windsor, for the man who found chief delight in reading the reports of British spies was George III himself. The agent mainly responsible for collecting this royal literary matter was that same Dr. Bancroft who so completely bamboozled Franklin and who was to find so many American apologists in the course of a century. Merely to dip into these twenty-five volumes shows that Americans have committed a great injustice in making Benedict Arnold the arch-traitor of the Revolution. That eminence rightfully belongs to Dr. Bancroft. Arnold was guilty of one act of treason, which failed, and so did no harm, while Bancroft, for eight years, was daily betraying his country, and doing so successfully. The prolongation of the contest was owing, more than to any other single cause, to the information which this man was constantly supplying — for money — to the ministry in London.

4

He was a gentle and scholarly soul, this Edward Bancroft — a man of some standing, too, especially in scientific circles. Even the British *Dictionary of National Biography* devotes a quarter page to "Edward Bancroft, M.D., F.R.S. (1744–1821), naturalist and chemist, a man of versatile talents, a friend of Franklin and Priestley," treating seriously his discoveries in dyeing and calico printing. He was a native of Westfield, Massachusetts, a pupil, so John Adams records, of Silas Deane in his schoolmaster days, and afterward was educated as physician in England. Apparently he possessed social graces that made him welcome in respectable circles. One of his closest friends was Paul Wentworth, member of a distinguished New Hampshire family, also resident in London, a man of greater mental attainments than Bancroft and of higher connections. Wentworth was a cultivated gentleman; he spoke French so perfectly that, among Frenchmen, he had no difficulty in passing as one of themselves; "Monsieur Wintweth," wrote Beaumarchais in a letter to Vergennes, "speaks French as well as you do, and better than I." Wentworth was distantly related to the Marquis of Rockingham, was the owner of a sugar plantation in Surinam, on which he had once installed Bancroft, then experimenting in "Tyrian dyes." Beaumarchais, in this same communication, describes "Wintweth" as "one of the cleverest men in England." Unfortunately Wentworth's mentality was devoted to base uses, for he early became a spy *de luxe* in the British service, expecting as rewards financial compensation, a baronetcy, and a seat in Parliament. His reports on American affairs — all now accessible in the Stevens papers — have a certain grace and are full of literary allusions and historic parallels. They are also replete with bitterness and chagrin. Nothing set Wentworth's nerves tingling so much as that word "spy" which he knew was frequently applied to himself; and, while many midnight hours were spent penning reams of betrayal, he also filled pages of recriminations against his English employers, who showed inadequate gratitude for his services and treated him with disdain. Probably the only really bright spots in Wentworth's life were his visits to France, for, on these occasions, he sometimes became the guest of Franklin and Deane at Passy. The fact that Arthur Lee, on Deane's arrival in France, had written him to keep away from Wentworth, as a dangerous character, was entirely forgotten.

According to Bancroft the irresistible Wentworth had been

the cause of his downfall. He tells the story in a written account of his misdeeds, a brochure which forms one of the most extraordinary bits of biographical literature in existence.   In 1874 the British government, the war with the former colonies having ended, evidently became weary of their old retainer; Bancroft's pension of £1000 a year was suddenly stopped, leaving the gentleman destitute.   As a plea for its renewal, Bancroft wrote Lord Caermarthen, then Foreign Secretary, giving a résumé of his services to the British crown, which consisted chiefly of a long list of treasons against his native land.   Thus over Bancroft's own signature we have a conscientiously catalogued list of betrayals.   How Bancroft, after spending two or three weeks with Deane in Paris in June 1776, returned to London; how there, meeting Paul Wentworth, he told the whole story of French and American negotiations; how Wentworth took him to Lords Weymouth and Suffolk, Secretaries of State, before whom Bancroft unbosomed himself — all these details the learned physician sets forth.   Naturally the noble lords decided permanently to link Bancroft to the British cause.   The first interview, and the written memorandum, in themselves secured a pension of £200 for life, but that proved only the beginning of an employment that lasted until 1784.   "As an inducement for me to go over and reside in France and continue my services there, until the Revolt should terminate or an open rupture with that nation ensue, his Lordship further promised, that when either of those events should happen, my permanent pension of £200 should be increased to £500 *at least.* [Italics in original.]   Confiding in this promise I went to Paris, and, during the first year, resided in the same house with Dr. Franklin, Mr. Deane, etc. and regularly informed this government of every transaction of the American commissioners; of every step and vessel taken to supply the American colonies, with artillery, arms, etc.; of every part of their intercourse with the French and European courts; of the Powers and instructions given by Congress to the Commissioners, and of their correspondence with the Secret committees, etc. and when the government of France determined openly to support the Revolted Colonies, I gave notice of this determination, and of the progress made in forming the two treaties of Alliance and Commerce, and when these were signed, on the Evening of the 6th of February, I at my own Expense and of a special messenger, and with unexampled despatch, conveyed this Intelligence to this City [London] and to the King's Ministers, within forty-two hours, from the Instant of their signature, a piece of information for which many individuals here, would, for purposes of speculation, have given me more than all that I have received from Government. . . . To fulfil the promise made by my Lord Suffolk my permanent pension was increased to £500 per annum, and regularly entered, in Book Letter A, payable to Mr. P. Wentworth, for the use of Edw. Edwards, the name by which, for greater secrecy, it had been long before agreed to distinguish me."

Amazing as this confession may seem, the contract entered into by Bancroft with the British government is more astounding still. The document is probably unique; is there any other instance in history of such an espionage bargain — a bargain in which the party of the first part, in writing, agrees to tell his secrets, definitely stipulating what they are to consist of? The handwriting in this contract — a contract now to be read in the Stevens Facsimiles — is that of Paul Wentworth, and the agreement was one to correspond with that gentleman. The subjects on which information was promised appear under two heads — that intended for Wentworth and that for Lord Stormont, British ambassador at Paris. Since Wentworth resided, for the most part, in London, and had immediate access to the British government, he was chiefly interested in diplomatic concerns — such as America's negotiations for alliances with France, Spain, and other powers; the details of commerce carried on between the West Indies and the Northern colonies; and in banking matters. Of particular importance were American attempts to obtain foreign credits, "the channels and agents used to supply them; the secret moves about the courts of France and Spain and the Congress agents and tracing the lines from one to another." Bancroft agreed — in writing — to furnish Britain with copies of all Franklin's and Deane's letters to and from the Continental Congress, and of all transactions and correspondence with foreign powers. For Lord Stormont, information was to be supplied that would aid in his daily task of protesting violations of neutrality; thus Bancroft contracted to furnish details about every ship sailing from France to America — its officers and crew, its cargo, especially war munitions, its port of departure, destination, and date of sailing, its projected course — so that British warships might be most advantageously placed for interception.

The manner in which all this intelligence was to be conveyed one would hesitate to transcribe did it not formally appear in this written contract. Anyone who might accidentally discover Bancroft's letters would think that he had stumbled upon an illicit love affair; they were to be written, "in gallantry," upon white sheets of paper, with liberal spaces between the lines. The apparent writing was to comprise confidences such as one would address to his sweetheart, but in the empty voids the real literary matter was to be inserted, containing news on the subjects listed above; but all this was to be written in "white ink," — that is, invisible ink, — "the wash to make which appear is to be given to Lord Stormont." Transmission of these letters was to be under the favoring auspices of darkness. "Mr. Jeans [a member of the British Embassy] will call every Tuesday evening after half past nine at the tree pointed at the south terrace of the Tuileries and take from the Hole at the root a bottle containing a letter and place under the Box-tree agreed upon a bottle containing any communication from Lord Stormont to Dr. Edwards [Bancroft]. All letters to be numbered with white ink. The bottle to be sealed and tyed by the neck with a common twyne about half a yard in length. The other end of which to be fastened to a peg of wood, split at the top to receive a very small piece of a card.[1] The Bottle to be thrust under the tree and the peg into the ground on the west side."

How sedulously Bancroft made use of these postal facilities is evident in the collection of his literary performances now available in the Stevens Facsimiles. But he was not the only one Wentworth had enticed into his syndicate of betrayal. He enlisted, indeed, a fair-sized brigade, all recruited from Americans resident in London: George Lupton; John Williams, uncle of the Jonathan Williams in charge of American shipping affairs at

---

[1] Evidently to make the spot accessible in the dark.

Nantes; Joseph Hynson, that pleasure-seeking sailor who succeeded in stealing six months' correspondence of the American
commissioners and passing it on to Downing Street; the Reverend
John Vardil, once Canon of Trinity Church, New York, who,
by boarding in a London sailors' resort which was little else than
a house of prostitution, made Hynson's acquaintance and engaged
him for this work; William Carmichael, of Maryland, for 1776–
1777 private secretary of Deane and Franklin at Passy, who, if
not a traitor, — his exact status has never been fixed, — was the
associate of men whom he must have known to be traitors. Of
all these British mercenaries — far more dangerous to the American cause than those imported from Hesse and Brunswick — the
man of overshadowing importance was Bancroft. Wentworth,
in London, served as a kind of clearing house, receiving Bancroft's missives, forwarded by Stormont from the "Box-hole"
of the Tuileries, transmitting such as seemed desirable to Lord
Suffolk and William Eden, condensing others, to save their lordships the trouble of wading through repetitious memorials, and
using them as the basis of "Informations" of his own. Wentworth supplemented these documents by occasional visits to Paris,
and at other times met Bancroft, for verbal communications, at
Dieppe and Dover. As a result his Revolutionary writings make
a picture of American diplomacy from 1776 to 1781. Especially
insidious are Wentworth's little papers called "Port Intelligence."
Probably no documents did the American cause such harm,
for they contained details of the sailings of ships carrying supplies
so sorely needed by Washington's troops. Ship after ship cleared
French ports for America, only to be scooped in by the British
cordon and taken to England. From May 1777 to April 1778
— almost a year — Congress received no messages or correspondence of any kind from its representatives in France, for all
ships carrying them had been captured.

Another aspect that startles one even to-day is the constant
use which Bancroft made of Franklin's correspondence. Arthur
Lee, in his unprinted journal, relates: "Count Vergennes had
complained that everything we did was known to the English
ambassador, who was always plaguing him with the detail. No
one will be surprised at this who knows that we have no time or

place appropriate to our consultation, but that servants, strangers and everyone was at liberty to enter and did constantly enter the room while we were talking about public business and that the papers relating to it lay open in rooms of common and continual resort." If the public had such a free access, a confidential secretary, like Bancroft, would find no difficulty in purloining and copying letters. He not only sent duplicates to Wentworth but sometimes originals. There are many references to them in Wentworth's essays. "Bancroft left them for my perusal," he writes, referring to a packet of letters from Passy, "I also retained originals of those of which he brought me duplicates."

Francis Wharton, the scholar who, as late as 1889, published his defense of Bancroft, says that his relation to Franklin was that of Boswell to Johnson. This perhaps explains the many Boswellian intimacies that enliven both Bancroft's and Wentworth's pages. Wentworth especially had a gift for portraiture and adjectives. We catch glimpses of Deane, "strutting like a cock on his dunghill," cursing France and all Frenchmen, expanding in "his Republican pride," quoting John Winthrop as his favorite political philosopher and outlining terms of possible peace at supper in the Café St. Honoré. An unforgettable sketch from the life is that of Franklin, shedding tears at the inevitability of American separation from Britain — tears that involved no disloyalty, for it was a regret common to most intellectual Americans, even those strongly devoted to independence. Bancroft rages now and then over the free use made of his reports; he would steal a paper, pass it on to Lord Stormont, who next day would protest to Vergennes, using terms and details that were almost exact quotations from the original. If this goes on, wails Bancroft, exposure is certain! Wentworth even gives vignettes of himself. He calls on Arthur Lee "to pay his respects," and, while waiting for the Virginian to appear, rifles Arthur's cardcase, lying on the table. At another time he sups "with Deane and a woman whom he believed to be Deane's mistress." His sizings-up of the commissioners are worth recording: "Franklin is taciturn, deliberate and cautious; Deane vain, desultory and subtle; A. Lee suspicious and insolent; W. Lee peevish and ignorant; Mr. Izard costive and dogmatical — all of them insidious and Bancroft vibrating between hope and fear, interest and attachment." Evidently, in Wentworth's eyes, Deane was a more important figure than Franklin. The following is from one of his "Statements of Information": "Franklin . . . seldom passes a day without seeing Deane. The latter appears to be the more active and efficient man, but less circumspect and secret, his discretion not always being proof against the natural warmth of his temper and being weakened also by his own idea of the importance of his present employment." Here is a glimpse of a dinner party at Passy at which Wentworth was present: "The conversation at dinner was offering bets that America would be independent. That Vandalia was to be the Paradise on Earth; that his (Deane's) own family and the Chaumonts were determined to go there." Vandalia and the Whartons make more than one appearance: Samuel Wharton is "a creature of and supported by Dr. Franklin, of an artful Jesuitical turn," "jealous and designing."

Bancroft, in addition to his spying, had another occupation which, at times, seemed to absorb him even more. As with most intriguers his passion for speculation was intense. George III, strict moralist on matters of this sort, reprehended this phase of his hirelings, for His Majesty abhorred stock gambling, and unimpeachable evidence that Bancroft was fond of such flings even led him to distrust the accuracy of his reports. "The man is a double-spy," the king would exclaim, meaning that, while betraying American secrets to the British, he was also revealing British plans to the Americans. Bancroft's frequent trips to England might possibly have awakened Franklin's suspicions, but the explanation was plausible enough: the man always returned with a budget of information, about the movement of British troops and the British navy, the plans of the ministry and the like — news which seemed important, but which was really false or inconsequential. Bancroft even drew a salary from Congress for services of this kind, and once wrote a protesting letter when his compensation was slow in arriving. The British ministry, to lend color to American confidence that Bancroft was their agent, even had him arrested as an American

spy. Bancroft made these visits to London for two purposes:
to confer with his employers in Downing Street, and to attend
to his personal speculations in the funds, undertakings in which
Wentworth was frequently a partner. In his letter to Lord
Caermarthen, already quoted, Bancroft refers to his rapidity
in bringing news of the signing of the French treaty, adding,
almost ruefully, "a piece of information for which many individuals would, for purposes of Speculation have given me more
than all I have received from Government." In writing this
the man was reminiscent. For Bancroft made tidy sums, not
only on this news, but on many other items that necessarily came
his way as confidential man at Passy.

In these speculations his associates seem to have been the
Whartons and Sir Thomas Walpole, all co-workers in Vandalia
days. Bancroft furnished the information while the Whartons
and Walpole supplied the cash. "If," Joseph Wharton wrote
Bancroft, November 8, 1777, "you could communicate any important news to me speedily on its arrival it might prove bene-
ficial to me." He transmits Bancroft his "direction" — that is,
the place where he could be addressed, for in those days, when
letters were constantly opened by the government, "covers" for
the reception of correspondence were the rule. In a letter of
November 10, 1777, addressed to his "good friend" [Bancroft],
J. Wharton becomes specific: "Your opinion may be a stimulus
to much further speculation. Why may not subsequent contacts
be mutual between him, you and me? [This letter does not quite
indicate who "him" was, probably Walpole.] I will engage thus
far with you, on your communicating to me the best intelligence
respecting war, or any other essential matter from a relation to
America, upon which you would have the insurance made, that
my friend and I will advance the premium, and admit you to an
equal share with us, holding you engaged for one third out of the
premium." Unfortunately the essential parts of Bancroft's letters to the Whartons are not available, for they were written in
that "white ink" so popular at the time, "the wash to make which
appear" not having been handed down to posterity. Paul Wentworth was not ignorant of these transactions. On December 11,
1777, he writes to William Eden: "He [Bancroft], I think, is

gone to London, by Dieppe and Brighthelmstone, and may be found at Mr. W—p—le's Town or Country or Mr. S. W—t—n's" — hardly impenetrable disguises for Walpole and Samuel Wharton. This peregrination concerns the greatest of Bancroft's speculative coups. The news of Burgoyne's surrender at Saratoga did not reach Paris until December 4, 1777, but rumors had reached Passy in November that the invasion from Canada was sure to prove a great disaster to British arms. So Bancroft writes to Walpole, November 30, telling him of Burgoyne's retreat, and there are evidences that the crowd "cleaned up" well on this advance information. One of the most conclusive is the change in Bancroft's behavior. Paul Wentworth's reference to his aid, in an undated letter (about the end of 1777), portrays a new aggressive, independent spirit: "Bancroft is not as he should be. He offered to repay all he has received. The cursed journey to London has spoiled all. Petrie went with them and Van Zandt is left behind in confidence. He is flush with money. Has large shares in the cargoes going out and, I suppose, has been bribed by Walpole."

Others besides the Lees knew that something was wrong at American headquarters. Franklin's equanimity was frequently disturbed, especially when Vergennes protested that his embassy was sheltering a traitor. Vergennes insisted that William Carmichael was the man; as a consequence of this, Carmichael was shipped home, without bringing to an end the flow of information to England. Bancroft, ready for this emergency, as for all, quickly solved the problem: the traitor, he insisted, was Beaumarchais! But the Lees, though by no means inclined to give a clean bill of health to Carmichael, and at this time entertaining no friendly opinion of Figaro, — who, in their judgment, was more interested in personal money-getting than in promoting American independence, — unerringly pointed the accusing finger at Edward Bancroft. Arthur's letters contain many references, in his usual slashing fashion, to the Bancroft-Wharton alliance. "Two notorious speculators," he writes to Dr. Gordon, September 22, 1779, "as desperate in their fortunes as in their principles, I mean Mr. Wharton and Dr. Bancroft, are the only confidants and advisers at Passy. I leave to you to judge whether they who have jobbed away the secrets of the state would make much hesitation in jobbing the state itself."

In the early months of 1778 came the celebrated Major Thornton incident. This gentleman, whose beginning and whose end seem equally obscure, was sent, in December 1777, by the American Commission to London, with the acquiescence of the British government, to alleviate the misery of American prisoners of war in England. On his return, on January 3, 1778, he submitted the following intelligence to Dr. Franklin and Mr. Deane: "Mr. Hartley told me that Lord North had informed him 'that he knew of Dr. Bankcroft's [sic] being in London, and was informed he had been sent there by the American Commissioners to stock job.' " Arthur comments on this as follows to the Foreign Affairs Committee of Congress: "The above is the declaration of Mr. Thornton, whom the Commissioners sent with their letter to Lord North, touching the prisoners. He informed me as above on his return and told me at the same time that he had given the same information to Dr. F[ranklin]. Dr. Bankcroft lived in the house with Dr. F. and Mr. D. at the public expense. He set out express for London, immediately on our receiving the news of Burgoyne's surrender. He has been trusted since by Dr. F. and Mr. D. with the secrets of state communicated to the three commissioners only, with such strict injunctions of secrecy that the commissioners thought they were not at liberty to communicate them to the commissioners of Vienna and Tuscany and Mr. Lee would not do so without their concurrence. Dr. Bankcroft still remains in the confidence of Dr. F. and conveys everything to the Messrs. Wharton in London, who seem to be acting on both sides."

This Major Thornton, for two months, after his return from London, acted as Arthur Lee's secretary. Subsequent events have disclosed that he was a British spy. For the brief period of their association, most of which time Thornton spent in England, where Lee had sent him to gather information on British naval and military preparations, he sought to maintain the position towards Lee that Bancroft held towards Franklin for eight years. In this he failed. As soon as Lee discovered the man's true character, which he did very quickly, he was promptly dismissed. It was Bancroft himself who instilled this suspicion in Arthur's mind. Thornton, he whispered to Lee, was speculating in the funds. Arthur confronted Thornton with the suspicion: was the statement true? No, replied Thornton, but he added that Bancroft and the Whartons were doing so all the time. Arthur presently discovered that, in their mutual recriminations, both men were telling the truth. In June 1778, facts came to Lee showing that Bancroft, the Whartons, and Thornton were corresponding; Thornton vanished from his employ and so ended his brief connection with the Lee establishment at Chaillot.

Franklin, however, could not be persuaded to abandon Bancroft. All the denunciation of the Lees only seemed to link him stronger to the man. That he sincerely trusted him is unquestioned; that all the secrets of the American Embassy at Passy were transmitted to the British government is not attributed to any worse qualities on Franklin's part than carelessness, devotion to an old friend, and lack of perspicacity. And then again that Vandalia business is constantly stalking across the stage! The American Revolution did not quiet this aspiration. Even in the thick of the fight the Franklin-Walpole-Wharton group were centring solicitously on the American Northwest, though, instead of seeking their grant from the British government, they now began petitioning Congress. Lee refers to this rejuvenation of an old scheme in a letter to John Page, May 27, 1778: "Since I last wrote to you I have discovered that a company, which has at its head, and which obtained some time since from the crown of Great Britain, an immense grant on the Ohio, within the Dominion of Virginia, are intriguing to interest members of Congress in it so as to get a confirmation of their grant from Congress, which would be invading the right of our state. The grant was called Vandalia. Many Englishmen are members of the company and the Americans are Dr. Franklin, Mr. Joseph Wharton, in London and a Dr. Bankcroft. These are the persons by whose intrigues it is expected the business may be affected."

Benjamin Franklin went to his grave without losing confidence in the associates who so successfully sold out his country. Bancroft remained his associate all through the war, and after, for Franklin even took him in a confidential service to the peace conference that ended the Revolution, Bancroft, of course, being still on the British pay roll.   In 1783 the adroit creature came to Philadelphia, again on a spy mission for the Foreign Office, bearing warm letters of introduction from Franklin.   "I have long known him," he writes, "and esteem him highly."   In 1785, after Bancroft had returned to England and Franklin had returned to America, the hospitable philosopher wrote him in most friendly terms.   "My best wishes and those of my family attend you.   We shall be happy to see you here when it suits you to visit us; being with sincere and great esteem, my dear friend, yours most affectionately, B. Franklin."   And so ends what was perhaps the most calamitous instance of misplaced confidence in American history.

5

Meanwhile an event had taken place of more inspiring character.   On December 5, 1777, Jonathan Loring Austin arrived in Passy as special messenger of Congress.   Franklin's anxiety as he greeted the emissary has passed into history.   "Is Philadelphia captured?" he tremblingly asked, and when Austin replied "Yes, sir," the old man, wringing his hands, turned to enter the house.   "But I have much greater news than that," Austin exclaimed at the retreating figure: "General Burgoyne and his whole army are prisoners of war!"   What the battle of the Marne proved to be to France in the recent European conflict the battle of Saratoga was to the American cause.   Paris celebrated the great American victory as though it had been her own.   The city was illuminated with bonfires; bells were rung and cannons fired; Americans appearing in the streets were almost mobbed by joyful Parisians; the Prime Minister sent his congratulations to the American envoys, requesting to be informed of all the details. For the fateful happenings of the next few months no better guide can be asked than the diary of Arthur Lee.   The aspect that stands out most clearly is French eagerness for an alliance. The battle of Saratoga immediately settled an issue that had been simmering for a year; French statesmen interpreted this triumph as a certainty that the United States would win its independence, and their only fear now was that France would be left outside the breastworks. One will recall the argument that Arthur Lee, in London in the winter of 1775–1776, was constantly pressing upon Beaumarchais. France, he kept insisting at that time, could not take the risk of failing to support the American cause. If the United States and England composed their quarrel, he argued, they would form a power that would be dangerous to France and would, in all probability, despoil her of her West Indian empire. Saratoga put this same fear in the hearts of Frenchmen. That, after this display of martial power, Great Britain would approach her erstwhile colonies in friendly guise seemed to French statesmen inevitable. Indeed, immediately after Saratoga, Paul Wentworth approached Franklin and Deane as unofficial agent, to see if the quarrel could not be settled; that Great Britain would now concede any terms, so long as America remained a part of the British Empire, was no secret. And it was to ensure against this very possibility that France had already taken the dangerous step of surreptitiously assisting the American cause.

Arthur Lee records in his diary how, two days after the news of Saratoga, Gérard, secretary to Vergennes, came to Passy. "He said as there now appeared no doubt of the ability and resolution of the states to maintain their independency, he could assure them it was wished they would reassume their former proposition of an alliance, or any new one they might have, and that it could not be done too soon." A few days afterward the Americans and Vergennes met in most secret session. Arthur's entry on December 12 follows: "My colleagues did not reach Versailles till half after eleven o'clock, when, upon sending notice by a servant to Mr. Gérard, his servant came with a hackney coach and carried us to a house about half a mile from Versailles, where we found Count Vergennes and his secretary. The minister [Vergennes] made us some compliments upon the present prosperous state of our affairs and conversed some time upon the situation of the two armies. He said nothing struck him so much as General Washington attacking and giving battle to General Howe's army. That to bring an army raised within a year, to this, promised everything." After a little more conversation on military matters, Vergennes passed to the subject of a Franco-American treaty. "The Count said that it was the resolution of his court to take no advantage of our situation, to desire no terms of which we might afterward repent and endeavor to retract; but to found whatever they did so much on the basis of mutual interest, as to make it last as long as human institutions would endure."

A few days later Vergennes sent his secretary to explain the royal purpose. "He was now at liberty to inform us that it was resolved to conclude that treaty [of amity and commerce] with us immediately, for which he was authorized to give us his majesty's parole. That, further, it was determined to enter into another treaty, offensive and defensive, to guaranty our independency, upon condition of not making a separate peace, or relinquishing our independency; that he had been ordered to draw up these two treaties, which he expected to lay before the council the next day, and of which he would send us copies in a few days. He said the King was not actuated by ambition, or a desire of acquiring new territory, but solely by the desire of establishing the independency of America." That was the one point at issue: France would not even ask the return to her of Canada, in case of American success. Since 1763 French policy had aimed at separating Great Britain from her American possessions, as a way — so French statesmen thought — of destroying the British Empire, and now the one promise exacted from the United States was that no peace would be made with the ancient foe that did not leave the American colonies an independent state.

One ceremony was necessary to confirm this new relation to France — the presentation of the American envoys to the king and queen. But here difficulties arose. The treaties were not yet avowed — at least officially; moreover, they were not in effect, not yet having been ratified by the American Congress. In reality, that is, the treaties did not exist; how then, could the king and queen receive American ambassadors? This fact probably accounts for the very informal presentation that, six weeks after the signing in France, took place at Versailles. The king and queen did receive Franklin, Deane, and Lee, and, at the same time, did not receive them — did not extend to them, that is, all the elaborate courtesies usual on such occasions. The informality of the presentation, as described by Arthur Lee, seems studied — as of course it was; royal France, while it evidently wished to recognize America at court, was forced to do so in a way that did not amount to complete diplomatic acknowledgment. One detail of this proceeding has passed into history. No man in those days could appear at the French court without a wig. Yet no wigmaker in Paris had a headdress large enough to fit Franklin's huge cranium. "It is not that the wig is too small," the distracted *perruquier* informed Franklin, "but that your head is too big!" Thus the philosopher was forced to greet royalty in his own carefully brushed gray hair, black velvet suit, knee breeches, white silk stockings, and silver-buckled shoes; in the eyes of both court and populace, Franklin could do no wrong, and his costume on this occasion only added to his *réclame*. But Arthur adhered punctiliously to etiquette — a large wig concealing his youthful tawny hair, sword dangling at his side, and chapeau, according to regulation, tucked under arm. And probably the most accomplished French courtier could not have rivaled Arthur's bow to the Majesty of France.

Arthur's description of this semi-presentation is the only one we have. The commissioners "were led to the anti-chamber of the King and after a few minutes they with all the crowd were admitted into the King's dressing room, where he had a sort of levee and where they with the two other commissioners [that is, Ralph Izard and William Lee] were presented by Count Vergennes to the King, who said, *'Je serai bien aise que la Congrès soit assuré de mon amitié'* [1] and then went out. He had his hair undressed, hanging down on his shoulders, no appearance of preparation to receive us nor any ceremony in doing it. The King appeared to speak with manly sincerity. After this they were presented to Count Maurepas, Mons. de Sartine, Ministre de la Marine, le Prince de Montbarey, Ministre de Guerre, Mons. Bertin and Mons. Amelot, two ministers for home affairs. The Chancellor was in town and two of the Ministers not within. I

---

[1] "I shall be very happy that Congress be assured of my friendship."

XII

THE VIRGINIAN AND THE CONNECTICUT YANKEE

I

POSTERITY has no quarrel with Arthur Lee for unmasking Edward Bancroft and can only regret that his efforts did not succeed. Neither does his complete understanding of Silas Deane, that other object of his "suspicions" and denunciations, reflect either on his judgment or on his patriotic motives. For here again the historic whirligig is ringing in its revenges. Not that, even in Revolutionary days, much doubt existed concerning Deane's character. Certainly that crusty commentator on men and things, John Adams, never entertained any illusions. "Mr. Deane," writes Adams in his *Autobiography*, "was not well established at home. The good people of Connecticut thought him a man of talent and enterprise, but of more ambition than principle. He possessed not their esteem or confidence. He procured his first appointment in 1774 to Congress by an intrigue. Under the pretext of avoiding to commit the legislature of the state to any act of rebellion, he got a committee appointed with some discretionary powers, under which they undertook to appoint the members to Congress. Mr. Deane, being one, was obliged to vote for himself to obtain a majority of the committee. On the third of November, 1774, the representatives indeed chose Mr. Deane among others, to attend Congress the next May; but on the second Thursday of October, 1775, the general Assembly of Governor and Company left him out. . . . Instead of returning home to Connecticut, he [Deane] remained in Philadelphia soliciting an appointment . . . first in the West Indies and then in France."

This last sentence presents Deane as the original of what was mention this to show how little of ceremony there was in the business or of previous preparation.   The commissioners, accompanied by Mr. Gérard, walked through the streets to their different dwellings.   Between two and three we dined at Count Vergennes, where there was a grand company of nobility. . . .

"22nd [of March].   The commissioners went again to Versailles to be presented to the Queen [Marie Antoinette].   It was with great difficulty they could pass through an unordered crowd, all pressing to get into the room where the Queen was, it being levee day.   When they got in, they stood a moment in view of the queen, and then crowded out again.   They were neither presented nor spoken to and everything seemed in confusion.   They went next to Mons. and Madame, the king's eldest brother, and his wife; then to Madame, the king's maiden sister.   The youngest brother, Count d'Artois, was at this time under a temporary banishment from court, for having fought a duel with Duke Bourbon, a prince of the blood.   They then visited the Chancellor, whose office is for life and he is obliged always to wear the robe of it.   After this they dined, with the Americans in their suite, at Mons. Girards."

Unhappy as was Arthur Lee over this not especially dignified ceremony, there was another man in Paris who liked it even less. Lord Stormont, the British ambassador, evidently interpreting the appearance of Franklin and Lee at Versailles as recognition of the rebellious colonies, immediately left Paris, without taking leave of the king.

to become a persistent type in American politics. Apparently he was the first "lame duck" in American history. Service in the national legislature had exercised an irresistible spell; just as to-day defeated Congressmen and Senators, on failure of reëlection, return to Washington and haunt the purlieus of former greatness, so Deane, in September 1775, came back to Philadelphia and roamed, ghostlike, the outskirts of the chamber now closed to him. And in 1775, as in 1935, there was only one consolation for such frustrated ambition — public office. So unchanging is the political character that, one hundred and sixty years ago, as now, the Congressional heart grew tender towards a colleague repudiated by his "deestrict." Deane wished to serve his country, preferably in some line in which his commercial shrewdness could be used; at this time he hardly aspired to diplomatic honors, for which he had no training or fitness; he did, however, possess trading talents, and such aptitudes were as useful to the embryo nation as the ability to shine in foreign courts. In Deane's Congressional career one powerful friend had been made who might help in realizing this desire. The letters of Robert Morris and Deane show that the two men were on more than official terms; Deane was evidently a familiar guest at the rich merchant's Philadelphia home. Morris has gone down in American history as "the financier of the Revolution," and justly, for his efforts in the cause constitute a powerful claim on the gratitude of his countrymen. Born in 1734, in England, of humble parents, emigrating to America as a child, quickly rising to power and wealth when apprenticed to the great Philadelphia firm of Willing, Robert Morris becomes an early type of that familiar American character, the self-made man. He displayed a gift for public affairs in Stamp Tax days, taking stand against parliamentary pretensions, yet at the same time opposing separation. A member of the Continental Congress in 1776 and a supporter of the John Dickinson point of view, Morris voted against the Declaration of Independence; like many others, however, after the adoption of that document, he became a "signer" and thenceforth a faithful devotee of the Revolutionary cause. Yet the character of Robert Morris, in spite of his patriotic work, has always been a matter of argument. His habit of mingling private advantage with public duty brought a burst of criticism in his lifetime that is not silenced yet, and his association with Silas Deane in personal ventures, when both men were supposed to be concentrating their energies on the business of Congress, is one of the chief counts against Morris as a public man.

The influence gained by the able Philadelphian in Congress facilitated Deane's plans as well as his own. His experience in commerce gave him a commanding position on all matters affecting trade and finance, and in 1775 he became a member of both Secret Committees having foreign matters in charge. His power increased from day to day until Paul Wentworth, writing to Lord Suffolk in October 1777, declared that Congress was ruled by "Richard Henry Lee, the Adamses and Robert Morris," who, he said, was "of great mercantile experience . . . fertile in expedients . . . is much confided in by all the cabals." Such a friend as this was naturally a great accession to a man who, like Deane, in 1775, had been turned adrift by his state. He at once sought Morris's assistance in obtaining public employment, and successfully. The man's first appointment was purely commercial. The original Secret Committee — that on commerce — was formed, in the main, of a group of New York and Philadelphia Tories, all working at that time against American independence — John Alsop, Francis Lewis, Philip Livingston, Robert Morris; and all of them apparently detected in the confused trade situation an opportunity for private profit. This is what John Adams meant in his comment to John Jay, when that gentleman made his approach in hopes of detaching Adams from the Lees: "I believe too many commercial projects and private speculation were in contemplation by the composition of these committees."

To understand the situation, the new prospect opened for American trade must be kept in mind. The Revolution of 1776 was not only political but economic, for it changed a trade system that had prevailed between Great Britain and America since 1651. Those Navigation Laws which had compelled America to trade only with England and her colonies and in British bottoms now suddenly went into the discard; Congress closed all American ports to Britain and opened them to the rest of the world. That a European scramble would take place for the commerce that had poured such wealth for more than a hundred years into England could be assumed. As already described, these new trade prospects became America's best diplomatic card, the bait constantly held forth by Franklin and the Lees for European help and alliances. Moreover, the falling off in trade with England in the two years preceding separation — caused by non-importation agreements and "associations" — everywhere thinned the merchants' shelves. Robert Morris, probably America's leading importer, appreciated the new opportunities more keenly than most of his compatriots. In his letters to Deane, after the latter arrived in Europe, Morris's mouth fairly waters at the prospect. As early as August 16, 1776, he writes in a paragraph which delightfully exhibits his practice of mixing private and public interests: "It seems to me that the present oppert'y [opportunity] of improving our fortunes ought not to be lost, especially as the very means of doing it will contribute to the service of our country at the same time. I have in a former letter told you the whole continent [that is, continent of America] would be in want of woolen goods the ensuing winter and you may depend that sufficient quantities cannot be sent in time. . . . All sorts of Cutlery Ware, Copper, Tin, Lead and every kind of goods fit for Winter wear must bring any price. . . . These goods may if you please came out 2/3rds on account of Willing, Morris & Co., 1/3d on your account." And, at about the same time: "There has never been so fair an opportunity of making so large a fortune since I have been conversant in the world." And so on *passim*. As Simeon Deane expressed it in a letter to brother Silas: "One fortunate adventure at this critical time makes a large fortune." Yet one difficulty quickly presented itself. Americans, after all, were Englishmen and had for decades been accustomed to English goods. What they really wanted were not French and Spanish manufactures, but that clothing and furniture and farm equipment which William Lee was accustomed to purchase in London markets for his Potomac friends, and those muslins, cambrics, lawns, calicoes, and silks which his wife, Philippa Ludwell, used to adapt to the taste of her feminine compeers at home. The fact that America and

England were in a state of war did not discourage Robert Morris and Silas Deane. One of Paul Wentworth's "Statements of Information" tells the story. A company was formed with a capitalization of £400,000. Morris and Deane were the Americans concerned; French members were that Ray de Chaumont whose house at Passy sheltered the American Embassy and M. Grand, who was banker to the American Commission, and another partner was Thomas Walpole, — Vandalia again! — member of Parliament, ostensibly an enemy alien to Morris and Deane, both of whom held positions of trust under the American government. The plan was to purchase goods in England, — this was obviously Walpole's department, — ship them to Havre and thence to American ports. The vessels were to carry no arms or ammunition, which, at that time, were more pressing needs of America than muslins and seersuckers. According to Professor Thomas P. Abernethy, of the University of Virginia, who recently unearthed this interesting case of trading-with-the-enemy, "This arrangement was carried into effect, and there is every reason to believe that it was successful."

2

That Deane came to France with the purpose, among others, of pushing his private fortunes is therefore clear. His life ambition was to become a great merchant, like Morris, and his chief idea in accepting the commission to France was to lay the basis for a trading firm with his brothers, Simeon and Barnabas, as partners. In fact he did establish such a firm while in France, but his dismissal prevented it from gaining much headway. That Morris, as member of the Secret Committee, obtained Deane's appointment to Paris, largely because he could be useful in pushing the business of Willing, Morris and Company, seems also to lie upon the surface. Deane at once embarked on the "trading plan" — the expression is that of Robert Morris. His "ventures" started before Franklin and Lee had been added to the American Commission, and the hold Deane obtained on American affairs, from July to December, 1776, was never relaxed. The two men who might have thwarted his schemes — Lee and Franklin — had practically nothing to do with the commercial side of American affairs. How Arthur Lee was elbowed out of Passy and stationed in lonely exile at Chaillot has already been described. The fact is that, in a brief period, the American Commission on its business side passed into the hands of Deane — and its concerns, for the first year, were largely business, the purchase of ammunition and supplies and their shipment to America.

In these details Franklin quite willingly permitted himself to become a cipher. The philosopher who landed in Bordeaux that cold and foggy December, 1776, after the hard winter voyage, was a weary old man, now in his seventy-first year and subject to attacks of gout. Thrifty as Poor Richard's advice had always been to his readers, carefulness in business affairs was not a trait of his own. That one should watch his pennies was part of the Franklin doctrine, yet the actual man had always abhorred account books — once, in a dissertation, he described his futility in the bookkeeper's art. The unprecedented acclaim which he had received from the French people signalized the part he was to play — the diner-out, hero of French intellectuals, pet of duchesses and salons, negotiator in matters diplomatic, maker of treaties and alliances, and the gentleman skilled in wheedling loans out of the depleted French treasury. Here was Franklin's job, and effectually did he do it. Lee the old man did not like, and that there was constantly at his elbow a shrewd Connecticut Yankee, only too glad to relieve him of such matters as cargoes and shipping, was a tremendous relief. One could quote many passages in the spy letters of Wentworth and others showing that, in all business matters, Deane was unquestioned master. There are constant references to "Franklin's apathy," his "lethargy," his "phlegmatic" attitude towards routine. Arthur Lee, in his dairy, quotes M. Grand, French banker to the Americans, as follows: "Mr. Deane seemed much affected and complained that it was hard upon him that he was obliged to do all the business himself, Dr. Franklin being generally occupied in philosophic studies."

A belief exists to-day that Deane's diplomatic career was destroyed by the "intrigues" of the "jealous Arthur Lee." The letters he was constantly writing, we are informed, to his brothers, to Samuel Adams and other leading members of Con-

gress, setting forth his colleague's villainies, eventually led to
Deane's recall. Yet the fact of the matter is that Arthur Lee
had nothing to do with that recall. The time came — months
after Deane's cashiering — when Lee did write caustic letters, the
most severe addressed, as was proper, to Congress itself, but
they could not have caused Deane's elimination, for Lee's charges
were not submitted until several months after Deane had been
deposed and John Adams had been sent to Paris as his successor. The vote of Congress recalling Deane was passed November 21, 1777. Students of Revolutionary history knew that from
about May 1777 to April 1778 no letters from their representatives in France reached Congress. Ship after ship, carrying out
letters, was "taken" by the British fleet — thanks to the accurate
"Informations" of sailing schedules supplied by Bancroft and
Wentworth. On April 30, 1778, James Lovell, for the Committee on Foreign Affairs, wrote Franklin and associates that
Congress had had no news from the commissioners in Paris since
the preceding May — nearly a year. In January 1778 came the
famous Captain Folger incident: he had sailed almost eight weeks
before from France, bearing a packet of letters from the American Commission in Paris; but when this was opened nothing but
white paper was found; through the connivance of one of England's American spies, Captain Hynson, — not unknown in Passy,
— the official communications had been seized and sent to the British government — which still retains them. Not only letters but
war cargoes were intercepted; had supplies of blankets, shoes,
tents, and clothes, dispatched from Europe to Washington's army,
not been "taken" by British ships, through information given
by Bancroft, the experiences at Valley Forge would have been
much less distressing.

Thus it is apparent that, even though Arthur Lee had transmitted his accusations against Deane, — as a matter of fact he
had written no such letters at this time, — they would not have
reached their destination. The cause of Deane's humiliation was
something quite different. His supercession by Adams was a
matter exclusively between the Connecticut statesman and Congress. Silas had never been a favorite in that body, and a few
months after his dispatch to France things began to happen that

infuriated the gentlemen of Philadelphia. One of the charges that has been brought against the Lees is an unfriendliness to Washington and a desire to displace him from the command of the Continental army in favor of Gates. There is a passage in a letter of Lafayette accusing "les Lees" of some such purpose; sentences in Richard Henry Lee's letters, highly praising Gates's military prowess, — and this at the time of the "Conway Cabal," — lend certain color to the charge. More significant still, it was the faction of which Lee was a member in Congress that led the campaign against Washington. If this charge against Lee were proved, it would be a serious stain on his record as it is on that of Samuel Adams. While there is no certainty, so far as Richard Henry Lee is concerned, there is pretty definite evidence that Silas Deane was not well disposed to Washington, and, at one time, was working in favor of another commander in chief. In a letter to the Secret Committee (December 6, 1776), he suggested that "it might be politic, as it would give a credit and character and credit to your military and strike perhaps a greater panic to our enemies . . . if you could select a great general of the highest character in Europe, such, for instance as Ferdinand, Marshall Broglie." This nobleman was prepared not only to take command of the American forces, but to become "stadtholder" of the new American nation, provided proper financial settlements were made upon himself and a large assortment of retainers and kinsmen. His magnanimity failed to stir the hearts of Congress, but proved to be only the first of many similar approaches. The long train of Frenchmen and other Europeans armed with contracts, signed by Deane, assuring them commissions in the American army, from lieutenancies to major generalships, guaranteeing high pay, back pay, and life pensions, now form a diverting episode in our military history, but at that time were not regarded as a joke, least of all by Washington, who wrote despairing letters to Richard Henry Lee, asking if the thing could not be stopped!

A few of these officers, notably Lafayette and De Kalb, proved assets to the American cause, but the average importation was a mere adventurer, discredited at home, involved in debt, and anxious, for varying causes, to get out of France. One of them was that same Thomas Conway [1] who led the conspiracy against Washington in the latter part of 1777. Employment of such volunteers meant the displacement of Americans, ambitious for commissions, in the Revolution as in all our wars; had Deane's "contracts" been approved by Congress, there would have been few native generals or colonels; the American army would have been officered by a collection of nondescript Frenchmen, unable to speak English, unacquainted with the country, disliked by the American soldier, men whose American career represented merely a chance to save their fortunes. A typical illustration was Du Coudray. Congress had authorized Deane to engage four French engineers, gentlemen of this profession being sorely needed in the Continental army, but there was no intention of bestowing high commissions or extravagant emoluments. Instead Deane engaged Du Coudray, an engineer of some importance, but of little military reputation, guaranteed him a life commission as major general, with a year's back pay and a life pension, and command of all the artillery forces in the American army, with power to fill all vacancies, and subject only to the orders of Congress and Washington. Du Coudray brought with him a company of nearly a hundred Frenchmen, most of them soldiers of fortune like himself, similarly assured high posts. Du Coudray's personal behavior, and that of his underlings, was insolently condescending, while his standing as a military man was evidenced by the fact that genuine French officers, to whom Congress had granted commissions, refused to serve under him. In the American forces the arrival of the Du Coudray troops caused almost a universal breakdown. Generals Knox, Sullivan, and Nathanael Greene announced their resignations, in case Congress approved the Deane "contracts"; Congressmen, assailed by their "constituents," whose popular militia leaders would have stood no chance of appointment if these foreign adventurers had been preferred, spent most of their time cursing Deane and working against his commitments. Happily, a benevolent Providence solved the problem. One morning in October

---

[1] Conway was not a Frenchman, but an Irishman. However, he had lived in France most of his life, and, at the time Deane gave him a commission, was a colonel in the French army.

1777 Du Coudray, gayly caparisoned and astride his charger, embarked on a Schuylkill River ferryboat. Bystanders urged him to dismount, for the horse was spirited and the vessel small and flimsy, but Du Coudray haughtily ignored the injunctions. Probably startled, the animal jumped or fell overboard, and, with his rider, disappeared beneath the waves. The most heroic attempts at rescue failed, and next day the recovered remains of the difficult Frenchman were buried in the near-by Catholic graveyard. "This dispensation will save us much altercation," wrote the grim John Adams. Congress promptly repudiated all Deane's "contracts," and, in the next few months, the great Du Coudray cavalcade sailed for France, threatening lawsuits against Congress and breathing imprecations upon the land of freedom.

This repudiation made Deane's recall inevitable; any self-respecting diplomat, under such circumstances, would have resigned. The simple truth is that Deane had violated his instructions in a matter of the most serious consequence, and for such infractions the penalty must be paid. Richard Henry Lee moved Deane's recall, acting for the Foreign Relations Committee; the extent to which he represented the Congressional desire was immediately apparent, for the resolution passed without a dissenting vote. Though the pill was sugared a little by instructing Deane to return to enlighten Congress on "European affairs," the recall was final and absolute, for almost simultaneously John Adams was appointed his successor. Thus the displacement was in no way connected with what was afterward known as the Deane-Lee "feud." The force of this powerful clan was subsequently directed against the repudiated Yankee, but the end of his public career was the unanimous will of Congress, caused by official acts which most distressfully embarrassed that body, and for which it refused to admit any palliation.

3

The prospect of reviewing this celebrated Franklin-Lee-Deane imbroglio, in any detail, is rather appalling. It excited, humiliated, and wearied the American people in 1778–1780, — a difficult period in the crisis, when public interest should have been concentrated on the immediate task, — and it has wearied several generations since. The struggle represented more than an impeachment of Deane. It represented an attack on the whole tribe of Lee. Passions that had been stirred in Virginia politics long before the Revolution, jealousies that had been fired by the importance that family had achieved in the contest, now burst into flame. The success of the Lee-Adams alliance in forcing the Declaration of Independence on an unwilling Congress had naturally enhanced its prestige. In the two or three succeeding years its power had vastly grown. A writer of the day declared that this dominant group ruled Congress by acting as the balance of power: "they meet regularly, debate upon and adjust the manner of their proceedings." Circumstances favored the Lees, the Adamses, and their associates, for they were "old stagers," and knew intimately the proceedings of Congress from the beginning; Congress as a whole was a changing body, the vast majority composed of new, inexperienced members, while this ruling bloc consisted not only of the ablest men, but men who year after year returned to Philadelphia, and thus had public affairs at instant disposal. Paul Wentworth, as quoted above, reported to his English employers that the Lees and the New England contingent and Morris were the rulers of Congress; Carter Braxton, the ancient enemy, was exercising against them his vitriolic tongue; John Dickinson disapproved the concentration of so much power in so few hands; and John Jay, still nourishing resentment, was directing jibes against this American "family compact," more arrogant, more grasping, than that which had been for a quarter century so disturbing an influence in the politics of Europe. The charge of selfishness, of overweening lust for power, was constantly leveled at the Lees. Certainly the American landscape at that time evidences the family influence. Congress contained two Lees, both signers of the Declaration of Independence and both holding dominating positions in legislation. There were five American embassies to European courts — Paris, Madrid, Vienna, Berlin, and Florence. With the exception of that to France, the Lees dominated them all, and in Paris Arthur Lee was joint commissioner with Franklin and Deane. Besides this, Arthur was sole commissioner to Spain.

William Lee was sole commissioner to Vienna and Berlin — besides being commercial agent in France; and Ralph Izard, in devotion and temper himself almost a Lee, was accredited to the Grand Duke of Tuscany. Certainly this family, powerful in Congress, accredited to most of the diplomatic stations in Europe, playing a decisive part in Washington's army, illustrated again the conception of Virginia grandees — that public affairs were a matter set aside for a few lofty families born and trained for the task. Necessarily such preëminence aroused antagonisms and hatreds, which came to full fruition in the dispute over Silas Deane.

Had modern conditions prevailed in 1778, the nation would have been edified by a Congressional investigation of heroic proportions — a kind of life-insurance inquiry or a proceeding resembling Teapot Dome. One can picture Silas Deane and his cosmopolitan group under the pitiless quiz of a Charles E. Hughes or a Thomas J. Walsh; and even the great Benjamin himself, subjected to such inquisition, would have had his unhappy moments, not necessarily explaining acts of guilt, but tenderness to relations, "lethargy" in the midst of disorder, indolent trust in unworthy associates, failure to perceive things that were apparent to casual observers and a matter of daily gossip in every European capital. Despite the absence of such an official record, the merits of this, the first great scandal in American history, are fairly plain. Lacking the ten or a dozen huge volumes of printed testimony that would have issued from the public printing office had Congress, in 1778, inaugurated the methods of inquiry that have since become so familiar, one must fall back on the disorderly literature that survives — collections of letters, minutes and votes of Congress, communications to the public press, addresses to "the virtuous people of America," "narratives," "replies," "vindications," and "refutations." These miscellaneous writings were promulgated by "Senex," "Plain Truth," "Candid," "Common Sense," — Mr. Thomas Paine was one of the most strident contributors on the side of the Lees to the general din, — "Lysander," "Philalethes," and other pundits of the ancient and modern world. Out of this bewildering potpourri two charges against Deane and his com-

panions stand conspicuous. He was "in trade," to use Arthur
Lee's expression, an occupation the fastidious Virginian regarded
as beneath ambassadorial dignity, not to question its propriety.
This meant that Deane, in partnership with Robert Morris and
French associates, — Ray de Chaumont, Grand, Monthieu,
Holker, Beaumarchais, perhaps Gérard, Vergennes's secretary
and first French minister to the United States, — was engaging
in "private adventures," commerce for personal profit, chiefly in
those materials that the cessation of British commerce had made
so scarce in America. The second accusation was even more
serious. Deane's accounts, said Lee, — accounts involving the
expenditure of 5,000,000 livres, — were in a state of "studied
confusion" that gave reason to suspect the malversation of public
funds. The likelihood that public money had been used to purchase and load ships for this private trade, as well as for privateering, was not ignored. Neither Arthur nor William Lee
hesitated to frame these accusations in bold terms. The first
reference appears in Arthur's letter to Richard Henry, dated
January 9, 1778 — nearly two months after Deane's recall.
"Let me know whether it is not proper that I should write to
the secret committee that in my judgment the public business
here is turned to private emolument, that my advice and endeavors have not the least influence." "Remember," wrote William
Lee to Congress, "I pray you, not to let any of his [Deane's]
accounts for the expenditure of the publick money finally pass
without the most authentic vouchers. Upon proper inquiry into
this business I can boldly assert that most infamous transactions
will be brought to light. From the apprehension rises Mr.
Deane's and Dr. Franklin's mortal hatred to myself." And
Richard Henry had his own pungent characterization, directed
chiefly at Franklin, who, in his correspondence, usually appears
as "that wicked old man," the "fox" who is "artful," "malicious,"
and "cunning," while his seat of operations is thus described:
"The corrupt hot bed of vice at Passy has produced a tall tree
of evil."

Clearly there was nothing indefinite about the accusations.
There were other charges, personal and official, and an abundant
list of mutual incriminations — that Arthur Lee was a "traitor,"

in correspondence with Lord Shelburne, that he conveyed to the opposition party in England news of the signing of the French-American treaty, that he was antagonistic to the French alliance and secretly coveting reconciliation with Great Britain. It was urged also that Deane was a "traitor," that he was speculating in British funds, and that his loose tongue, in Parisian cafés, was a constant embarrassment to the cause. There were plenty of reverberations of this kind, but there is no need, in the present review, of confounding the main issues with a mass of inharmonious details. The two really important charges were that the American Embassy had a "jobbing character" and that public money was spent without obtaining receipts. The most cursory examination of the existing literature substantiates both these indictments. The first has already been touched upon. One needs only to read the Deane-Morris correspondence of 1776–1777, which, on almost every page, has references to what the Philadelphia financier, then chairman of the Secret Committee of Congress, describes as his "trading plan." This avocation of a distinguished statesman had nothing to do with the public business; it was a matter purely of private profit. As one reads these letters, the facts stand out plainly enough: from the start Deane was chiefly interested in private commerce; his thoughts turned only incidentally to war supplies and treaties of alliance.

Extracts have been given above showing Deane's entire willingness to coöperate in the Morris trading plan. A few may be added at this point indicating that the plan was carried into effect. Thus M. Ray de Chaumont writes to Robert Morris, January 7, 1777: "Upon the friendship which I have for Mr. Deane I have accorded him 100,000 livres in the ship *Union*, Captain Roche, the half of which is upon your account. . . . The merchants may address their vessels to me and Mr. Deane, and we will return in them whatever commodities they shall desire, and in which we have an interest. If in acquiting yourself with Mr. Deane you return merchandise it is natural to suppose that you will address them to me conjointly with Mr. Deane, for in case of his death I should then have an opportunity of recovering my advances." Robert Morris writes to Deane, January 11, 1777: "Should you obtain a French fleet come out here, then will be the time to speculate" (meaning that then their cargoes would be protected from British attack). Deane writes Robert Morris, January 6, 1777: "Herewith I send you invoice of cargo of goods shipped by M. Chaumont. . . . The money was advanced for the goods by M. Chaumont and every advantage taken for our joint interest . . . you will see I engage for one third. . . . M. Chaumont is a capital man in France and makes this as his first experiment on the success of which he proposes to regulate his future connections in America. . . . The net profits, if any, hold for the use of my wife and son, payable to order of Mrs. Deane, or my brother Barnabas Deane, Esq." Deane to Jonathan Williams, December 18, 1777: "I hope you will be able to procure a freight for my brother's goods in Montieu's vessels, if there is room over the goods of the public" — an especially interesting passage, for it indicates a desire by Deane to ship his cargoes in bottoms carrying the sadly needed supplies to the Continental army. Arthur Lee, in his journal, reports on visits with French lenders on this subject: "M. Grand observed that our meddling so much with mercantile affairs had reduced us in the opinion of people in general and of the ministers. That the ministers had great reliance in Dr. Franklin's good faith and in mine but that they suspected Mr. Deane from the detours he had used." By accident Arthur met M. Paulze, head of the Farmers-General, "who expressed his opinion that Deane had some private views in tobacco."

Here therefore appear, on one hand, an American agent, sent abroad to obtain and rush aid to his native land, then almost dying for the lack of the materials of war, and on the other a member of Congress, at that time chairman of the committee having this particular matter in charge, diverting a considerable part of their energies to personal money-making. At times both clearly realized that they were engaging in a doubtful business. The arrival of Captain Roche's cargo in Charleston, where it was sold "at a considerable advance," caused embarrassment, for the merchant to whom it had been assigned began talking indiscreetly. "You seem," Morris wrote Deane, June 29, 1777, "to rely much on this gentleman's prudence, but he has told to everybody the concern you and I had in the *Union's* cargo, with many circumstances that I knew little about. Colonel Harrison, who happened to be in Virginia when he arrived, says the people in that country are acquainted with the whole concern, and from hence it is not improbable that they may conjecture by and by that Private gain is more our pursuit than Public Good." That really puts the matter in a nutshell.

But other mercantile matters engaged the Passy group. There was, for example, the exceedingly profitable business of privateering. From this occupation Robert Morris excused himself, not, however, from American motives. "Those who have engaged in privateering," he writes Deane, September 12, 1776, "are making vast fortunes in a most rapid manner; I have not meddled in this business which, I confess, does not square with my principles, for I have long had extensive connections and dealings with many worthy men in England and could not consent to take any part of their property." Others of the American group were not so chivalrous. Their operations in the English Channel in the summer of 1777 — fitting out vessels in French ports, seizing enemy ships and bringing them into France for condemnation and sale — enraged Vergennes and resulted in at least one enterprising American landing in the Bastille. The Lee opposition asserted that in many cases these private expeditions were financed with public money, — that 5,000,000 livres advanced by France and Spain for the American cause, — and there is little doubt that they were. Another matter that a modern legislative investigation, such as imagined above, could have profitably probed was the sale, in French harbors, of prizes taken by American ships. That these were purchased, at absurdly low prices, by Chaumont and friends, and subsequently sold at handsome profits, was another scandal of the time.

4

These latter matters will always remain obscure, for the reason that Arthur Lee's second charge was also well founded — that there was no bookkeeping at Passy and that no adequate record was preserved of expenditures. It was his tempestuous insistence on "accounts" that caused Franklin and Deane to regard him as a pest. When Arthur returned from Berlin, in late July, 1777, he discovered that 5,000,000 livres of public money had been spent, and a debt incurred in addition, but that it was impossible to discover in what channels the money had gone. He made most persistent efforts to discover, but in vain. Acrid interview and more acrid correspondence with Franklin failed to satisfy. Franklin, of course, was as much in the dark as Arthur, for he had left these details to Deane; still Arthur's complaints seemed only to stiffen his reserve, and increase his already profound dislike for the Virginian. On March 31, 1778, Lee writes Franklin again, "to repeat the request I long ago and repeatedly made that we should settle the public accounts relating to the expenditure of the money entrusted to us for the public," and, on April 4, 1778, to the Secret Committee: "I am obliged to say that this gentleman [Deane] took to himself the entire management of the business, in which I could obtain no share without a quarrel; that my advice and assistance were always rejected and he would never settle accounts." When John Adams appeared in Paris, as Deane's successor, the conscientious New Englander turned his attention to the same subject, with the same result as Lee. "The public business," he confided to his diary, "has never been methodically conducted. There never was, before I came, a minute book, a letter book, or an account book, and it is not possible to obtain a clear idea of our affairs." On May 21, 1778, John Adams wrote to Cousin Samuel: "Our affairs in this kingdom are in a state of confusion and darkness that surprises me. Prodigious sums of money have been expended and large sums are yet due, but there are no books of account nor any documents from whence I have been able to learn what the United States have received as an equivalent. Sir James Jay insisted that Mr. Deane had at least been as attentive to his own interest, in dabbling in the English funds and in trade, and in fitting out privateers, as to the public; and said he would give Mr. Deane fifty thousand pounds and that Dr. Bancroft too had made a fortune." "The expenses of Mr. Deane never have been known and never, I presume, can be known," was Adams's summation of the matter.

Congress was as unsuccessful in penetrating the mystery as

Lee and Adams. Deane, when he left France in early April, 1778, knew that he would be called upon to explain his accounts, that his financial course in France was under sharp suspicion, yet he brought no documents that would have exculpated him. Called twice before Congress, he simply submitted excuses; he had left France in a "hurry," he did not know he would be called upon for an accounting, he had deposited his papers in a "safe place," and so on. His only document was the banker's statement of money paid under Deane's administration, — the total reaching 4,046,988 livres, — but no vouchers were forthcoming. One item in this banker's statement would have stirred the interest of a Congressional investigating committee, as imagined above. On February 17, 1778, Silas Deane had sent Samuel Wharton, living in London, 19,520 livres. Why should the American Commission in Paris have sent this large sum to the Philadelphia Quaker in London? An eighteenth-century Charles E. Hughes might have asked: "Why should American money find its way into the enemy's country?" Was there anything significant in the date, the very time Samuel Wharton and the rest were speculating in the news — not yet generally known — of the Franco-American alliance? This item has never been explained, and, of course, never will be. But Deane's enemies in Congress, all through the summer and fall of 1778, kept demanding enlightenment on this and other subjects. From now on something like a chorus arose from the opposition: "Vouchers! vouchers!" But no vouchers appeared then or afterward. Up to the present writing (1935) no papers have been submitted showing how the American Commission — which means Silas Deane — dispersed these 5,000,000 livres. Any fiduciary who presents a list of persons to whom he has paid money, but submits no corresponding receipts from these payees, is subject to any suspicions the public chooses to entertain. That is Silas Deane's position in American history, and there one may leave the matter.

Benjamin Franklin's eyes were never opened to Edward Bancroft, but the time came when he saw Deane in his true colors. When Deane left for America, in March 1778, Franklin gave him a fine letter of recommendation, and also secured one of the same tenor from Vergennes, but these gestures must have become a rueful memory. After his humiliating appearance in Philadelphia, Deane sailed for France, ostensibly to secure his "vouchers" and present his complete accounts to Congress. Instead of clearing his name, Deane turned against his own country and began to plead the British cause. After 1778 Britain was in sorry pass in the American war. She was willing to compromise on any ground short of independence; ready to admit all her errors since 1763, to wipe from the slate all colonial legislation passed since then, and begin life anew with her erring child on a basis of mutual respect and confidence. And just as, in the midst of the late World War, there arose the cry of "Peace without Victory," so, in the latter days of the Revolution, came the cry of "Peace without Independence." But independence now was the ineluctable goal of America and her allies. The United States had no choice with honor; the French treaty had pledged her to make no peace except upon this basis, and loyal Americans had no intention, after all their suffering, of dropping this aim when the object was so near. In the eyes of the people, to preach "peace without independence" was virtual treason. But in the autumn of 1781 *Rivington's Gazette,* in New York, — a Tory organ, — began the publication of a series of letters by Deane advocating submission to England on these obnoxious terms. The letters made three points: that independence was a mistake, that the French alliance was an even greater blunder, and that the United States should accept the proffered English terms. The letters, addressed to Robert Morris, — of all men! — had been seized by a British ship on a captured American vessel. The time of publication was unhappy, for they appeared almost on the eve of Cornwallis's surrender at Yorktown. Their authenticity once established, Deane became an object of universal execration. Yet his contemporaries never knew the whole story; that appeared only with the publication of the letters of George III, the last edition in 1932.

For these pretty clearly show that Deane was in the pay of the British government. On March 3, 1781, His Majesty wrote to Lord North: "On returning last night from the oratorio I received your box. I think it perfectly right that Mr. Deane should be so far trusted as to have £3000 in goods for America. The giving him particular instructions would be liable to much hazard, but his bringing any of the provinces to offer to return to their allegiance on the former foot would be much better than by joint application through the Congress; for if by the breaking off of some the rest are obliged to yield, no further concert, or perhaps amity, can subsist between them, which would not be the case in the other mode, and the fire might only be smothered, to break out again on the first occasion." His Majesty was not the clearest writer of English that ever lived, but his meaning can be fathomed. He wished Deane instructed to advocate that the ministry deal with the former colonies individually, not with that collective nation known as the United States of America. This would not only accomplish the immediate purpose, but leave the "provinces" so angry with one another that future union would be difficult. Again, on July 19, 1781, George III wrote Lord North: "I have received Lord North's boxes containing the intercepted letters from Mr. Deane for America. I have only been able to read two of them, in which I form the same opinion of too much appearance of being connected with this country and therefore not likely to have the effect as if they bore another aspect." In a subsequent letter the king expresses the same opinion; Deane's letters were "too strong in our favor to bear the appearance of his spontaneous opinions." And then George outlines the kind of letter that Deane should write!

These letters have proved a great difficulty to Deane's apologists, who profess to see in them a British hope to bribe the American, not a realization; but to an impartial reader their whole style and implications indicate that the king's communications refer to an agent with whom the British government had established a close understanding. "From the publication lately made of the letters of George III," wrote Charles Francis Adams in 1874, "it appears certain that Deane was more or less in the pay of the government during the war." Franklin never knew of these letters of the British king, but he learned enough of Deane's transgressions. That his former colleague was consorting in England with Benedict Arnold ended the last vestiges of illusion. When Deane returned to Paris, in January 1781, he did not seek the old familiar shades of Passy; all his former companions were shunned, his denunciations of America and France making him obnoxious to both countries. According to Vergennes, the former commissioner was *"furieux contre sa patrie."* All leaders in the cause now abandoned him. "I hand him over to the buffetings of Satan," said John Adams. "He is a wretched monument of the consequences of a departure from right," was Jefferson's comment. Perhaps the cruelest thrust came from John Jay, Deane's old-time Congressional friend, his thick-and-thin supporter in the Deane-Lee controversy, and arch-enemy of the Lees. When Deane called on Jay in London, in January 1784, the New Yorker, now minister to Spain, refused to see him, and in a painful letter to Deane explained why his presence was unwelcome. "I was told by more than one, on whose information I thought I could rely, that you received visits from, and was on terms of familiarity with, General Arnold. Every American who gives his hand to that man, in my opinion, pollutes it." Deane's final years were miserable and squalid, much like Arnold's; like his abhorred compatriot he received occasional recognition from the king, but the mere attempt to keep body and soul together proved exhausting. Deane died — there have been suspicions of suicide [1] — in Deal, England, 1789, just as he was about to sail for America, in a final attempt to recoup fame and fortune, and was buried in the churchyard of that town.

And just as Arthur Lee was right when he insisted that Passy was a nest of spies, and that Edward Bancroft was a paid agent of the British government, so was he also right in his declaration that Deane and his associates were "in trade" and that there was "studied confusion" in money matters at the embassy. Yet Deane enjoyed one parting triumph at the expense of Lee. In his downfall he dragged the Virginia brothers with him, for the scandal brought to an end the diplomatic careers of Arthur and William Lee. That, of course, was inevitable. Arthur's champions in Congress, such as Samuel Adams and Henry Laurens, fought valiantly for his retention; but circumstances

[1] John Quincy Adams refers to this in his diary. Vol. I, p. 108.

were not on their side. The fact that France had recognized American independence made necessary a regular diplomatic establishment, and the selection of a single minister in place of the three-headed Cerberus that had lived so distractedly for three years. Naturally Benjamin Franklin was the only man seriously considered for this post. Any other choice would have caused a crisis with the French government. Whatever justice Arthur Lee may have had for his complaints, however right he may have been in his charges against Bancroft and Deane, the fact remained that he had lost the confidence of the French government. No man is of any use as a diplomatic agent under such disqualification.

But Arthur was not only joint commissioner to France, but sole commissioner to Spain. His friends, acknowledging the futility of attempting to keep him at Paris, now struggled to secure his appointment as minister at Madrid. In this too they failed, and John Jay, the family foe, accompanied as secretary by William Carmichael, — Arthur's enemy since his first days in France, — received the honor. This also was probably just, for France and Spain were so intimately joined by the Family Compact that a minister unacceptable to one court would be shied at by the other. But Arthur could not be expected to see the justice of all this. For the rest of his life he grieved and descanted in his usual vein against the ingratitude of republics. The fact that the inspiration and co-worker of pre-Revolutionary days, John Dickinson, voted against him caused particular sorrow, which found expression in a bitter letter addressed to the "Farmer." Its tenor is sufficiently indicated in the last words: *"Et tu, Brute!"* Dickinson replied in dignified fashion. "The conduct you object to," he wrote, "was influenced by two reasons, that, leaving the qualities of your head and heart unimpeached, would have led me to the same conclusion if you had been my brother. These were a coolness in the Court of Versailles towards you and the difference with Dr. Franklin. When it was considered that the connection between the House of Bourbon is so intimate, and that harmony between ministers who are to negotiate between them, especially on the same subject, is so necessary, all private regards give way to the superior force of public opinion. To wound and mourn falls to the lot of more than 'Brutus.' "

And John Adams, sound, utterly sincere, and careful as always in his choice of words, wrote his judgment in his diary: "I am fixed in these two opinions, that leaving the Doctor [Franklin] here alone is right and that Mr. Lee is a very honest and faithful man." It was a judgment from which Adams never departed. In 1819, when Adams himself was eighty-four, and when all the Lees had been in their graves for more than twenty years, he wrote his opinion of the clan, "that band of brothers," as he called them, "intrepid and unchangeable, who, like the Greeks at Thermopylæ, stood in the gap, in defense of their country, from the first glimmering of the Revolution in the horizon, through all its rising light, to its perfect day. Thomas [Ludwell] Lee, on whose praises Chancellor Wythe delighted to dwell, who has often said to me that Thomas Lee was the most popular man in Virginia, and the delight of the eyes of every Virginian, but who would not engage in public life: Richard Henry Lee, whose merits are better known and acknowledged, and need no illustration from me: Francis Lightfoot Lee, a man of great reading well understood, and sound judgment, and inflexible' perseverance in the cause of his country: William Lee, who abandoned an advantageous establishment in London from attachment to his country and was able and faithful in her service: Arthur Lee, a man of whom I cannot think without emotion: a man too early in the service of his country to avoid making a multiplicity of enemies; too honest, upright, faithful and intrepid to be popular; too often obliged by his principles and feelings to oppose Machiavellian intrigues, to avoid the destiny he suffered. This man never had justice done him by his country in his lifetime and I fear he never will have by posterity. His reward cannot be in this world."

Another witness — and what an entertaining one he would have made had a modern Congressional committee held an inquisition on American diplomacy at Paris! — would have been Beaumarchais. Yet there is no intention of entering into this tangled story in this place. It is doubtful whether the merits of Figaro's controversy with Arthur Lee and the Continental Congress will ever be determined. The fact that Beaumarchais, after his splendid early work in behalf of a struggling nation, should have become involved in an angry dispute with that nation — and a dispute on so squalid a matter as money — is one of the Revolutionary episodes on which present-day Americans look with little pleasure, and it has brought down on Arthur Lee the anathemas of all the biographers of the witty Frenchman. Yet for this sorry predicament Beaumarchais was not entirely blameless. In the summer of 1776, after receiving the first subsidies from France and Spain, Beaumarchais, partly to conceal the source of French supplies and partly to engage in a "trading plan" of his own, organized the firm of Roderique Hortalez et Cie, — the Spanish influence that led to the choice of his subjects for plays also directed the selection of a title for this fictitious commercial house, — installed himself and a large force of clerks in the ornate building of the Banque de Hollande, and began operations on a huge scale. The grandiloquent manner of life now assumed by the expansive genius is evident from the fact that he maintained, for his own use, eleven coaches and three coachmen. The dispatch of munitions to the American colonies frequently assumed a theatrical character extremely damaging to the secrecy with which the enterprise was supposed to be conducted. Thus, when the first ships sailed from Havre, — a proceeding in which absolute silence was requisite to success, — Beaumarchais celebrated the departure by moving a theatrical troop to the port and producing his most successful plays. Manifestations like this disgusted the less imaginative Lee, and he also had personal reasons for disgruntlement. Chief of these was that on the arrival of Silas Deane, in July 1776, Beaumarchais had suddenly dropped his association with Lee and entered into the closest relationship with Deane. Beaumarchais's explanation for his change in allegiance was reasonable enough. Deane had been made official American representative in France; Arthur Lee at that time was the secret agent of Congress in London — his appointment as American commissioner to France came several months afterward; naturally Beaumarchais should deal with the gentleman officially designated for that purpose. But Lee saw more in the matter than this. Beaumarchais, like Deane, was interested in "trade" on his personal account; like Deane, he hoped to reap great profits from the opening of American ports to France; and a partnership for this purpose with Deane would — so the "suspicious Lee" argued — be a valuable means to that end. That Beaumarchais, under the ægis of Hortalez et Cie, did embark on extensive "ventures" of his own is a matter of official record.

It is this dual relationship — a transporter of war supplies to America and a private trader for personal profit — that makes the Beaumarchais story so complicated and baffling. On the subject immediately in question, however, the facts were on Arthur Lee's side. This concerned the 1,000,000 livres which the king of France, in early June, 1776, had delivered to Beaumarchais for American aid. This was a subsidy — a gift, not a loan — to the colonies. It will be recalled that Grimaldi, in his meeting at Vitoria with Arthur Lee, specifically insisted that the money promised was simple largesse, that Spain expected no payment and would not receive any. The position of the French king was precisely the same, and for the same reason; for these courts to make a loan would be almost equivalent to a recognition of American independence. In the deal with France, it was provided that America should send cargoes of tobacco in payment; but this stipulation, Arthur always maintained, was merely a blind — a method of giving the character of a commercial transaction to what was really a present from France. Hardly had the supplies started for America when Beaumarchais began demanding payment from Congress — payment to him personally, insisting that the 1,000,000 livres had been advanced by him and his friends. In early 1778, his representative, de Francy, appeared in Philadelphia and began dunning Congress for the money. Though startled by the man's importunities, Congress, in gratitude for this timely help, would probably have paid the bill — or at least have recognized it, for in the depleted state of American finance at that time actual payment was impossible — had it not been for Arthur Lee. In his usual direct manner, he informed Congress that the money was a gift from the French king, that Beaumarchais was making a fraudulent demand, and that his agent should be disregarded; and this advice was accepted. That is the basis of the Beaumarchais controversy — a controversy that dragged along for fifty years, until Congress, in 1831, settled the matter with Beaumarchais's heirs by a cash payment of 800,000 francs — a payment based not so much on the merits of the dispute, but intended as a recognition of the great service the dramatist had rendered America in difficult times. As to the dispute itself, the whole question is definitely treated in *Beaumarchais and the Lost Million,* by Charles J. Stillé, lawyer and historian, who irrefutably shows that the money was a direct gift from France, and that Beaumarchais had no basis for his demand. It is another case in which Arthur Lee was right, though his attitude of hostility to a lively genius, notoriously irresponsible in money matters, who deserved so well of the American Republic is regrettable.

5

To all these transactions, as to most of the sad proceedings of American Revolutionary diplomacy, there came a culminating episode of comic relief. Arthur Lee's famous "treason" — his alleged act of informing Lord Shelburne of the signing of the treaty with France — was a matter of public gossip at the time, as it has been with Lee's detractors since. That the British cabinet learned of the French alliance almost as soon as it was adopted is the fact; Lord North acknowledged in Parliament that he had had inklings of it. Where the information was obtained is to-day no secret; in his catalogue of crime, submitted by Bancroft to Lord Caermarthen in 1784, he specifies the intelligence of the treaty which he took such pains to bring immediately to England. In his letters, Horace Walpole says that he learned the news from his cousin, Sir Thomas Walpole, the Vandalia magnate, to whom Bancroft constantly supplied such news for speculative purposes. In the third volume of his history of *French Participation in the Establishment of the United States,* Henri Doniol publishes a cryptic piece of writing, which, he says, Vergennes attributed to Arthur Lee. The passage is said to be in the handwriting of Vergennes himself, and is endorsed by that statesman as "an extract from a letter of Arthur Lee to Lord Shelburne, written immediately after signing the treaty between France and the United States of America." It is as follows: "To-day the new partnership was signed and sealed. The French firm is about to begin operations. If the old one wishes to preserve some interest it should act without delay." On the evidence of these few words rests the charge of "treason" against the Virginian. Possibly the paragraph appeared in some document intercepted by Vergennes's spies, but no evidence is presented that Arthur Lee wrote it. Lee's secretary for two months, as already said, was Major Thornton — a British spy whom Arthur dismissed as soon as he discovered his true character. Thornton's brief term of service covered the period when the French treaty was signed. The latest American scholar to study the mystery is Dr. Edward S. Corwin, professor of jurisprudence at Princeton University. In his *French Policy and the American Alliance,* Professor Corwin, after quoting this extract, says: "The letter referred to was probably the work of Lee's secretary, Thornton, who was undoubtedly a British spy. . . . Lee's loyalty to the Alliance is, in fact, above suspicion."

Lord North's statement in the House of Lords, announcing knowledge of the French treaty, naturally started a good deal of buzzing in Paris. The information now available in the Stevens Facsimiles, telling of Bancroft's betrayal of this news, was not then public property, and thus speculation as to the "traitor" had wide scope. It came to Arthur Lee's ears that a certain Samuel Petrie, an Englishman allied with the Anglo-American speculative group in London, was spreading rumors that he was the guilty man. Immediately one of the Virginian's peremptory letters was dispatched to Petrie, demanding to know whether he was circulating such reports. Petrie replied that he had made no such remarks about Arthur Lee, but admitted that he may have said something like it concerning Arthur's brother William. As William Lee was then in Frankfort, awaiting a chance to take up diplomatic business with Vienna or Berlin, Petrie may have thought this accusation a safe one

to make; however, Arthur sent word to his brother of the slander, and William, sardonic, high-tempered, at times fairly ferocious, at once took action. He wrote Petrie demanding retrac-
tion or proof; receiving no reply, he sent challenge to a duel,
proposing Spire, on the borders of France, as meeting ground.
"The journey will be horrible to me in this weather," William
wrote Arthur, "but I can't let the wretch escape."

Petrie failed to keep the appointment; instead he sent another
letter, telling of his poor health, but promising to give satisfaction at Lisle, in Flanders. William arrived there on the day in
question, but again the accuser disappointed him. Another letter
from Petrie said that he would appear as soon as his health
permitted. William was not in the best health himself, and long
journeys, in post chaise, over the roads of that day were not
his favorite form of recreation, but, with trunk stuffed with
pistols, he kept hard on Petrie's trail. In order not to give
Petrie the slightest excuse for declining a meeting, William wrote
his antagonist a letter, which was made up largely of the most
insulting epithets at his command. Petrie was, William now informed him, "such an abandoned and worthless wretch that it
is in truth a disgrace for a gentleman to have any connection
or contention with you. . . ." He further informed Petrie that
he was "the dirty tool of as dirty a junto as ever disgraced
society in the worst of times." Petrie replied that he would
be at Valenciennes on August 2 or the succeeding day. Arriving at the Flemish frontier, Lee was held up by the commandant;
he had no passport, and could get no horses without such a document. He sent word of the situation by courier to Petrie and
his friends, who had reached the Post House at Valenciennes,
and said that he would start as soon as horses could be procured.
Petrie sent back word suggesting that William walk! However,
Petrie added that he would be at an indicated spot the next day,
and would wait until one o'clock. Having procured his horses,
Lee started and reached the rendezvous at ten — three hours
ahead of time. Here he received word from Petrie that his
carriage had broken down, that a smith was working hard on
it, and that the repairs would unquestionably be finished in time.

Evidently the smith was not equal to the task and Petrie did not show up, and thus the insult remained unavenged.[1]

In reviewing this celebrated episode, one wonders whether, even though Arthur or William had sent this information to Shelburne, the crime would have been a great one. The question assumes an especial pertinency because, although the Lees committed no such indiscretion, we now know that Franklin did this very thing. The fact is that Lord Shelburne and his group held a special relation to the American Revolution: in this connection they were almost as much Americans as Franklin and the Lees themselves. Lord Shelburne had championed the American cause from the start; had opposed all the measures of the North administration; and, all through the war, had been heartily on the American side. Franklin, while representing the United States at the court of France, was in constant touch with the British statesman. Franklin's biographer, James Parton, so vindictive in his treatment of Arthur Lee, takes pride in setting forth the philosopher's wisdom in maintaining confidential terms with Shelburne. "I have remarked before," writes Parton, "that Dr. Franklin habitually made use of his acquaintance with the leaders of the English opposition to convey to England correct information of the state of things in America. The interests of America and the interests of that opposition were identical." That Franklin was corresponding with British statesmen during the Revolution was known at the time. Lord Stormont, British ambassador to France, wrote to Lord Weymouth, January 15, 1777: "I have reason to believe that Franklin has at least an occasional correspondence with the following persons, viz.: Lord Shelburne, Lord Camden, Mr. Samuel Wharton, Mr. Thomas Wharton, Suffolk Street, Mr. Williams, Queen Street, Cheapside." James Parton describes the most striking case of Franklin's communication with the British opposition. "During the progress of the negotiations [the negotiations with France for the treaty of alliance] Dr. Franklin resolved upon sending to England Mr. Austin, for the sole purpose of giving

---

[1] In fact, as Arthur Lee wrote, William, at the time in Frankfort, knew nothing of the signing of the Franco-American treaty until six weeks after that event.

Lord Shelburne, Mr. Fox, Mr. Burke, Lord Rockingham and the liberal members of parliament such a complete insight into American affairs as would enable them to demonstrate the impossibility of reducing the states to submission. The strange spectacle was then afforded of the most eminent British statesmen associating with and entertaining within houses, a commissioned emissary of the King's revolted subjects." In a memorandum published by Mr. Austin's family after his death it appears that in his English sojourn, for the purpose of giving pro-American English statesmen "a complete insight into American affairs," — which must necessarily have involved the Franco-American alliance then under negotiation, — Mr. Austin was "domesticated in the family of the Earl of Shelburne."

PART IV

THE LEES OF LEESYLVANIA

XIII

LEE VERSUS LEE

I

WHILE the sons of Stratford were doing their part in Congress and European capitals, another branch of the family was upholding the Revolutionary cause in Washington's army. The Lees of Lee Hall and Leesylvania now for the first time emerge as powerful figures in their nation's history. Their founder was Henry Lee, sixth son of the second Richard and younger brother of President Thomas Lee, who, in the early part of the eighteenth century, established himself at Lee Hall on the Potomac, not far from Stratford; a seat from which proceeded a succession of descendants, the head always named Henry, like the reigning princes of the House of Reuss. For the first two generations these Henrys had been a rather prosaic lot — prosperous country squires, not marked for leadership in the state, quite cast in shadow by the brilliance of their Stratford cousins. Lee Hall in Westmoreland, and its successor, Leesylvania, in Prince William, were gathering places of hospitality, but never attained the eminence that Stratford held in Virginian eyes. The second Henry (1727–1787), indeed, served as burgess contemporaneously with Richard Henry Lee and Francis Lightfoot, being one of the seven Lees who adorned Williamsburg in that time; he, too, displayed a genuine patriotism in the days of stamp acts, and was as earnest in the colonial cause as the Stratford scions themselves, but no important act of statesmanship stands to his credit. The Leesylvania Lees were worthy, substantial, placid, high-minded citizens, without a touch of the genius that was domiciled at Stratford.

These first two Henrys were more distinguished for their

marriages than for personal achievement. The fact that their branch should culminate in such men as Major General Henry Lee ("Light Horse" Harry) and his son, the leader of the Confederate armies in the Civil War, perhaps is not unrelated to their good fortune in this respect. The wife of the first Henry was Mary Bland, daughter of Richard Bland of Jordans, granddaughter of Theodorick Bland, Speaker of the House, and ancestor of a long line of Virginia statesmen and scholars. Mary Bland's brother was Richard, pronounced by Jefferson "the most learned and logical man of those who took prominent lead in public affairs, profound in constitutional lore." He proved a valiant champion of America's rights in stamp-tax days and in the Continental Congress — a leader of those moderates who wished to preserve American independence in American affairs and, at the same time, keep the British connection. His pamphlet, *An Inquiry into the Right of the British Colonies,* widely circulated on both sides of the Atlantic, outlined that conception of independence in local affairs and general allegiance to the mother country which is the basis of the present Dominion system of the British Empire. Bland was equally famous as an antiquary, and to him Virginia is indebted for the preservation of many of her early records, the basis of our knowledge of colonial Virginia history. "Staunch and tough as white leather," with "something of the look of old parchments," practically sightless in old age, unskilled at speaking, but with a mind full of historic instances and constitutional precedents, this Richard Bland, granduncle of the Leesylvania Lees, was a familiar phenomenon of their childhood, a patriarchal exemplar of good citizenship and instructor in the rights of freemen. The whole of Virginia could offer no more satisfactory ancestors, from the standpoint both of public spirit and of scholarship, than the Blands.

Somewhat more romantic was the marriage of the second Henry, son of Henry and Mary Bland. For this has inspired one of the most persistent legends in American history. His wife was Lucy Grymes of Morattico, Richmond County, usually referred to as that "lowland beauty" to whom an inarticulate and bashful boy of fifteen, named George Washington, wrote much halting "poetry," only to have his "chast and troublesome passion" despised in favor of the stodgy Henry Lee. The sentimental Washington Irving is chiefly responsible for this yarn. "Tradition states," he wrote in his life of Washington, "that the lowland beauty was Miss Grimes, of Westmoreland," — thus misspelling the lady's name and placing her in the wrong county, — "afterwards Mrs. Lee and mother of General Henry Lee who figured in revolutionary history as Lighthorse Harry and was always a favorite with Washington, probably from recollecting early tenderness for the mother." But Lucy Grymes has more substantial claims to distinction. In her children the lines of Leesylvania Lees emerged from obscurity. In this branch she played a part not unlike that performed by Hannah Ludwell in the Lees of Stratford, for, like Hannah, Lucy was the mother of famous sons — Henry, one of the finest soldiers of the Revolution; Charles, a leader of the American bar, attorney-general in the cabinets of Washington and John Adams; Richard Bland Lee, Congressman, Federalist champion, one of the men responsible for placing the Federal capital on the Potomac. This story concerns that deadlock which almost wrecked the Federal Union in its second year. New England and the North, under the leadership of Hamilton, were determined that the central government should assume the debts of the states — an assumption to which the Southern states were opposed. The South, in turn, was eager for the establishment of the new Federal capital on the Potomac, a site for which the Northern region had no enthusiasm. Congress was almost fatally divided on these two issues, when Jefferson, at the prompting of Hamilton, solved the problem. In brief, Jefferson agreed to get two Virginians to change their votes in favor of assumption if Hamilton, to "soothe" the Southern states, would guarantee the establishment of the national capital on the Potomac. Richard Bland Lee's was one of the two votes secured for this "deal." Perhaps, in changing his mind and securing this great advantage for his region, Lee had in mind the prophecy attributed to his granduncle, Thomas Lee of Stratford, that the capital of the future American nation would be placed in the very region where Richard Bland Lee's vote now assigned it. "The manœuvres concerning founding and assumption have been many and subtil," wrote Richard Henry Lee. "But truth is great and will prevail."

Thus the most striking quality of the Lees of Leesylvania, as distinguished from those of Stratford, is that they were all Federalists, fighters for the new constitution, leaders for "ratification" in Virginia at a time when the fate of that instrument was doubtful. Charles and Richard Bland Lee were too young to figure in the Revolution, but the accomplishments of their brother Henry served as militant prelude to the almost equally stormy part he was to play in civil life. Certainly his loyalty to Washington, an emotion almost religious in depth, was strengthened in war time. The great planter, however, Light Horse Harry had known from childhood. If Henry — his father — had supplanted the lord of Mount Vernon in the affections of Lucy Grymes, that proceeding apparently left no sting, for the Henry and Lucy Lees and the George and Martha Washingtons were intimate friends. Among Harry Lee's earliest memories were his childhood visits to Mount Vernon with his mother and father — visits antedating the Revolution. Just what impression the yellow-haired, blue-eyed, and hero-worshiping child made upon the sedate soldier is not recorded; the mere allusion to these trips is about all that has survived of Henry Lee's earlier days.

Another circumstance that distinguished him from the Stratford cousins was Henry's education. No English schools and universities for him; in the eyes of his father, Princeton was the greatest educational institution extant, and here, at the age of thirteen, Henry began serious studies. Just why the elder Lee regarded this as the one place worthy of nurturing a brilliant boy is not related, but perhaps the fact that its president was John Witherspoon influenced the selection. Certainly no sturdier upholder of Lee principles could have been found. President Witherspoon was a living refutation of that almost morbid obsession of Arthur Lee — that no Scotsman could be a decent citizen of any country, least of all America. For Witherspoon was a Scot of the Scots, a descendant of John Knox, born on Scottish soil, trained in Scottish universities, steeped in Presbyterian theology, imparting wisdom and preaching democratic principles in the broadest of Scottish burrs. He began his stewardship of

CHARLES LEE, 1758–1815

ATTORNEY-GENERAL IN CABINETS OF
WASHINGTON AND JOHN ADAMS

ANNE LEE, HIS WIFE

Portraits by Gilbert Stuart, Courtesy of Frick Art Reference Library

Princeton in 1768, a year when the air was full of the British-American discussion, promptly turning his back on his native land and becoming one of the most eloquent champions of the American cause — afterward a member of the First Continental Congress and signer of the Declaration of Independence. Nor in those pre-Revolutionary days did Dr. Witherspoon make any attempt to separate religion from politics; his sermons were frequently tirades against British pretension and incitements to rebellion. This required courage, for the royal governor of New Jersey, from 1763 to the Revolution, was William Franklin, Benjamin's son, a Tory of the Tories, always on the alert to crush sedition. Yet Witherspoon did not hesitate, in his commencement exhortations, with the governor sitting officially on the platform, to denounce King George and his abettors. And the president had educational ideas new to men in his position. He was fond of history and literature; at this early stage he introduced English as a common study, and insisted on writing and public speaking as essential items in undergraduate life. From a character such as Witherspoon, and from studies such as prevailed at Princeton, Henry Lee was the kind of youngster to profit.

Perhaps Witherspoon's genius in training boys explains the fact that so many students of Lee's day attained celebrity. Among his companions at Nassau Hall — then the only university building — were James Madison, pallid and ill from overstudy; Aaron Burr, prize winner in several branches of knowledge; Philip Freneau, already conspicuous as a writer of denunciatory verse; Brockholst Livingston, afterward Justice of the United States Supreme Court; priggish little Philip Fithian, upraised from obscurity by his diary, discovered and published more than a century after his death; and Henry Brackenridge, afterward poet, dramatist, jurist, clergyman, and a leader of that "Whiskey Rebellion" in western Pennsylvania which Major General Henry Lee was appointed to suppress. In this miscellaneous assortment of potential genius the young gentleman from Virginia was not the least promising. Already the qualities which captivated Washington and gave tinges of romance to his army were manifest. Henry Lee's personal graces made him popular among his fellows. Though not above medium stature, his well-proportioned figure showed the effects of out-of-door training in Prince William; that quickness of movement and "dash," so desirable in cavalry leaders, were apparent; and the large oval face, crowned by a mass of tawny hair, — always, even in college days, powdered and frizzled, — and the active, searching eyes, indicated a coming leader of men. That insistence on costume and display which lent charm to the Revolutionary forces was also in evidence at Princeton. Fithian suggests this characteristic in his reference to Lee at graduation: "The stage covered with gentlemen and ladies, amongst whom was the governor and his lady; and that he might not appear singular Lee was stiff with lace, gold lace." Evidently that tendency to green jackets, gold epaulettes, and flaming plumes that so signaled Harry Lee amid the ragged forces of Washington's army was innate.

But he had academic qualities as well. He was a serious student, his progress, as President Witherspoon wrote the father, "has always been in all respects agreeable," his chief interests being mathematics, "Natural philosophy," — that is, science of the Ben Franklin kind, — history, English literature, and, above all, the classics. Other records disclose that on one occasion Henry Lee received first prize for translating English into Latin, and all his days he was airing his proficiency in the Roman tongue. On another occasion, the third prize for reading English — probably what to-day would be called "declamation" — went to the future orator from Virginia. Despite his physical activity and good fellowship, the wilder phases of undergraduate life had little attraction, Harry Lee being especially marked for his interest in religion. With the endless round of prayer meetings, at that time, these predilections could be satisfied, but Harry was also given to song, to conversation, and, above all, to friends. He readily fell in with Dr. Witherspoon's insistence that a college was a place not only for intellectual improvement, but for education in citizenship. One of its functions, in his view, was "to produce a spirit of liberty and independence." Two undergraduate clubs that still exist had recently been organized to carry out this ambition, the Cliosophic, upholding the Tory interest, and the Whig, championing the new day. Harry Lee, in this tender period, was clearly a person of comprehensive tastes, for at different times he belonged to both societies. Evidently the thirteen-year-old stripling, when he landed at Princeton, was not an overzealous patriot, for he joined the Cliosophic, yet at graduation he was enrolled under the banner of the American Whigs, which indicated that President Witherspoon's policy of instilling correct political principles had had its effect. Probably even more important was the influence of James Madison, a political philosopher from his cradle and already imbued with many of the ideas which he was to embody in the Federal Constitution; with him Harry Lee formed an enduring friendship.

In this early period Lee's inclination was not for arms but the law. He planned on graduation to go to London and study, in good Virginia fashion, at Inns of Court. But daily increasing tension between America and England made this impossible. In consequence Lee passed three rather aimless years at the ancestral demesne, helping his father in the care of the estate, though probably the greater part of his time was spent attending parties, dancing, playing cards, riding with the hounds, and making love in the Potomac houses, where he immediately became a favorite. He found a congenial associate in his uncle, Squire Richard of Lee Hall; Stratford was one of his stopping places, and he was a special darling of the Carters of Nomini Hall. Suddenly, however, the idling paragon vanishes from these purlieus, and appears in an environment not so brilliant with silk coats and lace ruffles. The Carters were still drinking loyal toasts to king and queen, but for most Potomac hopefuls — above all, for Harry Lee — the hour of decision had come. And so far as his career was concerned, the outbreak of war was propitious. In the practical realities of life Harry Lee had little concern, but nature had created him a soldier. He was one of those characters so unpopular at the present time, but not without their uses in crises of conflict — a man to whom fighting was in itself a worthy occupation, and war a glorious business. That he was stirred by British "tyranny" and American independence was undoubtedly the fact, but the mere circumstance that armies were moving, that battles were being lost and won, was sufficient incentive to action.

Thus Lee had no difficulty in exchanging the festivities of Nomini Hall and Stratford for Washington's cold and bedraggled camp at Morristown. Inevitably a man of his dashing temperament would enter the cavalry. His first appearance typifies his enthusiasm for the mere panoply of war. The sight of an unequipped command was disheartening. Could not all his men, he asked, be provided with caps and boots? If so, "their appearance into Morristown would secure me from the imposition of carelessness as their captain and I have vanity enough to hope would assist me in procuring some little credit to the Colonel and the Regiment." This letter is a fair expression of Henry Lee's military character, which was entranced by parade and "glory." Vastly as he admired Washington, that general's wish to make Harry Lee an aid-de-camp was declined, because the duties seemed too sedentary. "I am wedded to my sword," Lee replied, "and my secondary object in the present war is military reputation . . . to deserve a continuance of your Excellency's patronage will be a stimulus to glory, second to none in power of the many that operate on my soul."

Lee's very appearance suggested the heroic mood. The uniform in which he delighted was a tall leather helmet, with horsehair plume streaming in the wind, green jacket, white lambskin breeches, shining boots reaching to the knees. Seated on his favorite Virginia mount, rushing with sabre drawn at the head of his three hundred troopers, against the foe — that was Henry Lee's conception of the military art. As to the brilliant appearance of these troops Washington is himself a witness; "the perfection in which he has kept his corps as well as the handsome exploits he has performed" are among the reasons advanced to Congress by the commander in chief for Lee's promotion. To Washington's army he performed a service not unlike that rendered by Jeb Stuart to the army of northern Virginia in '61–'64. There was much hand-to-hand fighting, there were scouting expeditions for information, raids in search of munitions and food, sudden attacks led by the redoubtable Harry, accompanied by the screaming of his followers — harbinger, perhaps, of the coming rebel yell. In Harry Lee was a good deal of the swashbuckler, and he had other qualities of the character — a grandiloquent manner of speech, boastfulness about his deeds, even now and then a touch of cruelty. Once, as a discouragement to desertion, he caused a fugitive to be hanged, sending to his brothers-in-arms the victim's severed head, an act that brought from his beloved Washington a letter of rebuke. Encountering, in a North Carolina campaign, a group of Americans who had joined the British cause, he ordered his troopers to attack and sabre them all, thus immolating to the Goddess of Liberty a hecatomb of ninety men. But other more praiseworthy transactions made him indispensable to Washington. He was that commander's greatest consolation at Valley Forge, for Lee had a gift for accomplishments desirable at that crisis; especially was he skillful in diverting food from British forces to American troops. Farmers in the Schuylkill region who withheld supplies from American soldiers in order to sell, at higher prices, to British became Lee's particular quarry. So successful was he in intercepting their activities that the British decided to eliminate the pest. About two hundred Englishmen one day surrounded Lee's quarters, a small-sized house, and attempted to take him prisoner. Ten followers were ambushed with their captain; these, placed at windows, poured such a murderous fire upon the British cavalrymen, receiving almost none in return, that, after three Englishmen had been killed and a considerable number wounded, the enemy retired. This brought Lee the one thing he valued above all others, a warm letter of admiration from Washington, commending his "gallant behavior," and approbation from a body not so given to appreciation — Congress, which rewarded Lee with a commission as major and an independent or "partizan" command.

This detachment of cavalry was small, never exceeding three hundred men, and as lightly equipped as possible, — hence the nickname of its commander, — but it performed constant and valiant service. Always Harry was looking for some "deed," some act of daring that would lift him above the commonplace and give him "fame." Mad Anthony's success in storming Stony Point prompted him to emulation. Lee's scouting, he believed, had made that performance possible, and the absence of his name in Congressional praise, or public rejoicing, was not endured in too gentle a spirit. But another opportunity almost as useful lay near. A hook of land extending between New York Harbor

and Hackensack River — the present site of Jersey City — lay
unprotected by the British, containing a garrison of one hundred
and fifty men.   To capture it could serve no military purpose,
for the Continentals entertained no hope of holding the fort permanently.   But such a deed would add lustre to American arms
and humiliation to the British and would thus serve an end in
building up American morale.   One August night, therefore,
Major Harry, with three hundred followers, made a silent march
into the English fortress, seized the whole garrison prisoner, and
escaped before the enemy could strike an answering blow.   It
was magnificent, even if, in the strictest sense, it was not war.
Envious fellow officers for a time dimmed Harry's "glory" by
bringing about his arrest and farcical court-martial, but Congress,
acting under promptings from Washington, quashed these proceedings, raised Lee to the rank of lieutenant colonel, and ordered
a gold medal to be struck in his honor, "emblematical of the affair."   Satisfactory as this recognition was, its tardiness, and
the dissensions of jealous rivals, somewhat diminished the reputation Harry Lee had been seeking.   The whole transaction —
the daring of the conception, the speed of execution, the laggard
praise of an ungrateful Republic — aptly symbolized Lee's career,
in which bitterness and sorrow figured as conspicuously as fame
and good fortune.   Perhaps the greatest reward was the comment
of his father, the senior Henry, who, from his Leesylvania home,
had been piously following his son's success in arms.   "The
surprise at Paulus Hook casts a shadow on Stony Point" was
the old gentleman's perhaps not disinterested comment.

2

Up to this point Harry Lee had been a dare-devil cavalry officer, but the time presently came when he displayed what Washington described as his "genius."   Soon after Lee's elevation
in rank the Revolutionary War assumed a new phase.   Up to
1780 operations had taken place almost exclusively in the region
north of the Potomac.   Though the British held New York and
had seemed victorious in other sections, the total results had not
been encouraging.   Evidently despairing of pushing hostilities

in this area to a decisive issue, Sir Henry Clinton suddenly turned attention to a new field. To invade the South, to conquer Georgia, the Carolinas, and Virginia, separate them from their Northern brethren, and "reannex" them to the British Empire — here loomed a more promising field of action than desultory and inconclusive performances in the North. A circumstance that promised success was that the South, particularly the Carolinas, was full of loyalists and that at least half the population, it was believed, would, if encouraged by the presence of British armies, at once raise the British flag. This proved to be the case. In the latter months of 1780, British forces, first under the command of Sir Henry Clinton, and afterward of General Cornwallis, had practically "restored" Georgia and the Carolinas to the British crown. Charleston and Wilmington remained in British hands — an enormous advantage, since the British fleet commanded the sea; American arms, under command of Gates, the "hero" of Saratoga, had suffered a humiliating disaster at Camden, and preparations were far advanced for an invasion of Virginia, under the direction of Benedict Arnold, now a brigadier general in the British service. The severance of the states south of the Potomac from the American Union would mean the end of the Revolution, and in January 1781 the success of the plan seemed practically assured. Washington now turned to General Nathanael Greene as his one recourse. To drive the British from the Southern department, to restore the supremacy of the Union, and to accomplish the task with an army ranging from 2500 to 3000 men — such was the responsibility entrusted to the Rhode Islander. Yet in large degree the impossible was accomplished. Several months of hard fighting practically cleared the British from Georgia and the Carolinas; and Cornwallis, advancing into Virginia, at last found himself on the promontory of Yorktown, between Washington's army and the French fleet. The army that was to split the nation in two and deliver the final, crushing blow to American independence was forced to march out of its *cul-de-sac* prisoners of war; the Revolution was ended, and the United States a fact.

On the part that Light Horse Harry played in this consummation his military reputation rests, not on "exploits" and disconnected deeds of valor. And that his contribution was vital General Greene bore testimony. "I am more indebted to this officer," Greene wrote Congress, February 18, 1782, referring to Lee, "than to any other for the advantages gained over the enemy in the operations of the last campaign and should be wanting in gratitude not to acknowledge the importance of his success, a detail of which is his best panegyric." This is certainly exalted praise when it is realized that among Greene's officers were Marion, Sumter, Pickens, and Morgan. Greene repeats his enthusiasm in a letter written to Lee in the heat of the campaign: "I have run every hazard to promote *your plan* of operation." This seems a clear acknowledgment, by Greene, that the strategy pursued in the Southern department was Lee's. It is a claim that all Harry's biographers have made, and which he seems to take to himself in his description of the campaign. The matter is of the utmost consequence, for the manœuvres adopted in the Carolinas and Georgia were largely responsible for sending Cornwallis into Virginia and ultimately into Yorktown; they had much to do, that is, with the collapse of the British military machine. To the biographer, alert for indications of inherited genius, these proceedings have particular interest; in boldness of conception, disregard of precedent, and reliance on enemy "psychology" as a directing influence in forming military plans, the Southern campaign suggests qualities subsequently manifest, nearly a century afterward, by Harry's son, Robert E. Lee.

After the battle of Guilford Court House, — on the whole an indecisive one, though technically a British victory, — the two armies found themselves in a difficult position. The Americans were camped at Ramsay's Mills, on the Haw River, while, about a hundred and fifty miles to the southeast, Cornwallis had safeguarded his army by marching it to Wilmington, his base of supplies and of reënforcements. Evidently the initiative lay in the hands of the Americans: what should they do with it? The question was anxiously debated at a council of war, for Nathanael Greene was one of those wise generals who did not act precipitately, but listened to the advice of his capable associates before deciding a programme. On this decision great events depended, — perhaps greater than those present had foreseen, — the losing of Virginia, and the consequent loss to the American Union of all the states south of the Potomac.   Henry Lee, in his *Memoirs,* describes this council in a good deal of detail, never mentioning himself by name, but modestly as "the Proposer."   At first the Proposer represented a minority of one, for all the rest of Greene's lieutenants centred upon the obvious plan and took issue with Lee's startling suggestion.   In the existing predicament the conventional mind saw only two courses: a march to Wilmington and an attack on Cornwallis, or an advance into Virginia, and an attempt to destroy Benedict Arnold, then raiding and terrorizing the whole region of the James.   Authority, then as to-day, insisted that the enemy's forces were the great objective in warfare; the destruction of his army, it was urged, would not only free the Carolinas and Georgia, but would save Virginia as well.   Lee now disconcerted the traditionalists by proposing an entirely new scheme; he records, in his grandiloquent way, how General Greene warmed to the idea as it was unfolded, which was natural enough, for "there was a splendor in the plan which will always attract the hero."   The Americans should make no advance upon Wilmington, asserted Lee, nor should they retire to a point near the Virginia boundary and there await a British attack.   Instead, they should march into South Carolina, form a junction with the able leaders stationed there, Marion, Sumter, and Pickens, assail the British communications with Charleston, and in this way, if successful, free the state from British rule.

Suppose Cornwallis should follow Greene and give battle somewhere in the South?   In that case, urged Lee, the chance would favor the Americans, for they would be reënforced by the troops and leadership of Marion, Sumter, and other brilliant commanders.   Suppose Cornwallis should take advantage of Greene's departure and invade Virginia?   In that case the Carolinas and Georgia would be free from British occupancy and the British campaign to subjugate the Southern states would be brought to an end.   This was indeed the great objective of Lee's proposal; if only Cornwallis would enter Virginia and leave the Southern department to the Americans!   He was positive that an invasion of South Carolina would have that result. The young man, then twenty-six, rested his confidence on his knowledge of Cornwallis and the British attitude towards colonials, just as his son, in outlining his campaigns, kept constantly in mind the mentality of opposing leaders. What were McClellan and Pope, from their innate character and nervous organization, likely to do in a given state of circumstances? Such was Light Horse Harry's state of mind, in advocating his plan. That Cornwallis should abandon the Carolinas for Virginia was, in Henry's view, the consummation above all to be desired, for that would destroy the whole British scheme of separating the South from the Union, and he was sure that an American advance into the Carolinas would produce that very result. He thought so because he had studied Cornwallis's mind and the mind of the average British commander. Their main characteristics were pride and contempt for American military prowess. To follow Greene's army and to accept battle where the Americans chose to exact it would be to give a despised foe the initiative — to make the rebels leaders and the British followers. Such a concession would be too much for the British stomach. "It would unequivocally declare," writes Lee, "the mastery of his opponent," and "the best and wisest men prefer any course to that which is coupled to an admission of their inferiority." Therefore, he insisted, Cornwallis would leave the Americans to such British forces as still remained in South Carolina and do the only thing left, march his men into Virginia, where they might have some preliminary successes and inflict considerable damage, but where, ultimately, they would have to cross swords with the whole American army. And meanwhile North Carolina, South Carolina, and Georgia would be redeemed.

Alexander Hamilton declared that this strategic plan "was not surpassed in boldness and wisdom by Scipio's famous determination to invade Africa." That it had tremendous historic consequences is now evident. For Cornwallis behaved precisely as Lee had predicted. After considerable hesitation, and much puzzlement over American manœuvres, he started for Virginia, where he wasted his energies in pursuit of "the boy," as he called Lafayette, then commanding the American forces in Virginia, engaged in several marauding expeditions that served no military purpose, and finally found himself cooped up in Yorktown, between Washington's army and the French fleet. Meanwhile Greene's expedition into Georgia and South Carolina was also working out in the manner foreseen. One by one the British military posts, Forts Watson, Granby, Motte, and Galphin, fell to the Americans — battles in which Lee performed a conspicuous part, in his usual "Light Horse Harry" style. These assaults form the most brilliant episodes in his military life, the result being that, in a few months, South Carolina and Georgia were freed from British rule and restored to the Federal Union.

After the last important engagement, that of Eutaw Springs, Lee, hearing that exciting events were taking place in his native Virginia, departed for the North, reaching Yorktown in time to participate in the siege and be present at the surrender. Yet that occasion was not without its bitterness. In many ways Lee was a child, given to jealous and sulky spells, and one of his most petulant outbreaks took place after Yorktown. Garbed in brilliant raiment, with hair powdered and queued in the back, he took his place in the line of officers as the British army marched out and Cornwallis surrendered his sword to Washington. But his mind was tormented by thoughts of neglect and inappreciation. Did anyone in this gathering understand the part that Lee had played in bringing the triumph to pass? Was it known that his had been the plan to force Cornwallis into Virginia, and at the same time rescue the lower South from the British flag? Evidently not, for there were no references to Harry or subsequent acknowledgments from Congress, and no reward, no promotion in military rank, not even a brevet. Lee began his Southern campaign as lieutenant colonel and remained a lieutenant colonel at the end of the Revolution. The title of "general" came to him many years afterward, in different service. Sensitive, proud, vain, even egotistical, pursuer of "fame" and "glory," this Yorktown proceeding, splendid as it was as the accomplishment of his country's freedom, was a humiliation to Harry Lee — only another sign of the misfortune that seemed to crown his most distinguished moments.

Sorrowful, angry, so melancholy in spirit that his condition alarmed his friends, Lee crept back to his native lair on the Potomac. The rebellion was over in which he had anticipated such renown, and though "Light Horse Harry" was a familiar name in all parts of the country, still that national recognition which he had looked upon as his right was not forthcoming. He made no secret of his repining; Harry, like most egotists, did his thinking out loud, and now he assumed the rôle of a man who had "deserved well of his country," but whom that same country chose to neglect. He even wrote reproaches to the commander whom he always referred to as "the illustrious Greene." "I candidly tell you, that I read some of your public reports with distress, because some officers and corps were held out to the world with a lustre superior to others, who to say the least deserved equally." Far from being offended, Greene tried to soothe his despairing favorite, and wrote that letter to Congress already quoted, in which he praised Lee as superior to Marion, Sumter, and other associates, but this recommendation produced no result on that torpid body. Lee, now at the philosophic age of twenty-six, became more and more misanthropic. Like most juvenile pessimists, he began to long for some "obscure retreat." In Byronic vein he writes, also to Greene, concerning his future plans. "I am candid to acknowledge my imbecility of mind and long time and eminence may alter my feelings; at present my fervent wish is for the most hidden obscurity; I want not public nor private applause; my happiness will depend on myself; and if I have but fortitude to persevere in my intentions it will not be in the power of malice, intrigue or envy to affect me. Heaven knows the issue. I wish I could bend my mind to other decisions. I have tried much, but the scars of my wounds are only irritated afresh by such efforts."

Harry Lee presently found his "retreat," but it was not a particularly "obscure" one. Consolation came in the form of one of the greatest estates on the Potomac. Stratford Hall was a different place from the modest Leesylvania in which Greene's favorite cavalry officer had spent his early years. And never had it been more attractive than in those spring days of 1782. For something new had happened to this establishment. Stratford no longer had a master, but a mistress, and this mistress a young lady in her nineteenth year. Philip Ludwell Lee died February 21, 1775; as his body was being lowered into the grave, his

MAJOR GENERAL HENRY LEE, 1756–1818

("LIGHT HORSE HARRY")

only son, presently christened Philip Ludwell, was born, a child who lived only a few months. Two girls, Matilda and Flora, were thus left to inherit the family estates, the larger part going to the elder, Matilda, at that time about twelve years old. Philip Ludwell Lee, as already noted, was not a lovable character, but he had an affectionate side, which appears most charmingly in his relation to his daughters. Music, which seems to have been Philip's chief æsthetic interest, is associated similarly with the girls. Almost the only bits of Philip's writing that survive concern these children. "Mr. Lomax," Philip writes William Lee (July 23, 1771), then living in London, "says he will make Matilda play and sing finely. He is fond of her ear and voice he says if you will send me Sartine's work Abels's and Campioni's and Scarleti's for the harpsicord he will always think on you when is playing them; if to dear to send all at once by degrees he has a great regard for you yet; and Corelli's music he wants." And Philip adds a word about the other daughter: "Our girl, your god daughter is called Flora signifies sweet as a flower."

Three years afterward Philip Fithian's diary recalls the arrival at Nomini Hall of the Stratford coach containing "young misses," all agog for a forthcoming party; an interesting item in social history, for these maidens at that date were about ten and eleven years old — a tender age, it would seem, for girls to be "out." These scraps are nearly all that we know of Matilda Lee. If the picture is a slight one, it is only as fleeting and fragile as Matilda herself, for she died at twenty-six, leaving no letters, not even one of those portraits or miniatures so popular in the day — nothing by which posterity can imagine her, except that word "divine" prefixed to her name by contemporaries. That she has always been known as the "divine Matilda" tells much. It was a title of the day, not idly used. About this time Arthur Lee was writing letters concerning a new Philadelphia friend whom he called the "divine Mrs. Bingham" — that social leader in Federal circles, as eminent for beauty as for political insight and cultivation; thus we may conclude that the adjective implied more than personal attraction, and one of Matilda's acts, as will appear, disclosed that she possessed character and determination. Harry Lee, of course, had known her from infancy;

not improbably, in those days, from 1773 to 1776, when he was
disporting in the Potomac houses, Matilda may have caught many
glimpses of her dashing cousin, regarding the young dandy with
all the suppressed excitement appropriate to a girl of her years.
She was thirteen when Henry left for Washington's army, and
nineteen when the disappointed hero returned to Prince William
in his hunt for "obscurity." A brilliant and lovely young woman
now placed herself between Henry and his quest. And not only
beautiful, but the owner of Stratford Hall, of more than six
thousand acres of tobacco soil, of a large retinue of slaves, and
of lands scattered all over northern Virginia. Virginians of those
days, in selecting wives, always had two purposes in view: "family and fortune." No Lee, from the first Richard to the end of
the story, ever permitted himself an experiment in pure romance:
no run-away marriages and no misalliances stained the family
escutcheon. Intermarriages between the different lines were
also constant. In this instance, a Lee not only fulfilled the ambition for "family and fortune," but also indulged in the luxury
of a love affair.

In after years Henry Lee was not the most constant and disinterested of men, where women were concerned, but that his love
for Matilda was spontaneous and deep there is no question. His
son, Robert E. Lee, — not, however, son of Matilda, — who
spent much of his time after Appomattox editing an edition of
his father's *Memoirs* and writing a brief biography, gives a picture of Henry riding up the oak- and poplar-lined road to Stratford soon after his return to Virginia. The girls, Matilda and
Flora, recognized the young officer "as he rode past the grove
of maples" and "welcomed him with joy." There was tea drinking in the garden, plenty of laughter, much reminiscence of the
war, anecdotes of the "great Washington" and of Lafayette and
Greene, while Henry sat marveling at the changes seven years
can produce in a gawky girl. Such an episode, of course, can
have only one end. The courtship was rapid, — as things were
likely to be with Harry Lee, — and in less than a month after
this cousinly call the young man who had hoped to spend his
life on a desert island, contemplating the wickedness of man, became, by virtue of his marriage with the richest and most beau-

tiful woman in Westmoreland, Lord of Stratford, gentleman farmer, and active power in building a new nation.

3

Peace, meanwhile, had brought new duties to other members of the clan. For Francis Lightfoot and William Lee the end of the war closed their public careers. The turmoil of Revolutionary statesmanship Francis Lightfoot Lee had never greatly liked. "What damned dirty work is this politics!" Such was his opinion of the daily transactions passing under view. Soon after the Deane excitement had subsided, Francis Lightfoot quietly departed for the Rappahannock, resumed his residence at Menokin, and again took up his traditional rôle of Atticus, devoting his remaining days — except for a brief and undesired service in the Virginia Senate — to farming, books, conversation, and friends. William Lee, after dismissal by Congress, tarried four years in Europe. Returning to Virginia in the fall of 1783, he retired to Green Spring, the old Sir William Berkeley estate that had come to him through his marriage with Hannah Phillipa Ludwell, and here passed the rest of his days, his life embittered not only by recollections of what he regarded as ungrateful treatment by his country, but by a steadily weakening eyesight which, at the end, made him totally blind.

The other two Revolutionary Lees, however, Arthur and Richard Henry, found themselves again in the forefront of politics. Though Virginia had not supported Arthur in the Deane affair, it showed its general approval of his Revolutionary efforts by sending him to the State Assembly, and subsequently made him member of Congress. In this latter post his work was important. The most far-reaching problem facing the Philadelphia statesmen in 1784 was that Northwest Territory in which the Lee family had always been so much at home. By this time the Lees, and most other patriotic Virginians, had decided on the wisest course to be adopted with this domain. The several states making claims to sections — Pennsylvania, Connecticut, New York, Virginia — should cease their discussions and surrender their rights to the Federal government. The letters of Richard Henry

Lee contain many references to this statesmanlike decision. Despite Richard Henry's subsequent opposition to the constitution, he was in essence a Union man; his chief argument for the cession of Virginia's title to the Northwest was to provide the central government with a territory out of which future states could be carved. The same insistence on union appeared in the two clauses which all the Lees insisted, with infinite iteration, should be included in the treaty of peace. The Newfoundland fisheries, for the advantage of New England, and the navigation of the Mississippi, from source to mouth, for the benefit of the Western lands, Virginia's great preserve — without these two advantages there could be no United States, and, largely as a result of their untiring determination, both points were ultimately won. Always at this time Richard Henry was thinking of the United States as a whole. The fisheries would be valuable, he wrote Sam Adams, as the training ground of American seamen, and thus as the nursery of an American navy. "In this idea" — this from a letter to Henry Laurens — "I shall ever include the fisheries and the navigation of the Mississippi. These, sir, are the strong legs on which North America can alone walk securely in Independence." And the Western empire, by the same token, should belong not to Virginia, but to "North America." And when the Virginia Assembly, in 1784, ceded this territory to Congress, Richard Henry, in a letter to Samuel Adams, defined the lesson of the act: "It will be the means of perfecting our union." In the document transferring this domain to the central government appears the signature of Arthur Lee, one of Virginia's representatives in Congress, appropriate symbol of the part the Lee family had played in making this territory American soil. The transaction was the one act, up to that time, which transformed the disorganized states into a federal union. The mere circumstance that these constantly quarreling entities possessed this inheritance in common in itself compelled them, despite their tendency to split apart, steadily to work towards the formation of a federal constitution.

The Six Nations did not accept this situation any too complacently. True enough, they had transferred their ancestral rights to Virginia and Pennsylvania in 1744, at the Treaty of

Lancaster, under the persuasions and "presents" of Thomas Lee; again, at Fort Stanwix, in 1768, they had said good-bye to the old hunting grounds. Despite all this, in 1784 the moment had come for a new convention, and Arthur Lee, son of the negotiator at Lancaster, was appointed one of a committee of three to obtain still another great refusal. Arthur, as usual, kept a day-by-day journal of his peregrination up the Susquehanna, and afterward to Cuyahoga — a trip to a wilderness of snow and ice, sleeping in log huts, the wind and snow penetrating the crevices, eating frontier food, depending, for guidance, on not over-trustworthy Indians; even Arthur's scaling of the Pyrenees, on his trip to Spain, was luxury compared to this. Parts of Arthur's journal survive; it is interesting for other reasons than his diplomatic achievements. It described a now thriving part of the United States that was then in wild condition: Pittsburgh, where he spent an icy Christmas, made a poor impression. "It is inhabited almost entirely by Scots and Irish, who live in paltry log houses and are as dirty as in the north of Ireland or even Scotland. . . . The place, I believe, will never be considerable." The journal is also full of retrospects and temperamental musings. Lying ill at Fort McIntosh, on the Ohio, — "high fevers" formed one of the burdens of the trip, — Arthur's mind reverts to early days in London, to his lodgings in the Temple, to his old English companions. What should he do with the rest of his life? "Should I settle and remain among my friends in Virginia; should I retire to Kentucky; or return to England and enjoy in retirement there all that a country great in arts and sciences affords? I entered life glowing with sentiments of liberty and virtue. I embraced the opposition with a double degree of enthusiasm, which the love of liberty and my country inspired. I devoted myself to the cause from its very infancy. From that time my life has been a continued scene of agitation and commotion. No calm has reposed, no repose has refreshed me." Should he marry and settle down? If so, he must act quickly, for Arthur Lee was now forty-four years old. "To live in Virginia without a wife is hardly practicable. But in Virginia boys and girls only marry, and they marry for almost any motive but love. A man at thirty, a woman at twenty, is old in Virginia and with my sentiments of love and marriage I am not likely to find a wife there."

And so on.   But the practical business of dealing with those creatures whom Arthur called "wolves" — that is, the honorable red men — soon roused him from fever and dreams.   The negotiation, of course, was a success.   Negotiations with Indian chieftains, when backed up by "presents," — rum, pipes of peace, belts of wampum, and "Jo-hahs!" — were likely to be.   Arthur's father had proved this at Lancaster forty years before, and Arthur repeated his triumph at Cuyahoga.   The Six Nations now made marks on another parchment, again transferring to the United States all their rights to the land Virginia had recently ceded.

Meanwhile Richard Henry Lee had again been elected to Congress.   This new summons was a genuine hardship, for Richard Henry was an invalid, frequent attacks of gout making life an agony.   However, he gathered his energies in November 1784, and again crossed the Potomac.   Trenton, New Jersey, to which a peripatetic Congress had adjourned, did not present, in the depths of winter, many suggestions of parliamentary dignity.   In fact Richard Henry found few Congressmen at hand; for weeks he sat disconsolately, nursing his illness and lamenting his country's indifferent state, waiting for a quorum: at that time there was really no government in the United States.   After January 1, the body changed its meeting place to New York, and now signs of life appeared.   At this session a great honor was bestowed on Lee.   Until then presidents of Congress had been selected in rotation, each state having its chance.   Congress now abandoned the practice and decided to choose the men deemed most worthy of the post.   The election fell unanimously on Richard Henry Lee.   His letters show that he immensely enjoyed the distinction.   "President of Congress" was then the nearest thing the country had to "President of the United States," and Lee entered on his career as national head with zest.   His outgivings at this time have a mellow, almost a jaunty ring; a new Richard Henry now emerges.   "I have taken a fine house," he writes his nephew, Tom Shippen, "on the same street where little Peggy lives" — Peggy and her mother, granddaughter and daughter of his sister Alice, then being the delights of the aging statesman's days.   Proudly he dates letters from "The President's House" and orders, from several places, new raiment, new horses, and a new chariot.

The "old President," he writes, "has been converted into a young beau."   "You will oblige me much by procuring and sending me two pair of socks — fine yarn, white and for a small foot as mine is very small when stripped."   "I must have a pair of black breeches — they suit my years, my station, and, above all, they please my inclination.   But though fashion will not permit me to wear black silk, perhaps it may permit me black of some kind.   Will the fashion permit an old grave member of Congress to wear black breeches, it being remembered always that he means to accompany the black breeches with white silk stockings and black shoes and knee buckles?"   "Now for the breeches — oh the Breeches — I must have a pair of black breeches!" — Probably the fact that the president of Congress, as head of the nation, gave dinners and receptions explains this jubilant insistence on wardrobe.   It was Richard Henry's business also to receive foreign diplomatists, who now, after the recognition of American independence, began to appear.   A happy meeting came on a day in May 1785, when the first minister from Spain called to present his credentials to the president of Congress.   He proved to be Diego de Gardoqui — that same Gardoqui who, eight years previously, had surreptitiously met Arthur Lee in Burgos, Spain, and arranged for secret aid from His Catholic Majesty to the struggling United States.

And again Richard Henry's thoughts turned to New England, "that vineyard of liberty," and to his New England friends.   The Virginian's letters are most genial, and the man himself most human, in his intercourse with the Northern clime.   William Whipple, of New Hampshire, sends Richard Henry "a quintal of fish" — the best that fishlike place afforded; Richard Henry responds with a cask of choicest Virginia tobacco, "for chewing."   Sam Adams, as always, is the man to whom Richard Henry turns for advice in public matters and to whom, above others, he unbosoms his spirit.   Richard Henry's love of New England reached a point that would probably outrage his descendants. He actually seems to prefer that country to Virginia! He was particularly solicitous that Massachusetts should be careful about its constitution. "Independent of general principles of Philanthropy," — thus Richard Henry writes John Adams, — "I feel myself much interested in the establishment of a wise and free Republic in Massachusetts Bay, where yet I hope to finish the remainder of my days. The hasty, unpersevering, aristocratic genius of the south suits not my disposition, and is inconsistent with my ideas of what must constitute social happiness and security."

4

But Richard Henry was to fight one more battle, and find his opponent in his own home circle — in that cousin Harry Lee who had recently married Matilda and set up as a great man in Westmoreland. The Lees, clannish as they seem, could be as cantankerous towards one another as the Adams tribe itself. And the clash between the two outstanding lines — the Stratford Lees and those of Leesylvania — came in the shaping of national parties into Democrats and Federalists, and in the first test of strength, the adoption of the constitution. It has been remarked that the statesmen and philosophers of the Revolution were likely to be Democrats, enemies of a centralized government, while the fighters in the field were inclined to insist on strong hands in the seat of power. Patrick Henry, Thomas Jefferson, George Mason, had never fought in battle — therefore they believed that the best government was the one which governed least; Washington and Hamilton had been soldiers, and were therefore advocates of a powerful constitution. A winter spent at Valley Forge, neglected by Congress, unsupplied with food, clothing, and ammunition, was an experience likely to make the victim advocate strong legislatures that had power to act. That Washington should emerge from the war with definite convictions on this subject thus need cause no surprise. These varying attitudes are exemplified in the Lee family. Richard Henry, scholar and statesman, was a Democrat, believer in a federated republic, but not in a "consolidated" one, while Light Horse Harry, who had

campaigned with Greene and Marion, fought with equal zeal for
the constitution.   And in many ways his championship, against
the antagonism of his kinsman, forms the finest chapter in his
life.

On July 5, 1787, Richard Henry, now almost helpless from
gout, arrived again in New York to assume his duties in Congress.
Though this body is generally regarded as an inept one, the fact
remains that its final session forms a brilliant page in the American story.   Two matters were giving it concern at the moment
of Lee's arrival: the Constitutional Convention, then sitting in
secret conclave in Philadelphia, and the ordinance under consideration for the proposed new government in the Northwest Territory.   Virginia's cession had been followed by invasion of settlers into the present states of Ohio, Indiana, and Illinois, and
the time had come for establishing a territorial government.   In
this subject every Virginian's interest was active.   "On the ninth
of July," says Bancroft, "Richard Henry Lee took his seat in
congress.   His presence formed an era."   On the committee appointed to consider the Northwest ordinance were two Northern-
ers and three Southerners, and of these, adds Bancroft, the
"two ablest were Virginians."   The statesmen to whom the historian refers were William Grayson and Richard Henry Lee.
Of Grayson history had been forgetful, but he was one of the
most powerful men of his time — one of those six-footers of
whom Virginia seemed so prolific, as remarkable for his intellect as for his physical frame, and scholarly, eloquent, witty, and
farseeing.   And, in his work on this committee, Grayson was
to share a noble achievement with Richard Henry Lee.   The report on the ordinance was the most democratic instrument proposed up to that time in America.   In every line it shows the influence of those Jeffersonian ideas which had recently caused
such heartburnings in the Old Dominion.   It struck at the system of entail by providing that property should descend in equal
shares to all children, with no discrimination on the ground of
sex.   At a time when most of the states maintained property
qualifications for voters, the Northwest ordinance insisted on
manhood suffrage.   It incorporated practically all the safeguards
of the Bill of Rights — religious freedom, freedom of the press

and assembly, trial by jury, and the like. One clause, says the historian of the constitution, "bears in every word the impress of the mind of Richard Henry Lee": this prohibited the passage of any measure which violated contracts; what Lee had in thought was the repudiation of public and private debts, and the efforts, rampant then as now, to debase the currency. There was nothing this at times acrimonious statesman hated quite so much as paper money. A new nation, standing for new ideals, should not begin its career with wholesale confiscation. It had been better, Lee wrote, "to remain the honest slaves of Great Britain than dishonest freemen."

All these provisions were excellent as the basis of a new America in the "back lands"; still the Northwest ordinance in its original form kept silence on a more vital matter. It contained no reference to slavery. This was not because the matter was not in everybody's mind; indeed, from the establishment of this territory as a national domain, the question whether it should be slave or free had been generally discussed. Many Southern settlers in Illinois, Indiana, and Ohio had taken their slaves with them, and the danger was looming that the land north of the Ohio, as well as that south, would be given up to the institution. Two members of Congress, both Virginians, now stepped forth and imposed a veto on this calamity. The two were William Grayson and Richard Henry Lee. Just which deserved priority is one of the disputed points of history. The probability is that they acted conjointly and that their separate parts in the transaction were indistinguishable. "Every one chose the part," says Bancroft, "which was to bring on their memory the benedictions of all coming ages."

The other matter then engaging the popular mind — the new constitution — did not offer such plain sailing. The slavery issue Richard Henry saw in all its clarity, but the "new plan" of government stirred mixed emotions. Governor Randolph had offered him an appointment as delegate to the Philadelphia Convention, which had been declined; Richard Henry declared that his position as member of Congress was inconsistent with the duties of framing a new constitution. The real fact is probably that Richard Henry felt only a mild enthusiasm for the proposal, though Bancroft is not just in saying that Congress, in electing Richard Henry Lee president, had "put at its head the most determined and the most restlessly indefatigable foe of any change whatever in the Articles of Confederation." Certainly the statement was not true in 1788, when the constitution came up for adoption or rejection. On his way to New York, in 1787, Richard Henry passed through Philadelphia, where the great convention was then sitting behind sealed doors; he met many old friends and picked up current gossip. "I found the convention at Philadelphia," he writes his brother, Francis Lightfoot, "very busy and very secret. It would seem, however, from the variety of circumstances that we shall hear of a government not unlike the British constitution. That is, an executive with 2 branches compromising a federal legislature and possessing adequate tone. This departure from simple democracy seems indispensably necessary, if any government at all is to exist in America. Indeed, the minds of men have been so hurt by the injustice, folly and wickedness of the state legislatures, and state executives that people in general seem to be ready for anything. I hope, however, that this tendency to extreme will be so controlled as to secure fully and completely the democratic influence acting within just bounds." This desire for a central body that would have "more tone" — that is, more authority, more energy, more decisiveness — than the existing régime appears in all his outgivings at this time.

That, when the proposed constitution became known, Richard Henry began to shift to the opposition, until he became almost its head, is true. Patrick Henry, George Mason, Richard Henry Lee — such is the triumvirate that marshaled the enemies of the new plan; Henry the emotionalist, Mason and Lee the constitutional statesmen, were aligned against a splendid group of Virginia advocates, including "Henry Lee of the Legion." The two kinsmen clashed on the very day the new constitution was presented to Congress. Richard Henry rose at once and offered amendments. The additions he suggested embodied no hostility to the new scheme of government; with certain emendations that "new plan" would be ideal. And the changes he proposed were not revolutionary. They were safeguards of liberty that were the

inheritance of a thousand years' struggle for Anglo-Saxon liberties — the several items in that Magna Charta that had figured
so heroically in Stamp Tax debates.   That Richard Henry's proposed amendments did not imply national destruction is evident,
for most of them, since 1790, have been part of the Federal Constitution, forming the celebrated first ten amendments.   Richard
Henry now suggested that these be added to the constitution as
sent to Congress and that the document, in this form, be transmitted to the states for ratification or rejection.   But up sprang
Light Horse Harry in opposition — joined by many of the most
distinguished members of Congress.   The suggestion, said Harry
Lee, was most irregular.   Congress had no right to tamper with
the work of the convention.   It could not add amendments; its
duty was merely to send the instrument to the states.   Harry's
position was unassailable; he and his party not only defeated
Richard Henry's motion, but did so in humiliating fashion, for
Congress, to give a sense of unanimity to their action, refused to
incorporate the elder statesman's resolution in their records.
First honors, in this family difference, clearly rested with the
veteran of Fort Motte and Eutaw Springs.

The battle now began in earnest.   Defeated in his attempt to
secure amendments before ratification, Richard Henry and his
followers changed their ground: they now fought for the rejection of the constitution and for a new convention, which should
draw up a new scheme.   Richard Henry began writing to his old
co-worker, Samuel Adams, in Massachusetts, and to Patrick
Henry and George Mason in Virginia, rallying them to the opposition.   Racked by his malady, unable to leave his Potomac
home, Richard Henry's literary activity was immense.   The controversy gave birth to his finest piece of writing, *Letters of the
Federal Farmer* — letters that, says Channing, "had a great vogue
and are still useful as containing an admirable statement of the
objections to the proposed organic law."   Lee's English was
tough, strong, hard-hitting rather than elegant; the argument is
not directed against a new constitution, for the uselessness of the
old system is granted, but for one that is more "democratic,"
that will preserve the states as independent republics.   He did
not wish Virginia to merge its individuality in a "consolidated

government"; the expression had not then gained vogue, but
States' rights was what the author had in mind.   Lee's book was
a literary success, for several thousand copies were sold, but it
angered many upholders of the constitution, above all Washington.   At that time nothing was so precious in Washington's
eyes as the new form of government, created by the body over
which he had presided.   His sense of order and of energetic administration had been outraged by the chaos the nation had presented in recent years.   Though not a constitutional expert, he
summed up, better than most lawyers, the argument for the "new
plan" when he said: "There is no alternative between the adoption
of it than anarchy."   Richard Henry Lee wrote Washington October 11, 1787, that, "in consequence of a long reflection upon the
nature of man and government, I am led to fear the danger that
will ensue to civil liberty from the adoption of the new system
in its present form," and that, on his return to Virginia, he would
stop off at Mount Vernon and discuss the matter in detail.   If
the meeting took place, Washington was not convinced.   James
Wilson, of Pennsylvania, made an elaborate speech, which was
generally regarded as a reply to Lee's *Letters,* and this Washington caused to be circulated in great quantities in Virginia.

The fact is that Washington, usually so even-tempered, was angered by Lee's activities.   He regarded him as the chief mischief
maker against the cause.   George Mason in particular, he thought,
had been led astray by the philosopher of Chantilly.   "The political tenets of Colo. M[ason] and Colo. R. H. L[ee]," he wrote
Madison, displaying more feeling than was usual in his letters,
"are always in unison.   It may be asked which of them gives
the tone.   Without hesitation I answer the latter, because I believe the latter will receive it from no one.   He has I am informed rendered himself obnoxious in Philadelphia, by the pains
he took to dessiminate his objections amongst some of the leaders of the seceding members of that state.   His conduct is not
less reprobated in this country; how it all will be relished *generally* is yet to be learnt by me."   "That the opposition should
have gained strength at Richmond," Washington writes Madison,
January 10, 1788, "among members of Assembly is not, if true,
to be wondered at, when we consider that the great adversaries to

the constitution are all assembled in that place, acting conjointly with the promulgated sentiments of Richard Henry Lee as auxiliary. It is said, however, and I believe it may be depended upon, that the latter (though he may retain his sentiments) has withdrawn, or means to withdraw, his opposition, because, as he has expressed himself, or as others have done for him, he finds himself in bad company, such as with M[ercer], S[mith], etc., etc. His brother, Francis L[ightfoot], on whose judgment the family place much reliance, is decidedly in favor of the new form."

Clearly, Washington was much wrought up by Richard Henry's warfare on his favorite scheme for establishing the new nation. Posterity would like to have a stenographic report of that discussion which Richard Henry had proposed at Mount Vernon!

5

Washington was mistaken in his belief that Richard Henry had changed his attitude. As the time approached for the Virginia Convention, the energies of the enemy not only increased, but met with great success. On a popular vote, it was said, more than three fourths of the people of Virginia would go against the new plan, and the array of talent selected for the deliberations at Richmond was imposing. Richard Henry himself did not attend this historic gathering, neither did Virginia's leading advocate of adoption, but the influence of the two men constantly hung over the proceedings, and Lee, from his Chantilly home, and Washington, from Mount Vernon, kept in immediate touch with the deliberations. This convention was perhaps the greatest assembly of freemen that had up to that time come together in America; in dignity, in scholarly and public-spirited consideration of the subject in hand, in the character and talents of the leaders, it can be compared only to the First Continental Congress. And in its influence on the American story it is almost as important as the early convocations in Philadelphia. Up to June 2, 1788, when sessions opened, neither Virginia nor New York had ratified the new system: obviously there could be no permanent government with these states left out; Virginia was then the largest state, in both area and population, even after the cession of the Northwest; it was also the richest. It is not too much to say that the real question before the convention was not merely whether Virginia should ratify, but whether there should be any constitution at all. The course of the American nation was fixed, for all time, by the deliberations that held Richmond spellbound for the next four weeks.

The chairman was Edmund Pendleton, then governor, but as the chairman of the committee of the whole was George Wythe, and as the debate took place chiefly in that committee, Wythe was in fact presiding officer. No more impressive choice could have been made. Possibly his slender figure — hollow chest, slight stooping shoulders, thin features, bald head, with a few wisps of white hair curling up at the back, long sharp nose, and bright inquiring eyes — seemed a little undistinguished in that company of Virginia giants; but Wythe's achievements, his greatness as lawyer and teacher, the part he had played in moulding many of Virginia's legal lights, several of whom sat in this convention, were in everybody's mind, and the fact that Wythe was an advocate of "the plan" gave it an initial advantage. As Wythe, from his rostrum, looked down on the 180 delegates, he had a panorama of the men who had guided Virginia's course — and, in considerable measure, the course of the nation — for the preceding twenty-five years. Foremost was that backwoods genius, now showing in bent form, gray hair, and lined features the effect of a hard life, but still alert, full of fire, and, unhappily for the constitutionalists, firmly opposed to ratification — Patrick Henry, destined at this gathering to make several of the most eloquent speeches of his life. Allied to him in this battle were other Virginians whose ability was a nation-wide story: George Mason, whose snow-white hair was offset by coal-black eyes, now burning with zeal against a measure which he regarded as enslavement for the country; William Grayson, as determined to destroy the new constitution as he had been to prohibit slavery in the Northwest, but mollifying the gravity of this convention by correcting the Latin quotations of the adversary and calling attention to false quantities in their Vergilian extracts; James

Monroe, who, although destined to become President, was not then a stalwart support to the cause — rustic in appearance, halting in speech, interrupting his remarks to read long passages from Polybius, which, in some occult way, were supposed to provide arguments against ratification; and Benjamin Harrison, still rotund, still jovial, still backbone of the James River Tories, and still adverse to close union of the Virginian empire with "leveling" New Englanders and shopkeeping Pennsylvanians.

Such were the leaders against approving the new system, a strong band, it must be granted — the mere fact that Patrick Henry led the opposition almost made it invincible. Indeed "the baffling of Patrick Henry" was recognized by the constitutionalists as their real occupation. Though their ranks enrolled no such mighty debater as this, the Federalists — as they were already beginning to be called — presented a formidable phalanx. That Edmund Pendleton ranged himself on their side seemed almost assurance of victory. This was the same Pendleton who, in 1765, had sought to moderate Patrick Henry's onslaughts on King George, and the two men had been at cross-purposes ever since. Pendleton was now sixty-seven, but he looked much older, for his once tall figure was shrunken and supported on crutches, he having broken a thigh some years before. He was the parliamentarian of the constitutional side, while its intellectual leader and expounder of governmental science was the ascetic who was afterward to serve as President — James Madison, recently engaged with Alexander Hamilton in writing *The Federalist,* and therefore well primed with ideas and arguments. Not only two future Presidents sat in this convention, but a future Chief Justice, and the greatest of them all, for here John Marshall, in the ensuing debates, unfolded many of the principles which he was afterward to embody in the interpretation of the instrument that he was now seeking to make fundamental law.

"Henry Lee of the Legion" or "Lee of Westmoreland" — titles that had temporarily displaced "Light Horse Harry" — was now thirty-two years old. He had reached the peak of vigor and comeliness. His marriage with Matilda had evidently saved him from the sad state in which the Southern campaigns had left the man; besides, that one thing which was indispensable to happiness — public applause — was now a regular part of his life. Washington had become more and more his friend; he had sat in the Virginia Assembly, in Congress, and now — an honor even higher — was a delegate in the Richmond Convention. Just under six feet tall, with pink-and-white oval face, blue eyes, light brown hair, with the same resonant voice that had sounded in his Carolina campaigns, he seemed adapted to the rôle the Federalists had assigned him. For in Madison, Pendleton, and Marshall there was learning in plenty; what was needed in addition was a "Rupert of debate" who could face Patrick Henry, George Mason, and the lumbering Harrison, hold them up to derision and score points. The rôle set for Harry Lee in the convention, that is, was not unlike the part he had played in the Revolution: he was not to be attached to any particular command, but was to head a "partizan" corps, to make forays, hitting the enemy hard when opportunity offered, and, when he had discomfited him, escaping and leaving the really serious business to the Big Guns. It was a task for which his acute and rapid mind was well fitted. Above all, Lee had eagerness for the cause, strengthened by the fact that his real leader in the new guerrilla campaign was the same general whom he had served in the Revolution — the gentleman at Mount Vernon who was following every step of his protégé with the same approbation he had displayed in his Revolutionary exploits.

Even with such encouragement a man of thirty-two might hesitate before assailing such a forensic veteran as Patrick Henry, then in his fifty-third year. And when Patrick Henry began to speak, the task seemed even more forbidding. Never, say the chroniclers, had the man whom Jefferson described as "the greatest orator who ever lived" displayed such skill. Day after day he denounced the work of the Philadelphia Convention and described it as a scheme to destroy all the good wrought by the Revolution. It must be admitted that, reading Patrick Henry's speech to-day, after a century and a half's experience under the instrument which he prophesied was to make "slaves" of all Americans, it is hard to understand the impression it produced; his fears for American liberties, under a standing army, the likelihood that the President would transform himself into an hereditary monarch, with American dukes, barons, and the like, no longer stimulate the patriotic goose flesh. But the interruptions of Henry Lee — for his job was to interrupt — have great contemporary interest. These covered several points that were subsequently to distract the nation and give much pause to Harry's son, military leader of the Confederacy. Thus one of the clauses in the constitution that most disturbed Patrick was the very first words, "We, the people." Why we, the people? Why not "We, the states"? There we are at once, in the very first day of this Virginia debate: was the United States an indestructible nation or merely a loose league of independent "sovereign" estates? In the next eighty years that question was to be debated and to be settled finally at Appomattox. To Harry Lee's mind, at that early moment, the issue was clear enough. The phrase "We, the people" did not frighten him any more than it had frightened Nathaniel Bacon, a century before, or than it was to make Abraham Lincoln quail, less than a century afterward. Lee was as dauntless in his nationalism as either of these men. He formulated the question of Nationalism with a conciseness that all its advocates subsequently never surpassed. "One would have thought," he said, "that the love of an American was in some degree criminal, as being incompatible with a proper degree of affection for a Virginian. The people of America, Sir, are one people — I love the people of the North not because they have adopted the constitution but because I have fought with them as such. Does it follow from thence that I have forgotten my attachment to my native state? In all local matters I shall be a Virginian. In those of a general nature I shall never forget that I am an American."

Another question that was to reach ultimate answer in 1861 found its way into this debate. It was propounded by George Mason and answered, with his usual eloquence and decisiveness, by Henry Lee. Suppose, said Mason, there should be "popular resistance to the constitution?" What then? Mason's precise words, in precipitating, at this early day, a question that was to lead to such bloody argument, are not recorded verbally, the reporter of these debates contenting himself with abstracting the remarks. Mason "expressed in emphatic terms, the dreadful effects which must ensue, should the people resist; and concluded by observing that he trusted gentlemen would pause before they would decide a question which involved such awful consequences." Harry Lee's instantaneous reply, however, is literally preserved: "Mr. Chairman, my feelings are so oppressed with the declarations of my honorable friend that I can no longer suppress my utterance. I respect the honorable gentleman, and never believed I should live to have heard fall from his lips, opinions so injurious to our country and so opposite to the dignity of this Assembly. If the dreadful picture which he has drawn be so abhorrent to his mind as he has declared, let me ask the honorable gentleman, if he has not pursued the very means to bring into action the horror which he deprecates? . . . God of heaven avert from my country the dreadful curse; but if the madness of some and the vice of others, should risk the awful appeal, I trust that the friends to the paper on your table, conscious of the justice of their cause, and recollecting their uniform moderation, will meet the afflicting call with that firmness and fortitude, which become men summoned to defend what they conceive to be the true interest of their country, and will prove to the world, that although they boast not in words of love of country, and affection for liberty, still they are not less attached to these invaluable objects than their vaunting opponents and can with alacrity and resignation encounter every difficulty and danger in defence of them."

"The madness of some" — are these words a forecasting of the fire-eaters on both sides, abolitionists of the North and impassioned upholders of "Southern rights" below the Potomac, who brought on the Civil War? "The vice of others" — is this likewise a divination of the selfish politicians who played with that issue for personal advantage? To his other talents Light Horse Harry seemed to add that of prophet. In the family story his attitude towards the problems that so distracted his son seems clear-cut. It would seem that Harry Lee was a nationalist, a believer in a strong central government, and that, should resistance to the constitution rear its head, he was prepared to resort to the final measure — that is, forcible suppression.

In this debate on the constitution, which someone has called the

greatest held in America in the eighteenth century, the Washing-
ton–Madison–Henry Lee contingent triumphed over the Patrick
Henry–Mason–Richard Henry Lee forces by a majority of ten.
Soon afterward New York ratified and the battle was won.

Richard Henry Lee took no such bold look into the future as his
cousin Harry.   He died unreconciled to the Federal Constitution,
even in amended form.   He became one of the first two United
States Senators from Virginia — the other being William Grayson — for the purpose of doing all in his power to secure amendments and possibly another convention for complete revision.
His letters, especially those written to Patrick Henry, exhibit him
as a States'-rights man to the end.   "The most essential danger
from the present system, in my opinion," he wrote, "arises from
its tendency to a consolidated government, instead of a Union of
Confederated States."

"Confederated States."   Ominous words!

XIV

DREAR DAYS AT STRATFORD

I

THE campaign for the ten amendments was Richard Henry Lee's last service to his country.   As soon as these had been imbedded in the Federal Constitution, he resigned the Senatorship from Virginia and retired to Chantilly.   The place was not a pretentious one, but formed a pleasant haven for his declining years. It was a wooden structure, situated on a point that commanded one of the most beautiful views of the Potomac.   Richard Henry's chief consolation, in his last days, was found in his children, especially his daughters.   Of these, Mary married John Augustine Washington, and Hannah, Corbin Washington, while another, Nancy, married her cousin Charles Lee, in due course to become a member of Washington's cabinet; still another, Sarah, also became the wife of her cousin, Edmund Jennings Lee.   All these alliances, as well as that of Richard's son Ludwell to a cousin, Flora, sister of the "divine Matilda," were delightful to the invalided statesman.

The Lee girls of this period were a particularly vivacious and charming lot.   A favorite niece, Lucinda, daughter of Thomas Ludwell Lee, kept a diary for a few weeks in 1788 [1] which forms the best description available of life along the Potomac in that time.   The scene, for the larger part, is laid at Chantilly, but other Potomac establishments — Stratford, Pecatone, Bushfield, Belleview, Nomini, Lee Hall, and Chatham — serve as background.   In this small volume we have the daily existence that surrounded Richard Henry in his last days.   His own daughters, Hannah, Nancy, and Molly, his niece Flora, — the latter "very

---

[1] *Journal of a Young Lady of Virginia, 1782,* published in Baltimore, 1871. The date, 1782, is shown by internal evidence to be wrong.   The correct date is 1788.

genteal and wears monstrous bustles," but haughty in manner, saluting her cousin with a distant kiss, — are the main figures in the story, and the conspicuous events are their walks in the garden of Chantilly, their dressings for dinner, and their dancings of the minuet to the tunes of a solitary darkey scraping his "fidle." Sometimes visits of "beaux" proved inopportune. "Lucy and myself are in a peck of trouble for fear they should return drunk" — a justifiable apprehension, for presently "the gentlemen arrived and we had to scamper. Both tipsy." Race meets at Fredericksburg, arrivals of "chariots" from neighboring plantations, tea drinkings, card playings, strolls in the woods — the final days of the Revolutionary Lees would be incomplete without this precious literary memorial, discovered several years ago, yellow and torn, in a Potomac attic.

Especially do the glimpses of Richard Henry's daughters, Hannah, Nancy, and Molly, linger in the memory. "Cousin Nancy and myself have just returned from taking an airing in the chariot. We went to Stratford, walked in the garden, sat about two hours under a butifull shade tree and eat as many figs as we could." Here is a picture of Hannah: "I forgot to tell you Cousin Hannah's dress yesterday. It was a blue lute-string habit, taffety apron and handkerchief, with the most butiful little hat on the side of her head I ever saw." And of Nancy Lee: "About sunset, Nancy, Milly and myself took a walk in the garden. We were mighty busy cutting thistles to try our sweethearts, when Mr. Washington caught us, and you can't conceive how he plagued us — chased us all over the garden and was quite impertinent. . . . I have been filling out tea, and, after that, we took a walk by the river by moonlight. The garden extends to the river. Nancy observed that walking by moonlight, she thought, reminded us of our absent friends." Other scenes were not so tranquil; a free-and-easy manner about this old existence in Westmoreland at times almost startles. "I must tell you of our frolic after we went into our room. We took it into our heads to want to eat; well, we had a large dish of bacon and beaf; after that a bowl of sago cream, and, after that, an apple pye. While we were eating the apple pye in bed — God bless you! making a great noise — in came Mr. Washington, dressed in Hannah's short gown and petticoat, and seazed me and kissed me twenty times, in spite of all the resistance I could make; and then Cousin Molly. Hannah soon followed, dressed in his coat. They joined us in eating the apple pye and then went out." Other diversions had a literary quality. Mr. Pinkard sits solemnly in the large sitting room of Chantilly and entertains the young ladies by reading a play, which the diarist calls *The Bell Strattagem.* She herself is fond of *Evelina* and *Telemachus,* the latter being "really delightful and very improving." "I have for the first time in my life just read Pope's 'Eloiza.' Just now I saw it laying in the window. . . . The poetry I think beautiful, but do not like some of the sentiments. Some of Eloiza's is too Ammorous for a female, I think."

Such a lively environment must have provided relaxation from the gout that finally destroyed the author of the Resolution for American Independence. Richard Henry Lee died June 19, 1794, and was buried in the old family plot, Burnt House Fields, Westmoreland.

The last days of Arthur Lee were lonelier. From 1782 to the establishment of the new government, in 1789, he lived in New York, first as a member of Congress and then as one of the three commissioners of the Treasury. When Alexander Hamilton assumed the duties of this department, Arthur retired to Virginia, settling on a thousand-acre farm at Urbana, on the Rappahannock. All through the "critical period," 1783–1787, Arthur was busily upholding the Lee tradition and serving the state; other distinctions came to him also, one that was especially prized being the honorary degree of Doctor of Laws, from Harvard University. But Lee's chief delight at this time was his correspondence, which includes many famous names on both sides of the Atlantic. With his American favorites — John and Samuel Adams, Joseph Warren, William Whipple, John Marshall, James Madison — he discusses all questions then disturbing the country, and his personal aspect comes out in his letters to his niece, Nancy Shippen Livingston, and her brother Tom. Nancy Livingston was Arthur's confidante in the most tender concerns of existence. His journal, already quoted, betrays a longing for domestic life, but in love, as in so many other things, Arthur Lee was unhappy. "He is courting Miss Sprig," wrote Jefferson from Annapolis to James Madison, February 10, 1784, "a young girl of seventeen and of thirty thousand pounds expectation." Possibly Jefferson's malice was affected by the fact that one of his followers, James Francis Mercer, was Arthur's rival for the eligible Marylander — and a successful one, for Mercer, afterward governor of Virginia, and Sophia Sprigg were married the ensuing year.

This failure, however, did not discourage the persistent Lee, but once again fate proved unkind. His letters to Nancy Livingston, from 1787 to 1789, are full of passionate outpourings to some beautiful unknown living in Sunbury, Pennsylvania. Since the lady evidently treated Arthur harshly, declining his visits and correspondence, he is compelled to do his "swaining," as he calls it, through his niece, her intimate friend, and those rhapsodies on his lady's eyes, pale cheeks, and other charms, most suitably transmitted to the person concerned, are embalmed in these epistles to Nancy. The proxy is exhorted to act as go-between and advance her uncle's courtship; evidently the young lady did not succeed, for Arthur, after the establishment of the new constitution, retired to the Rappahannock and there spent the solitary remainder of his days. And here he found consolation in the things which, after all, constituted his interests — books, flowers, gardening, farming, and correspondence.

His letters to Tom Shippen are full of judicious criticism on passing events. Tom, like his uncle, was a scholar, and so the extracts scattered over these papers, in Greek, Latin, Italian, French, and Spanish, and quotations from Dante, Tasso, Rousseau, Voltaire, to mention only a few esteemed authors, are not incongruous. Frederick the Great was Arthur's favorite statesman, despite his broken promise to recognize American independence after France; Voltaire was the greatest writer of ancient and modern times; and the model whom Thomas Shippen should take for the education of his son, just born, was Rousseau's *Émile*. As for the American Constitution, this was the favorite abomination of Arthur Lee. He was an unblushing monarchist. On May 7, 1787, on the eve of the Constitutional Convention, he writes Shippen, then in England: "It is painful to me to write

Etching by Richard Thomas Walker

STRATFORD HALL ON THE POTOMAC

BUILT BY THOMAS LEE ABOUT 1730; HOME OF THE REVOLUTIONARY LEES AND
BIRTHPLACE OF ROBERT E. LEE

on the people and politics of these U. S.   The utmost that charity
can say is that they do not improve.   The same unprincipled
pursuit of private speculations — the same sacrifice of the public
honor and interests to the selfish objects of Individuals — the
same antipathy in the dishonest to the payment of public and
private debts — the same open, and sometimes studied, violations
of their faith pledged in the confederation, by the respective
Assemblies, and the most baneful of all luxuries, the luxury of
the common people, who are more extravagant than any people
in the world of the same rank — all these conspire the dissolution
of government, the corruption of manners, the insecurity of
property and the destruction of national faith, character and
confidence. — For remedy of these evils, the Convention is now
meeting in Philadelphia.   Genl. Washington, Mr. Henry, and
your uncle, R. H. Lee have refused to attend it.[1]   I do not hope
anything from this meeting — because, in fact, the evil is rooted
in the very assemblies who are to confirm the acts of the Convention.   This renders it too probable that a plan of dignity
and effect will not even be proposed, and if proposed, will not
be accepted.   It is plain to me that what is doing, is tampering
with the disease, disserving the people, and endangering some
violent commotion.   It is now manifest that we have not the
public virtue and private temperance which are necessary to the
establishment at least of free Republics; but that we have courage,
enterprize and high mindedness enough to make a great and even
illustrious people, under one Sovereignty consisting of an imperial head, a Senate for life, and an elective house of Comms.
All things short of this appear to me to be the frippery of little
politicians, whose minds are incapable of deep reflection and
exertion."

Arthur's European correspondents — Burke, Barré, Sir William Jones, Richard Price, the Baron de Breteuil, Abbé Reynal,
Duc de la Rochefoucauld, and others — added to the zest of life,
but of them all the favorite was the Earl of Shelburne, now become the Marquess of Lansdowne.   Harsh as are Arthur's com-

---

[1] This was true at the time the letter was written, but Washington changed
his mind and became a delegate and presiding officer of the convention.
Patrick Henry also changed his mind.

ments on prevailing British policy, — the retention of the Western posts and the refusal to admit American ships to West Indian trade, — the Genêt performances had made him even more bitter against France. Disagreements with England, however, he regarded as temporary, but there was something, he thought, in the Gallic temperament that would forever prevent close fraternizing between France and the United States. "It seems to me that there is such an utter and unalterable difference between the people of France and those of England and between the former and those of the United States that no permanent connection or intimacy can exist between them. Similarity of genius will naturally draw and bind our two nations together when the temporary causes, which now oppose it, shall have ceased. It will be then only, in my judgment, that the liberties which are peculiar to the two people, will be secure against the world in arms." Perhaps as a pledge of this happier time, Arthur sent his English friend a painting of Washington,[1] and in honor of this friendship named his Rappahannock estate Lansdown.

In one of his last letters to Tom Shippen, dated March 26, 1792, Arthur Lee gives a picture of himself in his latest phase. "I have been occupied totally with my farm, planning fields, ditches and enclosures. I have sowd eight acres with clover seed alone; two with the addition of plaister of Paris; you shall know the result. I have planted some hundreds of locust, weeping willows, rose bushes, etc., etc. about my house, which I intend to make a wilderness of sweets. We shall be in our Infancy when you come to see us in the summer, but very happy in receiving you. The 22d of May I shall be at Richmond — the 1st of July at this place (Williamsbg.) upon the revision at which we are now working. I leave this for Lansdown in a few days. I have thus given you all my intended travels history. Kiss Betsey and her Baby for me and give my love to all with you."

Six months later, on a cold December day, Arthur spent several hours planting the orchard which was to be the delight of his old age. A rainstorm came on, but he kept hard at his task,

[1] This is not, as might at first be supposed, the famous full-length Lansdowne Washington, painted by Gilbert Stuart. Arthur sent his gift in 1790, while Stuart did not return to the United States, after a twenty years' absence, until 1792.

finally retiring, wet and frozen, to his bachelor hall. What in that time was called "a pleurisy" at once set in, and in a few days Arthur died, at the age of fifty-two. Three years later William, blind and bent with rheumatism, ended his career, at the old Green Spring estate of Sir William Berkeley. Appropriately, William found his grave in the Jamestown churchyard. In 1797 the line of the Revolutionary sons of Stratford came to an end, with the death of Francis Lightfoot Lee, at Menokin.

2

And with the passing of these Stratford Lees, headship of the family shifted to the younger branch — those Lees of Leesylvania whose representative, Light Horse Harry, by marrying his cousin, had become master of the Potomac estate. But Harry's happiness with Matilda was brief. He took her with him to New York, where for three years he represented Virginia in Congress; there are occasional references in letters to the popularity of the young couple, the gayety they contributed to official society, and the rising influence of the statesman. But there were times of sorrow, too. The first child, named Nathanael Greene Lee, in honor of Harry's commander in the Carolinas, lived only a year. Matilda had three other children, Philip Ludwell, who died in his eighth year, and Lucy Grymes and Henry, both of whom long survived her. Other troubles darkened Matilda's short married life. The irresponsibility in financial matters that wrecked Light Horse Harry's career early made its appearance. Probably it was no great surprise when Harry's father, dying in 1787, left him the larger part of the family property, as oldest son, but excluded him as executor, naming to that post the younger brothers. This action was not due to lack of affection or pride — indeed, the old gentleman had followed Henry's career as soldier and statesman with satisfaction; he did not believe, however, that his favorite son could be safely entrusted with money. It was an attitude several other relations subsequently manifested. Even Matilda Lee, great as was her love for her husband, had been alarmed by his tendency

to risk family property in harebrained speculations. Was Stratford, pride of the Lees, to be sacrificed to Henry's grandiose
plans and her children beggared? Such a fate was probable,
for all Matilda's property, under Virginia law of the time, became her husband's, and could be pledged or sold by his fiat alone.
That Matilda Lee was a young woman of determination and
foresight is shown by her prompt action in face of this danger.
She firmly took the ex-cavalryman in hand and made him sign
a document by which Stratford and property in Loudoun were
to be transferred, on her death, to her two sons, and meanwhile
to be held in trust for that purpose by Richard Bland Lee, her
husband's brother, and Ludwell Lee, son of Richard Henry.
The transaction was especially pathetic, for at that time, August
1790, Matilda was dying. She was only twenty-six years old,
was in her finest bloom, and her death left the distracted husband desolate. "Something always happens," he wrote years
afterward, "to mar my happiness." Never was this, regarded
by Henry as the maxim of his life, more true than in the loss
of Matilda. Henry Lee was himself at this time only thirty-
four, and found relief by plunging into public life. His speeches
at the Virginia Constitutional Convention had extended his
fame; the greatest American of the day was his friend and
backer; and thus Light Horse Harry's election, in 1791, as governor of Virginia — an office that had been filled by Patrick
Henry, Thomas Jefferson, Edmund Randolph, and other great
Virginians — seemed quite in keeping with the eminence he had
attained.

Henry Lee served as governor for three years, being reëlected
twice; the period was important, both in his personal life and
in his growth as a public man. In particular his governorship
witnessed the development of questions that figured conspicuously
in the later history of his family. The constitution was in an
experimental stage; the Patrick Henry school of thought had
by no means been reconciled; John Marshall had not yet established its principles in permanent form; and its precise authority,
the extent to which good Americans owed it allegiance — all these
matters were in dispute. The questions that afterward split
the nation in two — the relative power of federal and state gov-

ernments, States' rights, the possible right of a state to nullify the laws of Congress, even to secede from the federal "compact" — first came into life during Henry Lee's preëminence at Richmond. It was in these three years that the constitution met its first supreme test — its power to assert itself, to maintain its dignity, and to put down insurrection, even by force of arms. It will be recalled that this difficult point had come up for discussion at the Virginia Convention. What, George Mason had almost tauntingly asked Henry Lee, will you do if the people resist your wonderful constitution? That, the delegate from Westmoreland replied, would be a painful crisis; yet his speech indicated that he was ready to meet such contingencies in the one logical way. Undoubtedly this little debate with Mason remained vividly in Lee's mind, as in that of most thoughtful Virginians; the prospect suggested was not a pleasant one, and not many expected it to become a practical matter so soon. It seems almost fateful that the issue should have risen while a Lee was governor of Virginia, and called for decisive action on his part. The faction responsible for forcing the question was not the most thoughtful section of the American population, for it proved to be the destiny of the frontiersmen in the new West to precipitate a situation that, in far greater proportion, came up for arbitrament in 1861.

The constitutional crisis of 1794 has suffered in heroic aspect because the question at issue involved a matter so ignoble as whiskey. In the American story the outburst is usually called the "Whiskey Rebellion," but in the lively disputations of the time it is almost invariably referred to more fittingly as the "Western Insurrection." The facts are plain enough: in 1792 Congress, seeking revenue for the new government, laid a tax — just as it does to-day — on distilled spirits. This fell with particular severity on the rough-and-ready inhabitants in the Western region. The farmers' only salable crop was wheat; inadequacies of transportation made it practically impossible to send this to market in bulk, but by distilling it into whiskey and transmitting it across the mountains to civilization, — the extent to which our ancestors consumed raw spirits makes one's blood run cold, even in this cocktail-drinking generation, — the frontiersmen eked out a humble subsistence. Laying a tax of seven cents a gallon on this staff of life deprived of occupation a thrifty people, who, almost in mass, rose in opposition to the law. The way government inspectors were mobbed calls to mind the treatment of stamp vendors in 1765; the seat of trouble was trans-Alleghany Pennsylvania, with headquarters at Pittsburgh, but riots took place also in bordering sections of Virginia and Maryland, and in North Carolina. One of the worst disturbances broke out in Morgantown, and Martinsburg, Virginia, was also a seat of tumultuous dissaffection. Presently these outbursts led to open rebellion, the "Whiskey Boys" ultimately recruiting an army of 7000 men prepared to resist Congress and the constitution, while the leader, David Bradford, announced as one item in his programme "secession from the Union." Modern writers have sought to minimize the affair, but the President of the United States, at the time, George Washington, regarded it most seriously. He saw the uprising for what it was, an attempt to defy the constitution, the first that had been made, and he determined to meet the issue. "Actual rebellion against the laws of the United States," Washington wrote Charles M. Thruston on August 10, 1794, "exists at this moment, notwithstanding every lenient measure, which could comport with the duties of the public officers, has been exercised to reconcile them to the collection of taxes upon spiritous liquors and stills. What may be the consequences of such violent and outrageous proceedings is painful in a high degree even in contemplation. But, if the laws are to be so trampled upon with impunity and a minority (a small one too) is to dictate to the majority, there is an end, put at one stroke, to Republican government; and nothing but anarchy and confusion is to be expected hereafter. Some other man or society may dislike another law, and oppose it with equal propriety, until all laws are prostrate, and everyone (the strongest I presume) will carve for himself." Washington wrote in the same tenor to several correspondents, especially to Henry Lee. "No citizens of the United States," he said in a letter to Lee, on the latter's appointment as commander of the anti-Whiskey expedition, "can ever be engaged in a service more important to their country. It is nothing less than to consolidate and to preserve the blessings of that revolution, which, at much expense of blood and treasure, constituted us a free and independent nation. It is to give to the world an illustrious example of the utmost consequence to the cause of mankind. I experienced a heart-felt satisfaction in the conviction that the conduct of the troops will be in every respect answerable to the goodness of the cause and the magnitude of the stake."

That is to say, the possibility suggested by George Mason in the Virginia Convention had now come to pass. A considerable element in Pennsylvania, Virginia, Maryland, and North Carolina were "resisting" the constitution. And the probable response to such an uprising, intimated by Henry Lee at this same session, was about to come into effect. Washington had decided to suppress the insurrection and sustain the constitution by military force. All attempts at conciliation having failed, he called upon the militia of New Jersey, Pennsylvania, Maryland, and Virginia, states that responded with 15,000 well-equipped men. This was the largest army the United States had ever summoned into being. As Washington reviewed it, splendidly uniformed and munitioned, he must have thought ruefully of the ragged battalions which he had commanded, in a contest with the world's most powerful nation; had he had any body like this at Long Island, at Brandywine, or Monmouth, he would promptly have ended British rule in the colonies. So important did Washington consider this expedition, and especially the issues at stake, that he had at first intended to lead it in person; his Presidential duties requiring his presence at Philadelphia, however, he gave supreme command to Henry Lee, governor of Virginia, making him a major general for the purpose. Lee accepted the mission without hesitation. His promptness is significant to those interested in historic parallels. It afterward became a Southern contention that force could not be used to suppress resistance to the constitution, yet Light Horse Harry, in 1794, was apparently not squeamish about coercion. More important still, the Western insurrection even involved the same question as that which led to war in 1861, for separation from the Union was included in the programme of the extremists. Again, Robert E. Lee, in 1861, defended his championship of the Confederacy on one ground, and one ground alone: he could not take up arms against Virginia. Yet this is what his father, in 1794, actually did, for the insurrections of that time, as already said, included not only the people of western Pennsylvania, but the mountaineers of western Maryland, Virginia, and North Carolina. And Major General Lee, at the head of the greatest military force ever assembled by his country, started out to defend the constitution against this formidable rebel host. Washington also gave the enterprise his blessing, accompanying the army to its two bases, Bedford, Pennsylvania, and Cumberland, Maryland, where he reviewed the troops.

That this force was not compelled to fight has dimmed the importance of the proceeding, but the point in question is not affected. Except for its arrival, resistance to Federal authority would have grown and probably have reached destructive proportions, but the mere appearance of General Lee's command on the frontier had the desired effect. The insurrectionists melted away to their homes, and, instead of firing upon his fellow citizens, all that Lee had to do was to accept their surrender. Seldom has the wisdom of tackling a problem boldly, not piecemeal, but by irresistible force, been so justified. Jefferson, when he retired from Washington's cabinet, ostensibly to pursue philosophy and agriculture, but really to build up a party of his own and obtain a nomination for the Presidency, began ridiculing Washington's "insurrection," not hesitating to misrepresent the facts. John Marshall, in quite a different spirit, tells the story in his *Life of Washington*. "Thus," he writes, "without shedding a drop of blood, did the prudent vigor of the executive terminate an insurrection, which, at one time, threatened to shake the government of the United States to its foundations."

3

With this exception, Henry Lee's three years as governor were uneventful. On the personal side, however, the period was important. Matilda's death in 1790 had produced another of those spells of melancholy to which Lee was so subject. And as usual

he began to think of desperate remedies. To most of the tribe
of Lee the French Revolution had not appeared as the sunrise;
Richard Henry never ceased to mourn the execution of Louis
XVI and Marie Antoinette, endeared to him for their help in
the American war, and Arthur's usually adequate vocabulary
could find no terms sufficiently opprobrious to visit upon Robes-
pierre and his co-workers. But to Henry Lee, looking for an
escape from sorrow and eager to resume an occupation in which
he always shone, events in Europe came as a possible relief.
Would he not be received in the army of Revolutionary France?
French friends led Harry to believe that a high commission
awaited him and that the French would embrace him as an American Lafayette. Washington, it is true, threw cold water on the
proposal; that even-balanced statesman did not admire the performances of Revolutionary France, and there was work enough
for Henry Lee, he thought, in his own country. That Washington's advice had its effect is apparent from a letter soon afterward sent from Mount Vernon to the governor's mansion. "As
we have been told" — the date of Washington's letter is July 21,
1793 — "that you have exchanged the rugged and dangerous
field of Mars for the soft and pleasurable bed of Venus, I do
in this as I shall in everything you may pursue like unto it, good
and laudable, wish you all imaginable success and happiness."
Instead of going to France, Henry Lee had married Ann Hill
Carter of Shirley, June 18, 1793. He was thirty-seven and his
bride twenty.

It was a distinguished alliance, even for a member of the
House of Lee. It did not mark the first time the Lees and Carters
had come into conjunction, though their earlier association had
been of less amiable kind. Ann Hill Carter was great-granddaughter of that Carter of Corotoman, in Lancaster, contemporary and rival of Thomas Lee. King Carter's fortune, like that
of the first lord of Stratford, had been gained as agent of the
Fairfax proprietary; at his death, in 1732, — he left an estate
of 300,000 acres, one thousand slaves, and £10,000 cash (a large
sum in a time when hard money was almost nonexistent in Virginia), — he was probably the richest Virginian of his day. The
pride of King Carter, his overbearing character, his fierce energy,

and his piety had long since passed into Virginia legend. Piety may seem incongruous with Carter's imperious traits. Yet religion had been perhaps the man's most conspicuous virtue, as it became that of his descendants, manifesting itself most strikingly in the King's son, Robert the Councilor, who was successively Anglican, Baptist, Swedenborgian, and Catholic. Of all Virginians of his time, probably only one was not overawed by King Carter's greatness: that was Thomas Lee, who, as a young man, regarding the Potomac region near the falls as his own perquisite, successfully withstood certain Carter encroachments in the neighborhood.

Any family ill-feeling these conflicts may have bred had naturally vanished by the time Light Horse Harry appeared as suitor for the favorite daughter of the clan. In the intervening years both families had increased their power, though in different ways. The Lees represented the graces of Virginia life, while the Carters stood for its more sombre virtues. The Lees had become distinguished writers, diplomatists, scholars, soldiers, and Revolutionary patriots, even "democrats" and upholders of popular rights against patrician arrogance; the Carters were important rather as social leaders, defenders of ancient privilege, maintainers, as long as it could be maintained, of the British connection — at first reluctant, though ultimately loyal, supporters of revolution. Two of Richard Henry Lee's bitterest opponents in the Continental Congress were Benjamin Harrison and Carter Braxton, both Carters on the mothers' side. Whereas the Lees were famous for intellectual diversion and plain living, the Carters were given to unbounded hospitality, to social predominance and to the accumulation of wealth. For that last talent had not died with King Carter. His sons and grandsons, by alliances with the most opulent families in Virginia, constantly increased the Carter possessions. It was one of their habits to add, by intermarriage, other estates to their own, so that, by 1793, when Light Horse Harry entered the circle, Carter properties and Carter families were found in almost every section of Virginia. Thus the father of Charles Carter had joined his fortunes with the family of Hill, owners of Shirley on the James, a beautiful house filled with many mementoes of the past, including that Charles Wilson

Peale portrait of Washington which many prefer to those of Gilbert Stuart. Here Ann Hill, named for maternal ancestors, had spent a girlhood in the best Virginia tradition, with all the education deemed suitable to a young lady of her time, and with all those social occupations looked upon as the more desirable aspects of the feminine career. If loneliness became the dominant note of Ann Carter's married life, she certainly could not have lacked for companionship in her early days. By two marriages Charles Carter had twenty-one children. Yet so extensive were his riches that each was popularly estimated as an heir or heiress. This Charles Carter seems to have had gentler qualities than those usually associated with the family. High liver like all his tribe, devoted to church and social caste, he was also genial, a pleasant companion, a man of upright principle, conscious always of his duties of citizenship, attached to friends and children, especially his daughter Ann. Among the effects of that daughter was found a newspaper obituary which she had preserved through all her years of affliction. "His long life," it read, in the language of the time, "was spent in the tranquillity of domestic enjoyments. From the mansion of hospitality his immense wealth flowed like silent streams, enlivening and refreshing every object around."

Not until the advent of Light Horse Harry at Shirley had there been any disagreement between Charles Carter and his daughter Ann. That Governor Lee should start a rift at first seems strange. Though Ann Hill Carter, now twenty years old, a beauty and prospective heiress, was undoubtedly one of the most sought-after girls on the James, General Henry Lee was a bridegroom who was not to be despised. He was a close friend of Washington, with a fine military record, member of Congress, eloquent debater in the Virginia Convention, at the moment in question governor of Virginia — one whose name, in modern parlance, was being "mentioned" as successor to Washington in the Presidency of the United States. Carter's objections were ostensibly based upon Lee's desire to join the armies of Republican France, but undoubtedly lay deeper. Even Harry's financial irresponsibility does not provide a complete explanation. The fact is that one did not have to be a fine Virginia gentleman, with all the chivalrous Virginian's attitude toward women, to resent Harry Lee's manner of courtship. Not far from Shirley lived another charming Virginia girl, Maria Farley, born at Westover of fine family — a family into which other Lees married. Maria was Ann's closest friend, and to these two young ladies Harry's association had an aspect somewhat triangular. It is too late in the day to recover the whole story, but a letter recently unearthed is sufficiently explicit. Maria Farley married William Champe Carter, of Blenheim, Albemarle County, Virginia, nephew of Charles Carter of Shirley, father of Ann. The letter given below was written in 1821, by Judge Samuel Appleton Storrow, Judge Advocate General of the United States Army, and husband of Maria Farley's granddaughter.

FARLEY 6th Sept. 1821

MY DEAR SISTER

I have delayed writing to you for some days, & a visit from Mrs. Lee has been the cause. She is our relation & our Mother's earliest friend. It is fitting that I should explain the reason why I do now what I ought to have done a week since, & as the cause is Mrs. Lee [widow of Light Horse Harry] I cannot do better than explain Mrs. Lee. In fact I am glad of this chance — I have an overflowing of the heart whenever I think of her & an outpourring of the spirit is the only relief.

Very fine women (you may doubt me) are rather rare here. Female talent has generally received a wrong direction. I have seen many a worn out coquette, many a heartless Belle that wonted but the first impulse to have been made useful & happy. I have heard of many instances of rare capacities, but waist followed possession as tho' it were irresistible. In fact it may have been so — society (that of Va. I mean) was full of splendid meteors: if a woman had been inclined to pursue a right path there was no steady light whereby she could discern it. But Mrs. Lee need not have been in Va. to have been pronounced excellent — there is no circle — none on earth — of which she would not be an ornament. She commenced life a spoilt child — a beauty & fortune — but Heaven has used her as its purest gold & all that died under the torture were her imperfections.

My Mammy you know was a beauty & fortune too in her day
— Nancy Lee & herself were pretty much brought up together —
Mrs. Lee the eldest by a year.   Gen. Lee, at that time the head
of everything in Va., was in love (honestly they say) with Mrs.
Carter.   He was handsome, of splendid talents, & Governor of
the State.   Mrs. Carter, then Miss Farley, & Mrs. Lee, then
Miss Carter, were living together during the Gen.'s suit to Miss
Farley as desperately as was Gen. Lee in love with Miss F——
was Miss Carter with Gen. Lee & at the same time compelled
to witness his devotion to another object.   His repeated visits to
Miss F—— & utter neglect of her preyed upon her health —
but drew nothing from her of unkindness to her fortunate cousin.
& her only interference, & that against herself, was when General
Lee had made his offer & Miss Farley avowed that she should
reject it — she then said "O stop, stop Maria — you do not
know what you are throwing away."   Maria however persisted
in throwing it away.   & then in the face of decency & delicacy
he made an offer to her, which she *could not* resist, & became his
delighted wife, but to find in the short space of a fortnight that
her affections were trampled on by a heartless & depraved profligate.   I am right as to time.   One fortnight was her dream
of happiness from which she awoke to a life of misery.   Her
fortune was soon thrown away upon his debts contracted previous
to marriage: She was despised & neglected.   & he, who in his
outset of life bid fairer for a glorious termination of it than
perhaps any man in America died a vagrant & Beggar.   Gen.
Lee at the time of his marriage with her was a widdower.   By
his first marriage he had two children — one daughter married
and proved to be everything that was abominable, the other a
son, was the kindest & to his new Mother & her children the most
affectionate relation on earth.   Mrs. L—— herself had five children.   Just as Carter Lee (whom you recollect in college) had
proved himself a fine fellow, her eldest daughter Ann was attacked with a dreadful complaint in the hand, & after a year's
residence in Philadelphia for the sake of medical assistance &
after sufferings of a most horrible sort, was informed that her
life was to be saved only by the amputation of her arm.   The
Mother had infused a portion of her own heroism into her daugh-

ter & about six months since — after eighteen months exercise of it the sweet little creature was pronounced convalescent.

One misery ceased but to prepare the way for a greater. Henry Lee[1] — her husband's son — a gentleman of great fortune & talents — more distinguished perhaps than any young man in Virginia for excellence of various sorts. His genius, liberality, his devotion to his Mother's family & promise of eminence being the theme of everyone was convicted of crimes of the blackest dye. He married a Lady of fortune & her sister lived with him. He was guardian. He seduced her under circumstances too — too horrible to mention & blackened with his disgrace everyone that bore his name. This is the last fatal-fatal stroke seems to have left no phial unemptied. And yet when you see her you do not require the consideration of her suffering to give interest to her. Her simple dignity, her most admirable understanding & manners excite enough of admiration without any appeal to sympathy.

This is the history of the Lady who has kept my letter back & it is a most edifying one. Misery & temptation have beset her from the outset & their only effects have been to raise her nearer to Heaven. Carter & her youngest daughter Mildred were with her. They left us this morning. Sept. 10th. After writing the foregoing I stopt for breath, as well I might. You see that this parting continued for four days. Finding myself better in mind than I was, I go at it again.[2]

Such was the life tragedy of the mother of Robert E. Lee — a tragedy her affectionate father foresaw but was powerless to prevent. That the head of the House of Carter should object to a son-in-law who had "paid his addresses" to another girl, and turned to Ann only after that girl had rejected him, is understandable. But Harry's definite decision not to go to France gave Ann's father an excuse for reconciling himself to the inevitable. "You have declared upon your honor," Carter wrote the impending son-in-law, "that you have relinquished all thoughts of going to France, and we are satisfied with that assurance.

[1] This Henry Lee — last of the name — was the surviving son of Matilda and Light Horse Harry. He was born in 1787 and died in 1838.
[2] The rest of the letter is lost — perhaps destroyed.

As we certainly know that you have obtained her consent, you shall have that of her parents most cordially, to be joined together in the holy bonds of matrimony, whenever she pleases; and as it is determined on, by the approbation and sincere affection of all friends, as well as of the parties immediately concerned, we think the sooner it takes place the better."

Following the suggestion in the last sentence, the wedding — a splendid one, for which old Shirley offered the propitious background — at once followed, June 18, 1793. Ann Carter Lee accompanied her husband to Richmond and performed the rôle of governor's wife. And Maria Farley presently married Ann's cousin, William Champe Carter.

Of this woman, whose son was destined to play so momentous a part in American history, little is known. Beyond the fact that she was of medium height and brunette in coloring, even her physical appearance cannot be described. No well-authenticated portrait survives. In the crypt of the Lexington church that contains the body of Robert E. Lee hangs a painting, discovered in Italy, said to be that of Ann Carter. The lady wears, as her most conspicuous ornament, a miniature of the first President, inscribed "from Washington to his dear Ann." The former owner of this painting declared in writing that Mildred Lee, daughter of the Confederate general, said that it was a portrait of her grandmother, and that the Washington locket had been a wedding gift. As Mildred Lee was born thirteen years after Ann Lee's death, the identification is unsatisfactory; yet the likeness itself, that of a handsome, well-poised lady, with slightly wistful eyes, reënforces impressions handed down from Ann's contemporaries. Certainly Ann Lee's character inspired admiration in all who knew her. Judge Storrow, in the above epistle, bears evidence of her sterling traits, and William H. Fitzhugh, in his letter to the Secretary of War, recommending Robert E. Lee as a candidate for West Point, says that his mother was "one of the finest women the State of Virginia has ever produced." For a more definite insight a few of Ann Lee's letters survive. There is something in the very appearance of these withered manuscripts — a dozen or so — preserved in the Library of Congress that tells the story of character. The handwriting is as neat, and of as copper plate a variety, as that of Thomas Jefferson himself. Those niceties of punctuation, capitalization, and spelling, not too scrupulously observed by the most highly placed men and women of the time — as the letter printed above shows — are here handled with respect. The whole tenor of thought is similarly sincere and unaffected. Not an intellectual woman, the predominating trait of Ann, as of her son, was simplicity; old-fashioned religion, old-fashioned virtues, and old-fashioned manners made her moral world. All she asked of her boys was that they "be honorable and correct," that they "practice the most inflexible virtue," and "indulge in such habits only as are consistent with religion and morality." The love of relatives and connections which was such a persistent Lee trait was marked also in the daughter of the Carters. The communications are largely filled with queries about the members of the clan, expressions of affection for them, and requests for their letters; her sons, Ann insists, must cultivate the epistolary art; without this grace no man or woman can go far! That Ann Lee was poor, neglected, lonely, and in wretched health is now no secret, but this is not reflected in the correspondence, beyond a humorous reference to her lack of a carriage and doubts as to whether she will ever have one again. In adverse circumstances she possessed patience and fortitude of the highest kind, for it was the kind that said nothing about them. Ann Lee's one accomplishment, so far as these letters show, was singing — a talent frequently exercised for the benefit of her children. Especially significant is her silence about Light Horse Harry. The thirty pages of manuscript contain one reference to the writer's husband — to the time, in 1799, when he was absent electioneering for Congress. His success in that attempt, and the two winters Ann Lee spent in the national capital in Philadelphia, constituted the bright spot in this long period of disappointment and failure.

4

For Harry Lee's life is divided into two phases: the first, in which he plays the part of a soldier and statesman; the second, in which his failure in practical matters brought misery to himself

and his family.   It was Matilda's fortune to share the era of
fame and splendor; it was the fate of Ann to participate in the
time of collapse and squalor.   Still, there were a few flashes in
this disconsolate period — such as that election to Congress in
1799, largely through the influence of Washington.   Harry's
greatest achievement in Philadelphia was not as lawmaker or
political leader, but as rhetorician; Washington died soon after
his labors began and Lee was chosen to deliver the eulogy at
the old German Lutheran Church.   This is Harry Lee's one last
brilliant moment before his lapse into obscurity.   For his oration contains one undying phrase: it was the sentence in which
Lee described his hero as "first in war, first in peace and first in
the hearts of his countrymen."   That Light Horse Harry, in
the heat of emotion, could strike off such a tribute shows that
he possessed a quality which Washington himself assigned him
— of genius.   In the main, however, the decades from 1790 to
1810 offered little scope for Henry's talents.   After one or two
rather inconstant years he went over, bag and baggage, to the
Federalist Party; and the rapid eclipse of that organization in
the era following Washington's administration carried Henry
into political oblivion.   All measures of the Washington and
Adams administrations he supported, and with increasing fervor
— the attitude towards France, the proclamation of neutrality,
the Alien and Sedition Laws; while the Virginia and Kentucky
resolutions proclaiming, as early as 1798–1799, the doctrine of
Nullification — really a mild form of secession — aroused
Henry's fury.   Not unnaturally his great political aversion was
Thomas Jefferson.   Bad feeling between the two men reached
the boiling point when Lee, at a dinner party with the great
Democrat, heard him make remarks which he regarded as insulting to Washington.   Henry at once put the President on
guard; news of this reached Monticello, and letters and epithets began to stir the atmosphere.   Despite Jefferson's pseudo-indigna-
tion, the merits of this argument were on Lee's side, for Jefferson
certainly was abusing Washington in secret, and his denunciations of Lee as a "tergiversator," as one who was "dirtily employed in sifting the conversations of my table," now have a
hollow ring.   Lee carried his antagonism so far as to vote for

Aaron Burr for President in preference to Jefferson when, in 1800, the election was thrown into the House of Representatives. Under these circumstances Jefferson's accession to the Presidential chair boded no good to Lee's political career. He still remained on friendly terms with his old Princeton classmate and co-defender of the constitution, James Madison, despite Madison's "going over" to the new Democratic-Republican régime, but after 1800 there was no political future for Harry Lee — and for other reasons than the new political line-up.

By this time Harry was a broken man. It is a dreary picture that emerges from Stratford in this final decade. Under the prosperous Lees, Thomas and Philip Ludwell, and even under Matilda, the solemn pile, with its beautiful gardens, could easily take on an air of gayety; under the poverty that afflicted Henry and Ann, however, its lively charm disappeared. The living quarters consisted of a single floor — an assemblage of small apartments grouped around a central hall of fine proportions, adorned with family portraits, but with its hangings and other furniture growing shabbier year by year. This great living room had no provision for heating — only by carrying a charcoal brazier from place to place could invalid Ann create an illusion of warmth; "our poor old dwelling," as she calls it in one of her letters, presented an icy contrast to the cheery Shirley in which her childhood had been passed. Here, with her small children, Ann spent weeks and months alone, for Harry was constantly absent, chasing the will-o'-the-wisps that he believed could bring fortune and release. In February 1799 she writes to her favorite confidante, Mrs. Richard Bland Lee, that, with the exception of dining twice with neighbors, she had not left the house since the preceding August. "So confined is the sphere in which I have moved for the last six months that I am almost totally ignorant of every occurrence beyond the distance of fifteen or twenty miles, and, excepting the friends who do and always will retain their places in my memory and in whose remembrance I hope I shall exist I may with much truth be said to live 'The world forgetting, by the world forgot.'" Yet there is no complaining. "I do not find it in the smallest degree tiresome; my hours pass too nimbly for that."

Yet the truth is that every day the family was being more pinched for that ready cash without which domestic machinery cannot move. Henry had no profession except soldiering, and in that his occupation had long since gone; he had no taste or ability as a farmer — and, indeed, Westmoreland was steadily losing ground as a tobacco country. For several years he had frantically sought to mend his fortunes by schemes of land speculation and the like. In these the available assets left him by his father, and those he could squeeze from his wives, had long since disappeared. The family interest in Western lands was manifest in him, but with direful results. The dreams of Richard Henry and the other Lees for a Western American empire have heroic aspects. But Harry was thinking more of "the millions in it" than of the growth of the American realm. The Potomac River, as the destined transportation route to the West, seized on his imagination, as it had on Washington's. Washington's plans, however, centred in engineering problems, clearing the river of obstructions and canalizing around the Falls, but Henry's ideas concentrated on building cities, acquiring huge tracts of lands that were ultimately to reap the profits of these improvements. At the Falls he purchased five hundred acres as site of the great city he confidently believed would rise on that point. He called his future metropolis Matildaville, a melancholy tribute to his first wife; here a few sawmills and working buildings were constructed, but the exact location of the "city" is to-day unknown, although the name pathetically lingered on the map until modern times. Even though a second New York or Philadelphia had been destined to sprout in this region, Henry could not have profited, for he had purchased land to which no solid title could be provided, and thus he was unable to give deeds to the optimistic purchasers of corner lots and factory sites who really did appear. Besides this speculation Henry bought the mythical rights of an English family to large territories in the Potomac region — with the result that usually follows such aspirations. His final coup was the acquisition of what was left, or what he thought was left, of the Fairfax domain: here again Henry obtained an empty shell, for no title to the property could be granted. But all these Potomac schemes, even Washington's "Powtowmack Company," were doomed at the start. The idea of making the Potomac a highway by digging a shallow channel here and there, and removing rocky obstacles to navigation, was a mistake, as De Witt Clinton demonstrated, a few years afterward, by building the Erie Canal and thus appropriating for the Hudson River and New York that vast Western traffic that Washington and Lee had envisioned for their darling stream.

Lee was irretrievably ruined. And now begins his unhappy final era: living on small loans, hiding from creditors, piling up debt wherever credit could be obtained, crossing to the other side of the street and disappearing down alleys to avoid pursuing tradesmen; yet all this time maintaining an optimistic temper, cheerfully lending to one friend the money he had extracted from another, full of engaging conversation, fertile in epigram and anecdote, always willing to entertain strangers with recollections of Washington and Lafayette, fond of making bombastic speeches, of parading the highway in his old military cape, his head topped by a gorgeous white high hat — an adornment which, as legal proceedings disclosed, had not been paid for. As Ann and Henry huddled in that cold room at Stratford, one sound in particular sent the chills down their spines. That was a knock heralding the approach of sheriff or dun. Henry would tiptoe to the window, glance at the intruder, and if, as was usually the fact, a hard-faced creditor was discovered waiting admittance, some plan of denying access would be improvised. Finally, less obvious methods having failed, a chain was stretched across the door, which the most energetic bailiff found it hard to circumvent. Occasionally a persistent representative of the law would outwit the old cavalry officer, and then an episode ensued much like one of the favorite scenes of the comic stage. Light Horse Harry, his hair now grizzled, his clothes threadbare and shiny, would greet the stranger with the most ceremonious courtesy. Even a bottle of old wine might now and then be brought out; the conversation would be deftly turned to old campaigns and politics, and, after two or three entranced hours, Harry's guest would be bowed out, not, indeed, with any financial culmination to his call, but satisfied that his time had been well spent.

Many stories are told, most of them probably apocryphal, illustrating Harry's carelessness in money matters. One pictures him borrowing a pair of horses of a friend for a journey into a near-by county, the obliging friend sending a slave to care for the animals and bring them back. Two or three weeks passed with no news of Henry, the horses, or the negro. Then the owner accidentally met his faithless retainer. "What became of my horses?" he asked. "Well, you see, Marse Henry sold dose horses." "He did, did he? Why didn't you come back and tell me about it?" "Well, you see, Marse Henry sold me too." Yet Harry was as generous with his own property as this tale represents his being with that of others. His miseries really started with the purchase of the illusory Fairfax domain in partnership with Robert Morris. Morris was to furnish the cash, and, after completing negotiations, Henry went to Philadelphia to get his money. Instead of fulfilling his agreement, Morris borrowed from Henry all his remaining capital, about $40,000; the Philadelphian's failure to repay the loan left Henry helpless when creditors began pounding on the doors of Stratford. There was a fine Colonel Sellers touch in that transaction, but probably its humor was lost on Ann, child of luxury and of dignified living. Had it not been for her father, she would probably have wanted for bread. The kind old gentleman would provide for his daughter, but would do nothing to facilitate Harry's schemes. In 1806 Charles Carter died, leaving Ann a fair-sized property, in trust, the income to be paid for life, the principal, at her death, to go to the children. Her sister Mildred, dying in 1807, left her property also to the Lady of Stratford, with the similar safeguard against its appropriation by Harry Lee.

And, like Robert Morris, Henry found his Marshalsea — that courthouse and jail of Montross in which, as justice of the peace, he had once himself passed judgment on delinquent debtors. For two years previous to his incarceration the sheriffs of Westmoreland and Spotsylvania counties had searched for their victim, armed with papers authorizing them "to have the body" of Henry Lee and bring it before the court; but Henry had not been a cavalry leader in vain and proved as skillful in avoiding these diligent agents as he had, when necessary, Cornwallis himself. But the avalanche of court orders and pursuing sheriffs finally proved too strong. One pitiless merchant had claims for "a fine hatt, rope, powder, gunflints and two and one half quires of paper," an inventory that gives a fairly complete picture of Harry's occupations in his decline — the hat for his handsome public appearances, the gun and shot for diversions conformable to a Virginia gentleman, the paper for the ferocious diatribes which he loved to compose against Jefferson. These claims and others of larger scope kept Lee in the debtors' prison for more than two years. The little greensward outside, at which he could gaze, held precious memories. Ten years before he had been a candidate for Congress; in accordance with custom of the time, the voters appeared in person in this open space, calling out their preference *viva voce*. Things at first did not go propitiously for Harry — a Federalist candidacy, at that time, represented the forlornest of hopes; but suddenly a tall stalwart gentleman, whose presence caused a silence, dismounted from his horse, walked up to the talesmen, and said, "I vote for General Lee." That ballot had turned the tide in Harry's favor, for the voter was ex-President Washington. And now, in almost the same spot, Henry Lee was a prisoner, supported by the county at the rate of seventeen cents a day.

But Henry did not lose courage. He decided to pay his debts by the labor of his pen. Scribbling had always been a pleasure and there was one subject he knew well — those campaigns in the Carolinas in the last days of the Revolution. So Henry started furiously to work. The book, he insisted, would not only pay his debts and release him from prison, but launch him on a new career. "It will have a great run!" Harry told his friends — in error again, for the book had trouble in finding a publisher, and though, in the course of a hundred years, it has passed through three editions and is the original source for the history of the subject it treats, the money return was negligible. In this book Henry describes his own exploits modestly enough, always referring to himself in the third person, like Cæsar. He exalts his favorites, and does not mind rapping now and then those not admired. The work would rouse such antagonism that Henry first thought of publishing it anonymously, for he had no wish to spend an old age, he said, fighting duels. Jefferson's friends came at Lee furiously for the reference to a not particularly glorious episode in that sage's career — his hurried retreat from Monticello on the approach of Tarleton's troopers. Only by a hair's breadth did the British miss capturing the governor of Virginia and author of the Declaration of Independence! Harry Lee disposes of the incident in a brief paragraph, but its very terseness infuriated Jefferson. "The attempt to take the Governor, who was at his house in sight of the town, failed. Apprised of the approach of the dragoons he very readily saved himself by taking shelter in an adjacent spur of the mountain." Rather neatly expressed! — though probably Henry would have been the first to admit that Jefferson's humiliation did not consist in this strategic exit, for no governor has a right to permit himself to be captured, but in so neglecting the defense of his state that the precipitation was unavoidable.

Two years before Henry's translation to Montross an event had taken place at Stratford not particularly sensational in view of more exciting perturbations in the family, but of immense significance for the future. By 1806 Ann Lee had had three sons and one daughter, and, in the summer of that year, she felt the premonitions of another child. In all her attendant woes, Ann is perhaps pardonable for not rejoicing at the prospect. The rearing and education of three children — the oldest, Algernon Sydney, had lived only a year — seemed burden enough for the future. Her father's death in the same year, soon followed by that of Mildred, "the darling sister of my heart," to say nothing of the circumstances of her life, added to the distress of the time. Thus it was that Ann, in a letter to her sister-in-law, Mrs. Richard Bland Lee, who was also awaiting a child, penned an amazing sentence. "You have my best wishes for your success, my dear, and truest assurance, that I do not envy your prospects, nor wish to *share in them.*" (Italics in the original.) The confession is amazing, and indicates the mental state to which Ann had been reduced — for, eight days after it was written, January 19, 1807, Ann's child, a boy, was born. The birth took place in the southeast room of Stratford, the same chamber in which two signers of the Declaration of Independence and two diplomats of the Revolution had first seen light. Of all her brothers, Ann's favorites were Robert and Edward, and to this son, so undesired, was given the name of Robert Edward Lee.

5

As not infrequently happens with unwanted children, Robert presently became his mother's inseparable companion and the chief comfort of her life.   It is no wonder, the child was so handsome and sweet-tempered.   Some have held that Robert E. Lee was a Carter, not a Lee, and certainly in temperament, in character, in method, in sense of responsibility, in habit of mind and taste, — always excepting that supreme taste for military life, — the Confederate leader bore little resemblance to Light Horse Harry. In mental tranquillity and spaciousness of outlook the man seemed more adapted to Shirley beside the James than to Stratford on the Potomac.   The fact is that Robert Lee's association both with Stratford and with his father was slight.   Properly he was not a Stratford Lee; the house in which he was born was not that of his ancestors; only the circumstance that Henry Lee had married his second cousin, Matilda, and thus acquired a life tenure on the estate, made it Robert Lee's birthplace.   Nor could Robert have had vivid memories of his father.   From Robert's second year to his fourth Henry Lee was in a debtors' prison; the next year he underwent a terrible experience that left him a disfigured invalid, and in 1813, when Robert was six years old, the battered veteran, now fifty-seven, left Virginia never to return.   Probably Robert E. Lee's most lasting memory of his father was when the old man, with gray hair, bent shoulders, face scarred with recent injuries, almost blind, took the child in his arms, kissed him good-bye, and left his home in search of health.   Virginia never knew the presence of Light Horse Harry again, until, exactly one hundred years afterward, in 1913, his body was brought from the distant island in which he died and placed in the chapel of Lexington, Virginia, beside that of his famous son.

Before his departure, one balm came to Lee, proffered by his old Princeton classmate, James Madison, then President of the United States. War having broken out a second time with England, Madison wrote Lee offering him a commission as major general in the American army. Perhaps the fire, certainly the gratitude, of the old campaigner was stirred, but Lee's days of warfare were at an end. His generous spirit had involved him, a few months previously, in an adventure from which he never recovered. The story of the Baltimore riot has been frequently told; it remains one of the most infamous episodes in American politics. Why Lee should have become involved is at first puzzling: the quarrel did not concern him; his only motive seems to have been to come to the rescue of a friend. The disturbance was one result of the passions aroused by the war. The still existent, somewhat flickering Federal Party was opposed to the declaration against England. In Baltimore the leading opponent of hostility was Alexander Hanson, editor of the *Federal Republican,* which, in June 1812, published an editorial attacking Madison and his war policy in the best journalistic style of an exciting era. In that time, and for a considerable period afterward, the opposition had one favorite way of replying to such arguments: that was to assemble the faithful, gather in front of the offending printing office, and hurl brickbats and firebrands into the premises. So effectually was this riposte leveled at Hanson that in a brief time his building had entirely vanished, his printing equipment destroyed, and his newspaper brought to an untimely end, while the editor himself was nursing his wounds in exile in a near-by town. A month afterward he opened headquarters again in another part of Baltimore. The paper was to be printed in Georgetown, sent to Hanson, and distributed by him to subscribers. That the enemy would not tamely submit to such defiance Hanson well knew; when, therefore, Henry Lee, a friend of his father, dropped in for a friendly call at the very moment it had been planned to issue the first number of the revitalized sheet, the dashing campaigner was pressed into service. In his obliging way Harry Lee agreed to assume command — his final command, as it proved. The captain who, with half a dozen followers, ensconced in a farmhouse, had fought off more than a hundred British cavalrymen perceived no great military difficulty in his new assignment. A combination of circumstances — Lee's unwillingness to fire upon civilians, the great size of the mob, the cowardly behavior of the authorities and the militia — produced a bloody tragedy. After two days and nights of rioting a heap of bodies was discovered outside the jail — into which the victims had been moved, ostensibly for their protection — surrounded by a gang of roughs who, not satisfied with having clubbed and beaten the enemy into insensibility, was now applying several forms of torture. Light Horse Harry was stabbed twice in the face, and was aroused from unconsciousness by the efforts of one of the rioters to cut off his nose with a penknife. After three hours of this sort of thing, the mob abandoned the prostrate forms, believing they were dead. In fact the news of Light Horse Harry's death was sent broadcast, obituaries and eulogies appearing in several newspapers.

A clever and humane physician had succeeded in sequestrating the bleeding men and removing them to a hospital. One was indeed dead, but the rest were restored ultimately to some semblance of their former selves. And Light Horse Harry was at last taken to his home in Alexandria. Several painful months followed; unable, for the most part, to read or write because of his face wounds, barely able to hobble around his room, the invitation from President Madison to take the field, in high command, merely increased his sufferings. Instead, a plan that had been forming some time in his head now assumed definite shape. He wished to leave the country — to get away from his debts and sorrows, and seek restoration of health in a warmer climate. Once Brazil seemed the indicated refuge; now Henry's desires turned to the West Indies, where warmth and sunshine might renew vitality. And so Harry Lee spent his last five years wandering from one island in the tropics to another, separated from family and friends, though everywhere his personal charm and powers of conversation made new companions, especially among those English officers who were warring with his country.

Yet the period was for Henry one long time of loneliness and physical pain. A batch of his letters survive, written to the oldest and evidently favorite son, Charles Carter Lee, at that time a student at Harvard, described by Henry as "the seminary of my choice." Modern university students would regard these communications as rather ponderous and Polonius-like. They are exhortations to the practice of "virtue"; Carter is enjoined to tell the truth, never to deceive, not to swear, especially in presence of "his inferiors," not to be insolent in prosperity, to love his "best of mothers," to speak no derogation of God, to acquire self-command, to be plain and neat in dress, to read the best poets — and the best poets were Sophocles and Pope, not Shakespeare and Milton — and the best orators, to eschew "skeptical writers" and novelists, and let "John Locke be the director of your mind and the guide of your lucubrations." One admonition must have come from the bottom of Henry's soul. "Avoid debt, the sink of mental power and the subversion of independence, which draws into debasement even virtue." More interesting to modern readers than these heavy aphorisms are certain personal touches. The longing for family and home shows the writer in his most affectionate mood. What he craves above all else are letters from Virginia! Day after day, he says, does he watch the horizon for a sail from his native land; eagerly he meets it at the dock, hoping for something from "darling Carter." Usually he asks in vain. Ten months pass — not a letter from home; then a letter from Carter arrives. "It infused into his father's heart," writes Harry, "an overflow of delight, in defiance of the torturing pain of disease." Harry carries it around with him for days, reading and rereading. Presently another comes, enclosed in a letter from Ann, and, at this double good fortune, the wanderer once more finds relief from pain. All the references to his wife are affectionate. "This is the day of the month," he writes from Nassau, June 18, 1817, "when your dear mother became my wife — a happy day, marked by the union of two humble lovers." Soon afterward Henry's repeated attempts to find a boat sailing to Virginia succeed. "At length I get off. The ship *Betsy* is in harbor, taking in her cargo, and is destined to some southern port; in her I go; and shall be landed, I dare say, as soon as you get this letter. I fear you will be puzzled to read it, but it cannot be altered by one afflicted as I am daily. God bless my dear Carter."

One day in February 1818, a fifteen-year-old boy, engaging in sports near the shore of Cumberland Island, off the coast of Florida, observed a schooner approaching the landing of Dungeness, an estate that, after the Revolution, had been the home of General Nathanael Greene, now occupied by his daughter, Mrs. Shaw. The ship in due course came to anchor; a boat was lowered, and a much debilitated old man, accompanied by captain and mate, slowly walked to the rail, was assisted into the skiff, and rowed towards the shore. Two sailors made a chair with hands and arms, lifted their charge, and carried him to the beach. The stranger's face was pale and thin, and marked by deep scars under the eye; his whole body was emaciated and apparently tormented with pain. The hair was thin and almost white; the clothes were extremely shabby; yet the whole effect was not ignoble, for there was still a keenness in the eye, and signs of military bearing in the frame. But the visitor's weakness was profound. Leaning upon the young man, he advanced a few steps, then stopped and sank wearily upon a log. The sailors placed beside him a much-worn haircloth trunk and a cask of Madeira wine. This was all that was left of Light Horse Harry Lee and his possessions.

After a few moments, gaining breath, he asked the boy his name. It was Nightingale, the lad replied, proudly adding that he was a grandson of General Nathanael Greene. At this his unbidden guest arose, threw his arms around the boy, and held him for a long time in embrace.

"Tell your aunt," Harry said, striking a pose, dramatic to the last, "that General Lee is at the wharf and wishes the carriage sent for him. Tell her I am come purposely to die in the house and in the arms of the daughter of my old friend and compatriot."

That Mrs. Shaw received her father's favorite officer affectionately goes without saying. The house was a large and beautiful one, the room in which Lee was placed looking on one side to the Atlantic and on the other side to a garden of orange trees and flowers. Only infrequently could Henry leave this apartment, but now and then, leaning on young Nightingale, who became his constant companion, he would take a walk in the garden,

entertaining the lad with reminiscences of his grandfather, interspersed with denunciations of Jefferson and the Democrats, and
high praise for the Federals.   An American fleet lay at the time
in Cumberland Harbor, prepared to take over Florida when the
cession had been finally made by Spain, and the officers did all
in their power to honor the old companion of Washington and
to comfort his last days.   When, after a week or two, Henry
became too feeble to leave his bed, the younger officers acted as
nurses, sitting up all night, vainly attempting to relieve the sick
man's sufferings, which at times were terrible, for wounds received in the Baltimore riot had injured the internal organs.

At times Lee was an intractable patient, venting his anger on
the person nearest, but almost immediately, after an explosion,
becoming penitent.   Always, even in the intensest agony, he was
human.   One day an old negro woman, "Mom Sarah," entered
the room, having been selected by Mrs. Shaw as a possibly satisfactory attendant, many other experiments having failed.
Henry seized a shoe and hurled it at the intruder.   The old
negress promptly picked it up and threw it back at the sick man.
A broad smile spread over Henry's face, and from that moment
he and Mom Sarah were understanding friends.   But Henry
Lee did not long burden Mr. and Mrs. Shaw.   He died March 25,
1818, at the age of sixty-two.   All the American ships in the
harbor lowered their colors and fired military salutes as he was
placed in the grave.   And so Light Horse Harry found his
final resting place, not among his native Virginians as had his
ancestors, but in the burial plot of the Greenes.   For fifteen years
his grave was unmarked, and then foot and head stones came
from Matilda's son, Henry, Jr.   Not until 1862, forty-four
years after his death, did any member of the family visit the
grave.

In January of that year General Robert E. Lee was in South
Carolina, strengthening coast defenses against expected attacks
from the fleets of the United States.   "While in Fernandina,"
he wrote his wife, "I went over to Cumberland Island and walked
up to Dungeness, the former home of General Green.   It was
my first visit to the house and I had the gratification at last of
visiting my father's grave.   He died there, you may recollect,

on his way from the West Indies, and was interred in one corner of the family cemetery.   The spot is marked with a plain marble slab, with the name, age and date of his death.   Mrs. Green is also buried there, and her daughter Mrs. Shaw and her husband. The place is at present owned by Mr. Nightingale, nephew of Mrs. Shaw, who married a daughter of Mr. James King.   The family have moved into the interior of Georgia, leaving only a few servants and a white gardener on the place.   The garden was beautiful, enclosed by the finest hedge I have ever seen.   It was of the wild olive.   The orange trees were small, and the orange grove which, in Mrs. Shaw's lifetime, during my tour of duty in Savannah in early life, was so productive, had been destroyed by an insect that has proved fatal to the oranges on the coast of Georgia and Florida.   There was a fine grove of olives from which, I learn, Mr. Nightingale procures oil.   The garden was filled with roses and beautiful vines, the names of which I do not know.   Among them was the tomato vine in full bearing, with the ripe fruit on it.   There has yet been no frost in that region of the country this winter.   I went into the dining room and parlor in which the furniture still remained. . . .   The house has never been finished, but is a fine large one and beautifully located.   A magnificent grove of live oaks envelope the road from the landing to the house."

Another reference to his visit comes from Lee's companion, A. L. Long.   "We came to a dilapidated wall enclosing a neglected cemetery.   The general then, in a voice of emotion, informed me that he was visiting the grave of his father.   He went alone to the tomb, and after a few moments of silence, retraced his steps. . . .   We returned in silence to the steamer and no allusion was ever made to this act of filial devotion."

XV

END OF THE LEE CLAN

I

THE half century preceding 1861 was an important time in the history of the United States. It was the era that witnessed the rise of the slave power, and of a brilliant line of statesmen, ranged in opposing sides in the great sectional struggle — the period of the Missouri Compromise, Nullification, Kansas-Nebraska debates, fugitive-slave laws, Dred Scott decisions, and other harbingers of irrepressible conflict. In all these discussions the family of Lee played little part. The gift for public activity seemed to have departed with the fifth generation. Another significant change had taken place. No longer are the Lee estates found bordering the Potomac; the family, for the most part, abandoned the locations that had furnished sustenance and prestige for two hundred years. No longer are the Lees great tobacco planters; they are, in the main, gentleman farmers, lawyers, merchants, city dwellers, sometimes pioneers in the country to the west. Ludwell Lee, son of Richard Henry, upheld Virginia traditions of living at Belmont, in Loudoun — a house still standing in excellent condition; his cousin Thomas — whose chief distinction is that the late Edward D. White, Chief Justice of the United States, was a descendant — lived near by in Coton, a name that recalls the seat of the Lees of Shropshire; while the town of Leesburg sheltered a liberal representation of the tribe in whose honor it had been named. Above all, however, the city of Alexandria became a family suburb. Here Edmund Jennings Lee, younger brother of Light Horse Harry, and his wife Sally, daughter of Richard Henry Lee, made their home, and Richard Bland Lee, Charles Lee, and others not so widely known, added to its legal and political importance.

Almost the only Lee of the sixth generation who showed much aptitude for public life was Henry, son of Matilda Lee and Light Horse Harry.   But the fourth Henry Lee and last master of Stratford is a name that the family would willingly forget. This Henry, born in 1787, was apparently a charming child, quick, vivacious, much devoted to his stepmother, Ann Carter, who reared him as conscientiously as her own children.   Henry manifested all the family interest in books and public life; he likewise evinced literary talents, a considerable array of printed volumes ultimately standing to his credit.   At an early date less desirable qualities came to the surface.   That irresponsibility so marked in Light Horse Harry assumed an uglier form in the son.   Judge Samuel Appleton Storrow, in the letter printed above,[1] refers to the episode — the seduction of his sister-in-law — that wrecked Henry Lee's career and made him a social outcast.   Of the truth of this charge there is not the slightest question.   In a lengthy letter preserved in the Library of Congress, Henry Lee not only admits his offense, but attempts justification.   The girl was a member of his household at Stratford, and their constant association Henry evidently regards as sufficient excuse for his transgression.   This astonishing missive is addressed to Richard Brown, of Windsor, but it was really written for the benefit of John Tyler, then Senator from Virginia, afterward President of the United States.   It is mainly an attack on Thomas Jefferson, Tyler's friend and political exemplar, and reviews old Jefferson scandals, evidently on the theory that delinquencies in the patron saint of the Democratic Party provide sufficient excuse for his own.   Was his conduct, Lee wrote, any worse than Jefferson's?   And he rehearses, in much alluring detail, the story of Jefferson's alleged attempt to mislead the wife of an intimate friend, when that friend was engaged on a mission to the Western Indians.   If you can accept Jefferson as your leader, — so ran this *apologia,* — why do you cast me out?

It was through this Henry Lee that the Stratford estate was lost to the Lee family and passed to strangers.   This misfortune

[1] Pages 380–82.

was again the consequence of the man's relation with his wife's sister. For he was the girl's guardian, trustee of property left by her father. When Lee's ward became of age it was found that her entire inheritance had disappeared. Naturally her representatives seized, as reparation, all Lee's available assets: the most valuable was the Stratford estate, which the court awarded the young woman as part reimbursement of the defalcation.

Henceforth Henry Lee was little better than a vagabond, cast out by his relatives, ostracized by his social class, forced to pick up a living in odd ways, chiefly by acting as ghost writer for politicians. On him was fixed, in ironical distinction from his father, the name "Black Horse Harry," by which he is known in Virginia to this day. Virulent controversy now became his stock in trade. When Jefferson's letters were published, after that statesman's death, containing attacks on Light Horse Harry, the son responded with an acrid pamphlet, consisting chiefly of an unfriendly dissection of Jefferson's character and career — a valuable but by no means impartial study. When William Johnson published his life of Nathanael Greene, mildly criticizing passages in Light Horse Harry's *Memoirs,* Henry again responded with a bulky and tedious volume, upholding his father's statements. John Quincy Adams thought that Black Horse Harry had positive talents. "Lee's reputation," Adams wrote in this diary, "is bad with regard to private morals and his political course is unprincipled; but he writes with great force and elegance, and Mr. Calhoun had used him for that purpose." The reference to Lee's "political course" is reminiscent, for Adams had appointed Henry Lee assistant postmaster general, in which post, it was said, he had schemed in the interest of Andrew Jackson, Adams's great enemy. The appointment of Henry Lee as consul general to Algiers, President Adams afterward wrote, was his reward for treachery to me, and libels against me, and of sycophancy to the later President Jackson." Yet Lee had enough political influence to receive twelve electoral votes for vice president in February 1833. This was the result of his intimacy with Jackson, who found the man's literary talents useful, frequently employing him to write his speeches; in all probability Jackson's first inaugural was Lee's work in large part. In 1826–1827 Lee spent several months at Jackson's home, the Hermitage, near Nashville, Tennessee, examining that statesman's papers for biographical purposes. The manuscript of this proposed life, so far as written, is at present in the Library of Congress.

Lee wrote one charming letter, worthy of being rescued from oblivion. It is dated Monticello, July 1, 1826, where Lee had gone to examine documents relating to Jefferson's conduct as governor of Virginia. He found Jefferson, then eighty-three, seriously ill — on his deathbed, as it proved, for he died three days afterward. "As soon as I arrived," Lee writes Jackson, "he sent out for me, and though he seemed to look upon his end as approaching, he spoke of it as an event rather unpleasant than terrible, — like a traveller expressing his apprehension of being caught in the rain. I was surprised at the energy of his grasp and the alacrity of his conversation, and could not but admire the general predominance of mind over matter in all his words and actions in so trying and critical a moment. His daughter, Mrs. Randolph, hovers around his bed with grief at her heart and comfort in her hands but I fear her misgivings will be verified in spite of her tenderness and care."

Since Lee's consular appointment had been an ad interim one, he was in Algiers, performing his official duties, when news came of his rejection by the Senate. There was no future for the exile in America, so he went to Paris, where his last days were spent. And here again Lee's personal graces and lively mind brought important friends. The most celebrated of these was Letizia Bonaparte, mother of the Emperor Napoleon. Madame Mère apparently liked to talk to the appreciative American of her son, whose death she had survived. "In the interview with which I was honored by this venerable lady in the autumn of 1830," Lee afterward wrote, "she conversed much about the birth and infancy of her great son; whose full length portrait, in his imperial robes, was at the head of the bed in which she was reclining. The portrait of her husband, representing a very handsome man, was on the right of her bed. Among other things she mentioned the extreme fondness and indulgence of Napoleon's father, who often saved his favorite from her correction, and controlled him frequently by threatening to tell her of his disobedience. 'Very well, sir, I will tell your mother, and she will teach you to behave better.' She added, as well as I can remember her remark: 'This threat usually checked Napoleon, but sometimes I had to switch him well.' "

Henry Lee presently put this material to literary use. His admiration for the Corsican was as extreme as William Hazlitt's, and, like Hazlitt, he constituted himself his defender. When Walter Scott's depreciating life appeared, Henry Lee set himself to writing another, devoted mainly to refuting Scott's "errors" and "detractions." The first volume was published in 1835; it handles Sir Walter without gloves, one half the space being given to pointing out his mistakes. No more volumes were issued, for miseries now began to close in on Henry Lee. The last master of Stratford died in extreme poverty, in Paris, in 1838. And with him disappeared Stratford, so far as the Lees are concerned. This Lee estate, monument of so much distinction, starting place of so much American history, cradle of leaders who had contributed so largely to founding the United States, thus came to an end full of tragedy and disgrace. All the other owners of Stratford lie in Virginia graveyards, — in Burnt House Fields, in the Stratford tomb itself, — but the last son of the line found his resting place in Père-Lachaise, Paris.

The years of neglect and decay that followed were quite in keeping with this melancholy exit. The Stratford gardens disappeared; the interior, stripped of Lee furnishings and mementos of a hundred years, became raw and desolate; the lawns and driveways were overgrown with weeds; and the farm lands passed into underbrush and waste. Isolated in a remote region of the Potomac, the approaching roads little better than quagmires, Stratford became almost a legend, a shrine that excited varied emotions. It is said that Robert E. Lee was never heard to mention the name of that half brother who brought the glories of Stratford to extinction, but that he entertained tender recollections of the spot his letters show. In the midst of civil war, when the Arlington home had passed into possession of the United States, — to remain there up to the present time, — he cast loving glances at Stratford. In November 1861, his daughter Mildred wrote of her visit to the old seat, and from Savannah, where he was engaged in strengthening Southern sea defenses, he replied: "I am much pleased at your description of Stratford and your visit. It is endeared to me by many recollections and it has always been a great desire of my life to be able to purchase it. Now that we have no other home, and the one we so loved has been so foully polluted, the desire is stronger with me than ever. The horse chestnut you mention in the garden was planted by my mother. I am sorry the vault is so dilapidated. You did not mention the spring, one of the objects of my earliest recollections." And again, on Christmas Day, to his wife: "In the absence of a home I wish I could purchase Stratford. That is the only other place that I could go to, now accessible to us, that would inspire me with feelings of pleasure and local love. You and the girls could remain there in quiet. It is a poor place, but we could make enough corn bread and bacon for our support and the girls could weave us clothes."

Fortunately Stratford's brick walls, two feet thick, and its interior, strongly built, have survived the obliteration that has assailed most Potomac houses, and it has thus, in all substantials, remained intact for modern restoration as a Lee memorial.

That the Lees should abandon their tobacco plantations and seek new careers in general farming and the professions was inevitable, for the tobacco culture that had sustained their ancestors was falling into decay. Virginia, after the Revolution, never regained the ascendancy in this staple that had been hers in the old time. For several years her annual exports to England had averaged not far from 100,000,000 pounds; in 1797, fourteen years after the peace, they had dropped to a quarter of that amount. The part most adversely affected was that Northern Neck which for generations had been a stronghold of the Lees. The land here was naturally much less fertile than in other sections of the state; when prices were high the planters could afford to compensate the defect with fertilizers; under the low prices that now prevailed, however, this was not profitable. Therefore the old tobacco princes had to find other fields of employment; the Church, the army, the navy, law, medicine, and general business became their recourse. Of the Lees now congregated in Alexandria one interest was prominent. This was religion. Edmund Jennings

Lee and his son Cassius were among the leading Virginia laymen of the Episcopal Church, their lives centring around that Christ Church in Alexandria of which Washington had been the historic vestryman, and their patron saint was that Bishop William Meade, himself a Lee, who looms so large in the annals of the state. Neither they nor their exemplars accepted sympathetically Jefferson's policy of confiscating church property; and largely owing to their persistent fight, Christ Church parish succeeded in preserving its glebe from the general spoliation. Though all these Lees were Anglicans, they were of the Low Church variety, as was their kinsman Robert, and fairly Methodistical in matters of discipline. Indeed, they seemed to approximate those New Englanders of whom the Revolutionary Lees were so fond, but who have not been especially popular with a more modern generation. No Puritan was ever more exacting in Sabbath observance, and in their eyes theatres, dancing, card playing, horse racing, and the like were to be eschewed as one would flee damnation. Many stories are told of the lengths to which the Lees would go in avoidance of Sabbath desecration. Edmund Jennings Lee became mayor of Alexandria, developing into one of those "crusading" magistrates familiar in recent times, aiming with particular ferocity at gamblers. They all had another quality that suggested a more Northern region: an intense hostility to slavery. Alderman William Lee's son and heir, William Ludwell, lived to be only twenty-eight years old, yet so intense was his feeling on this subject that he set free all his slaves. The story is told in Leesburg that Richard Henry Lee, grandson of the original bearer of the name, so detested slavery that he left Virginia and settled in Washington, Pennsylvania, that he might get away from it. Naturally, as political lines began to form after 1830, the Lees became Whigs, the party responsible for such resistance as was made to the increasing pretensions of slavery advocates.

2

It was in Alexandria that those "formative influences" regarded as so potent in making the man were brought to bear on Robert E. Lee. He was four years old when the exodus from

Stratford took place; his half brother, Henry, the owner of that estate, was twenty-four and, recently graduated from William and Mary, naturally wished to assume his inheritance. From 1811 until his departure for West Point in 1825, Robert spent virtually all his time in Alexandria; practically all his early instruction was obtained there. Here he attended the academy, studying the classics and mathematics with Mr. Leary; here he found his playmates — mainly his cousin Lees; and here he absorbed his standards of conduct and American tradition. The place was a fruitful field for such training. Alexandria was preeminently the city of General Washington. A few miles to the south protruded the peninsula on which Mount Vernon stood; near by was the Masonic hall immemorially associated with Washington's name; the most conspicuous structure was that Carlyle House in which the Braddock expedition had been organized — the military enterprise that first made the Washington name celebrated throughout America. Up the river five or six miles stood Arlington House, the home of that George Washington Parke Custis who delighted to be known as the "child of Mount Vernon" and Washington's adopted son — a unique character, spending his time in leisurely and not too thrifty cultivation of his acres, in making Fourth of July speeches largely devoted to eulogies of the great American, to writing pleasingly garrulous reminiscences of early days at Mount Vernon and composing plays for the "poor rogues of actors," as he called them, on such obvious themes as *Pocahontas,* the *Pawnee Chief,* and *Baltimore Defended.*

Arlington was replete with memorabilia of Washington; Custis was full of stories of the days when he was "dangled" on the great statesman's knee; the child Robert Lee was a frequent visitor and playmate of Custis's only child, Mary, who was in due course to become his wife. To be thrown into constant association with Washington — his deeds, his ideals, his conception of the American purpose — must have exercised a powerful influence on the growing boy. The chief devotion of Washington's latter days was the constitution and the Federal Union; Custis was himself a Whig; and Lee's love of the Union, marked even in the time of his great decision, probably here had its inspiration.

Washington's identification with Christ Church also stimulated the religious feeling that was innate. As to the child himself, the testimony is all to the same effect. The coal-black hair, coal-black eyes, sturdy figure, energetic and courteous bearing, give the impression of an unusually charming boy — charming both in appearance and in character. Though Robert lacked the literary bent, there still is something about him that reminds one of Walter Scott. Lee's allegiance to Virginia, its families, its legends, its standards of conduct, its martial past, recalls Scott's devotion to the soil of Scotland. This was Lee's strongest emotion, as love of the heather was of Scott. Yet this did not preclude Scott's loyalty to the greater kingdom and its king, any more than did a similar loyalty diminish Lee's love of the Union. And Scott's perfect courtesy, his kindness, his love of humbler folk, combined with a reverence for aristocracy and established things, are suggestive also of Lee. For Robert, genial as was his attitude towards Republican standards, was, in his inmost heart, an adherent of caste; there was nothing democratic about him in the sense of free-and-easy association with his brother men. He was as firm a believer in rule of family as had been his kinsman Arthur. Though his faith was manifested in more amiable fashion, Robert E. Lee harks back to the eighteenth century, a true son of that "golden age" in Virginia, when a few families were selected — undoubtedly by God — to stand guardian of the commonwealth, to hold its chief officers and lead it in peace and war.

All this, too, reminds one of Walter Scott. And with this restricted view there was an elemental largeness of soul in both men, and an allegiance to primeval virtues. "Walter, thou wast always good," an admiring relative of Scott's exclaimed, a phrase that recalls the earliest written allusion to Robert E. Lee, in his father's letter dated Nassau, February 9, 1817: "Robert was always good and will be confirmed in his happy turn of mind by his ever watchful and affectionate mother." This insistence on the "goodness" of Robert — his impeccable behavior as a schoolboy; his companionship as a child with his mother; his model conduct at West Point, where he was graduated second in his class, not having received a single demerit for four years; his abstention from certain tendencies regarded as essential to the manly Virginia character, for, while his fellow officers were consuming mint juleps, Lee stolidly drank ice water, had a loathing for the "stench" of tobacco that would have done credit to James I, was never known to swear, play cards, or visit the playhouse, to say nothing of more reprehensible enjoyments — has proved something of an embarrassment to commentators on his life. They seem to think it necessary to prove that the boy was not a prig. Yet the pictures we get of this early time suggest no need of such defense. Certainly the filial devotion described by Lee's son, in his delightful *Recollections and Letters,* is not displeasing to the most masculine soul. "His tenderness for the sick and helpless was developed in him when he was a mere lad. His mother was an invalid, and he was her constant nurse. In her last illness he mixed every dose of medicine she took and was with her night and day. If he left the room she kept her eyes on the door until he returned. He never left her but for a short time." That Lee was an austere character, as child, boy, and man, with whom one did not easily maintain backslapping relations, it would be absurd to deny, but to the charge of youthful priggishness there is one sufficient answer. The mere Sir Galahad never becomes the most popular man in his college class, but Lee achieved this position at West Point. And in the Mexican War he was to prove that a dignified bearing, abstention from frivolities, and elegance of deportment were not inconsistent with a personal bravery that would have done credit to a Hotspur.

It was in this Mexican War that Lee came into his own. There is no occasion, in this place, to detail the incidents of Lee's career as young man and army officer — his achievements at West Point, his labors as engineer, the many permanent works constructed on the Mississippi River, at Baltimore and New York Harbor — nor the incidents of his life, especially his typically Virginian marriage — for what could be more appropriate than the alliance of a Lee with the great-granddaughter of Martha Washington? Lee's twenty or thirty biographers have related all these facts with sufficient exhaustiveness, particularly the latest of them, Dr. Douglas S. Freeman, whose book, a fine specimen of the biographer's art, has now comprehensively and definitively assembled everything that is known — or that is likely to be known — concerning the man's preparation for his historic work. But any writer seeking his own interpretation of Lee and his career must emphasize those two momentous years in Mexico. On the ethical merits of this invasion Lee has little to say; he did not feel the moral indignation of Grant, who, like Lee, had his first military experience at this time — more obscurely than the Virginian, for Grant was fifteen years younger — and who has branded the war in his *Memoirs* as "one of the most unjust ever waged by a stronger against a weaker nation" and "an instance of a Republic following the bad example of European monarchies, in not considering justice in their desire to acquire additional territory." Lee took a milder view; the war "was continued if not brought on by Mexican obstinacy and ignorance," but he did not become personally aroused and, as far as the settlement of ticklish questions was concerned, he said, "Let the pedants of diplomacy decide." To Lee the Mexican War appeared as a military, not a political problem, and in this aspect he won the reputation that directed his afterlife. And this war demonstrated the fact that was afterward displayed on a wider field — that Lee was one of the military geniuses of all time. Not that he emerged from the conflict with any popular *réclame.* The young brevet colonel who returned from Vera Cruz in the autumn of 1849, bursting joyously into his home at Arlington for the much-longed-for reunion with wife and seven children, was only slightly better known to the American public than the Captain Lee who had left two years before.

His name, as the English say, had frequently appeared in "despatches," the more erudite students of campaigns had noted indications of brilliance, but the quality of the man was realized only by his superiors. There were few abler soldiers extant anywhere in those days than Winfield Scott, — a man whose "fuss and feathers" pursuit of the Presidency has obscured his talents as commanding general, — and this officer expressed in his reports what must have seemed at the time extravagant estimates, but which now appear as keen forecasts of the future. "This officer," Scott wrote of Captain Lee, "greatly distin-

guished at the siege of Vera Cruz, was again indefatigable, during these operations, in reconnaissance as daring as laborious,
and of the utmost value.   Nor was he less conspicuous in planting batteries and in conducting columns to their stations under
the heavy fire of the enemy." He described Lee's reconnaissance
on the Pedregal lava field as "the greatest feat of physical and
moral courage performed by any individual, in my knowledge,
pending the campaign."   Scott's opinion was succinctly summed
up afterward in the statement that Lee was "the very best soldier
that I ever saw in the field," and his desire to have Lee appointed
to the command of the Federal army, on the outset of the Civil
War, is well authenticated.   Practically all the other superior
officers under whom Lee served in Mexico paid similar tribute.
This is the more remarkable since Lee, in this conflict, never
commanded troops; he was an engineer, his business being to
reconnoitre, to study topography, to select the best places for attack, the best locations for entrenchments, for defense, for erect-
ing guns, for approach to the enemy's positions.   Such work,
well done, is the basis of victory, and so well did Lee accomplish
his task that Scott made him one of his little "cabinet of strategy,"
and came to regard him as his main reliance.   That audacity and
willingness to take chances which Lee afterward displayed in the
Virginia campaigns were first evinced in Mexico, and Lee possessed other military qualities, which are set forth in professional
studies, but which have no place in this book.   Had there been
no Mexican War there would probably have been no Civil War,
for it was the political passions unloosed by the new lands acquired in that conflict that led to the slavery discussion of the
fifties; certainly there would have been no Lee, in the spring of
'61, to be advanced immediately to command of the Virginia
forces, for it was the fame he then reaped that caused his selection.

3

Out of the Mexican War Lee emerged also with his character definitely formed.   His quality was so simple, so elemental,
that it probably changed little with the years: but it needed the

final touch of war to bring it into outline. "It is well war is so terrible," he remarked at Fredericksburg, "or we should grow too fond of it." But he had already learned this lesson at Vera Cruz and Chapultepec: "You have no idea what a horrible sight a battlefield is," he wrote home; and inevitably scenes like this sobered a nature not naturally given to levity. This quality of sombreness and reserve in Lee is easy to exaggerate; yet the appearance of the man, then and afterward, had a restraining effect. The Confederate private may have called him "Marse Robert," but to his children he was usually "the General." With men of less exalted station there was something, if not of familiarity, at least of friendly understanding. Dr. Freeman relates a precious story: that of a common soldier approaching Lee and asking for a chaw of tobacco, only to be referred most courteously to one of Lee's brother officers addicted to that habit. General Maurice tells of Lee passing a group of soldiers holding a prayer meeting; the general dismounts, uncovers, and remains in reverent attitude to the end; could anyone, the Englishman asks, imagine a German officer assuming such equality with his men, even in these circumstances? In the daily routine, too, Lee's existence was almost rustic. Virginia is not scattered with houses pointed out as "Lee's headquarters," as are New York and the Jerseys with Washington memorials, for the reason that Lee seldom lived in dwellings, but in tents, like his fellow soldiers. So much has been written of his splendid appearance at Appomattox — his full-dress uniform, gold epaulettes, sash and sword — that this is the commonly accepted image of Lee in war. One biographer suggests that Lee donned this raiment, not for ceremonial reasons, but because they were the only presentable clothes he had! For Lee, though always neat, customarily wore nothing but the ordinary Confederate uniform, with no sword or gold braid, and with nothing to indicate his rank except the three stars on collar. Despite this lack of ostentation, Lee's presence did make him a man apart. That mighty stature so characteristic of Revolutionary Virginians had been handed down to the Confederate leader, and though his hair grew whiter as the war progressed, and a white beard concealed part of the strong, handsome face, Lee was still the "marble model," as he was called at West Point, and his eye still had its piercing gleam and his face its ruddiness — undoubtedly the handsomest man in the army, as he had been in his student days.

This exterior, this reserve, can easily lead one astray in estimating the mainsprings of Lee's life. The soldier who planned and executed the operations of '62 was obviously a man of intellect; yet Lee's abiding qualities, which directed his entire career, affected his every judgment and determined every crisis, were the emotions. In fact, Lee apparently had few intellectual tastes. He was not a reading man. Even in the last days, when president of Washington College, he had no personal library and used to complain of the long winter evenings, which left him with nothing to do. Of his early classical training he retained few traces, and general literature, even English literature, was a closed book. Hundreds of Lee's letters survive, and, so far as the present writer recalls, do not contain a single reference to Shakespeare or great writers of his own era — an era that comprised such names as Byron, Shelley, Scott, Dickens, Wordsworth, Hawthorne, Emerson, Thackeray, to mention only a few. His active period was the time of Darwin, Herbert Spencer, Matthew Arnold, and other propagators of the new science and philosophy, yet to such expounders of modern ideas Lee was impervious. One glimpse exhibits Robert reading a *Waverley Novel* at Arlington, with Mrs. Custis and Mary as auditors; there are hints that he was fond of Marcus Aurelius; strangely enough, volumes of Rousseau appear among those borrowed from the library at West Point; he read Worsley's translation of the *Iliad* — a gift from the author — in the last days at Lexington; and these are almost the only books of general literature, as distinguished from professional subjects such as engineering and military science, that — so far as the record shows — occupied his time. Lee's one literary accomplishment was an ability to read French, and he studied many military works, especially those describing Napoleon's campaigns, in the original. His knowledge of the American constitutional system, appropriately enough, was derived from the *Federalist,* a classic which he seems to have made his own. Other topics that engaged his practical mind were geography, forestry, architecture, and navigation. That reading was regarded as a didactic process and not an imaginative stimulus appears in a letter to his daughter Mildred. "Read history, works of truth, not novels and romances. Get correct views of life and learn to see the world in its true light. It will enable you to live pleasantly, to do good, and, when summoned away, to leave without regret." Perhaps Lee's indifference to æsthetic literature, poetry, painting, and sculpture is explained by his absorption in two volumes that were his constant companions — the Bible and the Book of Common Prayer. He has recorded his belief that the Bible was sufficient for all the intellectual needs of humankind. "I only received a few days since your letter of 2nd September," he writes Markie Williams, December 20, 1865, "accompanying Thos: a Kempis imitation of Christ which you kindly sent me. I have read some of your favorite chapters and hope I may derive from the perusal of the book the good you desire. I prefer the bible to any other book. There is enough in that to satisfy the most ardent thirst for knowledge; to open the way to true wisdom; & to teach the only road to salvation and happiness. It is not above human comprehension, & is sufficient to satisfy all its desires. The difficulty is to conform the heart the mind & thoughts to its teaching, & to obtain strength to bring the body under controul of its spirit." Again one is reminded of Walter Scott, who on his deathbed, asked what book he would like to have read, replied, "The Bible! There is only one."

Thus Lee, on the mental side, was an exceedingly serious person, regarding even reading as a means to the certainties of life, and one form of preparation for the hereafter. He lived not in books, but in himself, and his outward aspect really concealed a nature not intellectual, but first of all emotional. And, as is common with emotional men, he had a feeling for the beautiful. His love of nature, apparent on all occasions, forms a pleasing contrast to other more stolid aspects. Whether campaigning in the Virginia mountains, or engaged in those solitary rides with Traveller that formed the main diversions of the last days, this absorption in external beauty, spontaneous, sincere, Wordsworthian in simplicity, exemplifies the texture of the man. Ordinarily not gifted with the pen, his vignettes of the surrounding scene frequently have a poetic quality. "The ground is covered with six inches of snow, and the mountains, as far as the eye can reach in every direction, elevate their white crests as monuments of winter." And here is a similar scene in summer: "The mountains are beautiful, fertile to the tops, covered with the richest sward of bluegrass and white clover, the enclosed fields waving with the natural growth of timothy." Merely to catalogue the flowers apparently gives delight. "Here," he writes of the country around Savannah, "the yellow jasmine, red-bud, orange tree perfume the whole woods and the japonicas and azaleas cover the garden." Such scenes frequently inspire serious thoughts. "I enjoyed the mountains as I rode along," Lee writes his wife from West Virginia, while engaged in that unsuccessful first campaign, "the valleys so beautiful, the scenery so peaceful. What a glorious world Almighty God has given us. How thankless and ungrateful we and how we labor to mar his gifts." Lee's love of solitude is another expression of this emotional side. For conventional diversions he had no taste — once he wrote his sons a severe rebuke for attending balls, especially in war time; the woods, the mountains, the rivers and meadows of Virginia afforded sufficient relaxation from life's weighty concerns. And he preferred to spend familiar hours with them alone. What were his thoughts on these excursions, especially those that followed Appomattox and retirement, has inspired much speculation; such intimacies Lee never confided to person or paper. "Traveller is my only companion, I may say my pleasure. He and I, whenever practicable, wander in the mountains and enjoy sweet confidences." "Most of my time is passed with Traveller in the mountains. . . . In the woods I feel sympathy with the trees and the birds." This solitary figure, clad in gray Confederate coat, — shorn of its buttons, in accordance with the decree of the War Department, for they bore the Confederate insignia, — astride his dappled gray mare, slowly winding in and out the mountain trails, is perhaps the most touchingly dramatic in American annals.

Lee's love of children — the man who ordered Pickett's charge at Gettysburg could talk baby talk with his little friends — and of animals — Nipper the cat was as important a part of his house-

hold in Lexington as were the favorite horses, Traveller and
Lucy Long — similarly indicates the gentler sides of his soul.
Most commentators have denied the man a sense of humor; certainly no epigrams or real witticisms stand to his credit; his tendency to teasing and banter can hardly be regarded as manifestation of this desirable quality, and his recorded jokes are rather
banal, sometimes even in bad taste, such as his fondness for
jibing women friends on their annual production of infants.
Significantly, though Lee could detect the good points of the foe,
he evidently had little regard for Lincoln or appreciation of his
rich human attributes.   No eighteenth-century Virginia gentleman could be expected to comprehend such a rough-and-ready
frontier genius.   Yet Lee did possess a grimness, almost a sardonic quality, that, in the absence of genuine humor, may pass
for it.   Not infrequently he turned this quality against himself,
as when he wrote Mrs. Lee, ten days after Gettysburg: "The
army has returned to Virginia.   Its return is rather sooner than
I had originally anticipated."   When, after establishment in Lexington, Lee was importuned to become president of the proposed
Valley Railroad, an undertaking that gave little promise of success, he replied: "It seems to me that I have already led enough
forlorn hopes."   Lee's dislike of certain of his opponents found
similar expression.   Only two did he actually despise, Butler and
Pope — a feeling with which there was little disagreement, even
in the North.   When his son, "Rooney" Lee, a Federal prisoner,
was moved to a new place of safety, Lee remarked that "any
place would be better than Fort Monroe with Butler in command,"
and his antipathy to Pope inspired several bitter comments.   That
his nephew, Louis Marshall, who fought on the Union side, was
part of Pope's entourage was particularly offensive.   "When you
write Rob tell him to catch Pope for me, and also bring in his
cousin Louis Marshall who, I am told, is on his staff.   I could forgive the latter's fighting against us, but not his joining Pope."

For Hooker Lee's contempt was more good-natured; he commonly referred to him as "Mr. F. J. Hooker," thus making his
own use of Hooker's nickname, "Fighting Joe"; while for Burnside Lee had a real affection, as had most people, friend or foe.
"We always understood each other so well," he commented, on

Burnside's supersession, "I fear they may contrive to make these changes till they find some one whom I don't understand." The most unfortunate victim of this strain in Lee was General David Hunter, the head of a Federal force in the Shenandoah in 1864. After the war, Hunter wrote Lee, asking his professional opinion of his strategy in that campaign. In particular "when he [Hunter] found it necessary to retreat from before Lynchburg, did he not adopt the most feasible line of retreat?" Lee replied with a cutting solemnity that would have done honor to Dean Swift: "I would say that I am not advised as to the motives which induced you to adopt the line of retreat which you took, and am not, perhaps, competent to judge of the question, but I certainly expected you to retreat by way of the Shenandoah Valley and was gratified at the time that you preferred the route through the mountains to the Ohio — leaving the valley open for General Early's advance into Maryland."

Thus any impression that "Marse Robert" was all sweetness of spirit and not subject to the baser irritations common to human nature is much beside the fact. He could greet General Pickett with a freezing disdain which made that officer an enemy for life — one of the few Southern soldiers who really hated Lee, "that old man," Pickett would say, "who commanded my men to massacre"; though his usual attitude towards subordinates was one of quiet courtesy, on occasion he could snap at them waspishly for dereliction, — once he ordered a private soldier shot for stealing a pig, — nor was his attitude towards the Northern enemy always the dignified one that has passed into tradition. "Those people," was the way in which he constantly referred to the foe, and the time came when he could storm at them as "vandals" and violators of all rules of war; in such moments his neck would turn red and chin and head flare upward, like a spirited horse. Plenty of instances are recorded of Lee's loss of temper, and the episode of the man lying ill on the North Anna, constantly shouting as he lay in bed, "We must strike them a blow! We must strike them a blow!" is a picture of a frantic and baffled hero — it so impressed one of his generals, who told him to his face that he was much too excited to command the army. Usually respectful to Davis, a message from the Confederate presi-

dent indicating delay in evacuating Richmond so angered Lee
that he tore it into bits.   At Gettysburg also the testimony is conclusive that Lee lost his poise and came close to an attack of
nerves.

If one seeks further instances in which a calm and restrained
nature gave way to passing emotion, it can be found in the man's
tendency to tears.   The instances cited by his daily associates
are astonishingly numerous.   His imperturbability at Chancel-
lorsville — discussing systems of education with the German
attaché, Scheibert, while the battle was raging fiercest — is usually quoted as picturing Lee's supreme self-command, yet when
news came of Jackson's wounding, he moaned aloud.   Dr. Freeman describes a similar scene, when Jeb Stuart died.   "Lee
put his hands over his face to conceal his emotion. . . .   Lee
could only say, 'I can scarcely think of him without weeping.' "
The mere thought of abandoning Richmond brought tears to his
eyes.   Bishop Meade's sermons would frequently have the same
result.   "I witnessed the opening of the convention yesterday,"
Lee writes his wife from Richmond, May 16, 1861, "and heard
the good Bishop's sermon. . . .   It was a most impressive scene
and more than once I felt the tears coming down my cheek."
Other evangelical preachers could move the general in the same
way.   Many episodes of the kind could be cited, but perhaps the
most touching occasion came when, in San Antonio, Texas, government property was seized by troops of that recently seceded
state.   Lee, then lieutenant colonel in the United States army,
asking his friend Mrs. Caroline Darrow what the pending excitement meant, was told that Texas had seized all Federal supplies
and that "we are prisoners of war."   At this Lee's lips trembled
and he burst into tears.   "Has it come so soon as this?" he asked.
The spectacle of Robert E. Lee weeping because Texas had
seceded and was performing rebellious acts against the Federal
government is one that does not quickly fade from memory.

4

There are other evidences that Lee's chief springs of action
were the emotions; thus his supreme interest was religion, and

religion of a highly emotional, even primitive type. Modern interpretations of the Bible would have been lost on Lee; in his literal acceptance of the Scriptures, his belief in miracles and the incessant participation of God in human affairs, the Confederate leader would to-day be classed as a Fundamentalist. His reference to the Bible as the book that "satisfies the most ardent thirst for knowledge" is quoted above. "There are many things in the old book," he wrote at another time, "that I may never be able to explain, but I accept it as the infallible word of God and receive its teachings as inspired by the Holy Ghost." Lee began and ended every day on his knees, and in his daily prayers all humankind were included, even to those Northern armies on whom he was preparing to train his artillery the following morning. Every act, every decision, was preceded by prayer. Every friend and acquaintance was entrusted to the Almighty. One day he had a visit from three of his nephews. "As soon as I was left alone," he records, "I committed them in fervent prayer to the care and guidance of our Heavenly Father." When one of his chaplains informed Lee that he was constantly present in their prayers, he again was reduced to tears. He was as stern a Sabbatarian as Stonewall Jackson, insisted on Sunday observance in camp, and was by no means lenient to infractions. That military operations often became imperative on the Lord's Day was a matter of deprecation. "One of the miseries of war," he wrote, "is that there is no Sabbath and the current of work and strife has no cessation. How can we be pardoned for all our offenses?" Probably the Confederate forces were the most religious that ever took the field; prayer meetings were part of the daily routine, and the whole army was frequently swept by revivals — manifestations which Lee encouraged. Only secondarily did Lee regard himself as responsible to President Davis and the Confederate government: above them he felt a direct accountability to Jehovah — for Lee's God was a palpable, communicable reality, a personal deity, to whom he could speak directly and who had an eye on his every act. The abstractions that satisfy the modern religious nature would have meant nothing to this primitive soul who had absorbed his conception from Bishop Meade and evangelical Alexandria. After the war, at Lexington, Lee was observed one day to be in a particularly absent mood. "I was thinking," he said in explanation, "of my responsibility to Almighty God for these hundreds of young men." He held the same attitude towards the vast assemblage under his direction in the war; if one man went morally astray, Lee would have to answer for the dereliction; he was severe, therefore, in holding the rank and file to their religious obligations. Judge Winston, in his *Biography,* tells how, amid the tents of Fredericksburg, regimental chaplains, under Lee's orders, "erected religious altars around which the ragged soldiers knelt and worshiped the Heavenly Father, into whose keeping they committed their course and from whom they expected final victory. The very rocks and woods rang with appeals for holiness and consecration." For anything resembling the religious fervor with which the Confederate army rushed at their Yankee brethren, we must consult the Old Testament. This ecstasy was generally characteristic of the South at the time, as it still is to a considerable degree; stimulated by the leader of the army of northern Virginia, its influence in rousing the soldiers to battle can hardly be exaggerated. The spirit of Robert E. Lee in this, as in all other matters, permeated the host.

Just as William E. Gladstone believed that God was every second at his elbow, writing tariff schedules, formulating budgets, indicating the make-up of cabinets, putting words in his mouth in every crisis of debate, so Robert E. Lee was conscious of the presence every moment, and attributed the slightest transaction to the interference of the Almighty. "Everything is in God's hands," was the expression perhaps most constantly on his lips. If victory perched on his banners, — as, in the first two years, it commonly did, — thanks were rendered to God; if failure or defeat proved the day's event, the general was similarly acquiescent: "God's will be done." Every triumph of Confederate arms was accepted with grateful prayers to the Being who had accomplished it. "We mourn the loss of our gallant dead in every conflict," Lee wrote after second Bull Run, "yet our gratitude to Almighty God for His mercies rises higher and higher every day; to Him and to the valor of our troops a nation's gratitude is due." On the eve of the unfortunate operations in western Virginia, Lee puts forth his prayer: "I hope the great Ruler of the Universe will continue to aid and prosper us, and crown at last our feeble efforts with success." When that campaign collapsed Lee then gives the reason: "The Ruler of the Universe ruled otherwise and sent a storm to disconcert a well-laid plan and to destroy my hopes." After Gettysburg the Confederate army, in retreat to Virginia, found that the Potomac had risen several feet; had Meade pursued in sufficient force the position would have been desperate. "Had the river not unexpectedly risen," Lee writes his wife, "all would have been well with us; but God, in His all-wise providence, ruled otherwise and our communications have been interrupted and almost cut off." Lee was not satisfied with the outcome of the "Seven Days' Battle" in the Peninsula, which, he thought, should have resulted in the annihilation of McClellan's army: "Our success was not so complete as we could have desired, but God knows what is best for us."

Rooney Lee, in August 1862, succeeded in capturing prisoners and papers of Pope; in this exploit his father saw the guiding hand of the Most High: "I am so grateful to Almighty God for preserving, guiding and directing him in this war: help me to pray to Him for the continuance of His signal favor." Even the greatest sorrows Lee met in this spirit. "Any victory would be dear at such a price," he said, when news was received of Stonewall Jackson's death, "but God's will be done." In matters of more mundane concern, this intercession of the Almighty was part of Lee's religious belief. While still in the Federal army an opportunity for promotion had started the usual scramble among junior officers, but Lee, although one of the most eligible candidates, refused to push his interest, for the following reason: "My trust is in the wisdom and mercy of a kind providence, who ordereth all things for the best." The repining in the Lee family for the loss of Arlington he disapproved, for "Our heavenly Father has found it necessary to deprive us of what He has given us."

Probably Lee went further than most of his Southern compeers, disposed as they were to see the hand of God in the transactions of men, for he had an explanation of the Civil War not flattering to Americans, North or South: he regarded it as a visitation sent by God to punish the nation for its sins. And in this condemnation Lee did not spare himself. "God has been very kind and merciful to us, and how thankless and sinful I have been." "I shall need all your good wishes & all your prayers," he wrote Reverend C. Walker, rector of Christ Church, Alexandria, — the letter is quoted by Judge Winston, — "in the struggle on which we are engaged & earnestly & humbly look for help to Him above who can save us & who has permitted the dire calamity of this fratricidal war to impend over us. If we are not willing that it should pass from us, may He in his great mercy shield us from its dire effects & save us from the calamity our sins have produced." "God alone can save us from our folly, selfishness and short sightedness," he wrote to Markie Williams, June 21, 1861, before hostilities had started. "I can only see that a fearful calamity is upon us and fear that the country will have to pass through for its sins a fiery ordeal." And in a letter written to his wife on Christmas Day, 1861, an unhappy hour in the Confederacy, he expresses the hope that all may become "sensible of our transgressions," and "penitent," so that the "heavy punishment under which we labor may with justice be removed from us and the whole nation." Gettysburg seemed to have afflicted Lee with similar thoughts. Again it was a punishment for mortal sins, — this time sins of pride, — and this diagnosis of the failure coincides with that of many military critics, who think the campaign was largely the result of Lee's depreciation of his opponents; he himself said that his fault was that he regarded his soldiers as "invincible." This explanation is given a religious turn in Lee's message to his troops after the battle: "Soldiers! We have sinned against Almighty God! We have forgotten His signal mercies, and have cultivated a revengeful, haughty and boastful spirit. We have not remembered that the defenders of a just cause should be pure in His eyes, that our times are in His hands and we have relied too much on our own arms for the achievement of our independence." The military leader of the Confederacy, searching his heart for an explanation of the defeat that sealed his country's fate, found it in that arrogance which was so displeasing to his God — an overweening disposition which the Almighty had avenged with destruction. The punishment of the South had been that of Lucifer.

<h1 style="text-align:center">5</h1>

Thus Lee's deity — in this phase of his life — was the deity of the Old Testament, anthropomorphic, with all the impulses and passions of men, jealous and revengeful, heaping benefits on those who pleased him, hurling Jove-like thunderbolts on those who had given offense, and, at the same time, a God of infinite goodness, mercy, and justice. Yet along with this emotional ideal of divinity there ran a vein of worldly sense which lifted Lee far above most other leaders of the Confederacy. Successful as he was in arms, it is a question whether he would not have been equally successful as a statesman. Had the Confederacy triumphed, nothing could have kept Lee out of the Presidential chair — not even his aversion to office; and the possibility is that, like Washington, he would have left a great reputation as father of his country. Most writers on Lee insist that he had no interest in "politics," or even in public affairs; his silence during the long discussion on the problems of the eighteen-fifties is instanced as proving the point. All this may be true, but it is equally true that probably no Southern leader had so accurate a view of the crisis of 1861 as Lee. When one passes in retrospect the speeches of a Yancey, a Toombs, a Rhett, even a Jefferson Davis, the clear-visioned, quiet opinions of Lee have penetrating wisdom. A fair-sized library has been written on Lee the soldier; at least a monograph could be composed on Lee the statesman. Such a book would rest chiefly on his attitude towards slavery, towards secession and the war. On slavery his views were those of the Lee family and the great Virginians of the Revolution. That Lee had read the speech of Richard Henry Lee in the House of Burgesses of 1759 is doubtful, for he was no student of history, even of his own family, but his views were the same. In this speech, it will be recalled, the young Virginian, then twenty-seven years old, sought means of ending slavery in Virginia, not because it was an injury to the black, but to the white. It was perhaps the most conspicuous instance of high-visioned

statesmanship in the Colonial era; had Richard Henry's programme not been brushed aside by an unthinking generation, the
American story would have presented a different aspect.   This
was the view that Robert E. Lee held in 1861.   Hinton Rowan
Helper could not have summed up the situation any more impres-
sively than did Lee, when he said: "Wherever you find the negro,
everything is going down around him, and wherever you see the
white man, you see everything around him improving."   With
the cotton states, the "deep South," Lee had no affinity; the kind
of plantation he was familiar with was that of Arlington, abode
of culture, gentle manners, and of slavery in its most benignant
form; the few bondmen Lee had he emancipated, and the provision of Mr. Custis's will stipulating for the freeing of all his
"servants" Lee joyfully carried out, even amid the tornado of
war.   Colonel Robert E. Lee commanded the Federal force that
captured John Brown; but for Brown himself, although he abhorred his plan of servile insurrection, he had no animosity; he
dismissed him as a madman — which was probably the fact.   It
is significant that in war, Lee, unlike most Southern officers, was
not served exclusively by negroes; his favorite mess steward
was Bryan, an Irishman.

The type of thinking that regarded slavery as not an evil, but
a good, — "evil, be thou my good," — and that proposed the legal
renewal of the slave trade, Lee regarded with horror, as did all
his family.   And the political theories called in being to substan-
tiate this conception also inspired in him no sympathy.   Secession, for example, was just as unpopular with Robert E. Lee as
it had been with his father, Light Horse Harry.   A good deal
of discussion has taken place about the study of Rawle's *On the
Constitution;* this book, which taught the constitutional right of
secession, was perhaps used as a textbook at West Point in Lee's
student days, and the question has been debated whether Lee
had not studied it as an undergraduate, and absorbed the ideas
that justified his course in '61.   Such a debate is a waste of time;
whether Lee ever saw Rawle's work is doubtful, but what is not
doubtful is that he never accepted its arguments.   For Lee's
ideas on secession, in 1861, were those of Abraham Lincoln.   On
January 22, 1861, after several states had seceded, he wrote to

Cousin Martha Williams one of the saddest letters that ever came from the pen of man: "The subject recalls my grief at the condition of our country. God alone can save us from our folly, selfishness and short-sightedness. The last accounts seem to show that we have barely escaped anarchy to be plunged into civil war. What will be the result I cannot conjecture. . . . I am unable to realize that our people will destroy a government inaugerated [sic] by the blood and wisdom of our patriot fathers, that has given us peace and prosperity at home, power and security abroad, and under which we have acquired a colossal strength unequalled in the history of mankind. I wish to live under no other government & there is no sacrifice I am not ready to make for the preservation of the Union save that of honor. If a disruption takes place, I shall go back in sorrow to my people & share the misery of my native state, & save in her defense there will be one less soldier in the world than now. I wish for no other flag than the Star-Spangled Banner and no other air than 'Hail Columbia.' I still hope that the wisdom and patriotism of the nation will save it. I am so remote from the scene of events & receive such exaggerated and excited accounts of the opinions and acts of our statesmen that I am at a loss what to think. I believe that the South justly complains of the aggressions of the North, & I have believed that the North would cheerfully redress the grievances complained of. I see no cause of disunion, strife, & civil war, & I pray it may be averted."

It will be observed that Lee uses the expression "civil war" as descriptive of the impending uprising. This is the term he always employed. After the battle of Antietam, in a letter addressed to his daughter Mary, in November 1862, he refers to the conflict as "this civil war." That in itself shows how far Lee was removed from the classic view of secession. To-day upholders of the Southern constitutional theory call the conflict of 1861–1865 the "war between the states" and avoid the term that Lee used. The Northern contention is that the transactions of 1861–1865 were rebellion; that for a state to separate from the central government was an act of violence, unconstitutional, illegal, to be justified only, as was the Revolution of 1776, — which no American to-day denies was a rebellion, — by a long series of wrongs impossible to right in any other way — and by success. The traditional Southern attitude is that each state was sovereign; that the constitution was a compact, not an indissoluble union; that a state could remain in or withdraw as it saw fit, and that the act of withdrawal was no excuse for subjection by force of arms. This latter conception is described by the rather awkward phrase, "war between the states." There is no reason for entering into this discussion in this place; enough learning and rhetorical skill have been expended on that subject; in his latter days, after four years of war, there are signs that Lee inclined, at least in part, to the Confederate view; but in the day of his decision he was a strong anti-secessionist, and used two words which eloquently portray his statesmanlike grasp of the problem. Secession was "Revolution," he said, and it was "Anarchy." In a letter written April 20, 1861, to his sister Mrs. Marshall, Lee writes: "The whole South is in a state of Revolution." On January 23, 1861, he said: "As far as I can judge by the papers we are between a state of anarchy and civil war. May God avert from us both. . . . I see that four more states have declared themselves out of the Union; four more will apparently follow their example. Then, if the border states are brought into the gulf of revolution, one half of the country will be arrayed against the other." And, on the same date: "As an American citizen I take great pride in my country, her prosperity and institutions and would defend any State if her rights were invaded. But I can anticipate no greater calamity for the country than a dissolution of the Union. . . . Secession is nothing but revolution. The framers of our constitution never exhausted so much labor, wisdom and forbearance in its formation, and surrounded it with so many guards and securities, if it was intended to be broken by every member of the Confederacy at will. It was intended for 'perpetual union'[1] so expressed in the preamble, and for the establishment of a government, not a compact, which can only be dissolved by revolution, or the consent of all the people in convention assembled. It is idle to talk of secession. Anarchy would have been established and not a

---

[1] Several Lee biographers have called attention to this mistake. "Perpetual union" is not in the constitution, but in the Articles of Confederation.

government, by Washington, Hamilton, Jefferson, Madison and the other patriots of the Revolution."

And Lee hit upon the fundamental argument against secession when he labeled it "anarchy." His meaning was clear enough: so long as any unit in government had the right to separate from the rest, government, in fact, did not exist. That a logical — possibly a constitutional — argument upholding this right can be made is true enough; but no successful nation ever built itself up on strictly logical lines. The forces of history, the impact of events, the teachings of commerce, are influences quite as significant in the development of a nation as rigid covenants. From the beginning the United States has operated under two constitutions — the written one, on which the Southern contention alone relied, and another, formed of precedents, court decisions, historic proceedings, the inescapable lessons of the situation. The Western insurrectionists of 1794, who first asserted the right to disregard laws of Congress, could put forth plausible arguments justifying their act. Washington, however, saw that this uprising was not sense, that no government can exist, whatever its constitution may be, unless it can enforce its decrees; he therefore sent Light Horse Harry, Robert E. Lee's father, with an army of 15,000, and so established the principle — afterward acted on by Andrew Jackson, when South Carolina started its Nullification in 1832 — that the central government had the right and duty of protecting itself from destruction. That secession was all of a piece with this Lee clearly saw. It is "anarchy" for a state to include in its form of government a principle that implies its own nonexistence, and just as the physical body, when invaded by death-dealing germs, manufactures antitoxins that destroy them, so the state, in the presence of such lethal poisons as nullification and secession, produces counteracting agencies of protection. That this secession was anarchy, as Lee described it, the Confederate states themselves were to discover. If these states could rightfully secede from the Union, it necessarily followed that any Confederate state itself could depart at will from the Confederacy; and, in fact, separatist tendencies quickly appeared, and before the war ended actual secession movements started in certain parts of the South. Moreover, not only could a Confederate state abandon the Confederacy, but any part of a state could detach itself from the rest; just as an area of Virginia "seceded" from the Old Dominion and became the sovereign state of West Virginia, so North Carolina, Mississippi, or Texas could split in two, three, or any number of entities; thus was secession "anarchy," writ large. The Civil War decided this argument in Lee's favor; since Appomattox, nothing has been heard of secession except by readers of history; but that Robert E. Lee saw this so clearly in 1861 must be put to his credit side as a statesman.

And he saw other things invisible to many purblind Southern leaders. The Southern air was full of speeches insisting that the North would not resist, that it was too cowardly to start a war, that any Southerner could lick four or five Yankees. Lee understood the situation better and estimated more accurately the power, resourcefulness, and determination of the North. A son, Robert, Jr., student at the University of Virginia, was eager to drop his studies and enter the Confederate army. "It will all be over before I get my chance!" argued the young man. Robert, Jr., in *Recollections and Letters,* prints his father's letter to Mrs. Lee, written in April 1861: "I wrote to Robert that I would not consent to take boys from their colleges and put them in the ranks at the beginning of a war, when they are not wanted and when there were men enough for that purpose. The war may last ten years. Where are our ranks to be filled from then?" It reminds one of Kitchener, in 1914, when Englishmen were expecting to reach Berlin by Christmas. On February 8, 1862, Lee wrote his wife: "The contest must be long and the whole country has to go through much suffering. It is necessary that we should be humble and taught to be less boastful, less selfish, and more devoted to right and justice to all the world."

It is indeed doubtful whether Lee, heroically as he served the Confederacy, ever believed, in his heart of hearts, that it could succeed. One day he detected an officer, busily calculating Southern chances of success, putting on paper comparative statistics of population, North and South, of resources, money, ships, industrial establishments, and the like. "Lay aside your pencil," Lee remarked. "Do not make any figures: figures are all against us."

His son quotes a remark made to General Pendleton a day or two before Appomattox: "I have never believed we could, against the gigantic combination for our subjection, make good in the long run our independence, unless foreign powers should, directly or indirectly, assist us." And Lee never expected foreign assistance; in this respect again his statesmanship rose superior to that of most Southern leaders. Jefferson Davis, Judah P. Benjamin, Mason, Yancey, and other Confederates had an ineradicable faith that the need of cotton in Great Britain and France would compel them to intervene on the side of the South. England especially was to play in behalf of the Confederacy the part that France had played in behalf of the revolting thirteen colonies. This belief in the power of "King Cotton" now figures as the great illusion of Confederate statesmanship. It was an illusion by which Lee was never led astray. "In answer to my question," wrote Herbert Saunders, an English journalist, in 1866, describing an interview with Lee at Lexington, "he replied that he had never expected us to give them material aid, and added that he thought all governments were right in studying only the interests of their own people and not in going to war for an 'idea' when they have had no distinct cause of quarrel." In November 1861, Captain Wilkes seized the British ship *Trent,* and removed from it the Confederate commissioners Mason and Slidell. As a result, England and the United States found themselves on the brink of war. The South was delirious with joy: the one event that would surely bring them independence, war between the United States and the greatest European power, was about to take place. But Lee was not deceived. On Christmas Day, 1862, when this "incident" was furiously boiling, he wrote his wife: "You must not build your hopes on peace on account of the United States going to war with England. She will be very loath to do that, notwithstanding the bluster of the northern papers. Her rulers are not entirely mad, and if they find England is in earnest, and that war or a restitution of the captives must be the consequence, they will adopt the latter. We must make up our minds to fight our battles and win our independence alone. No one will help us." Lee seems to have been almost the only Southern leader who at once saw the meaning of the greatest act of statesmanship of the war — Lincoln's emancipation proclamation. That ended all hope of European intervention, for it put the Confederacy in the light of fighting for slavery and the Union in the light of fighting for its destruction. The British and the French people so hated this institution that any government taking the Southern side in the American Civil War could not long have survived. Judge Winston publishes a letter written by Lee to Jefferson Davis, July 6, 1864: "As far as I have been able to judge this war presents to the European world but two aspects. A contest in which one party is contending for abstract slavery and the other against it; the existence of vital rights involved does not seem to be understood or appreciated. As long as this lasts we can expect neither sympathy or aid."

6

And this presents the ethical problem involved in Lee's career. Why, being such a lover of the Union and a believer in its principles, such a despiser of slavery and of secession, a man of so little faith in the wisdom of the Confederate cause, of no great hope in its success — why did he resign from the Federal army and cast in his fortune with the South? Here again the great simplicity of Lee's character gives the answer. The point is made above that Lee, while obviously a man of intellect, was even stronger on the emotional side. And it was the emotions, not the logical faculty, that determined his action. The mere fact that Lee was a Virginian did not automatically make him a follower of the Confederacy. Other Virginians, of high mentality and lofty conscience, took stand on the Union side. Virginia has produced few finer characters or abler soldiers than George H. Thomas, son of the Tidewater, graduate of West Point, veteran of the Mexican War, and, in 1861, major in the Federal army. Devoted as was Thomas to Virginia, he never hesitated a moment, but remained in the Union forces and became a bulwark of the Northern cause in Western campaigns. Winfield Scott was a Virginian, a native of so Virginian a town as Petersburg, and a student at William and Mary; Scott, in 1861 commanding general of the American army, not only retained his commission, but planned the campaign for the invasion of the seceding states. It may be urged that these men — and others — were not Lees, with that peculiar relation to the Old Dominion inherent in the historic Virginia clans; but there were Lees, with precisely the same family tradition as Robert Edward, who turned their backs on the Confederacy. His own sister, Mrs. William L. Marshall, was Unionist in sympathy, and her son, Louis Marshall, fought in the Union army. Perhaps the most interesting Lee engaged in high position on the Union side was Samuel Phillips Lee, grandson of Richard Henry. Phillips Lee, with his charming wife, Elizabeth Blair, for many years one of the chief adornments of Washington life, with a vein of political and social reminiscence that extended from a childhood in the White House in Jackson's time to the McKinley administration, was a fervid devotee of the Union cause. Just as Robert E. Lee had spent his active career in the Federal army, so Samuel Phillips had served the American flag in the navy, being captain on the outbreak of civil war. Thus Cousin Samuel was faced with the same problem as Cousin Robert: should he remain a Unionist, or join the seceders? His decision was immediate. "When I find the word Virginia in my commission," he said, "I will join the Confederacy."

That Samuel Phillips Lee should take this stand was no surprise to his family or friends. His decision had been foreseen for twenty years. Phillips Lee had always been a studious observor of American affairs. Though since his thirteenth year the American navy had claimed his active life, — an existence that had constantly led him far from the borders of the United States, — the struggle of parties in Washington, and particularly the conflict over slavery, had aroused his tensest emotions. And he was a man of eager and passionate nature — devoted to his allegiances, fiery in his opposition to injustice and wrong. He had one abiding admiration: he regarded the American Republic as the greatest achievement of the modern world. It was with Phillips Lee a matter of constant and enthusiastic conversation. Anything that tended to disrupt this consummation was abhorrent to his spirit. The slavery agitation was wicked, in his eyes, because it tended to produce that very result. In-

SAMUEL PHILLIPS LEE, 1812–1897

REAR ADMIRAL, U. S. N.

ELIZABETH BLAIR, HIS WIFE

Portraits by Thomas Sully

deed, Phillips Lee, long before Sumter, regarded civil war as inevitable. His daily conversation indicated the side he would choose, in that event. His love of Virginia was profound, but his love of the Union was stronger, and he made no secret of the fact that in case of war he was prepared to defend the flag even at the cost of bearing arms against his own state. In their attitude towards slavery, the Federal Union, secession, Robert E. Lee and his cousin Phillips were at one; the point on which they parted company was the question of whether they should give precedence in loyalty to the central government or to Virginia. Both men were lofty-minded and determined their course on conscientious grounds; the fact that two such men, inheritors of the same ideas, of the same family traditions, of the same social environment, brought face to face with the same question, should make such opposing decisions has a bearing upon that problem of "loyalty" worthy the attention of the psychologist.

Phillips Lee's course, in case of hostilities, was known not only to his friends, but to the Buchanan administration. The Secretary of the Navy, Isaac Toucey, was a Connecticut man; despite this fact, his Southern sympathies were notorious and had led to political ostracism from his own state. One of the charges made against Toucey, then and afterward, was that he had so far entered into the sympathy of the Southern majority in Buchanan's cabinet that, in 1860, he had dispersed many warships and many of the ablest officers to remote parts of the world, so that they would not be available on the outbreak of war. Whatever the justice of this accusation, it is a fact that Captain Samuel Phillips Lee, in the winter of 1861, was ordered, with his ship the *Vandalia,* to the East Indies. There were two reasons, Lee always believed, why Southern sympathizers wished him out of the way. First of all he was a Lee, and the possibility of a Virginia Lee taking the Northern side was not pleasing. Moreover, two of Captain Lee's intimate relatives and constant associates were his brother officers, Smith Lee, brother of Robert Edward, and John Augustine Washington, last proprietor of Mount Vernon. Both these men were opponents of slavery and strongly Unionist in feeling. John Augustine was grandson of Hannah Lee, daughter of Richard Henry, and thus cousin to Phillips Lee. Phillips was the strongest-minded of the triumvirate, and the possibility that he might persuade his companions to adhere to the Union was also something not to be endured. Both Smith Lee and John Augustine Washington followed Robert E. Lee into the Confederate cause; but the attempt to isolate Phillips Lee near the China coast — if such an attempt was deliberate — did not succeed. He was off the Cape of Good Hope when news came of the outbreak of war. In his eagerness to get into the fray Phillips committed a very serious offense: he disobeyed orders, and instead of proceeding to the East Indies he turned his ship homewards, safely reached an American port, and reported at Washington. Ordinarily a court-martial and serious punishment would have followed; the spectacle of a Lee frustrating what was regarded — rightly or wrongly — as a Southern plot to keep him out of service on the Northern side was too appealing. Instead of being put on trial, Captain Lee, after service off Charleston, was made acting rear admiral and commander of the naval force blockading Virginia and North Carolina.

Thus the mere fact that Robert Edward was a Virginian and a Lee did not make his championship of the South inevitable. In the excitement of disunion, Northern enemies sought to attribute his decision to unworthy motives. This is preposterous and little is heard of it to-day. If Lee had been seeking worldly advantage he would have remained in the Northern army. Probably — though the fact is not precisely established — he could have been commander of the Federal forces; with his military genius he would have become such a Federal hero that the nation would have showered its greatest honors on his head. Lee's only chance of keeping the Arlington estate lay in maintaining his Northern allegiance; if one can think of Lee as being guided by material considerations, — a very difficult assumption, — he would have stayed under the Federal flag.

The fact is that Lee, next to his religion, loved Virginia. That was his greatest emotion. His feeling for its soil was as tender as that of a lover for his mistress; merely to breathe its air gave the man the contentment that he found in no other way. He was really out of place anywhere else. Gamaliel Bradford says that Lee had one friend — God; but he is wrong, for he had two, and Virginia was a close rival to the one Bradford names. He did not reason about either of these faiths: he accepted them, felt them — they were a part of his being, bred in the flesh. This emotion for Virginia was elemental, intuitive, something that he could not resist, however logic might point out another way. "I felt so elated," he wrote to a cousin in 1840, on his return from the Mississippi River, "when I found my self within the confines of the ancient Dominion that I nodded to all the trees as I passed, chatted with the drivers and stable boys, shook hands with the landlords and, in the fulness of my heart — don't tell Mary — wanted to kiss all the pretty girls I met." And the gayety of the young man sobered into a deep abiding passion. His victories in the war were all gained defending his native land; whenever he left Virginia, failure and defeat became Lee's portion. His first campaign, in the far reaches of western Virginia, near the Ohio, was so unsuccessful that his reputation suffered a sudden decline and he was kept for a year from active command; this country was indeed included in the political confines of Virginia, but it was really a Northern region, in which Lee was not at home. When, in December 1863, things were going badly for the Confederacy in Tennessee, Davis wished to send Lee there to take charge of operations against Grant. Lee was aghast; the idea of leaving Virginia and battling in an unfamiliar country was a pang. "My heart and thoughts will always be with this army," he said, meaning the army of northern Virginia — his army.

The fact is that Lee's attachment to the Confederacy was a matter of slow growth. "The cotton states, as they call themselves," was his almost contemptuous reference in the weeks before the war. On March 15, 1861, he was offered a brigadier generalship in the Confederate army, but did not accept the appointment. Two weeks afterward he did accept a commission as colonel in the United States army, signed by Abraham Lincoln. Only one thing could move Lee from his allegiance to the Union — that prospect he so dreaded, Virginia's secession. This momentous event took place April 17, and three days afterward Lee resigned his commission in the United States army. Even then, however, Lee was not a full-fledged Confederate; to what degree his emotions had robbed him of the power of reason is evident from a strange illusion: that he could keep apart from the general situation and limit his activities to fighting in defense of his native state. Dr. Freeman quotes a conversation, in Texas, in February 1861, when a young man asked Lee whether, in case of conflict, he would "go North or remain South." "I shall never bear arms against the Union," Lee replied, "but it may be necessary for me to carry a musket in defense of my native state, Virginia." This notion — that he need not fight against the United States, but could fight for Virginia — appears in those famous letters written, on the day of his resignation, to General Scott, his brother Smith Lee, and his sister Mrs. Marshall. "Save in defense of my native state," he wrote General Scott, "I never desire again to draw my sword." "I am now a private citizen," Lee wrote his brother Smith, "and have no other ambition than to remain at home. Save in defense of my native state, I have no desire ever again to draw my sword." On the twenty-third of April, Lee, accepting before the Virginia Convention the commission of commander of the Virginia forces, did so in these words: "Trusting in Almighty God, an approving conscience and the aid of my fellow citizens, I devote myself to the service of my native state [not the Confederacy, observe] in whose behalf alone will I ever again draw my sword." Events quickly showed the absurdity of this position, — fighting defensively for Virginia and not offensively for the Confederacy, — but Lee came to the new attitude reluctantly. His earliest expressions of loyalty to the Southern government seem a little forced. In May, he was writing not so exclusively of Virginia, but of "my section of the country," and in a letter dated September 1, 1861, he speaks of "our southern cause." From this time forwards Lee became outspoken for the Confederate states; he displayed the utmost loyalty and deference to its president and government and gradually took on its political beliefs and its constitutional principles.

As to the much debated question of the rightness or wrongness of his decision, Lee himself uttered a few sentences that definitely dispose of the matter. Much has been made, by unfriendly critics, of Lee's "treason": he had taken, as Federal officer, an oath of allegiance to the constitution; to violate this oath, it is urged, and bear arms against the Union was clearly treason. There is not much in this contention. There is a time when "treason" becomes a duty, just as "rebellion" does; the present writer does not think that such justification existed in 1861, but Lee did, and his conscience, not that of outsiders, was properly his guide. Cromwell was a "traitor" to his king, and so was Washington, according to this narrow interpretation of the word. Lee did what he thought was right, and he was not the man to make such judgments lightly, and that really concludes the argument. In his letter to his sister, of Unionist sympathies, written April 20, the day he resigned from the United States army, Lee said: "I know you will blame me, but you must think as kindly of me as you can, and believe that I have endeavored to do what I thought right." And to a little girl in the North, who had asked Lee for his photograph, he wrote: "I cannot raise my hand against my birthplace, my home, my children." No analyst of the soul, appraising Lee's motives, has any right to go beyond that. A man who follows the dictates of his conscience performs his personal duty. Four years afterward, when his cause had ended in disaster, several of Lee's officers demurred at the proposed surrender. What would history say? "That is not the question," Lee replied. "The question is: is it right to surrender this army? If it is right, then I will take all the responsibility." The principle that determined his surrender was the same that had compelled him to take up arms in 1861. It was the principle that directed Lee's whole life, and more than that no man can ask.

And never was it more conscientiously displayed than in Lee's attitude in retirement. This is the period of his life that has probably elicited the greatest admiration. And it is all of a piece with his character and opinions. Even Lee's friends were astonished, and possibly aggrieved, at the calmness with which he accepted the result, at his exhortations to resume friendly relations with the enemy and to join hands with the North in the reëstablishment of a common country. Yet no one who has considered Lee's attitude during the four years of war finds any inconsistency. Certainly no one who has paid due regard to his profound religious faith finds Lee recreant to his principles. It was his belief that an all-wise and an all-beneficent power ruled the universe; that everything was the work of this supreme will, and that all divine decisions were for the good of mankind.   With Lee this was not mere theology, abstract thought, unconnected with the conduct of daily life; it was personally realized and the principle by which he measured his acts.   Over and over again, during the war, in letters to friends, in reports to his government, had he declared that the issue of the Confederacy was in God's hands and that he would accept the verdict.   "We must submit to His Almighty Will, whatever that might be," he wrote his wife immediately after Gettysburg, and, at the beginning of war, Lee replied to a clergyman who had asked if he were "sanguine of results": "At present I am not concerned with results.   God's will ought to be our aim, and I am quite contented that his designs should be accomplished and not ours."

Herein is sufficient explanation of Lee's course after the surrender.   The divine will, he believed, had been evinced at Appomattox.   This will, Lee concluded, had decided that, on this continent, there should be one Anglo-Saxon republic and not two. Not to have accepted the outcome, from Lee's point of view, would have been profanation.   When one studies Lee's life at Lexington after the war, and ponders his letters and acts, the question rises whether, after all, he was not reconciled to the result: whether that love for the old flag to which he had confessed on the eve of Sumter had been entirely stilled by four years of war; whether, if he were living to-day, he would not proclaim, as the majority of Southerners do, that the failure of the Confederacy was best for the South as well as for mankind.

Significantly, Lee's emotions, in this latter period, again reverted to Virginia rather than to the Confederate states.   "All you boys who fought with me," he said after the surrender, "go home and help build up the shattered fortunes of our old state."   And none of his remarks has been quoted quite so much as his reply to a kinswoman who asked him what fate had in store for Virginia: "You can work for Virginia, to build her up again — to make her great again.   You can teach your children to love and cherish her."   If many of Lee's acts and words before and during the war savor of the Old Testament, his behavior afterward showed that the New had become his rule of life.   And this statement

ROBERT EDWARD LEE, 1807–1870

must be understood literally. For two thousand years the world has been full of sneers for professors of the creed that Lee made his own, of men and women who give outward service to its teachings, but never attempt to reduce them to practice. Probably those who actually embody in daily life its principles of forgiveness, love of enemies, human brotherhood and unselfishness, are rare. But Lee was one of them. Two years after the war, when hatred both North and South was at white heat, Lee spoke his celebrated rebuke to a young woman whose own spirit was not entirely destitute of rancor: "I believe I may say, looking into my own heart, and speaking as in the presence of God, that I have never known one moment of bitterness or resentment." It would be hard to believe of most men, but not of Lee.

And so the story of the Lees ends, much as it began, in devotion to a lost cause. The two most glamorous lost causes in the history of the Anglo-Saxon race are that of the House of Stuart in England and that of the Southern Confederacy in the United States. The Lees championed the fortunes, remorselessly destined to failure, of both. And these lost causes had their uses. Both were full of wrong thinking, — wrong thinking not exclusively confined to one side, — but both also at times emblazoned the human spirit in heroic phase. Both causes have left fine traditions of loyalty and splendid exploits, and have thus become part of the history and character of the countries concerned. Without the Civil War the nation would not be the one we know to-day; it would not stand so firm in its institutions, for the problems that had vexed its first seventy years have forever vanished, and possibly the Civil War was as essential to national growth as was the Revolution to independence. But the leadership of the Lees in national matters is no longer a living force. There came one brief moment, in 1898, when a Lee again displayed the family gift for public service: Fitzhugh Lee, a nephew of the general, one of the most effective cavalry leaders on the Southern side, was American consul general in Cuba when the *Maine* was sunk, and by the tact, conciliation and good sense manifested at that crisis upheld the best standards of his clan and won national renown. Soon afterward war broke out between the United States and Spain; when

"Fitz" Lee donned the uniform of the United States and received a commission as major general of volunteers, his act was taken, both North and South, as the symbol of a united country.

As a great political power, however, the Lees have had to yield to a changed America. That individual Lees may reach distinction is not improbable, but the influence of the family, as family, once so powerful in American life, has gone forever. A daily enlarging democratic order makes impossible that idea of family leadership which grew up in Virginia and died finally with the surrender of '65. The desolate aspect of the Potomac shore manifests this change. One can search that region where the first Richard Lee assembled his plantations and find almost no trace of the ancient day. With the exception of Stratford, which has survived for two centuries, and Menokin, on the Rappahannock, — to-day a sad ruin, — all the Lee houses have disappeared. Cobb's Hall, Lee Hall, Mount Pleasant, Chantilly, Belleview, Leesylvania — of those Potomac places, once dispensers of hospitable friendship and headquarters of statesmen and leadership, hardly even the foundations can now be discovered. But a new fate, emblematic of the new time, has been reserved for Arlington, where the last of the great Lees fixed his home. It is now a national shrine — the house a Lee museum, the surrounding country the burial place of Federal soldiers and sailors, one section set aside as grave and monument of the Unknown Soldier in the World War. As one stands on the porch, the object mainly in view is the Lincoln Memorial, joined physically and spiritually to the home of Robert E. Lee by the beautiful new bridge across the river. Though the old Lee houses have disappeared, their work survives in the state and nation they did so much to build, and in the institutions they had so great an influence in creating.

The Lees of Virginia

(This genealogical table is not complete. It comprises the most notable of the Lees, especially those who figure in the present volume. If dates of birth or death are omitted, it is because they cannot be determined. More important characters are in bold type.)

RICHARD LEE d. 1664
m. ANN

1 JOHN c. 1645–1673 2 **RICHARD** 1647–1715 m. LÆTITIA CORBIN 1657–1706 3 FRANCIS c. 1648–1714 4 WILLIAM c. 1651–1697 5 HANCOCK 1653–1709 (From him descended, in fifth generation, ZACHARY TAYLOR, twelfth President of the United States and father of Richard Taylor, Lieutenant General, C. S. A.) 6 ELIZABETH 7 ANN 8 CHARLES c. 1656–c. 1700

1 JOHN (d. in infancy) 2 RICHARD (Merchant in London. Children settled in Virginia.) 3 PHILIP c. 1681–1744 (Ancestor of Maryland Lees and of Thomas Sim Lee, 1745–1819, Revolutionary Governor of Maryland) 4 FRANCIS 5 **THOMAS** 1690–1750 m. HANNAH HARRISON LUDWELL (From whom descend the STRATFORD LEES) 6 **HENRY** c. 1691–1747 m. MARY BLAND (From whom decend the LEESYLVANIA LEES) 7 ANN d. 1732 (m. William Fitzhugh of Eagle's Nest, King George County, who was grandfather of William Fitzhugh of Chatham who was grandfather of Mrs. Robert E. Lee)

1 JOHN c. 1724–1767 2 RICHARD c. 1726–1795 3 **HENRY** 1729–1787 m. LUCY GRYMES 4 LÆTITIA 1730–1788

1 PHILIP LUDWELL 1726–1775 m. ELIZABETH STEPTOE 2 HANNAH 1728–1782 3 THOMAS LUDWELL 1730–1778 (Many descendants, most famous ___ EDWARD D. WHITE, late Chief Justice of U. S. Supreme Court) 4 **RICHARD HENRY** 1732–1794 (___ny descendants, including ___UEL PHILLIPS LEE, Rear Admiral ___ Navy, and BLAIR LEE, Senator ___om Maryland, 1913–1917) 5 FRANCIS LIGHTFOOT 1734–1797 (No descendants) 6 ALICE 1736–1818 7 WILLIAM 1739–1795 (Descendants) 8 ARTHUR 1740–1792 (d. unmarried)

1 MATILDA m. Maj. Gen. HENRY LEE (Light Horse Harry) 2 FLORA m. LUDWELL LEE

1 **HENRY** 1756–1818 (Light Horse Harry) 2 CHARLES 1758–1815 (U. S. Attorney-General, 1795–1801) 3 RICHARD BLAND 1761–1827 4 THEODORICK 1766–1840 5 EDMUND JENNINGS 1772–1843 6 LUCY b. 1774 7 MARY 8 ANNE 1776–1857

m. (1) MATILDA LEE, of Stratford   m. (2) ANN HILL CARTER, of Shirley

1 LUCY GRYMES, 1786–1860 2 **HENRY** 1787–1837 (Last Master of Stratford. Died in Paris, France) 3 ALGERNON SIDNEY 1795–1796 4 CHARLES CARTER 1798–1871 5 ANNE KINLOCH 1800–1864 6 SYDNEY SMITH 1802–1869 7 **ROBERT EDWARD** 1807–1870 m. MARY ANNE CUSTIS 8 CATHERINE MILDRED 1811–1856

FITZHUGH 1835–1905 (Major General, C. S. A., Governor of Virginia, Major General in U. S. Army in the Spanish-American War)

1 GEORGE WASHINGTON CUSTIS 1832–1913 (d. unmarried) 2 MARY CUSTIS (d. unmarried) 3 WILLIAM HENRY FITZHUGH 1837–1891 m. MARY TABB BOLLING 4 ANNIE 1839–1862 (d. unmarried) 5 AGNES (d. unmarried) 6 ROBERT EDWARD 7 MILDRED (d. unmarried)

1 GEORGE BOLLING b. 1872 m. HELEN KENEY 2 ROBERT EDWARD d. s. p.

1 ANNE CARTER m. HANSON ELY, JR. (Issue) 2 MARY CUSTIS m. HUNTER DE BUTTS (Issue)

ROBERT EDWARD IV b. Dec. 25 1924

INDEX

INDEX

tion, 124; adopts Stamp Act, 126, 127; her need of money, 127–130; imposes new taxes, 149–151; and the "Farmer's Letters," 152; her endeavors to split colonies, 171, 180; passes Boston Port Bill, 186; Spain's antagonism to, 215, 216; her foreign trade, 217, 218; importance of West Indies to, 230–232; and Prussia, 249, 250; her relations with Holland, 257, 258, 260, 261; and American Civil War, 428, 429. *See also* Bancroft, Edward; Continental Congress

Faerie Queene, dedication of, 6
Fairfax, George, member of Ohio Company, 66
Fairfax, Lord, 44
Fairfax, Lady, 44; inherits Virginia proprietary, 59
Fairfax, Lord Thomas, and the Northern Neck, 44–46
Family Compact, 215, 317
Farley, Maria, and Light Horse Harry, 380–382; marries William Champe Carter, 380, 383
"Farmer's Letters." *See* Dickinson, John
Fauquier, Gov. Francis, and the Council, 75; his partiality for Robinson, 107; prorogues burgesses, 126; and Mercer, 131
Fisher, George, describes Philip Ludwell Lee, 88, 89
Fithian, Philip, his diary quoted, 52, 88, 345; at Princeton with Henry Lee III, 333, 334
Fitzhugh, Henry, member of Mississippi Company, 118
Fitzhugh, William, quoted, 33, 42; member of Mississippi Company, 118
Fitzhugh, William H., praises Ann Carter Lee, 383
Folger, Capt., famous incident regarding, 302
Ford, and Arthur Lee, 142
Fothergill, Dr., at Ham House, 24
France, her pretensions in America, 61–63, 69; her cession of American territory to England, 113; her interest in American rebellion, 215–218; importance of West Indies to, 230–232; and the subsidy to America, 236, 239; her new relations with America, 241, 242, 256; her estimate of Franklin, 267, 268; celebrates victory at Saratoga, 291–295; revolution in, 377. *See also* Beaumarchais
Francy, M. de, representative of Beaumarchais, 320
Franklin, Benjamin, 57; influenced by

Locke, 95; his loyalty to British crown, 124; and stamp-collector applications, 134; and Arthur Lee's tract, 169; elected Massachusetts agent in London, 172; presents Richard Henry Lee's petition at court, 195; at the Second Continental Congress, 200, 207, 211; leader of anti-proprietary forces, 207; on Declaration Committee, 211; his instructions to Arthur Lee regarding English mission, 214; gives up London agency, 218; makes memorandum of Arthur Lee's report, 238; myth concerning, 239; his opinion of "militia diplomacy," 240, 241; head of American Commission, 241; embarrassed by credentials to Spain, 242, 243; his conflict with William Lee, 255, 256; and the negotiations with Holland, 257–259; his treatment of Arthur Lee at Passy, 262–269; foundation of his feud with Arthur Lee, 269–275; his instructions to Deane, 276; blind to Bancroft's treachery, 277, 281, 284–286, 289–291; and Wentworth, 285, 286; and Thornton, 289, 290; receives Austin, 291; presented at court, 293–295; a cipher in business affairs, 301, 312; sees Deane in true colors, 313, 315, 316; his correspondence with British statesmen, 324, 325
Franklin, William, in the Continental Congress, 190; dismissed as governor of New Jersey, 209; member of Grand Ohio Company, 273; and Witherspoon, 333
Franklin, William Temple, secretary of American Commission, 263
Frederick the Great, his attitude toward America, 249, 250, 256, 257; and Arthur Lee's mission, 251; his opinion of Elliot, 253
Freeman, Dr. Douglas S., 408, 411, 417, 434
French and Indian War, Virginia in, 97
Freneau, Philip, at Princeton with Henry Lee III, 333
Fry, Katherine, her *History of the Parishes of East and West Ham,* 24 n.

Gadsden, Christopher, in the Continental Congress, 190
Galloway, Joseph, describes Samuel Adams, 188; in the Continental Congress, 190, 192; member Grand Ohio Company, 273
Gardoqui, Diego de, his negotiations with Arthur Lee, 246–248; minister from Spain to America, 351

Arthur's petition, 219; opposed to French intervention, 232; and Arthur's report, 238; secures William's appointment to Nantes, 255; receives Arthur's unfortunate letter, 268; and Washington, 303; moves Deane's recall, 305; on corruption at Passy, 308; and the Western territory, 348; again elected to Congress, 350; as president of Congress, 350–352; his clash with Light Horse Harry, 352, 355, 356; and the fight for the constitution, 355–364; comments on Philadelphia convention, 355; his *Letters of the Federal Farmer*, 356, 357; Washington's anger at, 357, 358; United States Senator, 364; retires to Chantilly, 365; and his daughters, 365–367; his death, 367; compared to Robert E., 422, 423

Lee, Mrs. Richard Henry I, 183

Lee, Richard Henry II, describes action of Westmoreland Association, 136; his *Life of Arthur Lee, 173 n.*; his hatred of slavery, 405

Lee, Gen. Robert Edward, son of Henry III, at Lee Hall, 49; his opposition to slavery, 74, 422; describes his father, 346; his birth (1807), 391, 392; his mother's inseparable companion, 392; at his father's grave, 397, 398; his fondness for Stratford, 403, 404; a Low Church Anglican, 405; "formative influences" of, 405–408; at West Point, 407, 408; his early career, 408; in the Mexican War, 408–410; his character formed, 410–417; his religion, 417–422; his grasp of public affairs, 422, 427; on secession, 423–426; never expected South to win, 427–429; ethical problem of, 429–435; his love of Virginia, 432; his feeling toward the Confederacy, 433, 434; in retirement, 435–437; his shrine at Arlington, 438

Lee, Robert Edward, Jr., his *Recollections and Letters* quoted, 408, 427

Lee, "Rooney," in the Civil War, 415, 420

Lee, Samuel Phillips, his determination to fight on Union side, 430–432

Lee, Smith, 431, 432, 434

Lee, Thomas I, influenced by Ham House, 24; builder of Stratford, 48; generously treated by his brother, 51; his lack of education, 51, 52; makes himself a foremost Virginian, 52, 53; his domestic life, 54, 55; compared to Washington, 57, 58; his feud with "King" Carter, 58, 59, 62, 378; agent for Lady Fairfax,

59; penetrates Western country, 60–62; "president" of Virginia, 63; his treaty with Six Nations, 63–65; president of Ohio Company, 66–68; his opposition to France, 66–68; president of Council, 67; his influence on western expansion, 68, 69; his attitude toward slavery, 77; end of his life, 81; education of his sons, 85, 86; his death, 87; his will, 89, 90; his pronouncement justified, 113

Lee, Mrs. Thomas I, an important accession to House of Lee, 54–57; treatment of her children, 157, 158

Lee, Thomas Ludwell, member of Ohio Company, 66; qualities of, 80; education of, 85–87; as guardian, 89, 90; as a burgess, 97; his popularity, 110, 111; member of Mississippi Company, 118; signer of Westmoreland Resolutions, 135; active in provincial disturbance, 209, 210

Lee, Thomas Sim, Revolutionary patriot, 50

Lee, Mrs. Thomas Sim, 50

Lee, William, describes "Emigrant" Richard, 4, 6, 7; describes Richard II, 31–33; describes Thomas, 52; traits of, 57, 159; education of, 85, 86, 89, 90; to be tobacco trader in London, 90; and the classics, 94; secretary of Mississippi Company, 118, 119; signer of Westmoreland Resolutions, 135; in London, 137; as a boy, 157, 158; treated harshly, 158; his London business, 159, 160; his marriage, 160, 161; and Johnson, 167; partner of Sayre, 172; elected alderman in London, 218, 219; and Wilkes, 219, 220; his difficulties at Nantes, 255, 256; appointed to Berlin and Vienna, 256, 257; his treaty with Holland, 257–261; his knowledge of Bancroft's treachery, 277; presented to king of France, 294; accuses Deane, 308; end of his diplomatic career, 316; his proposed dual with Petrie, 322–324; retires to Green Spring, 347; his death, 371

Lee, Mrs. William, shares in husband's business, 160, 161, 299

Lee, William Ludwell, his hatred of slavery, 405

Lee family, its rank in Virginia, 48, 49; its quarrels with the Washingtons, 49, 50; in Maryland, 50; compared with Washingtons, 57, 58; conspicuous in difficulties with England, 113; close friends of Adamses,